*h*agstrom®

Nassau County
New York

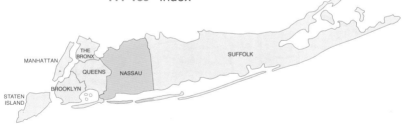

EIGHTH EDITION

Copyright © 2007
Hagstrom Map Company, Inc.
www.hagstrommap.com
Printed in China

Cover Photo: Long Beach, New York,
Photographer: Quang-Tuon Luong

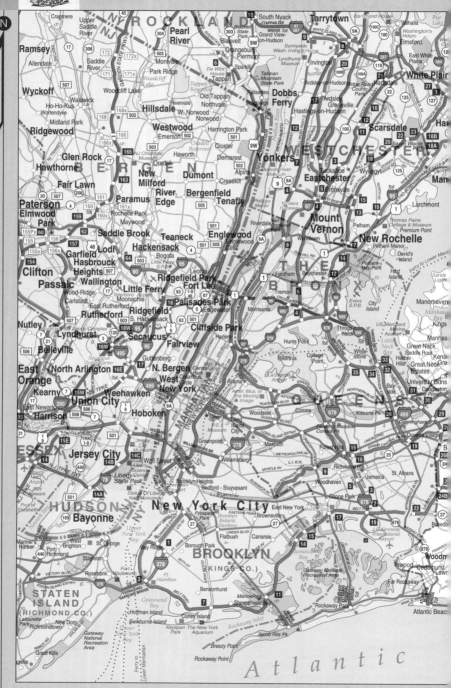

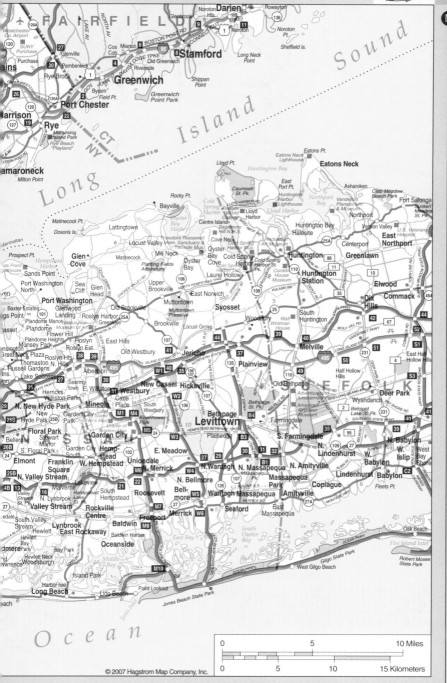

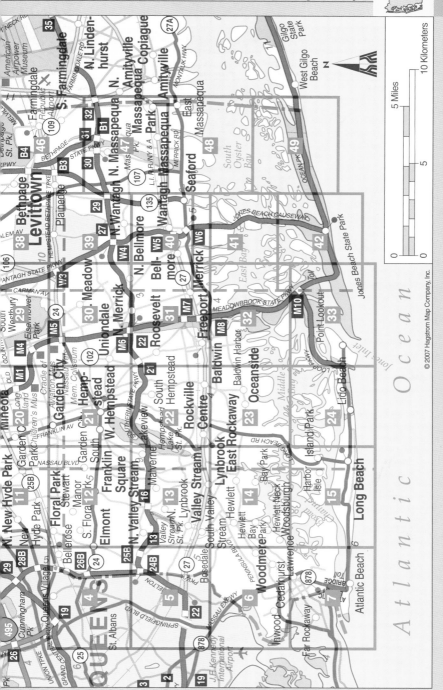

Gilgo State Park

West Gilgo Beach

N

5 Miles

10 Kilometers

5

0

0

© 2007 Hagstrom Map Company, Inc.

Jones Beach State Park

Atlantic Ocean

Inlet

27A

35

N. Linden-hurst

American Airpower Museum

Farmingdale

Republic Airport

S. Farmingdale

N. Amityville

Amityville

Copiague

N. Massapequa

N. Massapequa Park

East Massapequa

Massapequa

46

B4

32

31

B1

B3

30

47

48

49

Bethpage

Levittown

Plainedge

N. Wantagh

N. Bellmore

Wantagh

Seaford

38

29

27

39

W4

40

41

42

W. Meadow

N. Merrick

Roosevelt

Bell-more

Freeport

Merrick

30

M5

24

29

W3

W5

W6

31

W7

M7

M10

33

Uniondale

Hempstead

Baldwin

Baldwin Harbor

Oceanside

Point Lookout

Garden City

Hemp-stead

W. Hempstead

Garden City South

M1

M4

20

21

102

M6

22

21

M8

32

24

Mineola

N. New Hyde Park

Floral Park

Franklin Square

Elmont

Malverne

Rockville Centre

Lynbrook

East Rockaway

Island Park

Lido Beach

11

25B

12

21

13

16

13

22

23

15

24

New Hyde Park

Bellerose

S. Floral Park

Stewart Manor

N. Valley Stream

Lakeview

South Hempstead

Valley Stream

Hewlett

Bay Park

Long Beach

Garden City Park

Children's Mus.

Nassau Vets. Mem. Coliseum

Cradle of Aviation Mus.

Valley Stream N. St. Pk.

South Valley Stream

Hewlett Bay Park

Hewlett Neck Woodsburgh

Harbor Isle

28B

29

26B

24

25B

24B

27

14

6

7

Queens Village

Cunningham Pk.

St. Albans

Rosedale

Woodmere

Inwood

Cedarhurst

Lawrence

Atlantic Beach

19

495

26

25

3

2

19

5

22

878

Far Rockaway

J.F. Kennedy International Airport

QUEENS

Atlantic Ocean

5

School Districts

Reference Number	Administrative Office Address	Administrative Office Phone Number	Website	Map Number
HEMPSTEAD			Note: All phone numbers have area code 516.	
1 Hempstead UFSD	185 Peninsula Boulevard, Hempstead 11550	292-7111	http://www.hempsteadschools.org/	21
2 Uniondale UFSD	933 Goodrich Street, Uniondale 11553-2499	560-8800	http://www.uniondale.k12.ny.us/	21,22,29,30
3 East Meadow UFSD	101 Carman Avenue, East Meadow 11554	228-5200	http://www.eastmeadow.k12.ny.us/	29,30,39
4 North Bellmore UFSD *	2616 Martin Avenue, Bellmore 11710	992-3000	http://northbellmoreschools.org/	30,31,39
5 Levittown UFSD	150 Abbey Lane, Levittown 11756	520-8300	http://www.levittownschools.com/	30,39,40,47
6 Seaford UFSD	1600 Washington Avenue, Seaford 11783	592-4000	http://www.seaford.k12.ny.us/	40,41,42,47,48
7 Bellmore UFSD *	2750 S. St. Marks Avenue, Bellmore 11710	679-2900	http://www.bellmore.k12.ny.us/	30,31
8 Roosevelt UFSD	240 Denton Place, Roosevelt 11575	867-8600	http://www.rooseveltschools.net/	30,31
9 Freeport UFSD	235 N. Ocean Avenue, Freeport 11520	867-5200	http://www.freeportschools.org/	22,23,31,32,33
10 Baldwin UFSD	960 Hastings Street, Baldwin 11510	377-9200	http://www.baldwin.k12.ny.us/	22,23
11 Oceanside UFSD	145 Merle Avenue, Oceanside 11572	678-1226	http://www.oceanside.k12.ny.us/	14,15,22,23,24 32,33
12 Malverne UFSD	301 Wicks Lane, Malverne 11565	887-6405	http://www.malverne.k12.ny.us/	13,14,22
13 Valley Stream #13 UFSD ***	585 N. Corona Avenue, Valley Stream 11580-2099	568-6100	http://www.valleystream13.com/	5,12,13
14 Hewlett-Woodmere UFSD	One Johnson Place, Woodmere 11598-1312	374-8100	http://www.hewlett-woodmere.net/	6,14,15
15 Lawrence UFSD	P.O. Box 477, Lawrence 11559	295-7032	http://www.lawrence.org/	6,7,15
16 Elmont UFSD **	135 Elmont Road, Elmont 11003	326-5500	http://www.elmontschools.org/	4,12,13
17 Franklin Square UFSD **	760 Washington Street, Franklin Square 11010	505-6975	http://www.franklinsquareschools.com/	11,12
18 Garden City UFSD	56 Cathedral Avenue, Garden City 11530	478-1000	http://www.gardencity.k12.ny.us/	11,20
19 East Rockaway UFSD	Ocean Avenue, East Rockaway 11518	887-8300	http://www.eastrockawayschools.org/	14
20 Lynbrook UFSD	111 Atlantic Avenue, Lynbrook 11563	887-0256	http://www.lynbrook.k12.ny.us/	13,14
21 Rockville Centre UFSD	128 Shepherd Street, Rockville Centre 11570	255-8920	http://www.rvcschools.org/	13,14,21,22,23
22 Floral Park-Bellerose UFSD ** (N. HEMPSTEAD)	One Poppy Place, Floral Park 11001	327-9300	http://www.floralpark.k12.ny.us/	4,12
23 Wantagh UFSD	3301 Beltagh Avenue, Wantagh 11793	781-8000	http://www.wms.wantaghufsd.k12.ny.us/	39,40,41,47
24 Valley Stream #24 UFSD ***	Horton Avenue, Valley Stream 11582	256-0153	http://www.vsufsd24.com/	5,13,14
25 Merrick UFSD *	21 Babylon Road, Merrick 11566	922-7240	http://www.merrick-k6.org/	31,32,33,40,41
26 Island Trees UFSD	74 Farmedge rd, Levittown 11756	520-2100	http://www.islandtrees.org/	38,39,46
27 West Hempstead UFSD	252 Chestnut Street, West Hempstead 11552	390-3100	http://www.westhempstead.k12.ny.us/	12,13,21,22
28 Long Beach	235 Lido Boulevard, Long Beach 11561	897-2108	http://www.lbeach.org/	15,24,33
29 North Merrick UFSD *	1057 Merrick Avenue, Merrick 11566	292-3694	http://www.north-merrick.k12.ny.us/	30,31
30 Valley Stream #30 UFSD ***	175 North Central Avenue, Valley Stream 11580	285-9881	http://www.valleystream30.com/	5,6,13
31 Island Park UFSD	150 Trafalgar Boulevard, Island Park 11558	431-8100	http://www.ips.k12.ny.us/	15,24
Bellmore-Merrick CHSD *	1260 Meadowbrook Road, Merrick 11566	992-1000	http://www.bellmore-merrick.k12.ny.us/	
Sewanhaka CHSD **	77 Landau Ave., Floral Park, NY 11001	488-9800	http://www.sewanhaka.k12.ny.us/	
Valley Stream Central CSD ***	One Kent Road, Valley Stream 11582	872-5601	http://www.vschsd.org/	

School Districts

Reference Number	Administrative Office Address	Administrative Office Phone Number	Website	Map Number

NORTH HEMPSTEAD

1 Westbury UFSD	2 Hitchcock Lane, Old Westbury 11568-1624	876-5001	http://www.westburyschools.org/	9,19
2 East Williston UFSD	11 Bacon Road, Old Westbury 11568-1599	333-1630	http://www.ewsdonline.org/	18,19,20
3 Roslyn UFSD (OYSTER BAY)	Harbor Hill Road, Roslyn Heights 11577	625-6303	http://www.roslynschools.org/	10,18,19
4 Port Washington UFSD	100 Campus Drive, Port Washington 11050	767-5000	http://www.portnet.k12.ny.us/	1,2,8,9
5 New Hyde Park-Garden City Park UFSD ** (HEMPSTEAD)	1950 Hillside Avenue, New Hyde Park 11040	352-6257	http://www.nhp-gcp.org/	10,11,12
6 Manhasset UFSD	Memorial Place, Manhasset 11030	267-7700	http://www.manhasset.k12.ny.us/	2,3,9,10,19
7 Great Neck UFSD	345 Lakeville Road, Great Neck 11020	773-1405	http://www.greatneck.k12.ny.us/	1,2
9 Herricks UFSD	99 Shelter Rock Road, New Hyde Park 11040	248-3100	http://www.herricks.org/	10,11,19
10 Mineola UFSD	200 Emory Road, Mineola 11501	237-2001	http://www.mineola.k12.ny.us/	11,19,20
11 Carle Place UFSD	Cherry Lane, Carle Place 11514	622-6400	http://www.cps.k12.ny.us/	19,20
15 Jericho UFSD	Cedar Swamp Road, Jericho 11753	681-4100	http://www.bestschools.org/	19

OYSTER BAY

1 North Shore CSD	112 Franklin Avenue, Sea Cliff 11579	705-0350	http://www.northshore.k12.ny.us/	8,17,18,28,37
2 Syosset CSD	99 Pell Lane, Syosset, New York, 11791-2998	364-5600	http://www.syosset.k12.ny.us/	35,36,37,43,44
3 Locust Valley CSD	Horse Hollow Road, Locust Valley 11560	674-6350	http://www.lvcsd.k12.ny.us/	26,27
4 Plainview-Old Bethpage CSD	106 Washington Avenue, Plainview 11803	937-6301	http://www.pob.k12.ny.us/	37,44,45,46
5 Glen Cove SD	Dosoris Lane, Glen Cove 11542	759-7202	http://www.glencove.k12.ny.us/	8,16,17,25,26,34,35
6 Oyster Bay-East Norwich CSD	McCouns Lane, Oyster Bay 11771	624-6500	http://oben.powertolearn.com/	5,26,27,34,35,36
15 Jericho UFSD	Cedar Swamp Road, Jericho 11753	681-4100	http://www.bestschools.org/	18,27,28,36,37
17 Hicksville UFSD	200 Division Avenue, Hicksville 11801	733-6679	N/A	28,29,37,38
18 Plainedge UFSD	241 Wyngate Drive, P.O. Box 1669, N. Massapequa 11758	992-7450	http://www.plainedgeschools.org/	39,46,47
21 Bethpage UFSD	10 Cherry Avenue, Bethpage 11714	644-4000	http://www.bethpagecommunity.com/Schools	37,38 45,46
22 Farmingdale UFSD	50 Van Cott Avenue, Farmingdale 11735	752-6510	http://www.farmingdaleschools.org/	46
23 Massapequa UFSD	4925 Merrick Road, Massapequa 11758	797-6175	http://www.msd.k12.ny.us/	48

* Middle, Junior and Senior high schools within this district are covered by Bellmore-Merrick CHSD.
** High schools within this district are covered by Sewanhaka CHSD.
*** Junior and Senior high schools within this district are covered by Valley Stream Central CSD.

Note: The numbers used on this list and on the map pages to identify school districts are Hagstrom reference numbers only. Agreement with official school district numbers used by the Board of Cooperative Educational Services is coincidental.

The above table reflects 2004/2005 Union Free School Districts (UFSD) and Common School Districts (CSD). The district boundaries shown on the map are subject to periodic change due to development and/or district consolidation. School districts that cover portions of more than one town show the adjoining town(s) in parentheses.

Nassau Co.

Points of Interest

African American Museum
110 N. Franklin St, Hempstead
Special exhibits highlight a collection that examines the history and cultural heritage of Long Island African Americans.
(516) 572-0730 **Map 21, M 18**

Belmont Park Race Track
Hempstead Tpke., Elmont
Home of the third leg of thoroughbred racing's Triple Crown. Daytime races during the spring months.
(718) 641-4700 **Map 4, E 17**

Cedarmere
Roslyn Harbor
Home of nineteenth-century poet William Cullen Bryant. Estate contains Nassau County Fine Arts Museum, Nassau County Office of Cultural Development, education center, gardens, and poetry readings.
(516) 571-8130 **Map 18, L 10**

Cradle of Aviation Museum
Charles Lindbergh Blvd., Garden City
Discover Long Island's aerospace heritage at the Cradle of Aviation Museum. The museum is dedicated to military aircraft production in Long Island during World War II. Includes exhibits and IMAX Theater.
(516) 572-4111 www.cradleofaviation.org **Map 20, P 16**

Cow Neck Peninsula Historical Society Museum
336 Port Washington Blvd., Port Washington
Based in the Sands-Willets House, on the National and State registers of historic landmarks. The museum has displays of eighteenth century life and furnishings. Tours by appointment.
(516) 365-9074 www.cowneck.org **Map 9, H 9**

Earle-Wightman House Museum
20 Summit St., Oyster Bay
This restored 1720 saltbox house contains historical exhibits, colonial and federal period rooms, and a reference library. Home to the Oyster Bay Historical Society.
(516) 922-5032 members.aol.com/OBHistory **Map 35, U 5**

Garvies Point Museum and Preserve
50 Barry Dr., Glen Cove
Research center and resource for the study of the archaeology and Geology of coastal New York. Museum and nature trails.
(516) 571-8010 www.garviespointmuseum.com **Map 8, K 6**

Gregory Museum
Heitz Place, Hicksville
The museum is located in the Heitz Place Courthouse, and some of the original jail cells have been preserved. Other Long Island artifacts on exhibit include rocks and minerals, a collection of fossils, and dinosaur eggs. The museum also offers workshops in crafts and science.
(516) 822-7505 www.gregorymuseum.org **Map 37, V 13**

Grist Mill Museum
Memorial Park, Atlantic Av. and Wood Av., East Rockaway
Memorabilia featuring Native Americans and school exhibits from East Rockaway.
(516) 887-6300
members.aol.com/lynhistory/gristmil/grist1.htm
Map 14, J 23

Long Island Children's Museum
11 Davis Av., Garden City
The museum's new location can hold 10 times more visitors than the previous one. Children can touch and climb exhibits. Theater performances once a week.
(516) 224-5800 www.licm.com **Map 20, O 16**

Nassau County Museum of Art
One Museum Dr., Roslyn Harbor
The museum offers exhibitions, group tours and lectures. A museum shop, bookstore, and café are also on site.
(516) 484-9337 www.nassaumuseum.com **Map 18, L 10**

Nassau Veterans Memorial Coliseum
1255 Hempstead Tpke., Uniondale
This 18,000-seat arena is the site of professional and collegiate sporting events, concerts, shows, and other attractions.
(516) 794-9303 www.nassaucoliseum.com **Map 29, P 17**

Nautical Mile (Woodcleft Canal)
Woodcleft Canal, Freeport
Known for commercial fishing, charter and open boats, open air fish markets, restaurants, shops with a nautical flavor, and offshore casino gambling. **Map 32, Q 24**

North Fork Theatre at Westbury Music Fair
960 Brush Hollow Rd., Westbury
This theater presents music, musicals, and concerts. It is one of the top five theaters in the country that seats 3,000 or fewer.
(516) 334-0800 www.musicfair.com **Map 28, S 13**

Old Bethpage Village Restoration
Round Swamp Rd., Old Bethpage
Museum village depicts the rural life of the 1800s. Forty historic buildings, including an inn, homes, and a church, present life on Long Island before the Civil War.
(516) 572 8400 www.oldbethpage.org **Map 45, BB 13**

Old Westbury Gardens
71 Old Westbury Rd., Westbury
Over 100 acres of formal gardens, fields, and woods surround the elegant Stuart-style mansion of John S. Phipps. Summer lawn concerts and picnic areas.
(516) 333-0048 www.oldwestburygardens.org **Map 19, P 13**

Onderdonk House
1471 Northern Blvd., Manhasset
Built in 1836 by famous lawyer and judge Horatio Gates Onderdonk. On national, state, and county registries as a historical landmark. **Map 9, G 11**

Raynham Hall
20 West Main St., Oyster Bay
The twenty-room Raynham Hall was built in 1740. It was a British headquarters during the revolutionary war and the site of the first documented American Valentine. The Victorian wing contains 1851 period furnishings.
www.raynhamhallmuseum.org **Map 35, U 5**

Rock Hall
199 Broadway, Lawrence
Built in 1767, this Georgian Colonial Historic House is on the National Register of Historic Places. Period furnishings and annual exhibits.
(516) 239-1157 **Map 7, D 26**

Saddle Rock Grist Mill
Grist Mill La., Saddle Rock
Historic grist mill.
(516) 571-7900 www.saddlerock.org **Map 2, C 11**

Sagamore Hill National Historic Site
20 Sagamore Hill Rd., Oyster Bay
This Victorian mansion overlooking Oyster Bay was the summer White House of President Theodore Roosevelt, and later, his place of retirement. Includes a museum of personal items and audio-visual exhibits.
(516) 922-4447 www.nps.gov/sahi/home.htm **Map 34, W 4**

Tilles Center for the Performing Arts at LIU/ C.W. Post Campus
Northern Blvd., Brookville
Contains a 2242-seat main hall and the 490-seat Hillwood Recital Hall, and is home to the Long Island Philharmonic. Over 70 events presented each season in theater, dance, and music.
(516) 299-3100 www.tillescenter.org **Map 27, P 10**

US Merchant Marine Academy
300 Steamboat Rd., Great Neck
Academy on the site of the former Chrysler estate educates officers for the Merchant Marines or Naval Reserve. Memorial chapel and museum.
(516) 773-5000 www.usmma.edu **Map 2, A 10**

Government Guide

Department	Location	Telephone
Assessment Review Commission	240 Old Country Road, Mineola, 11501	(516) 571-2391
Board of Elections	400 County Seat Drive, Mineola, 11501	(516) 571-2411
Commissioner of Investigations	1 West Street, Mineola, 11501	(516) 571-0534
Consumer Affairs	200 County Seat Drive, Mineola, 11501	(516) 571-2600
County Assessor's Office	240 Old Country Road, Mineola, 11501	(516) 571-2490
County Attorney	1 West Street, Mineola, 11501	(516) 571-3056
County Clerk	240 Old Country Road, Mineola, 11501	(516) 571-2663
County Comptroller	240 Old Country Road, Mineola, 11501	(516) 571-2386
County Executive	1 West Street, Mineola, 11501	(516) 571-3131
County Legislature	1 West Street, Mineola, 11501	(516) 571-6636
Criminal Court	262 Old Country Road, Mineola, 11501	(516) 571-2800
District Attorney	262 Old Country Road, Mineola, 11501	(516) 571-2994
Drug & Alcohol Addiction (*)	40 Main Street, 3rd Floor, Hempstead, 11550	(516) 572-1900
Economic Development Administration	400 County Seat Drive, Mineola, 11501	(516) 571-0390
Health Department	240 Old Country Road, Mineola, 11501	(516) 571-3410
Housing & Intergovernmental Affairs	400 County Seat Drive, Mineola, 11501	(516) 571-0390
Human Rights Commission	1550 Franklin Street, Mineola, 11501	(516) 571-3662
Office for the Physically Challenged (*)	60 Charles Lindbergh Boulevard, Uniondale, 11553	(516) 227-7399
Office of Management and Budget	1 West Street, Mineola, 11501	(516) 571-4273
Office of Minority Affairs	1 West Street, Mineola, 11501	(516) 571-6174
Planning Commission	400 County Seat Drive, Mineola, 11501	(516) 571-5847
Police Department	1490 Franklin Ave, Mineola, 11501	(516) 573-7000
Public Works (*)	1100 Prospect Avenue, Westbury, 11590	(516) 571-3139
Purchasing Office	240 Old Country Road, Mineola, 11501	(516) 571-4200
Senior Citizen Affairs (*)	60 Charles Lindbergh Blvd, Uniondale, 11553	(516) 227-8900
Sheriff's Department	240 Old Country Road, Mineola, 11501	(516) 571-2113
Social Services	101 County Seat Drive, Mineola, 11501	(516) 571-4817
Supreme Court	100 Supreme Court Drive, Mineola, 11501	(516) 571-2904
Traffic And Parking Violations Agency (*)	16 Cooper Street, Hempstead, 11550	(516) 572-2700
Treasurer's Office	240 Old Country Road, Mineola, 11501	(516) 571-2090
Veterans Services (*)	1425 Old Country Road, Plainview, 11803	(516) 572-8452
Youth Board (*)	60 Charles Lindbergh Boulevard, Uniondale, 11553	(516) 227-7134

(*) Indicates outside map area

Government Seat: Mineola

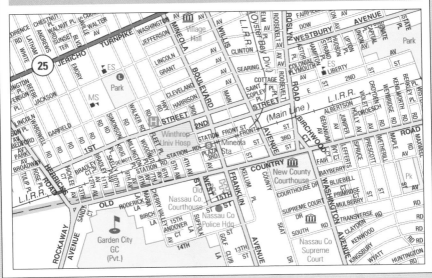

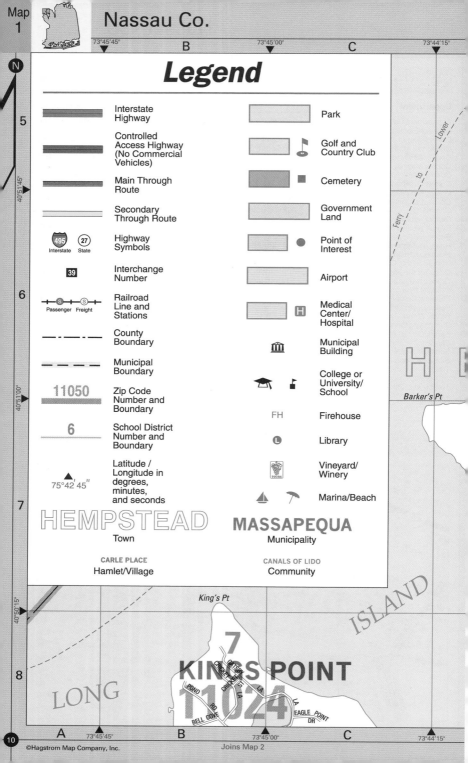

Map 1

Nassau Co.

Legend

Interstate Highway		Park
Controlled Access Highway (No Commercial Vehicles)		Golf and Country Club
Main Through Route		Cemetery
Secondary Through Route		Government Land
Highway Symbols — **495** Interstate, **27** State		Point of Interest
Interchange Number — **39**		Airport
Railroad Line and Stations — Passenger, Freight		Medical Center/ Hospital
County Boundary		Municipal Building
Municipal Boundary		College or University/ School
11050 Zip Code Number and Boundary		FH Firehouse
6 School District Number and Boundary		Library
75°42′45″ Latitude / Longitude in degrees, minutes, and seconds		Vineyard/ Winery
		Marina/Beach

HEMPSTEAD
Town

MASSAPEQUA
Municipality

CARLE PLACE
Hamlet/Village

CANALS OF LIDO
Community

Barker's Pt

Ferry to Lower

King's Pt

LONG ISLAND

7
KINGS POINT
11024

EAGLE POINT DR

BELL COVE

POND RD

Joins Map 2

73°45′45″ 73°45′00″ 73°44′15″

A   B   C

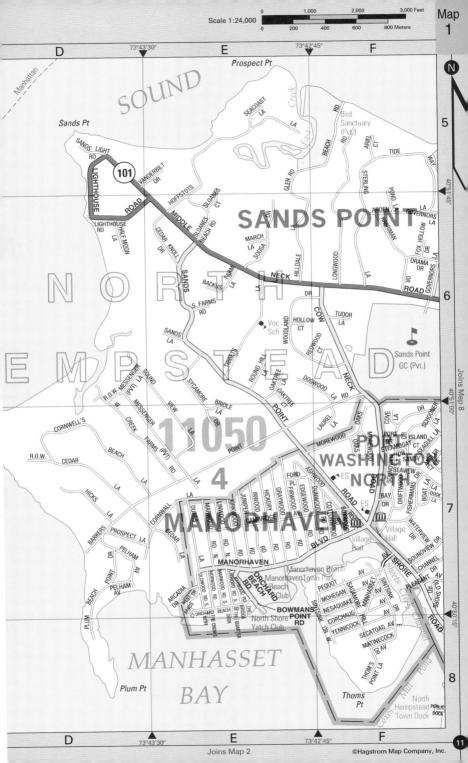

Map 1

Scale 1:24,000

SOUND

Prospect Pt

Sands Pt

SANDS POINT

N O R T H

H E M P S T E A D

11050

4

MANORHAVEN

POINT WASHINGTON NORTH

MANHASSET

BAY

Plum Pt

Thoms Pt

North Hempstead Town Dock

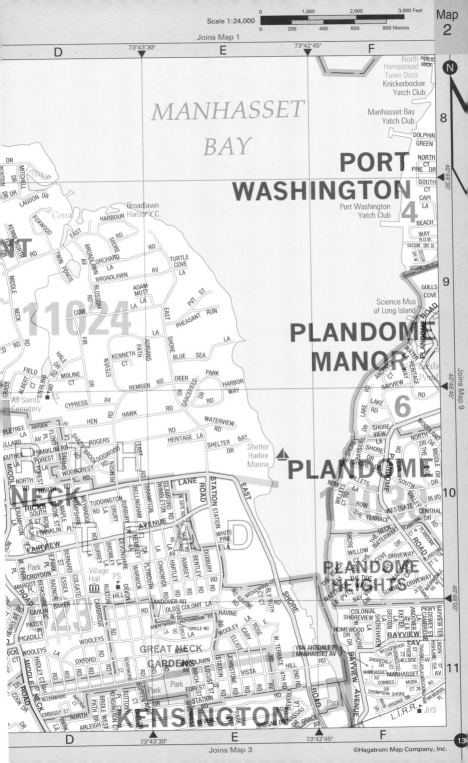

Map 2

Scale 1:24,000

0   1,000   2,000   3,000 Feet
0   200   400   600   800 Meters

D   73°43'30"   E   73°42'45"   F

N

MANHASSET BAY

North Hempstead Town Dock
PUBLIC DOCK
Knickerbocker Yatch Club

8

Manhasset Bay Yatch Club

DOLPHIN GREEN

PORT

NORTH PINE CT
SOUTH CT

40°49'30"

WASHINGTON

Port Washington Yatch Club

CAPI LA

4

BEACH WAY
R.O.W.

SECOR DR N
SECOR DR W
SECOR DR E
SECOR DR S

GULLS COVE

9

Science Mus of Long Island

PLANDOME

Leeds Pond

MANOR

WATER HERITAGE

ANDOVER WAY
BAYVIEW

6

40°48'45"

LAKE RD
SHORE VIEW LA

NORTH DR
MIDDLE DR

SHORE DR
BAYSIDE DR
WILLETS

PLANDOME

SOUTH DR

WESTGATE
CENTRAL

10

BLVD

THE TERRACE
THE NECK WATERWAY

PLANDOME RD

Shelter Harbor Marina

PLANDOME HEIGHTS

THE COVE DRIVEWAY

THE TIDE WATERWAY

11030

COLONIAL SHOREVIEW
CAMBRIDGE
GROTON LA
EXETER LA

40°48'00"

HOMEWOOD LA

BAYVIEW

PKWY
DEWEY ST
BAYVIEW TER

HIGHLAND AV

WEDGEWOOD DR
SHORELAND DR
HILLSIDE DR

1 VAN ARSDALE PL
2 MANHASSET AV

GREAT NECK GARDENS

MANHASSET AV
COMBES AV
MORA

DR THOMPSON SHORE

11

KENSINGTON

L.I.R.R.

JHS

D   73°43'30"   E   73°42'45"   F

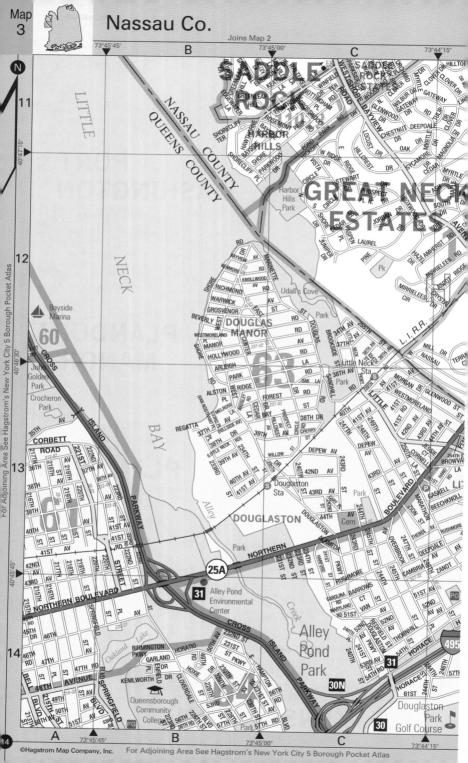

Map
3

Joins Map 2

Nassau Co.

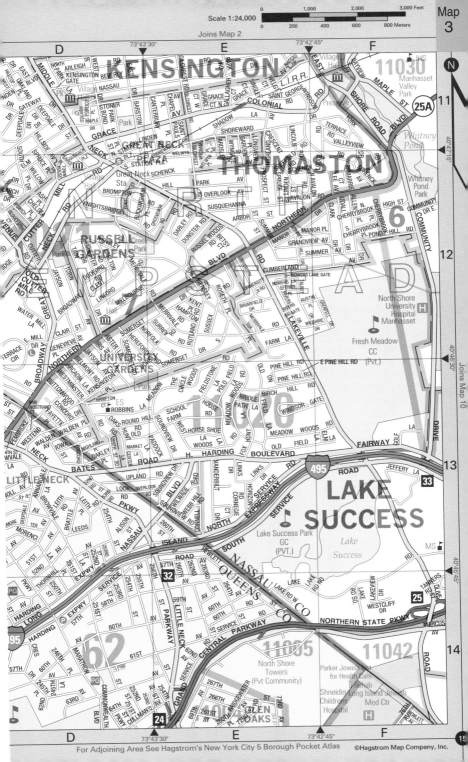

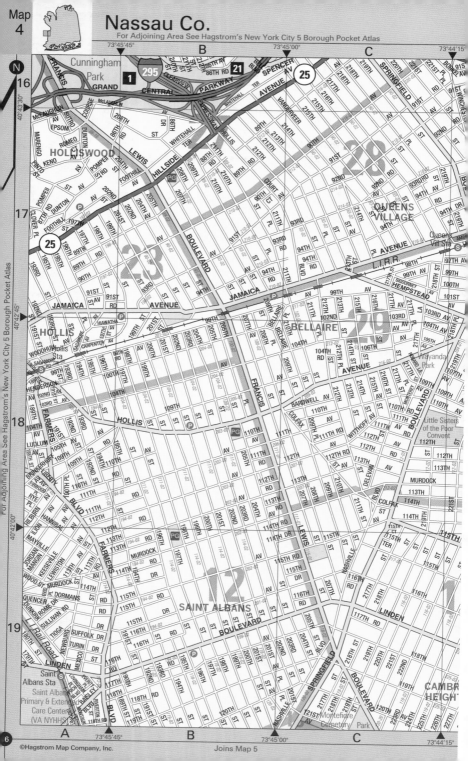

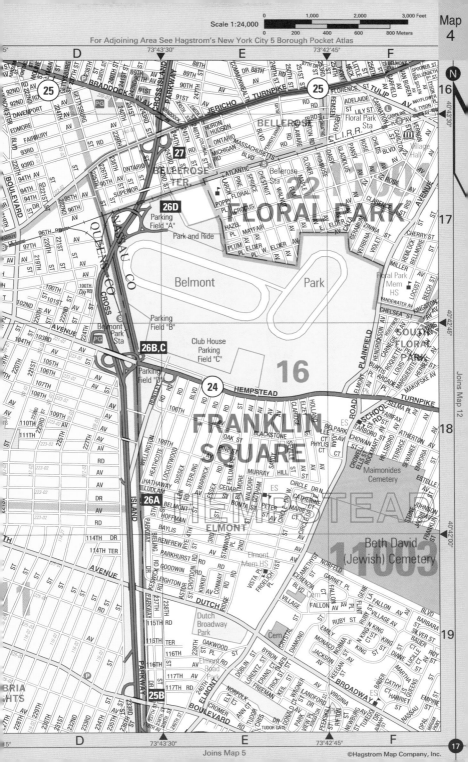

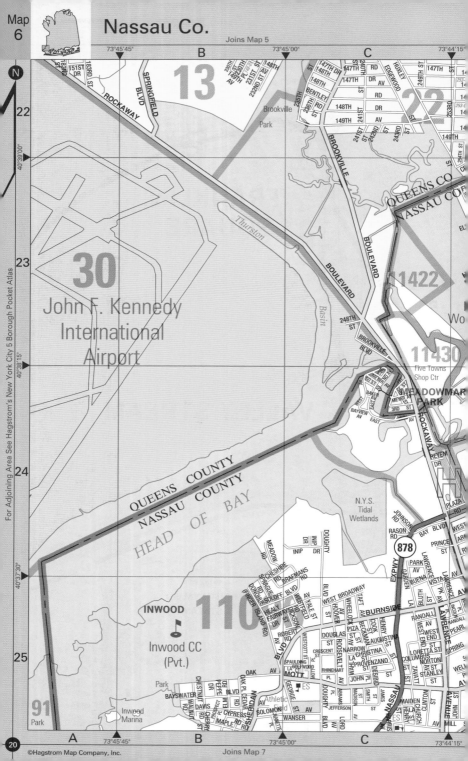

Map 7

Scale 1:24,000

Joins Map 6

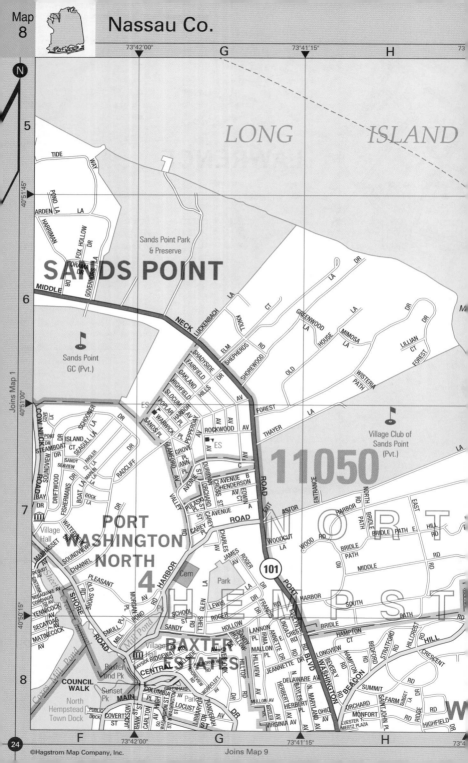

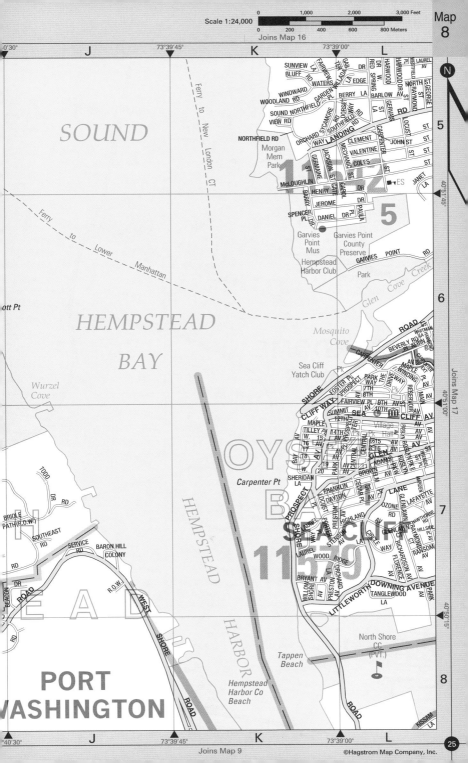

Map
8

Scale 1:24,000

| 0 | 1,000 | 2,000 | 3,000 Feet |
| 0 | 200 | 400 | 600 | 800 Meters |

Joins Map 16

J 73°39'45" K 73°39'00" L

SOUND

Ferry to New London CT

Ferry to Lower Manhattan

HEMPSTEAD

BAY

Wurzel Cove

ott Pt

11542

5

SUNVIEW BLUFF
WINDWARD
WOODLAND RD
SOUND
VIEW RD
NORTHFIELD RD
Morgan Mem Park
McLOUGHLIN
HENRY
SPENCER
JEROME
PL
DANIEL
Garvies Point Mus
Hempstead Harbor Club
Garvies Point County Preserve
Park
GARVIES POINT
RD

Glen Cove Creek

Mosquito Cove

Sea Cliff Yacht Club

ROAD

BEVERLY RD

CARPENTER

SHORE

CLIFF WAY

FOSTER PL
PROSPECT
PARK WAY
7TH
8TH
FAIRVIEW PL 9TH
SUMMIT 10TH
12TH
MAPLE
TILLEY PL 14TH
W. 15
16 AV
17 PL
18
W. 19
20
PARK
SHERIDAN LA

SEA CLIFF AV

Village

GLEN

SEA
CLIFF

Carpenter Pt

HEMPSTEAD HARBOR

PROSPECT

FRANKLIN
DAYTON
HIGHLAND

LANE

OZONE

SHORE
WAY
LAUREL
WOOD
RIDGE
BRYANT AV
WILLOW
PRESTON
STENSON

SEACLIFF
11579

DOWNING AVENUE
TANGLEWOOD LA
LITTLEWORTH

LAFAYETTE

HILLSIDE

RICHARDSON AV
FLORENCE
RANSOM AV

PARK

North Shore CC (P.V.T.)

Tappen Beach

PORT
WASHINGTON

BRIDLE PATH (R.O.W.)
SOUTHEAST RD
SERVICE RD
BARON HILL COLONY
ROAD
WEST SHORE
ROAD
R.O.W.

TODD DR RD

Hempstead Harbor Co Beach

J 73°40'30" K 73°39'45" L 73°39'00"

N

5

40°51'45"

6

40°51'00" Joins Map 17

7

40°50'15"

8

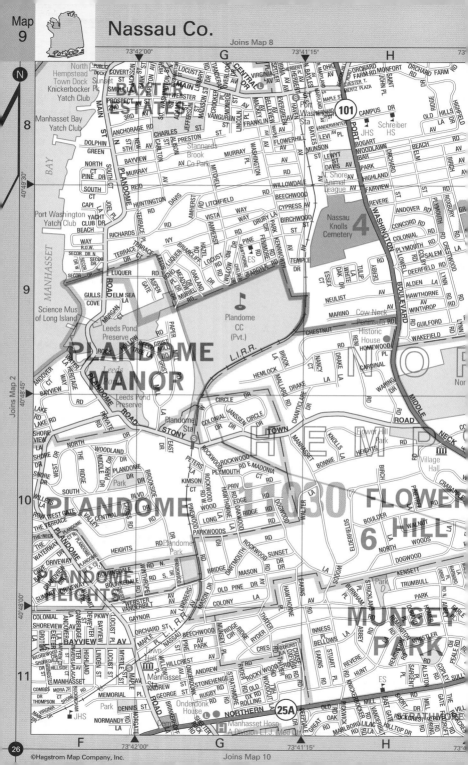

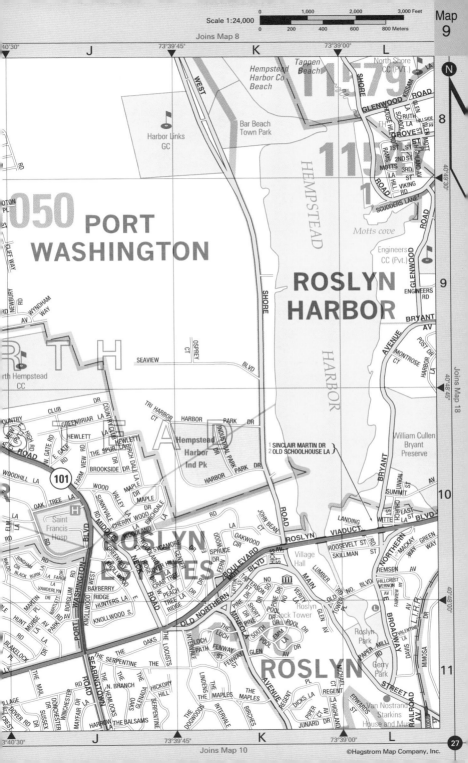

Map
9

Scale 1:24,000

1,000   2,000   3,000 Feet

200   400   600   800 Meters

Joins Map 8

N

Hempstead
Harbor Co.
Beach

Tappen
Beach

North Shore
CC (PVT.)

1157-9

KISSAM
LA

WEST

GLENWOOD
ROAD

GLEN
LA

GLEN
RUTH
LA

FH HILL
SCHOOL
LA

HILLSIDE
AV

8

Bar Beach
Town Park

Harbor Links
GC

GROVES

1ST ST

2ND ST

3RD
ST

LOW

115

MOTTS

ROAD

HILL
VIKING
RD

40°49'30"

050 **PORT
WASHINGTON**

**ROSLYN
HARBOR**

HEMPSTEAD

SCUDDERS LANE

ROAD

Motts cove

Engineers
CC (Pvt.)

GLENWOOD

ENGINEERS
RD

9

BRYANT
AV

40°48'45"

Joins Map 18

rth Hempstead
CC

SEAVIEW

OSPREY
CT

BLVD

HARBOR

MONTROSE
CT

POST DR

HARBOR
RD

AVENUE

TRI HARBOR
CT

HARBOR

PARK

DR

William Cullen
Bryant
Preserve

CLUB
DR

GREENBRIAR
DR

HEWLETT
DR

HEWLETT

COUNTRY CLUB DR

THE SPUR

BIRCH DALE LA

Hempstead
Harbor
Ind Pk

INDUSTRIAL PARK DR

1 SINCLAIR MARTIN DR
2 OLD SCHOOLHOUSE LA

BRYANT

SUMMIT
ST

CHURCH
ST

WITTE
ST

EAST
AV

N. E. GATE

E. GATE

BROOKSIDE DR

HARBOR

PARK

DR

101

FARM VIEW

WOODHILL LA

WOOD
DR

MAPLE
DR

VALLEY

MAPLE

CHERRY WOOD

OAK TREE LA

MIDDLE RD

RD

JOHN BEAN
CT

ROSLYN

ROAD

VIADUCT

NORTHERN

BLVD

10

Saint
Francis
Hosp

LA

SYCAMORE

OAKWOOD
CIR

LANDING

ROOSEVELT ST

SKILLMAN
ST

MACKAY
WAY

GREEN
WAY

ROSLYN
ESTATES

SPRUCE
DR

Village
Hall

REMSEN
AV

HILLCREST

VERNON
AV

ELM

KNOLLWOOD
WEST

BAYBERRY
RIDGE

HUNTERS LA

KNOLLWOOD S.

LA PEACH

TREE LA

RIDGE

PINE
DR

SHORT
DR

PINE
DR

MAIN

LUMBER
ST

OLD
NO. ROAD

Roslyn
Tower

ROSLYN

40°48'00"

L.I.R.R.

BROADWAY

MIMOSA

PORT WASHINGTON

BORGLUM

MINEOLA

BOULEVARD

GLEN
AV

POOL
DR

Roslyn
Park

PAPER MILL
RD

VALENTINE

Gerry
Park

THE OAKS

THE SERPENTINE

THE

LOCH

INTERVALE

LOCH
PATH

FENWAY
ST

FENWAY

GLEN

AV

MICHAEL
ST

PL

Van Nostrand
Starkins
House and Mus

SEARINGTOWN
ROAD

THE MALL

N. BRANCH

THE HEMLOCKS

THE OAKS

CANADA

HICKORY
HILL

SERPENTINE

THE LINDENS

THE MAPLES

THE
MAPLES

BIRCHES

REGENT

REGENT

DICKS LA

PIPER
CT

HIGHLAND

JUNARD DR

EDWARDS
ST

RAILROAD
AV

STREET

ILLAGE

DOVER RD

MAYFAIR DR

WINCHESTER

DORCHESTER

SUSSEX

HARROW

THE BALSAMS

THE DOGWOODS

INTERVALE

J   K   L

73°39'45"   73°39'00"

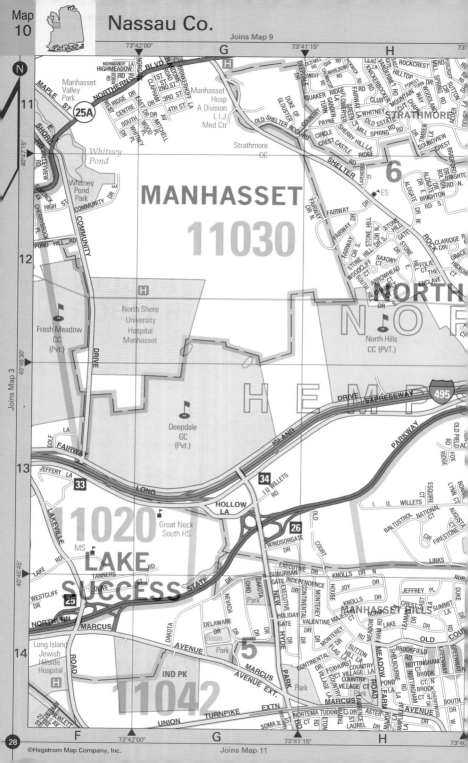

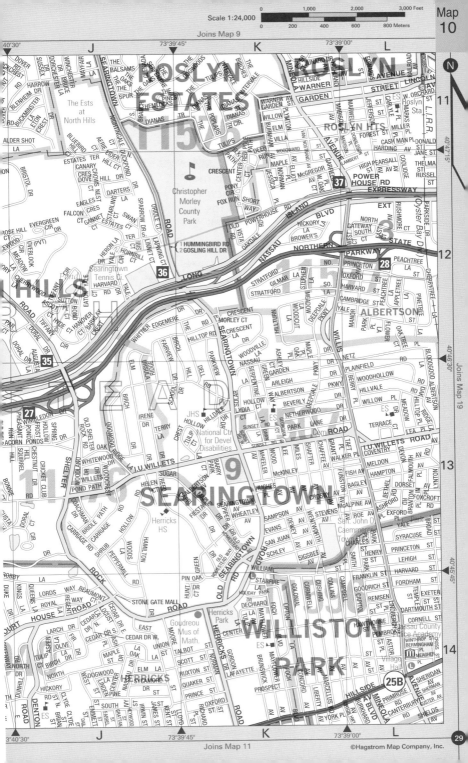

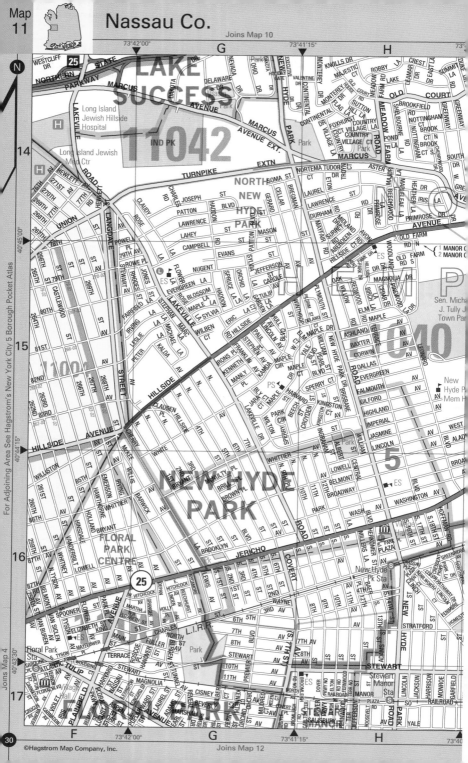

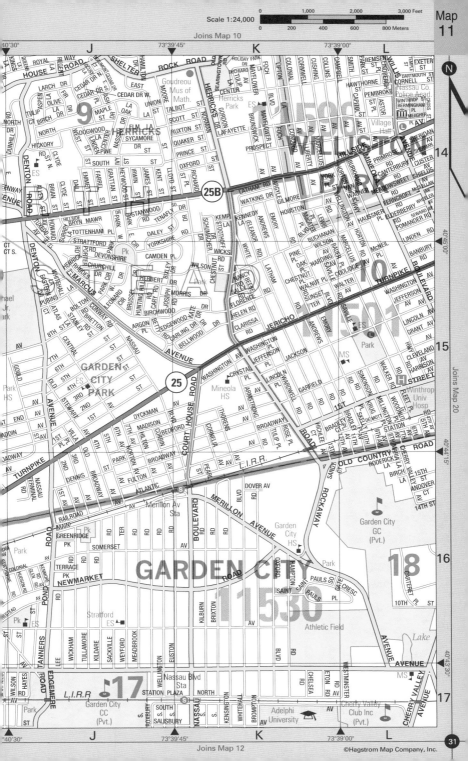

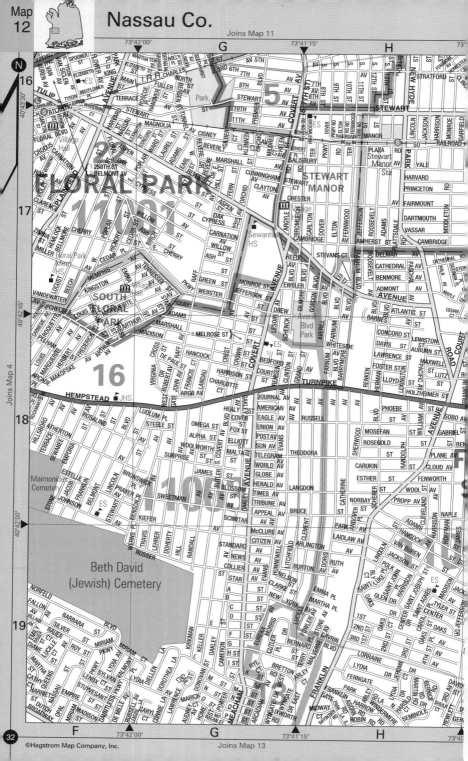

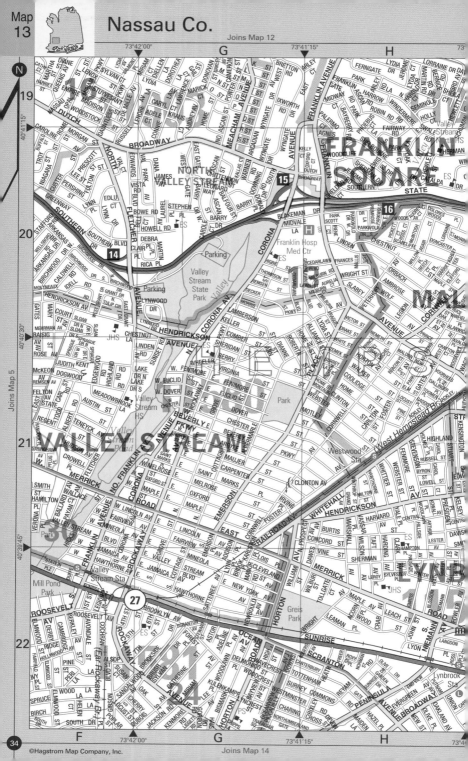

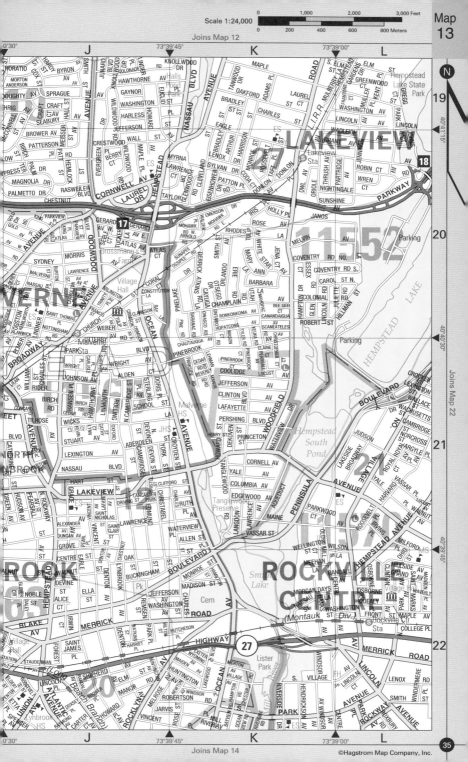

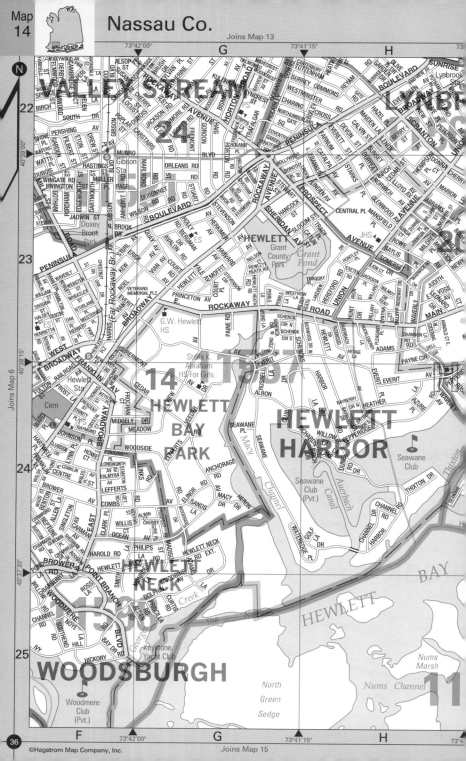

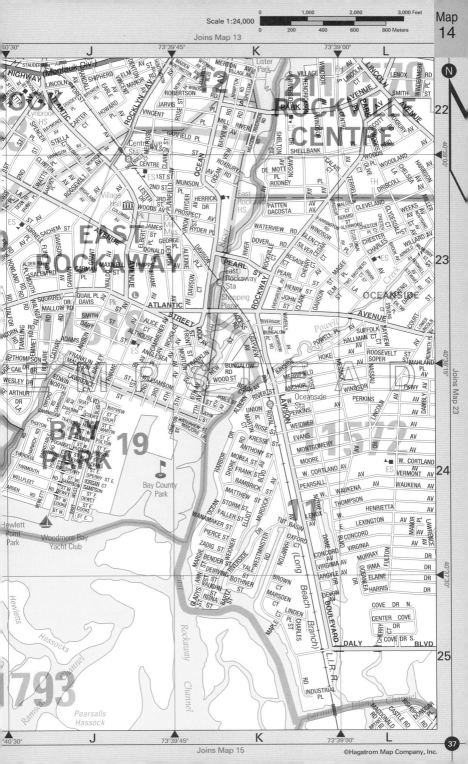

Map 15
Nassau Co.
Joins Map 14

N

WOODSBURGH

14

Woodmere Club (Pvt.)

The Narrows

North Green Sedge

Ney's Hole Creek

Ramsing

73°42'00" G 73°41'15" H 73°

25

40°36'45"

Stinking Pt

So. Green Sedge

Cedar Island

BROSEWERE BAY

Woodsburgh Channel

11

11793

Post Marsh

26

Big Hassock

LEAD

Charles Pt

CHANNEL

40°36'00"

LAWRENCE H E M P S

15

POST

Sand Bar Pt

Joins Map 7

11559

BROAD

Lawrence Marsh

R

27

REYNOLDS CHANNEL

City Beach

W. W. BLVD

ES W. BLVD F

H

ST BLVD M

WATER W. BLVD

11561

CHESTER

40°35'15"

Park

BAY
PARK
AV

ST
ST W.

PARK

ST

AV AV AV AV AV AV AV AV AV AV ST AV ST ST AV ST AV ST AV ST AV AV

NEW YORK NEW YORK AV

W. W.

PARK WALNUT

ATLANTIC BEACH BLVD BEECH BEECH STREET

OLIVE

BEECH

W.

PENN

CAPRI AV
CLAYTON
SWAN
MARK DR

MALONE
OSWEGO
MOHAWK
TROY
BUFFALO
ROCHESTER
TRENTON
BROOKLINE
NEVADA

OHIO
ILLINOIS
CONNECTICUT
FLORIDA
GEORGIA
KENTUCKY
OCEAN
INDIANA
LOUISIANA
MICHIGAN
MARYLAND
MINNESOTA
NEW HAMPSHIRE
TENNESSEE
VERMONT
VIRGINIA
WISCONSIN
WYOMING
ALABAMA
DELAWARE
OREGON
ARIZONA
VIEW
NEBRASKA
PENNSYLVANIA
CALIFORNIA

W. GRAND BROADWAY LINDELL WASHINGTON

LAFAYETTE

W. BOARDWALK

Park

ES

28

ATLANTIC

F 73°42'00" G 73°41'15" H 73°4

38

©Hagstrom Map Company, Inc.

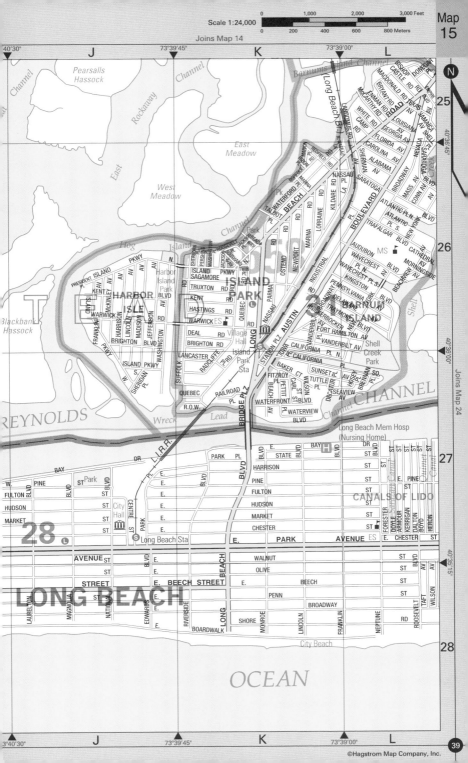

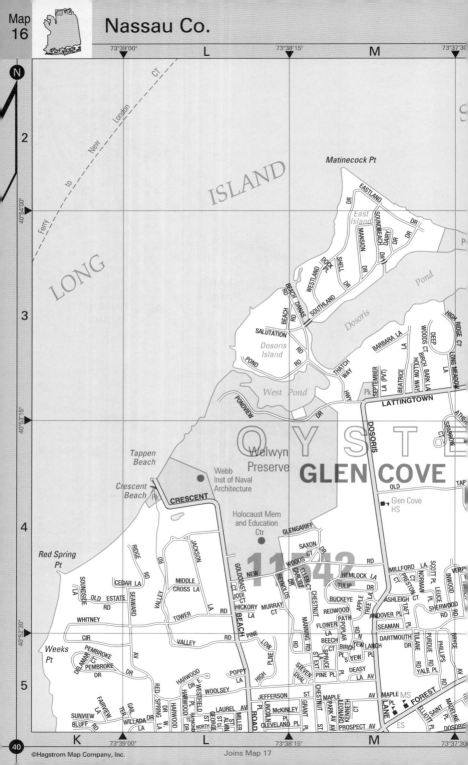

Map

16

Scale 1:24,000

0   1,000   2,000   3,000 Feet
0   200   400   600   800 Meters

SOUND

Fox Pt

Creek

N   O   P

73°36'45"   73°36'00"

Peacock Pt.

Frost

Creek

SHEEP LA

END RD LA

LANDS

THE FARM (PVT)

Park

Park

EAST

PITTLE VIKINGS COVE (PVT RD)

POMEROY LA

FROST CREEK PL

LATTINGTOWN

Glen Cove GC (Pvt.)

BEACH DRIVE

PEACOCK LA

MEUDON

GREAT MEADOW RD

DR

LEWIS

CREEK

DANTON LA S

PARISH RD

MINDY CT

11560

CREEK LA

The Creek Club (Pvt.)

ROBIN CT

SWAN CT

THEM

DR

CARDINAL

BEECHWOOD

R   B A Y

TAPPANWOOD Cem

WOODS CT

LATTINGTOWN CT

TAPPAN

OVERLOOK

RD

WINDING WAY

DR

Village Hall

ROAD

HORSE HOLLOW ROAD

HIGH

APPAN

RD

WALNUT

SWEET LA

BITTER

ELMS

LA

HOLLY TREE LA

MAPLE

VI

SUGAR LA

HITCHING

POST LA

BRIDLE

SPUR

STIRRUP

SPIRON

ARPLANK

RD

BRANDING LA

TIMBER LA

SADDLE LA

LA

DEEPDALE CT

KIRKWOOD

MEADOWFIELD CT

BRIARWOOD DR

HILLDALE PL

RIDGEFIELD PL

WOODALE DR

DRIFTWOOD DR

BROADFIELD PL

5

MEDICAL PLZ

BROOKDALE

LATTINGTOWN RIDGE CT

OVERLOOK

CT

FOXWOOD PATH

LATTINGTOWN

ROAD RD

PRIVATE RD

SKUNKS

LANE

MEADOW PL

WEIRS LA

MISERY

SHELTER LA

1 HILLCREST PL

LUDLAM LA

RYEFIELD RD

CORNEGARTH

BALDWIN

HILL ROAD

LINDBERGH ST

ALBERTA

BELLA VISTA ST

CHURCH ST

KATHERINE

RIGGS ST

SOUNDVIEW

CHERRY ST

NURSERY ST

BENJAMIN PL

WINANS PL

DAVIS

BIRCH

UNDERHILL AV

ASH ST

BIRCH ST

LOCUST ST

EDGEWOOD

BUCKRAM ROAD

N 2ND ST

CROSS

LEONA PL

13TH ST

14TH ST

2ND ST

1ST ST

12TH ST

10TH ST

11TH ST

9TH ST

8TH ST

7TH ST

W. 6TH ST

W. 4TH ST

NORTH

WOOD

S

LOCUST VALLEY Sta

AVENUE

W. 5TH ST

W. 3RD ST

5TH ST

6TH ST

4TH ST

ELM

E. 3RD PL

LINDEN ST

LINDEN FARMS RD

TOWN LANE

COCKS LANE

FARMS RD

AVENUE

PRESTWICK TER

CLINTON ST

JAMES ST

CAMBRIDGE ST

SAINT ANDREWS

HARRISON AV

FORD RD

FOREST RD

NASSAU RD

FOREST

LOCUST VALLEY

S

LANE

PIPING ROCK ROAD

H

ANDREWS

North Shore Univ Hosp at Glen Cove

WALNUT ROAD

TITUS ST

TOWNSEND RD

RD

MATINECOCK

THREE PL

BIS WAY

WESTGATE CT LA

Nassau CC (Pvt.)

(Oyster Bay Div)

QUAIL RIDGE RD

OVERLOOK RD

LINDEN FARMS RD

LA

N   O   P

73°36'45"   73°36'00"

Joins Map 25

Joins Maps 26

Joins Map 17

Map
17

Scale 1:24,000

Joins Map 16

3,000 Feet
1,000   2,000
200   400   600   800 Meters

11560
MATINECOCK

11545

OLD BROOKVILLE

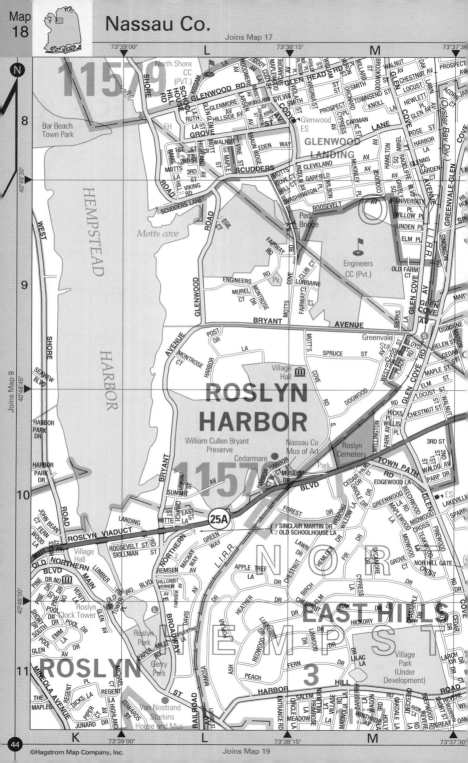

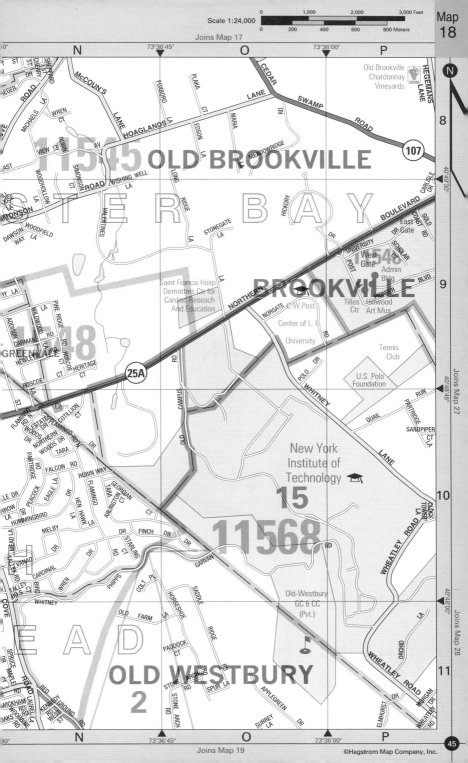

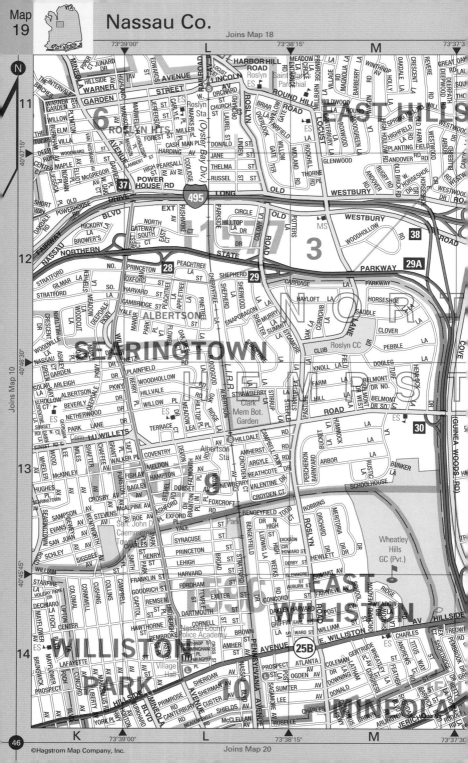

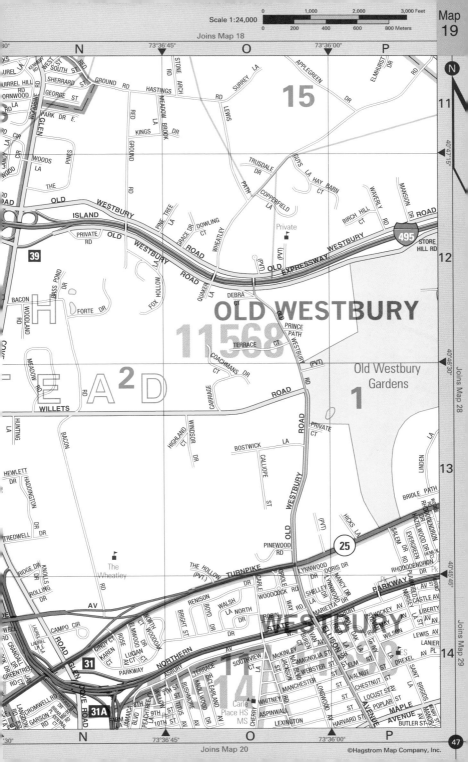

Map
19

Scale 1:24,000

Joins Map 18

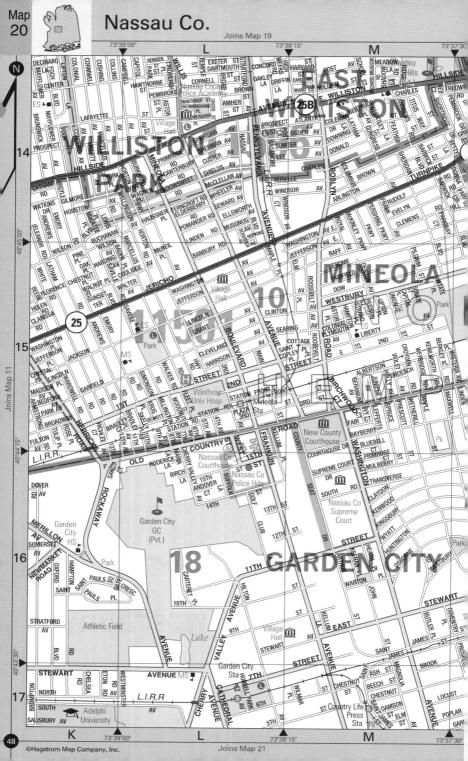

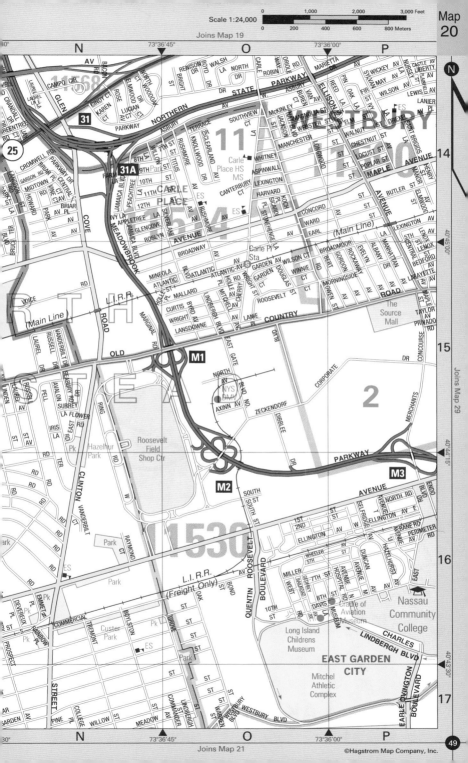

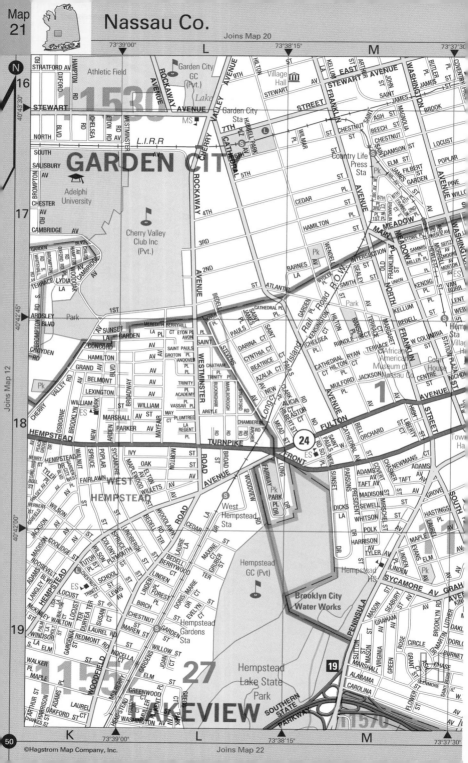

Map
21

Scale 1:24,000

0   1,000   2,000   3,000 Feet

0   200   400   600   800 Meters

N   O   P

73°36'45"   73°36'00"

Custer Park

Long Island Childrens Museum

Nassau Community College

EAST GARDEN CITY

Mitchel Athletic Complex

Park & Ride

Hofstra University

Weeb Ewbank Hall

North Campus Parking Field

HEMPSTEAD (FULTON AV) TURNPIKE

Shuart Stadium

UNIONDALE

102

2

Hempstead Island Med Ctr

HEMPSTEAD

JERUSALEM AVENUE

HEMPSTEAD AVENUE

Kennedy Mem Pk

JERUSALEM AVENUE

Lincoln Park

Park Northern

UNIONDALE AVENUE

BROOKSIDE AVENUE

NASSAU ROAD

Greenfield Cemetery

N   O   P

73°36'45"   73°36'00"

©Hagstrom Map Company, Inc.

16

17

18

19

40°43'30"

40°42'45"

40°42'00"

Joins Map 30

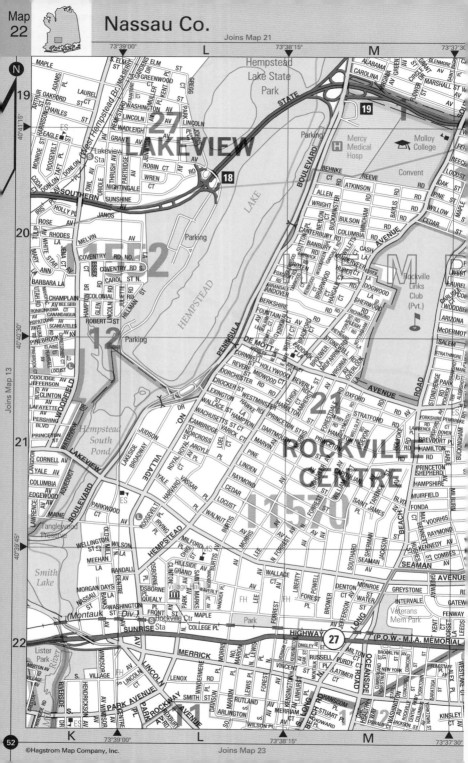

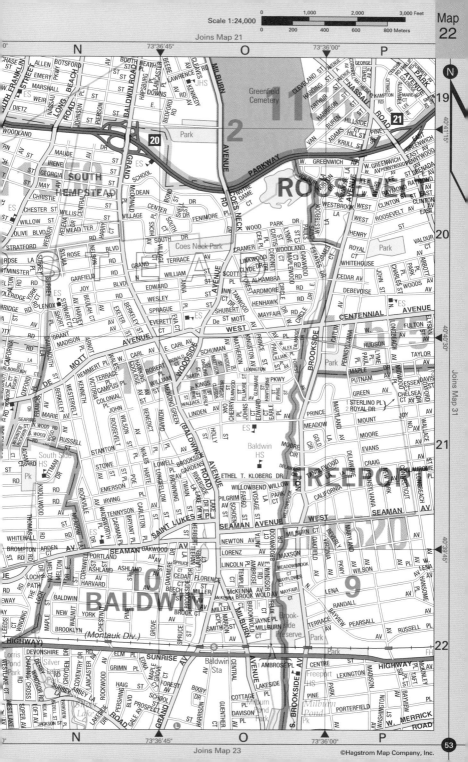

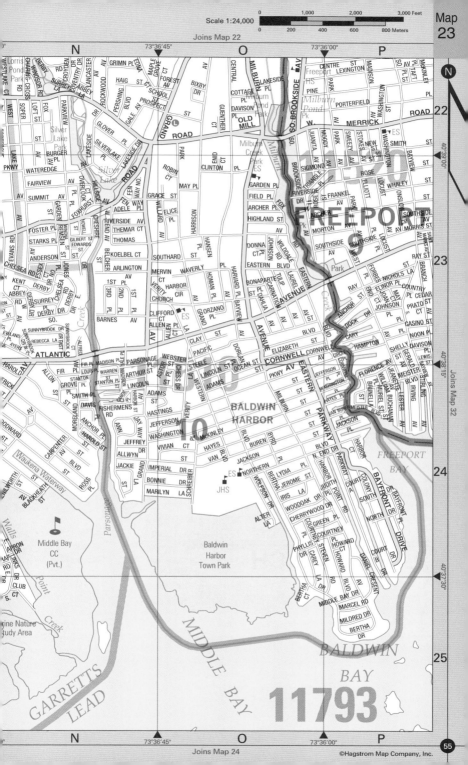

N   73°36'45"   O   73°36'00"   P

N

25

West High Meadow

40°36'45"

LEAD

MIDDLE

11

11793

Parsonage Island

Cinder Island

Seadog Island

26

BAY

STEAD

Channel

No Cinder Island

Long Meadow

40°36'00"

Joins Map 33

Cinder Island

Cinder Island

Ingraham   *Hassock*

Creek Channel

CHANNEL

Middle Island

Island

Channel

Lido Beach
Nat'l
Wildlife
Management
Area

11569

27

BOBSBAY RD
NEPTUNE RD
BAY LA
ANCHOR RD
CHANNEL RD
SWAREN DR
DANIEL
GARRY AV
DR
DONNA LA

LIDO BEACH

MARGINAL RD

BOULEVARD

Town of Hempstead
West Marina

♩
Lido GC

Nickerson
(Nassau) Beach
Park

Malibu Beach
(Town of Hempstead
Park)

40°36'15"

NANTWICK ST
BIARRITZ ST
ROYAL ST
LUCHON ST
WOODHAL ST
LEAMINGTON ST
SARATOGA ST
KENSINGTON ST
PRESCOTT ST

Lido Blvd
Park

BLVD

Beach

28

OCEAN

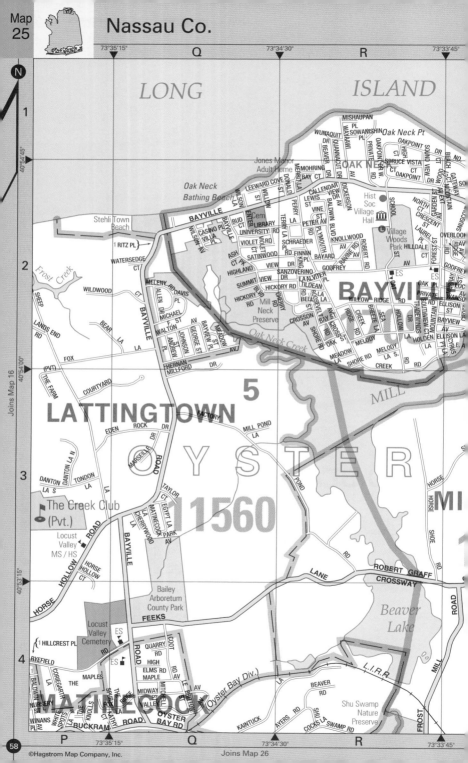

Map
25

Nassau Co.

73°35'15" Q 73°34'30" R 73°33'45"

LONG   ISLAND

N

1

40°54'45"

MISHAUPAN PL
WUNAQUIT DR SOWANISHIN
WANAMI Oak Neck Pt
QUANNAQUIT DR OAKPOINT
BEAVER OAKPOINT DR W. HIGH CT
MOHRING OAK NECK SPRUCE VISTA
Jones Manor OAKPOINT SOUND VIEW DR
Adult Home CALLENDAR OAKPOINT
VIEW AV DICKERSON BEACH
Oak Neck LEEWARD COVE LA LEWIS ST SCHOOL NORTH
Bathing Beach WILSON ST WILLOW ST VINE BALDWIN BLVD Hist CRESCENT
BAYVILLE BUD PERRY ST TERRY LA PETER AV Soc LAUREL
CT LIBRARY PLYMOUTH Village Hall FOREST ST
CASINO PL UNIVERSITY RD SCHRAEDER KNOLLWOOD Village HILLDALE
VILLA PL VIOLET ST RD FINNIN AV Woods OVERLOOK
1 RITZ PL BAYVILLE VIOLET SATINWOOD BAYARD ROBERT Park AV
WATERSEDGE ASH HIGHLAND VIEW DR GODFREY ST GODFREY
CT CT PL SUMMIT SANZOVERINO ES BAYVIEW
MELENY DAVIS BLVD VIEW LAVLITER ES PRIVATE
WILDWOOD ALLEN DR RD HICKORY RD TILDEAN WILLOW RIDGE RD BAYVILLE 11709
SHEEP MICHAEL BELL CHERRY ELLISON ST
BEAR ST HICKORY BELL BAY BREEZE LA BAYVIEW AV
LANDS END WALTON JOHNSON CROSSON AV SEA CROSS RIDGE ELLISON AV
RD ANDREW GEORGE ST OAK MEADOW HOLDEN LA
FOX LA MEADOW AV SHORE RD MELODY CHRIS LA
(PVT) HERNAN DR MELODY LA S. AV
THE FARM MILLFORD Oak Neck Creek MEADOW SHORE RD CREEK MELODY LA

BAYVILLE 11709

2

40°54'00"

Frost Creek

Stehli Town
Beach

BAYVILLE

BAYVILLE

Joins Map 16

COURTYARD

5

LATTINGTOWN

FACTORY

OYSTER

EDEN ROCK DR MILL POND LA

MILL

40°53'15"

MARSEILLE

ROAD

11560

DANTON LA N TONDON LA
DANTON LA S LA

TAYLOR CT
EGYPT LA
MATINECOCK LA
CHERRYWOOD PARK AV

POND RD

HORSE
HORSE
SHOE

MI

3

The Creek Club
(Pvt.)

Locust
Valley
MS / HS

HORSE
HOLLOW
CT

BAYVILLE

HOLLOW

ROAD

HORSE

Bailey
Arboretum
County Park

FEEKS

LANE ROBERT GRAFF
CROSSWAY

ROAD

Beaver
Lake

4

1 HILLCREST PL

RYEFIELD

Locust
Valley
Cemetery

ES

ES

MAPLES

QUARRY RD
HIGH
ELMS RD
MAPLE
MIDWAY

COOT RD
RD

CORIEGARTH

THE
MAPLES

SHIPE LA
KATHY

MITCHELL LA
LE BRETON AV

QUARRY
ROAD
ROAD
ROAD

L.I.R.R.

FROST
ROAD

MATINECOCK

BALDWIN

NURSERY

WINANS AV

WHITE
SPOTS LA

BUCKRAM

KNOLL LA
VALLEY
OYSTER
BAY RD

Oyster Bay Div.)

KAINTUCK

BEAVER RD

AYERS RD

COCKS LA

SHU LA
SWAMP RD

Shu Swamp
Nature
Preserve

ROAD

58

P 73°35'15" Q 73°34'30" R 73°33'45"

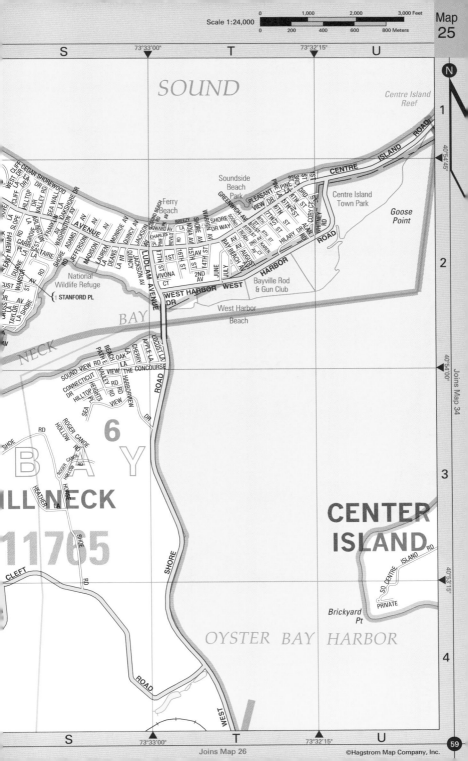

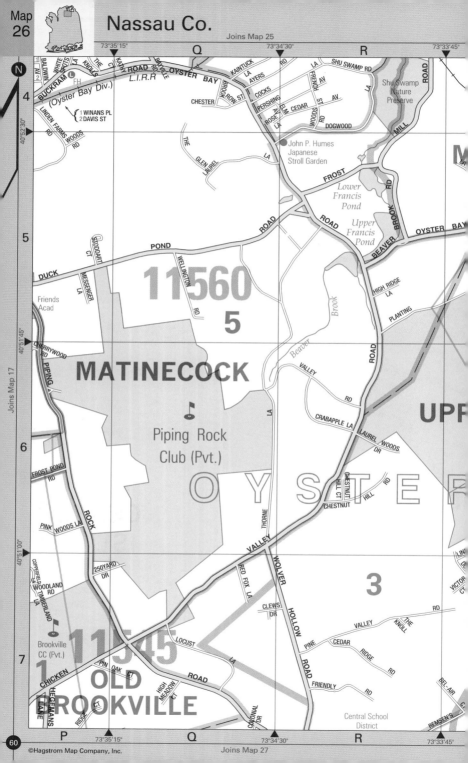

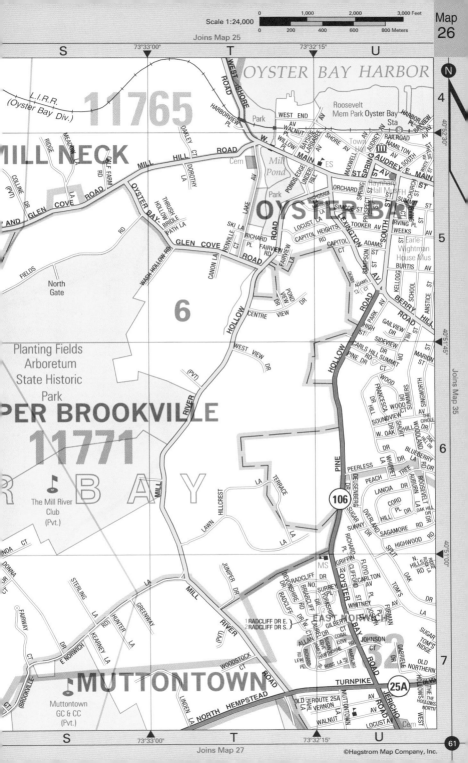

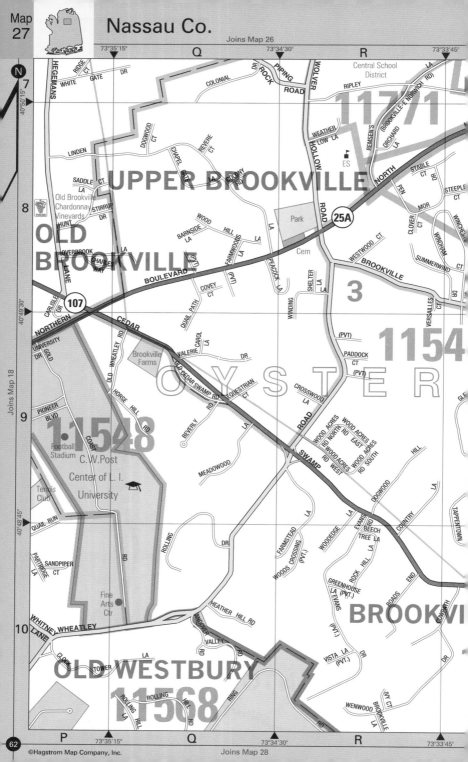

Map
27

Nassau Co.

Joins Map 26

N

7

8

9

10

Joins Map 18

UPPER BROOKVILLE

OLD
BROOKVILLE

Old Brookville
Chardonnay
Vineyards

Central School
District

117/1

25A

3

1154

OYSTER

1·11548

C.W.Post
Center of L. I.
University

Football
Stadium

Tennis
Club

Fine
Arts
Ctr

WHITNEY
WHEATLEY
LANE

OLD WESTBURY
11568

BROOKVI

Joins Map 28

Map
27

Scale 1:24,000

| | 1,000 | 2,000 | 3,000 Feet |

| | 200 | 400 | 600 | 800 Meters |

S | T | U

73°33'00" | 73°32'15"

N

7

40°50'15"

Muttontown
GC & CC
(Pvt.)

11732

TURNPIKE

LINDEN LA

WALNUT AV

MUTTONTOWN

LOCUST AV

Cem

HOLLOWS

THE

WEST
FARM LA

JERICHO

HILL LA

Chelsea Center-Nassau
County Office of
Cult. Devel.

11732

Hoffman Center
Nature Preserve

EMPSTEAD

ROAD

VILLAGE
HALL DR

8

6
MUTTONTOWN
11791

STONERIDGE
CT

WAKEFIELD DR

CHELMSFORD

SERENITE

SEREIN CT

Muttontown

HUNTERS
DR

106

NICHOLS
CT

LA

Private Burial
Ground

Preserve

40°49'30"

EASTWOODS

DORCHESTER
DR

DR

MUTTONTOWN

ROAD

WOOD
CT

MOTTOW

ROAD

ROAD

ROAD

Joins Map 36

5

LA

MORAINE
CT

B A Y

MIDLANE

FERNCOTE

LA

Bird
Sanctuary

CHESTNUT
CT

RD

Cem

EDGE

EDGE CT

RD

9

GLENBY

LA

RD

BLACK ROCK RD

PRIVATE

DR

FRANCES

LYNN
DR

40°48'45"

VICTORIAN LA

HOWARD
DR

LA

KNOLLWOOD
RD

KIRBY

IRONWOOD
RD

TITUS PATH

OYSTER BAY

FRUITLEDGE

Brookville
Nature
Park

CONN CT
(PVT.)

JERICHO

10

Tam O Shanter
Club Inc
(Pvt.)

BRIDLE PATH

CT

BELLE SONIA
CT

LA KIRBY

KIRBY
HILL

QUAKER

Cem

RIDGE

DR

DR

LA

MICHAELSON

LA

KARBY

ILLE

15

BROOK LA

DR

MacLEAN

ROAD

HEMLOCK

DR

WINDSOR

DR

PARKVIEW

ADEL
(PVT.)

LA

HEATHER LA

LA

JERICHO TPKE

NORDEN

DR

EAST NORWICH

106

ROAD

11753

25

EMERSON

MAYFLOWER RD

RD

107

KAROL
PL

KRISTI
DR

ELLEN
PL

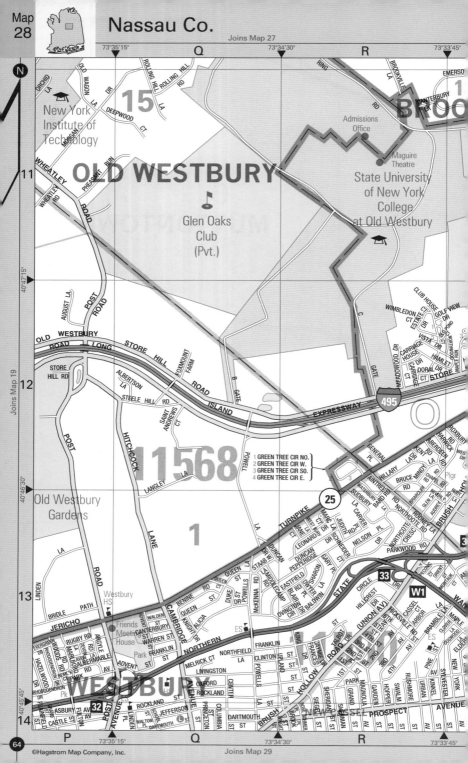

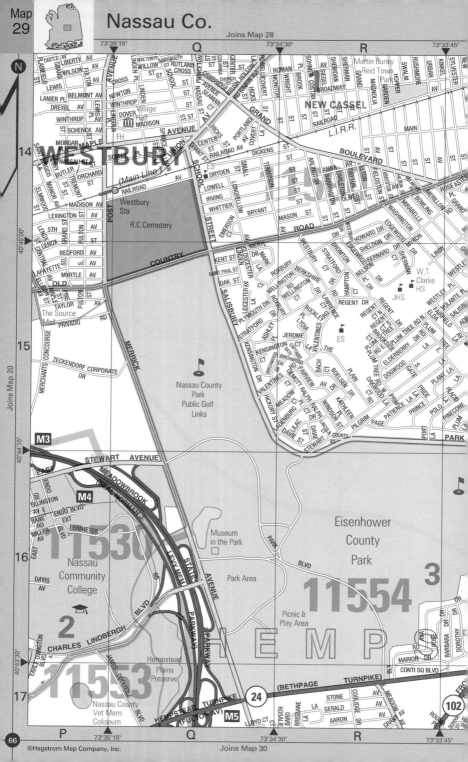

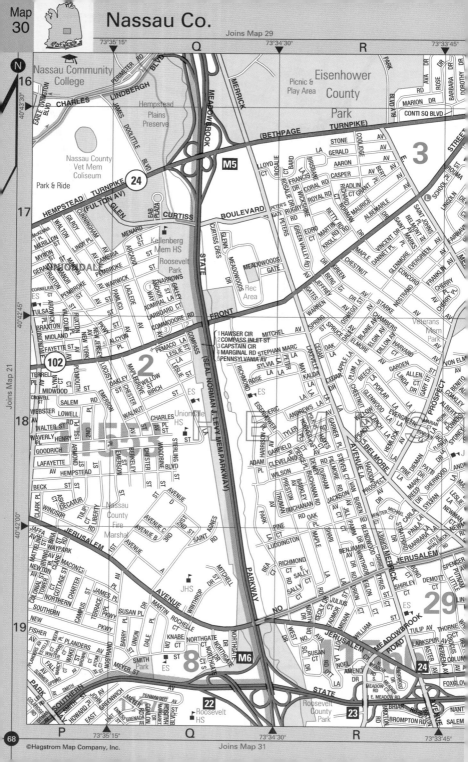

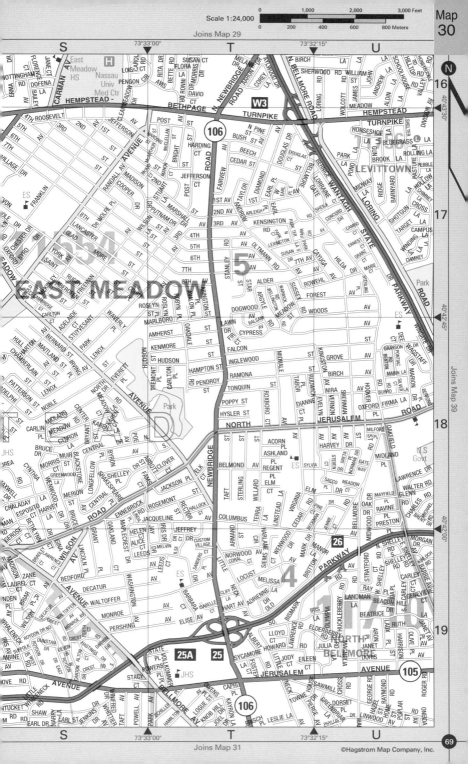

Map 30

Scale 1:24,000

EAST MEADOW

LEVITTOWN

NORTH BELLMORE

©Hagstrom Map Company, Inc.

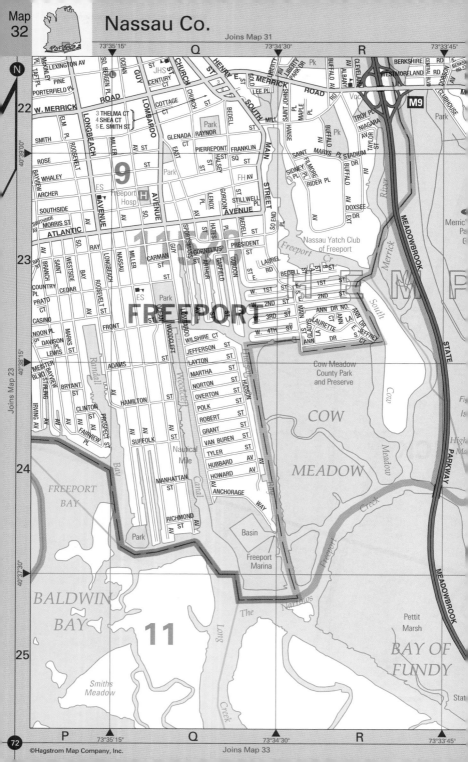

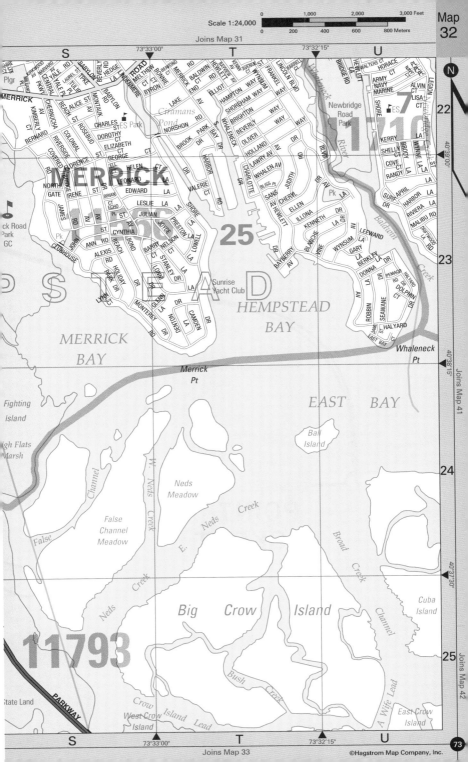

Map
32

Scale 1:24,000

0   1,000   2,000   3,000 Feet
0   200   400   600   800 Meters

73°33'00"   73°32'15"   N

MERRICK

S   T   U

22

11710

Wadleneck River

Newbridge Road Park

ARMY NAVY MARINE

WALTERS CT   HORACE

BRIDGE RD

HORACE
PL   CT

ALVIN CT   LISA CT

ES

KERRY LA

SHELLY CT
COVE CT

WYNNE LA

BRODY LA

RANDY LA

SURF DR
APRIL LA

HARBOR LA
RIVIERA LA

MALIBU RD

40°39'00"

MERRICK

25

Ciramans Pond

MERRICK
11566

STES Park

LAKE AV
NORSHON DR

CHARLES ST
DOROTHY CT
ELIZABETH CT
GEORGE CT

HELEN CT
LEONARD LA
EDWARD LA
LESLIE LA
JULIAN LA
CYNTHIA LA

BROOK PARK DR
BAY DR
WHALENECK DR

HARBOR DR

VALERIE CT
SHORE RD

PRESTON LA
LOWELL LA
LOWELL LA

BRIGHTON AV
OLIVER AV
HOLLAND AV

LAWRY AV

WHALEN AV
SANS AV

BLISS PL

ELLEN

CHERYL

ILLONA

KENNETH

BLANCHE

GARY LA

BERKLEY LA

LEEWARD LA

WYNSUM LA

DONNA LA

PEMACO CT

ROBBIN LA

SEAWANE CT

HALYARD

ISLAND

Sunrise Yacht Club

HEMPSTEAD
BAY

DOLPHIN DR

Whaleneck
Pt

40°38'15"

MERRICK
BAY

Merrick
Pt

EAST   BAY

Ball
Island

Fighting
Island

igh Flats
Marsh

W. Neds Creek

Neds
Meadow

Neds Creek

24

False
Channel
Meadow

E. Neds Creek

Broad Creek

40°37'30"

11793

Big   Crow   Island

Channel

Cuba
Island

25

Bush Creek

ate Land

PARKWAY

Crow Island Lead

West Crow
Island

A Wife Lead

East Crow
Island

S   T   U

73°33'00"   73°32'15"

Map
33
Nassau Co.

73°35'15"
Q
73°34'30"
R
73°33'45"

Stat

N

25

40°36'45"

Smiths
Meadow

West High
Meadow

Scow   Creek

High
Island

H E M P S

Seadog
Island

11

State

Boat

Channel

Creek

26

9 Me.
   Isl
   1

LOOP

40°36'00"

MIDDLE
BAY

Long
Meadow
Island

Alder
Island

Gun Club

Long Beach Thoroughfare

Point
Lookout

Joins Map 24

27

Town of Hempstead
West Marina

Town Of Hempstead
East Marina

BAYSIDE

DR

Firemen's
Tower

INLET

LIDO   BOULEVARD

PARKSIDE
BALDWIN
CEDARHURST
FREEPORT
GARDEN
GLENWOOD
HEWLETT
INWOOD
LYNBROOK
MINEOLA

BELLMORE

11569 POINT
LOOKOUT

Malibu Beach
(Town of Hempstead
Park)

28

BEACH
CITY
OCEAN
BLVD
AV
AV
AV
AV
AV
AV
ST
AV

DR

40°35'15"

JONES

Pa

28

ATLANTIC

P
73°35'15"
Q
73°34'30"
R
73°33'45"

Map
33

Scale 1:24,000

0	1,000	2,000	3,000 Feet
0	200	400	600	800 Meters

Joins Map 32

S   73"33'00"   T   73"32'15"   U

N

25

te Land

MEADOWBROOK

Crow   Island   Lead

Bush   Creek

West Crow
Island

Toll

40"36'45"

Middle Crow
Island

A Wife Lead

East Crow
Island

AY OF
UNDY

Swift

M10

S T E A D

Creek

Jones
Island

25

26

EN...
ISLAND...

eadow
sland

1793

PARKWAY

40"36'00"

Channel

Joins Map 42

PARKWAY

BAY

Sloop

JONES

BAY

DRIVE

OCEAN

PARKWAY

27

Parking

Boat Basin

Beach

Parking

40"36'15"

End

Parking

28

Parking

West

OCEAN

S   73"33'00"   T   73"32'15"   U

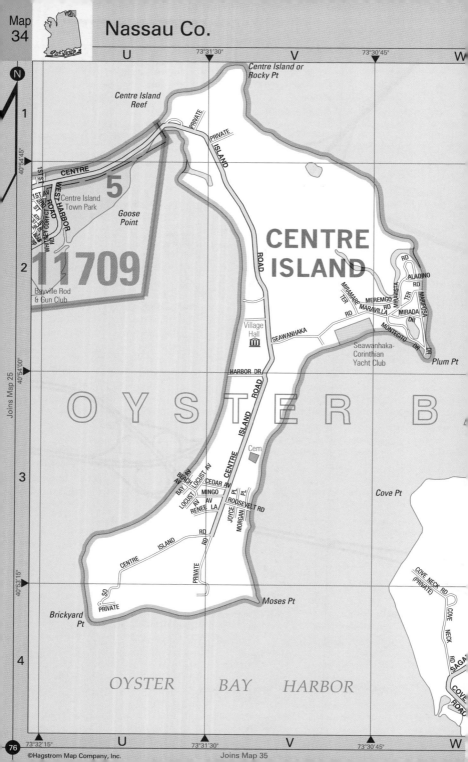

Map
34

Nassau Co.

N

U   73°31'30"   V   73°30'45"   W

Centre Island or
Rocky Pt

Centre Island
Reef

40°54'45"

CENTRE

1ST ST
WEST HARBOR
WHITNEY CORCTN RD
RD
RD
1ST ST
3RD ST

Centre Island
Town Park

5

Goose
Point

PRIVATE

PRIVATE

ISLAND

**CENTRE
ISLAND**

RD
ALADINO
RD
MIRANDSTA
TER
MARIPOSA
DR

11709

Bayville Rod
& Gun Club

40°54'00"

ROAD

Village
Hall

SEAWANHAKA

MIRAMARE
TER
RD
MARAVILLA
MEREMGO
RD
MIRADA
DR
MONTECITO
DR

Plum Pt

Seawanhaka-
Corinthian
Yacht Club

HARBOR DR

O Y S T E R   B

Joins Map 25

CENTRE ISLAND ROAD

Cem

Cove Pt

3

BEACH
BAY
BEAN
LOCUST AV
CEDAR AV
MINGO
LOCUST
RENEE LA
AV
JOYCE PL
MORGAN PL
ROOSEVELT RD
PL

40°53'15"

ISLAND

RD

CENTRE

PRIVATE

Brickyard
Pt

SS
PRIVATE

Moses Pt

COVE NECK RD
(PRIVATE)

COVE
NECK
RD
SAGA

4

OYSTER   BAY   HARBOR

COVE
ROAD

Map
34

Scale 1:24,000

0   1,000   2,000   3,000 Feet
0   200   400   600   800 Meters

73°30'00"

73°29'15"

73°28'30"

N

FT. HILL DR

Nature
Conservancy
Preserve

Caumsett
State
Historic
Park

R.O.W.

DOGWOOD LA

COUNT RUMFORD LA

HILL DR

LLOYD

LLOYD

HARBOR

ROAD

1

LH

Lloyd   Harbor

40°54'45"

Fort Hill Fleet
YC

Lloyd

HARBOR

R C Diocese
of Brooklyn

2

11743

WEST   NECK   ROAD

SUFFOLK

NASSAU

West
Neck
Beach

40°54'00"

Lloyd Harbor
Village
Park

A Y

COLD

COUNTY

COUNTY

Cooper
Bluff

3

SPRING

6

11771

ROAD

40°53'15"

SAGAMORE HILL ROAD

Sagamore Hill
National Historic Site

COVE NECK

HARBOR

4

ELRLAND CT

COVE NECK ROAD

GRACEWOOD
CT

TENNIS COURT RD

N

73°30'00"

X

73°29'15"

Y

73°28'30"

Z

For Adjoining Area See Hagstrom's Western Suffolk Pocket Map

Map
35

Scale 1:24,000

| 0 | 1,000 | 2,000 | 3,000 Feet |

| 0 | 200 | 400 | 600 | 800 Meters |

73°30'00"   X   73°29'15"   Y   73°28'30"

N

4

40°52'30"

COVE NECK

COLD SPRING HARBOR

TENNIS COURT RD

COVE

NECK ROAD

R.O.W

COVE RD

LAUREL RD

NORTH RD

RD

LAUREL (PVT)

RIDGE LA

(PVT)

(PVT)

Bay

SOUTH COVE

LAUREL TIFFANY

UPLAND RD

WELD-GLIDER RD

COVE RD

HOLLOW

(PVT)

DE FOREST RD

5

ARIANA CT

It's

erve

71

ROYSTON

LA

DAFFODIL LA

RD

HONEY BLOWER RD (PVT)

EDGE (PVT)

RD

PRIVATE RD

40°51'45"

6

SUNSET MORRIS

LA

LA

RD

RD

LAUREL HOLLOW

RD

TULIP RD (PVT)

(PVT)

ROAD

Joins Map 43

R.O.W MEADOW LA

COVE

SHUTTER

DRUMLIN LA

THE LA

LA

RD

HICKORY LA

HILL

LA

STEWART

6

B   A   Y

WOODLAND

YELLOW DR

PASTURE (ROW)

LA

MOORE'S

BIRCH CT

HEMLOCK CT

TIMBER RIDGE

RD

11

LAUREL

HOLLOW

ES

RD

(PVT)

(PVT)

YSTER BAY COVE

GATE

COTE

DR

St. John's Memorial Cemetery

SPRINGWOOD PATH

(PVT)

GLENINDALE

KOENIG

WENMAR LA

DR

HEMPSTEAD

BIRCH RD

TURNPIKE

WILDWOOD DR

ROAD

(PVT)

40°51'00"

ULINE CT

(NORTHERN BLVD)

TALL OAK

CRESCENT WHITE

Fox Hollow Preserve

WHITE RD

VISTA DR

ECHO HOME RD

7

HILL

SABINE

TALL OAK HUCKLE-BERRY CT

WOODVALE

WAYLOR LA

Pond

SHADY LA

11791

SKYVIEW CT

TIBER

PALATINE RD

OAK

FOREST CT

CRESCENT

OAK DR

TREE RD

HARBOR

LAUREL CT

LA

2

FOXHUNT

RD CRESCENT

TALL

NORTH CRESCENT EAST

FOXHUNT

CHERRY LA

CHERRY LA

THE HOLLOWS

SPRING

LAUREL LA

RATE ORD

ROAD

FOXHUNT

SOUTH CRESCENT

FOX CT

73°30'00"   X   73°29'15"   Y   73°28'30"

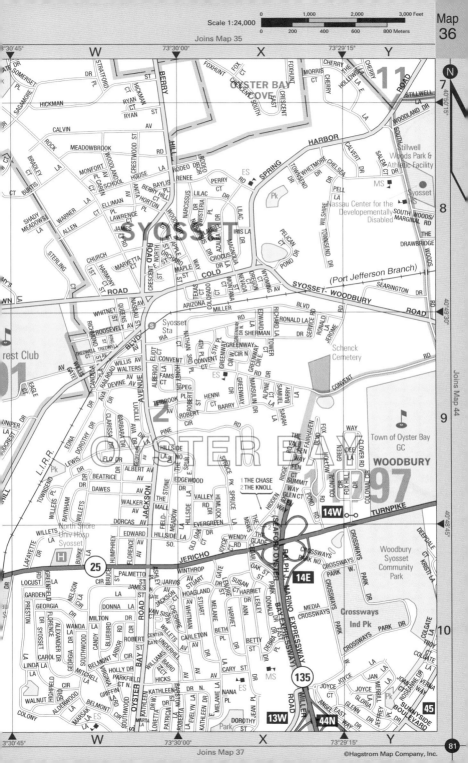

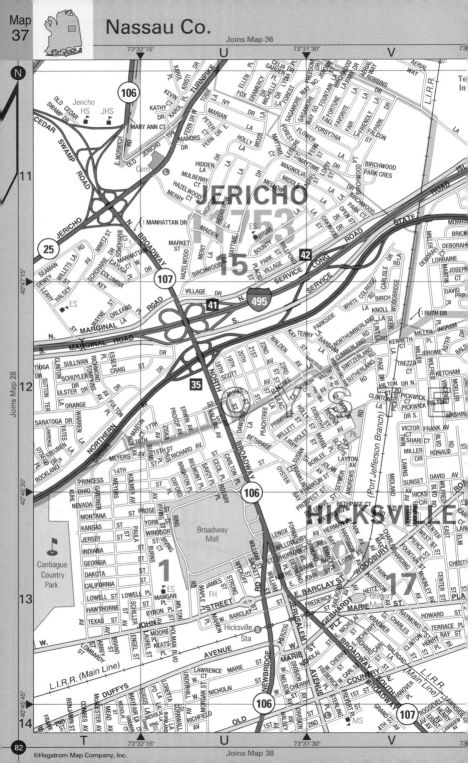

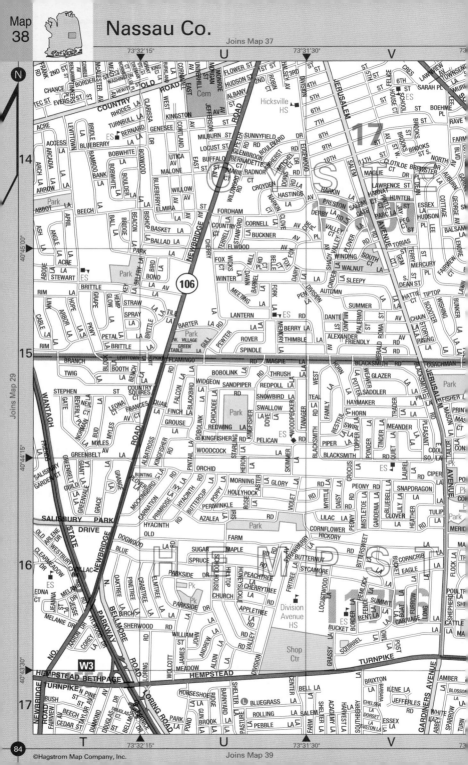

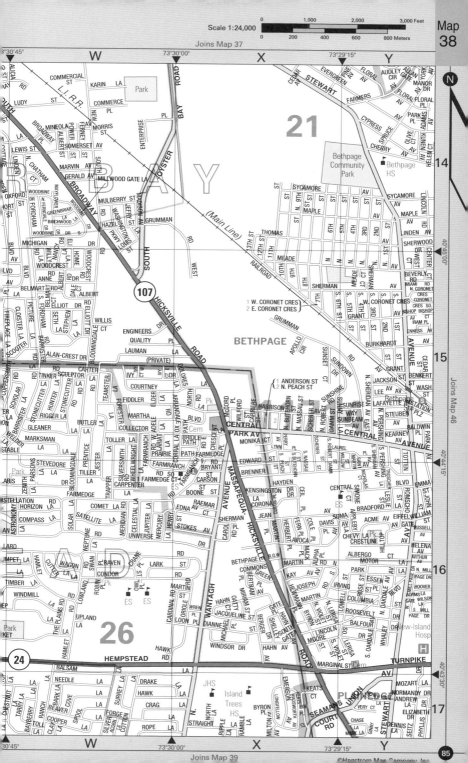

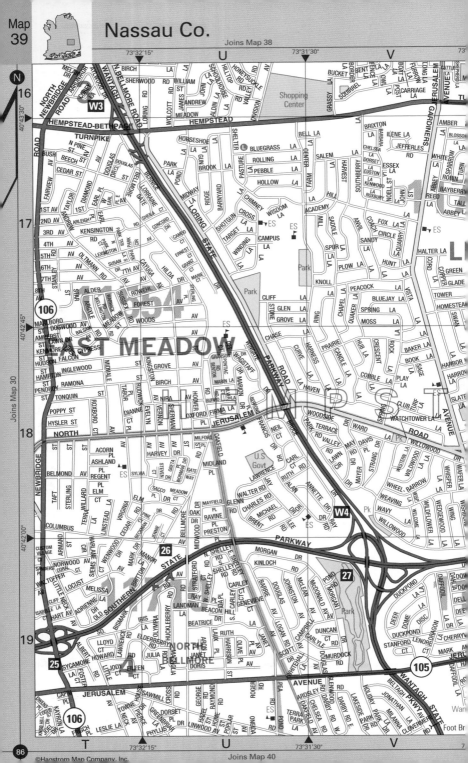

Map 39

©Hagstrom Map Company, Inc.

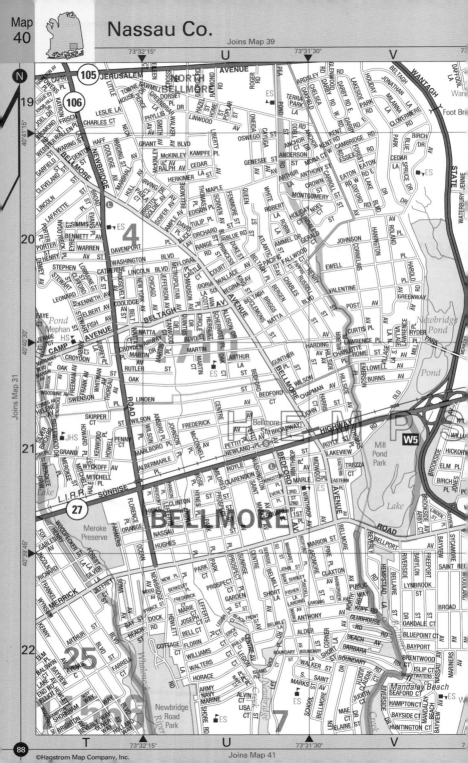

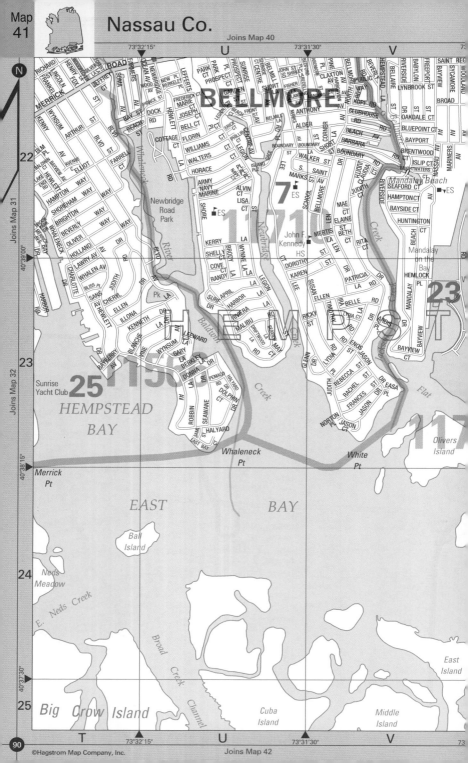

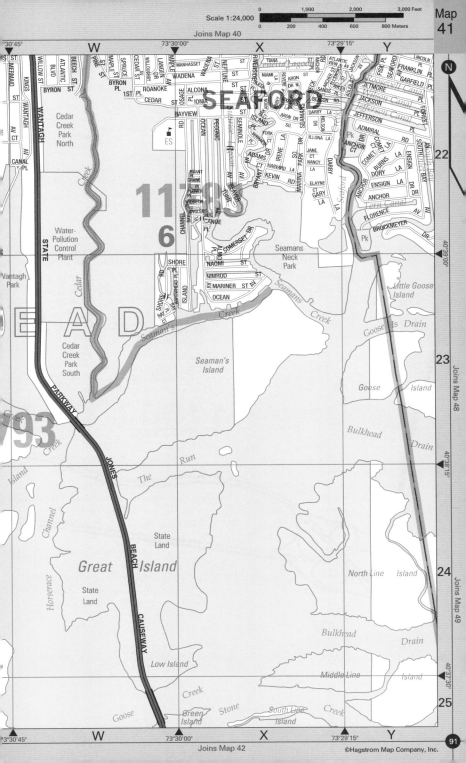

Map
42
Nassau Co.
Joins Map 41

N

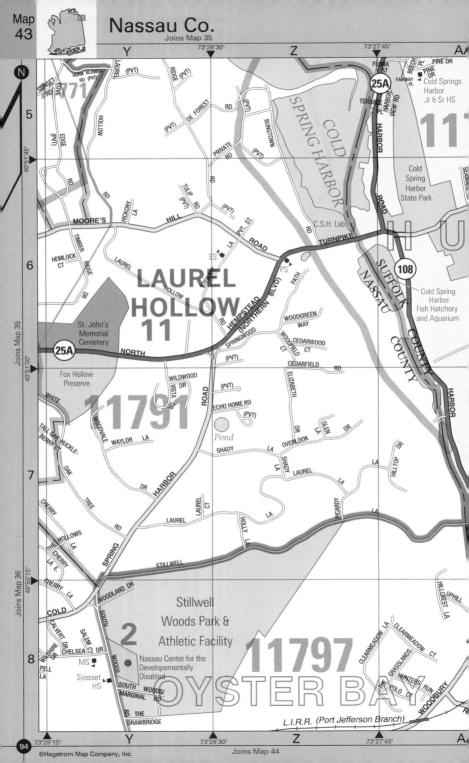

Map
43
Nassau Co.
Joins Map 35

LAUREL
HOLLOW
11

11791

2

11797

OYSTER BAY

Stillwell
Woods Park &
Athletic Facility

Nassau Center for the
Developementally
Disabled

Syosset
HS

Cold Springs
Harbor
Jr & Sr HS

Cold
Spring
Harbor
State Park

Cold Spring
Harbor
Fish Hatchery
and Aquarium

St. John's
Memorial
Cemetery

Fox Hollow
Preserve

L.I.R.R. (Port Jefferson Branch)

Joins Map 35
Joins Map 36

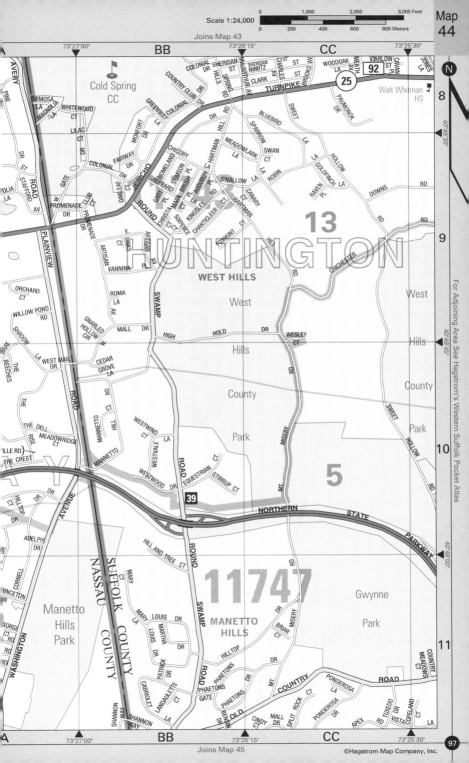

Map
44

Scale 1:24,000

Joins Map 43

For Adjoining Area See Hagstrom's Western Suffolk Pocket Atlas

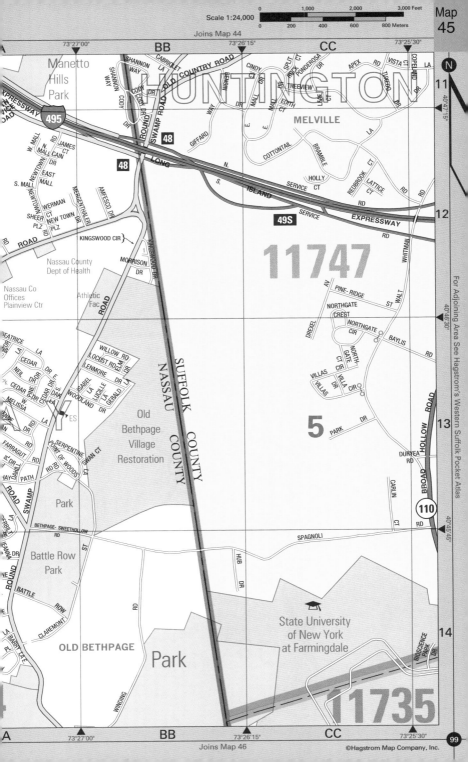

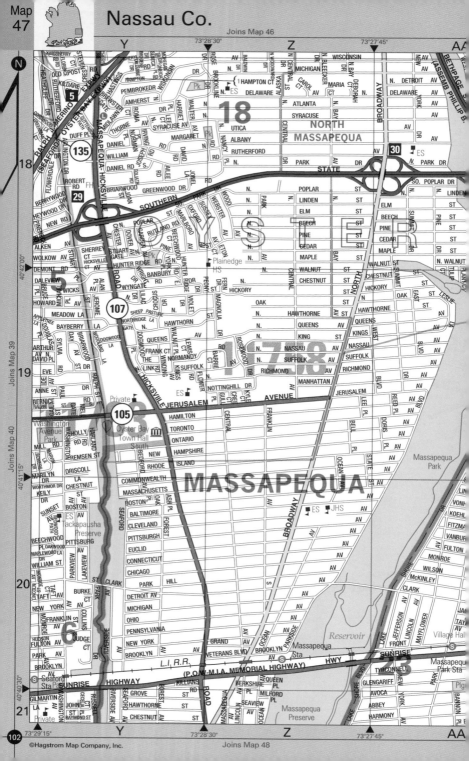

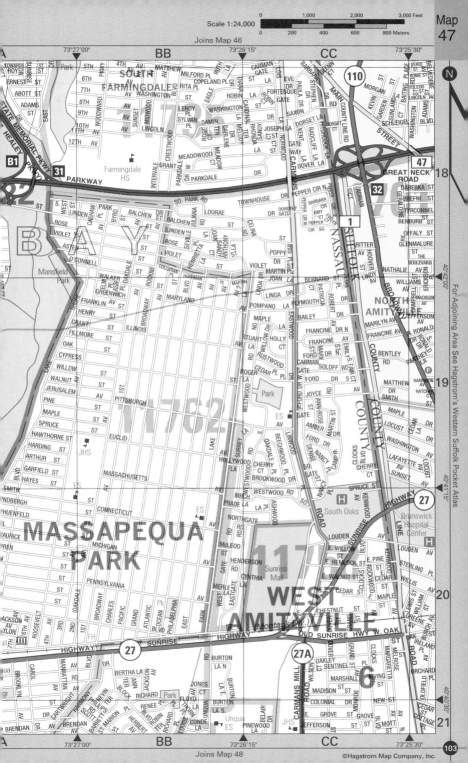

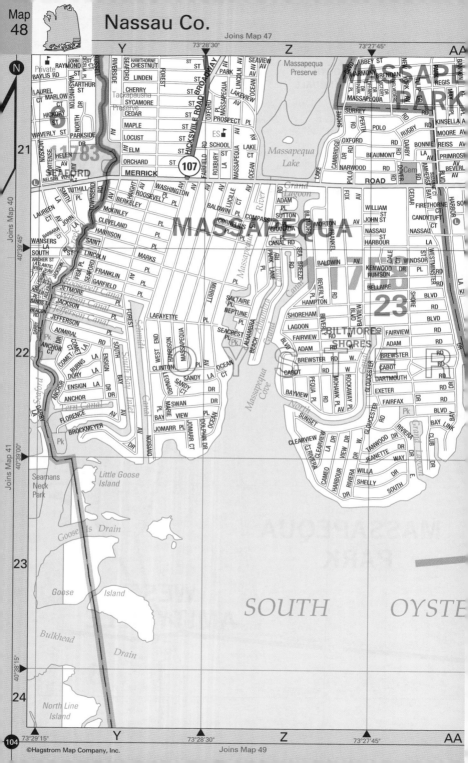

Map
49

Nassau Co.

Joins Map 48

N

24

Joins Map 41

40°37'30"

25

Joins Map 42

40°36'45"

26

40°36'00"

27

73°28'30" Z 73°27'45" AA

Bulkhead
Drain

North Line

Island

Little Squaw
Island

OYSTER

Bulkhead Drain Goose

Squaw
Island

Middle Line Island

SOUTH

1179

Stone Creek

South Line
Island

O Y S T E

25

Black
Banks

Sloop Channel

HEMPSTEAD

To.

High Hill
Beach

ZACHS
BAY

Bea

OCEAN Jones

Jones Beach
State Park

ATLANTIC

73°29'15" Y 73°28'30" Z 73°27'45" AA

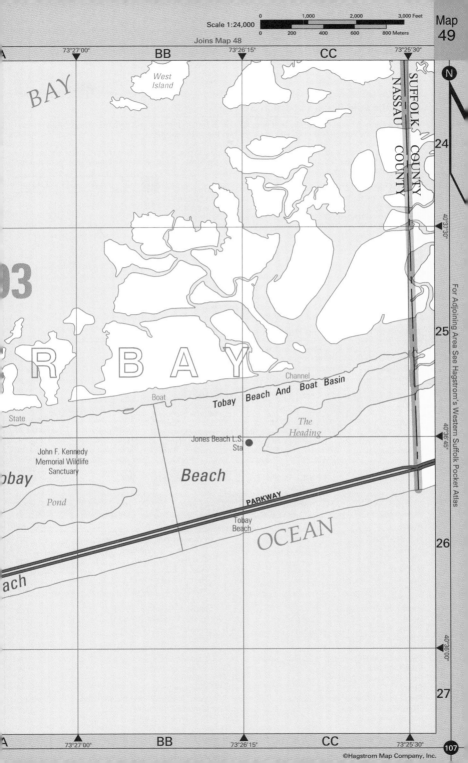

BB   73°26'15"   CC   73°25'30"

73°27'00"

West
Island

BAY

SUFFOLK COUNTY
NASSAU COUNTY

N

24

40°37'30"

03

R   B   A   Y

25

40°36'45"

Channel
Tobay Beach And Boat Basin

Boat

State

The
Heading

John F. Kennedy
Memorial Wildlife
Sanctuary

Jones Beach L.S.
Sta

Beach

obay

Pond

PARKWAY

Tobay
Beach

OCEAN

26

ach

40°36'00"

27

73°27'00"   BB   73°26'15"   CC   73°25'30"

Nassau Co.

Index Guide

Using the Grid Square Location System

Blue lines are drawn horizontally and vertically on the map, forming grid squares. These squares can be identified by letters and numbers appearing in the map margins.

Streets and roads are listed alphabetically in the index. When more than two streets of the same name appear the two-letter code in parentheses following the street name indicates municipality, incorporated village, hamlet, or city where the street is located.

The two letter code in the next column indicates the town in or nearest which the street is located. The three towns in Nassau carry the code of the town in which they belong: Hempstead (Hu); North Hempstead (Nu); Oyster Bay (Ou). Town codes are provided for all entries.

For example, to locate Hawthorne St. in the village of Massapequa Park (MS), find Hawthorne St. in the alphabetical listing as follows:

Hawthorne St (MS)........Ou 47 AA 19

This indicates that Hawthorne St. is in the village of Massapequa Park, in or near the town of Oyster Bay, and can be found on map 47 in grid AA 19, as shown to the right.

1	Z	AA	BB	CC
18				
19		X		
20				
21				
22				

Abbreviations Used on Hagstrom Maps

Al .... Alley	ES .... Elementary School	Riv .... River
Av .... Avenue	Expwy .... Expressway	RR .... Railroad
Blvd .... Boulevard	GC .... Golf Club	S .... South
Bk .... Brook	HS .... High School	Sq .... Square
Boro .... Borough	Hwy .... Highway	St .... Saint
CC .... Country Club	JHS .... Junior High School	St .... Street
Cem .... Cemetery	La .... Lane	Sta .... Station
Cir .... Circle	MS .... Middle School	Ter .... Terrace
CO .... County	Mt .... Mount	Term .... Terminal
Cor .... Corner	Mun Bldg . Municipal Building	Tpk .... Turnpike
Cr .... Creek	N .... North	Tr .... Trail
Cres .... Crescent	Pk .... Park	Twp .... Township
Ct .... Court	Pkwy .... Parkway	W .... West
Dr .... Drive	Pl .... Place	Wk .... Walk
E .... East	Rd .... Road	

Municipality and Hamlet Codes

Place	Code	Place	Code
HEMPSTEAD		Freeport (Village) .... FR	
Atlantic Beach (Village) .... AB		Garden City (Village) .... GA	
Atlantic Beach Estates .... ae		Garden City South .... gs	
Baldwin .... bw		Harbor Isle .... hi	
Baldwin Harbor .... bh		Hempstead (Town) .... Hu	
Barnum Island .... bi		Hempstead (Village) .... HV	
Bay Park .... ba		Hewlett .... hl	
Bellerose (Village) .... BL		Hewlett Bay Park (Village) .... HB	
Bellerose Terrace .... bt		Hewlett Harbor (Village) .... HH	
Bellmore .... bm		Hewlett Neck (Village) .... HN	
Cedarhurst (Village) .... CH		Inwood .... in	
East Atlantic Beach .... ea		Island Park (Village) .... IP	
East Garden City .... eg		Lakeview .... lk	
East Meadow .... ed		Lawrence (Village) .... LW	
East Rockaway (Village) .... ER		Levittown .... ln	
Elmont .... el		Lido Beach .... ld	
Floral Park (Village, part) .... FP		Long Beach (Independent City) .... LB	
Floral Park Centre .... fc		Lynbrook (Village) .... LY	
Franklin Square .... fs		Malverne (Village) .... ML	

Place	Code
HEMPSTEAD (cont.)	
Meadowmere Park	mp
Merrick	mr
Mineola (Village, part)	MI
New Hyde Park (Village, part)	NP
North Bellmore	nb
North Lynbrook	ny
North Merrick	ne
North Valley Stream	nv
North Wantagh	nw
Oceanside	os
Point Lookout	pl
Rockville Centre (Village)	RC
Roosevelt	rv
Salisbury	sl
Seaford	sd
South Floral Park (Village)	SF
South Hempstead	sh
South Valley Stream	sv
Stewart Manor (Village)	SM
Uniondale	un
Valley Stream (Village)	VS
Wantagh	wn
West Hempstead	wh
Woodmere	wm
Woodsburgh (Village)	WG
NORTH HEMPSTEAD	
Albertson	al
Baxter Estates (Village)	BE
Carle Place	cp
East Hills (Village, part)	EH
East Williston (Village)	EW
Floral Park (Village, part)	FP
Flower Hill (Village)	FH
Garden City Park	gk
Glenwood Landing (part)	gw
Great Neck (Village)	GN
Great Neck Estates (Village)	GE
Great Neck Gardens	gg
Great Neck Plaza (Village)	GP
Greenvale (part)	gv
Harbor Hills	hh
Herricks	hr
Kensington (Village)	KG
Kings Point (Village)	KP
Lake Success (Village)	LS
Manhasset	ma
Manhasset Hills	mh
Manorhaven (Village)	MH
Mineola (Village, part)	MI
Munsey Park (Village)	MK
New Cassel	nc
New Hyde Park (Village, part)	NP
North Hempstead (Town)	Nu
North Hills (Village)	NL
North New Hyde Park	nn
Old Westbury (Village, part)	OW
Plandome (Village)	PD
Plandome Heights (Village)	PH
Plandome Manor (Village)	PR
Port Washington	pw
Port Washington North (Village)	PN
Roslyn (Village)	RL

Place	Code
Roslyn Estates (Village)	RE
Roslyn Harbor (Village, part)	RH
Roslyn Heights	rt
Russell Gardens	RG
Saddle Rock (Village)	SR
Saddle Rock Estates	se
Sands Point (Village)	SP
Searington	sg
Strathmore	st
Thomaston (Village)	TM
University Gardens	ug
Westbury (Village)	WB
Williston Park (Village)	WP
OYSTER BAY	
Bayville (Village)	BY
Bethpage	bp
Brookville (Village)	BK
Centre Island (Village)	CI
Cove Neck (Village)	CN
East Hills (Village, part)	EH
East Massapequa	es
East Norwich	en
Farmingdale (Village)	FG
Glen Cove (Independent City)	GL
Glen Head	gh
Glenwood Landing (part)	gw
Greenvale (part)	
Hicksville	hk
Jericho	je
Lattingtown (Village)	LT
Laurel Hollow (Village)	LH
Locust Grove	lg
Locust Valley	lv
Massapequa	mq
Massapequa Park (Village)	MS
Matinecock (Village)	MC
Mill Neck (Village)	MN
Muttontown (Village)	MT
Nassau Shores	ns
North Massapequa	nq
Old Bethpage	ob
Old Brookville (Village)	OK
Old Westbury (Village, part)	OW
Oyster Bay (Town)	Ou
Oyster Bay (uninc)	oy
Oyster Bay Cove (Village)	OC
Plainedge	pe
Plainview	pv
Roslyn Harbor (Village, part)	RH
Sea Cliff (Village)	SC
South Farmingdale	sa
Syosset	sy
Upper Brookville (Village)	UB
West Amityville	wa
Woodbury	wy

*All municipalities are incorporated villages or cities that have definite, legal boundaries. The codes for these municipalities are shown in capital letters.

All hamlets are unincorporated areas and have no definite official boundaries. The codes for these are shown in lower case letters.

Population of Towns and Cities

Place	Population (*)	Place	Population (*)
Town of Hempstead	755,924	City of Long Beach	35,462
Town of North Hempstead	222,611	City of Glen Cove	26,622
Town of Oyster Bay	293,925	**Total County Population**	**1,334,544**

Index to Places/Population/Zip Codes

Place	Town	Pop.(*)	Map	Zip Code
Albertson	North Hempstead	5,200	19	11507
Atlantic Beach (Village)	Hempstead	1,986	7	11509
Atlantic Beach Estates	Hempstead		7	11509
Baldwin	Hempstead	23,455	22	11510
Baldwin Harbor	Hempstead	8,147	23	11510
Barnum Island	Hempstead	2,487	24	11558
Baxter Estates (Village)	North Hempstead	1,006	8	11050
Bay Park	Hempstead	2,300	14	11518
Bayville (Village)	Oyster Bay	7,135	25	11709
Bellerose (Village)	Hempstead	1,173	4	11426
Bellerose Terrace	Hempstead	2,157	4	11001
Bellmore	Hempstead	16,441	40	11710
Bethpage	Oyster Bay	16,543	46	11714
Biltmore Shores	Oyster Bay		48	11758
Brookville (Village)	Oyster Bay	2,126	18	11545
Canals of Lido	Hempstead		24	11561
Carle Place	North Hempstead	5,247	20	11514
Cedarhurst (Village)	Hempstead	6,164	6	11516
Centre Island (Village)	Oyster Bay	444	34	11771
Cove Neck (Village)	Oyster Bay	300	34	11771
East Atlantic Beach	Hempstead	2,257	7	11561
East Garden City	Hempstead	979	20	11530
East Hills (Village, part)	North Hempstead	6,822	18	11576
East Hills (Village, part)	Oyster Bay	20	18	11576
East Massapequa	Oyster Bay	19,565	48	11758
East Meadow	Hempstead	37,461	30	11554
East Norwich	Oyster Bay	2,675	26	11732
East Rockaway (Village)	Hempstead	10,414	14	11518
East Williston (Village)	North Hempstead	2,503	19	11596
Elmont	Hempstead	32,657	4	11003
Farmingdale (Village)	Oyster Bay	8,399	46	11735
Floral Park (Village, part)	Hempstead	13,667	4	11001
Floral Park (Village, part)	North Hempstead	2,300	4	11001
Floral Park Centre	Hempstead		11	11001
Flower Hill (Village)	North Hempstead	4,508	9	11030
Franklin Square	Hempstead	29,342	4	11010
Freeport (Village)	Hempstead	43,783	22	11520
Garden City (Village)	Hempstead	21,672	11	11530
Garden City Park	North Hempstead	7,554	11	11040
Garden City South	Hempstead	3,974	12	11530
Glen Cove (City)	Hempstead	26,622	16	11542
Glen Head	Oyster Bay	4,625	17	11545
Glenwood Landing (part)	North Hempstead	60	18	11547
Glenwood Landing (part)	Oyster Bay	3,481	18	11547
Great Neck (Village)	North Hempstead	9,538	2	11023
Great Neck Estates (Village)	North Hempstead	2,756	3	11021
Great Neck Gardens	North Hempstead	1,089	2	11023
Great Neck Plaza (Village)	North Hempstead	6,433	3	11021
Greenvale (part)	North Hempstead	1,981	18	11548
Greenvale (part)	Oyster Bay	250	18	11548
Harbor Hills	North Hempstead	563	3	11023
Harbor Isle	Hempstead	1,334	15	11558
Hempstead (Village)	Hempstead	56,554	21	11550
Herricks	Hempstead	4,076	10	11040
Hewlett	Hempstead	7,060	14	11557
Hewlett Bay Park (Village)	Hempstead	484	14	11557
Hewlett Harbor (Village)	Hempstead	1,271	14	11557
Hewlett Neck (Village)	Hempstead	504	6	11598
Hicksville	Oyster Bay	41,260	37	11801
Inwood	Hempstead	9,325	6	11096
Island Park (Village)	Hempstead	4,734	15	11558
Jericho	Oyster Bay	13,045	37	11753
Kensington (Village)	North Hempstead	1,209	2	11021
Kings Point (Village)	North Hempstead	5,076	2	11024
Lake Success (Village)	North Hempstead	2,797	3	11020
Lakeview	Hempstead	5,607	22	11552
Lattingtown (Village)	Oyster Bay	1,860	16	11560
Laurel Hollow (Village)	Oyster Bay	1,930	35	11791
Lawrence (Village)	Hempstead	6,522	7	11559
Levittown	Hempstead	53,067	39	11756
Lido Beach	Hempstead	2,825	24	11561
Locust Grove	Oyster Bay		36	11791
Locust Valley	Oyster Bay	3,521	16	11560
Long Beach (City)	Hempstead	35,462	15	11561
Lynbrook (Village)	Hempstead	19,911	13	11563
Malverne (Village)	Hempstead	8,934	13	11565
Manhasset	North Hempstead	8,362	10	11030
Manhasset Hills	North Hempstead	3,661	10	11040
Manorhaven (Village)	North Hempstead	6,138	1	11050
Massapequa	Oyster Bay	22,652	47	11758
Massapequa Park (Village)	Oyster Bay	17,499	47	11762
Matinecock (Village)	Oyster Bay	836	26	11560
Meadowmere Park	Hempstead		6	11559
Merrick	Hempstead	22,764	31	11566
Mill Neck (Village)	Oyster Bay	825	25	11765
Mineola (Village, part)	Hempstead	15	20	11501
Mineola (Village, part)	North Hempstead	19,219	20	11501
Munsey Park (Village)	North Hempstead	2,632	9	11030
Muttontown (Village)	Oyster Bay	3,412	27	11791
Nassau Shores	Oyster Bay		48	11758
New Cassel	North Hempstead	13,298	28	11590
New Hyde Park (Village, part)	Hempstead	3,975	11	11040
New Hyde Park (Village, part)	North Hempstead	5,548	11	11040
North Bellmore	Hempstead	20,079	30	11710
North Hills (Village)	North Hempstead	4,301	10	11030
North Lynbrook	Hempstead	742	13	11563
North Massapequa	Oyster Bay	19,152	47	11758
North Merrick	Hempstead	11,844	31	11566
North New Hyde Park	Hempstead	14,542	11	11040
North Valley Stream	Hempstead	15,789	13	11580
North Wantagh	Hempstead	12,156	39	11793
Oceanside	Hempstead	32,733	23	11572
Old Bethpage	Oyster Bay	5,400	45	11804
Old Brookville (Village)	Oyster Bay	2,167	17	11545
Old Westbury (Village, part)	North Hempstead	3,561	18	11568
Old Westbury (Village, part)	Oyster Bay	667	19	11568
Oyster Bay (uninc)	Oyster Bay	6,826	35	11765
Oyster Bay Cove (Village)	Oyster Bay	2,262	35	11771
Plainedge	Oyster Bay	9,195	46	11714
Plainview	Oyster Bay	25,637	45	11803
Plandome (Village)	North Hempstead	1,272	2	11030
Plandome Heights (Village)	North Hempstead	971	2	11030
Plandome Manor (Village)	North Hempstead	838	2	11030
Point Lookout	Hempstead	1,472	33	11569
Port Washington	North Hempstead	15,215	9	11050
Port Washington North (Village)	North Hempstead	2,700	8	11050
Rockville Centre (Village)	Hempstead	24,568	22	11570
Roosevelt	Hempstead	15,854	31	11575
Roslyn (Village)	North Hempstead	2,570	9	11576
Roslyn Estates (Village)	North Hempstead	1,210	9	11576
Roslyn Harbor (Village, part)	North Hempstead	714	18	11576
Roslyn Harbor (Village, part)	Oyster Bay	309	18	11576
Roslyn Heights	North Hempstead	6,295	10	11577
Russell Gardens	North Hempstead	1,074	3	11020
Saddle Rock (Village)	North Hempstead	791	2	11023
Saddle Rock Estates	North Hempstead	424	2	11021
Salisbury	Hempstead	12,341	29	11590
Sands Point (Village)	North Hempstead	2,786	1	11050
Sea Cliff (Village)	Oyster Bay	5,066	17	11579
Seaford	Hempstead	15,791	40	11783
Searington	North Hempstead	5,034	10	11507
South Farmingdale	Oyster Bay	15,061	46	11735
South Floral Park (Village)	Hempstead	1,578	4	11001
South Hempstead	Hempstead	3,188	22	11550
South Valley Stream	Hempstead	5,638	5	11581
Stewart Manor (Village)	Hempstead	1,935	12	11530
Strathmore	North Hempstead		9	11030
Syosset	Oyster Bay	18,544	36	11791
Thomaston (Village)	North Hempstead	2,607	3	11021
Uniondale	Hempstead	23,011	21	11553
University Gardens	North Hempstead	4,138	3	11020
Upper Brookville (Village)	Oyster Bay	1,801	26	11771
Valley Stream (Village)	Hempstead	36,368	5	11580
Wantagh	Hempstead	18,971	40	11793
West Amityville	Oyster Bay		47	11758
West Hempstead	Hempstead	18,713	21	11552
Westbury (Village)	North Hempstead	14,263	19	11590
Williston Park (Village)	North Hempstead	7,261	10	11596
Woodbury	Oyster Bay	9,010	44	11797
Woodmere	Hempstead	16,447	6	11598
Woodsburgh (Village)	Hempstead	831	6	11598

(*) Source: U. S. Census Bureau, Census 2000
Note: Populations are provided for incorporated areas only.

A

Nassau Co.

STREET	MUN.	MAP	GRID
Andover La	Ou	37 W	13
Andover Pl	Hu	12 H	18
Andover Pl	Ou	16 M	4
Andover Pl	Hu	21 L	18
Andover Rd (gg)	Nu	2 E	11
Andover Rd (pw)	Nu	9 H	9
Andover Rd (EH)	Nu	19 M	12
Andover Rd	Hu	22 L	20
Andover Rd	Ou	27 Q	10
Andrea Rd	Hu	30 S	18
Andrew Av	Hu	30 T	17
Andrew Ct	Ou	44 Z	8
Andrew La	Hu	38 U	16
Andrew La	Ou	46 Y	17
Andrew Pl	Ou	25 Q	2
Andrew Rd	Nu	9 G	11
Andrew Rd	Ou	46 Z	16
Andrew St	Nu	9 G	11
Andrews Av	Hu	31 Q	21
Andrews Dr	Ou	48 AA	22
Andrews La	Hu	30 R	18
Andrews Pl	Hu	40 W	20
Andrews Rd	Nu	11 K	15
Andrews Rd	Ou	37 V	13
Andrienne Dr	Ou	45 AA	13
Angel Wy	Ou	36 X	10
Angevine Av	Hu	21 N	18
Angle La	Ou	29 T	14
Angler La	Nu	8 F	7
Anglers Pl	Hu	40 X	22
Anglesea Pl	Hu	14 J	23
Anita Av	Ou	36 W	8
Anita Ct	Hu	22 O	21
Anita La (wn)	Hu	39 W	19
Anita La (sd)	Hu	40 X	20
Anita Pl	Ou	46 BB	15
Anjo Dr	Ou	46 Y	17
Ann Ct	Hu	4 E	19
Ann Ct (FR)	Hu	32 R	23
Ann Ct (pv)	Ou	45 AA	12
Ann Dr	Ou	36 X	10
Ann Dr E	Hu	32 R	23
Ann Dr N	Hu	32 R	23
Ann Dr S	Hu	32 R	23
Ann La	Hu	39 X	18
Ann Pl	Nu	8 G	7
Ann Rd	Hu	32 S	23
Ann St (VS)	Hu	13 G	21
Ann St (GL)	Ou	17 N	6
Ann St (HV)	Hu	21 N	19
Ann St (os)	Hu	14 K	25
Ann St (bh)	Hu	23 N	24
Ann Ter	Ou	47 BB	20
Anna Av	Nu	29 R	14
Anna Av	Hu	31 P	20
Anna Pl	Hu	22 O	20
Annandale Dr	Ou	35 V	7
Anne Dr	Ou	38 W	15
Anne Dr	Hu	39 X	19
Annette Av	Hu	31 T	22
Annette Ct	Ou	45 Y	13
Annette Dr	Nu	8 G	8
Annette Dr (os)	Hu	23 L	25
Annette Dr (os)	Hu	23 M	25
Annette Dr	Hu	39 U	18
Ann-Rose St	Ou	47 CC	19
Ansbro Pl	Hu	40 U	21
Anstice St	Ou	35 U	5
Anthony Av	Hu	40 U	22
Anthony Dr	Ou	46 Z	17
Anthony La	Ou	47 BB	18
Anthony St (os)	Hu	14 K	24
Anthony St	Hu	40 U	20
Anvil La	Hu	39 V	17
Apex La	Ou	29 T	14
Apian La	Ou	48 BB	21
Apking St	Hu	23 L	23
Apollo Cir	Ou	38 X	15
Apollo La	Ou	29 T	14
Appeal Av	Hu	12 G	18
Apple La	Ou	25 S	2
Apple La	Hu	30 R	18
Apple St	Ou	36 W	8
Apple Tree La	Ou	16 M	4
Apple Tree La	Nu	18 L	10
Appleby La	Ou	46 Y	16
Applegreen Dr	Nu	18 O	11
Appletree La (GN)	Nu	2 D	10
Appletree La (al)	Nu	19 L	12
Appletree La (cp)	Nu	20 N	14
Appletree La (lv)	Hu	38 U	16
Appletree La (sd)	Hu	39 X	19
April La	Ou	29 T	14
April La	Hu	41 U	23
Apron Dr	Hu	23 N	24
Aqueduct	Hu	13 K	21
Arbor Gate	Ou	45 AA	13
Arbor La (al)	Nu	19 M	13
Arbor La (nc)	Nu	28 R	13
Arbor La	Ou	29 T	15
Arbor La	Hu	31 S	22
Arbor Pl	Ou	17 M	6
Arbor Rd	Nu	19 M	11
Arbor Rd	Ou	36 W	10
Arbor St	Nu	3 E	12
Arbuckle Av	Hu	6 D	23
Arby Ct	Hu	40 V	21
Arcade Pl	Hu	4 F	18
Arcadia Av	Hu	30 Q	17
Arcadia Dr	Nu	1 E	7
Arcadia La	Nu	3 D	13
Arcadia La	Ou	29 T	14
Arcadian Av	Hu	13 G	20
Arch Av	Ou	46 BB	17
Arch La	Ou	29 T	14
Arch St	Hu	23 M	24
Archer Pl	Hu	23 O	23
Archer Rd	Hu	21 L	18
Archer St (FR)	Hu	23 O	23
Archer St	Hu	40 X	22
Arden Blvd	Hu	12 K	18
Arden Ct	Hu	22 N	22
Arden La	Nu	1 F	6
Arden Rd	Hu	14 J	24
Ardis La	Ou	45 Z	12
Ardis Pl	Hu	41 V	23
Ardmore Rd	Hu	22 O	20
Ardmore St	Hu	40 V	21
Ardsley Blvd	Hu	12 J	17
Ardsley Cir	Hu	22 L	21
Ardsley Gate	Ou	37 W	12
Ardsley Pl	Nu	3 E	11
Ardsley Pl	Hu	22 L	21
Ardsley Rd	Hu	39 U	19
Ardvin La	Ou	46 Y	17
Argo Av	Hu	12 G	18
Argon Pl	Nu	11 J	15
Argonne Pl	Ou	48 BB	21
Argyle Av	Hu	21 O	19
Argyle Av (os)	Hu	14 K	25
Argyle Pl (RC)	Hu	22 L	21
Argyle Pl	Hu	40 U	21
Argyle Pl	Ou	48 AA	21
Argyle Rd (pw)	Nu	9 G	9
Argyle Rd (SM)	Hu	12 G	17
Argyle Rd (CH)	Hu	6 D	24
Argyle Rd (MI)	Nu	11 K	14
Argyle Rd (al)	Nu	19 L	13
Argyle Rd	Hu	21 L	18
Argyle Rd	Nu	28 P	13
Argyle Rd	Hu	30 T	17
Argyle Rd (mr)	Hu	31 R	22
Argyle Rd	Ou	45 Y	13
Argyle Rd (wn)	Hu	40 W	20
Ariana Ct	Ou	35 W	5
Ariel Ct	Nu	1 F	5
Arizona Av (LB)	Hu	15 G	28
Arizona Av	Hu	22 M	20
Arizona Av	Ou	36 X	8
Arkansas Dr	Hu	5 E	20
Arleigh Dr	Nu	10 K	13
Arleigh Rd	Nu	2 D	11
Arleigh Rd	Hu	22 M	20
Arleigh Rd	Hu	30 T	17
Arlene Dr	Hu	29 T	16
Arley Ct	Hu	12 H	19
Arley Rd	Hu	12 H	19
Arlington Av (VS)	Hu	5 E	21
Arlington Av (fs)	Hu	12 H	19
Arlington Av (ML)	Hu	13 J	20
Arlington Av (RC)	Hu	22 L	22
Arlington Av (bh)	Hu	23 N	23
Arlington Ct	Nu	18 N	10
Arlington Dr	Hu	39 X	18
Arlington Dr	Ou	47 Y	18
Arlington La	Ou	25 S	2
Arlington Pl	Hu	6 D	24
Arlington Pl	Ou	17 L	7
Arlington Rd	Hu	6 D	24
Arlington St (ML)	Nu	19 M	14
Arlington St	Nu	29 R	14
Arlyn Dr	Ou	48 AA	21
Arlyn Dr E	Ou	48 BB	21
Armand St	Hu	30 T	19
Armon Dr	Ou	45 Y	14
Armond St	Hu	30 P	18
Armour St	Hu	24 L	27
Arms Av	Hu	31 S	20
Armstrong Rd	Nu	11 K	15
Army Pl	Hu	31 U	22
Arnold Av	Hu	23 L	23
Arnold Ct	Hu	30 S	17
Arnold Ct E	Hu	14 H	23
Arnold Ct W	Hu	14 H	23
Arnold Rd	Hu	13 K	20
Arnold St	Ou	37 W	13
Arnot Pl	Hu	22 N	21
Aron Ct	Ou	45 Z	14
Aron Dr	Ou	44 Y	8
Aron Dr E	Hu	40 X	22
Aron Dr N	Hu	40 X	22
Aron Dr S	Hu	40 X	22
Aron Dr W	Hu	40 X	22
Aron Pl	Hu	30 U	19
Arowick Pl	Hu	21 P	17
Arpad St	Ou	37 W	12
Arrandale Av	Nu	2 C	10
Arrandale Rd (lk)	Hu	22 L	20
Arrandale Rd	Hu	38 X	15
Arrow La	Ou	29 T	14
Arrow St	Hu	23 M	24
Arrowhead Ct	Nu	10 H	12
Arrowhead La	Hu	7 D	25
Arrowhead Pl	Hu	41 X	23
Arterial Hwy	Ou	17 N	6
Arthur Av (SF)	Hu	12 F	18
Arthur Av (LY)	Hu	13 H	21
Arthur Av	Ou	46 Y	16
Arthur Av N	Hu	39 X	19
Arthur Av W	Hu	39 X	19
Arthur Ct	Hu	22 M	22
Arthur Ct	Ou	45 Y	12
Arthur Dr (ba)	Hu	14 J	24
Arthur Dr (sd)	Hu	40 X	20
Arthur La	Hu	40 U	20
Arthur Pl (VS)	Hu	5 E	21
Arthur Pl (wy)	Ou	44 Z	9
Arthur Pl	Ou	45 Y	12
Arthur St (GA)	Hu	20 M	16
Arthur St (wh)	Hu	13 K	20
Arthur St (un)	Hu	21 O	19
Arthur St (bh)	Hu	23 N	24
Arthur St (mr)	Hu	32 Q	23
Arthur St (mr)	Hu	31 T	22
Arthur St (FG)	Ou	46 AA	16
Arthur St (MS)	Ou	47 AA	19
Arthur St	Hu	40 Y	21
Asbury Av	Nu	19 P	14
Asbury Av	Hu	31 R	20
Asbury Av W	Nu	20 O	14
Ascan Rd	Hu	12 H	19
Ascan St	Hu	13 G	20
Ascot Ct	Nu	10 J	12
Ascot Ridge	Nu	3 D	12
Ash Ct	Ou	25 Q	2
Ash Ct	Hu	21 M	19
Ash Ct	Hu	30 P	18
Ash Dr	Nu	3 C	12
Ash Dr	Nu	18 L	11
Ash La	Hu	5 F	22
Ash La	Ou	29 T	14
Ash Pl (GE)	Nu	3 D	12
Ash Pl (hr)	Nu	10 J	14
Ash Pl (ne)	Hu	31 R	20
Ash Pl (MS)	Ou	47 BB	19
Ash Pl (mq)	Ou	47 Y	20
Ash St (FP)	Hu	12 G	17
Ash St (VS)	Hu	5 D	21
Ash St	Ou	16 P	4
Ash St	Hu	12 J	18
Ash St (GA)	Hu	21 M	17
Ash St (WB)	Nu	19 P	14
Ashford Dr	Ou	37 W	11
Ashford Pl	Nu	19 L	13
Ashland Av	Nu	11 H	15
Ashland Av	Hu	22 N	22
Ashland Pl	Hu	30 T	18
Ashleigh Ct	Ou	16 M	4
Ashley Ct	Nu	10 K	12
Ashley Dr	Hu	5 E	20
Ashley Pl	Ou	17 M	8
Ashley Pl	Hu	29 Q	15
Ashley Pl	Ou	36 W	10
Ashley Ter	Hu	13 H	20
Ashwood Pl	Ou	47 CC	20
Ashwood Rd	Nu	1 E	7
Aspen Ct	Hu	39 W	19
Aspen Dr	Ou	44 Y	10
Aspen Gate	Nu	9 G	9
Aspen La	Nu	10 J	14
Aspen Pl	Nu	3 C	12
Aspen St	Hu	12 G	17
Aspinwall St	Nu	19 O	14
Aster Av	Hu	30 R	19
Aster Dr	Nu	10 H	14
Aster Dr	Ou	37 V	12
Aster La	Nu	3 D	12
Aster La	Hu	38 U	16
Aster Pl N	Hu	29 S	14
Aster Pl S	Hu	29 S	14
Aster St	Ou	47 AA	18
Astor Ct	Hu	21 M	18
Astor La	Nu	8 G	7
Astor Pl (VS)	Hu	13 G	22
Astor Pl (WP)	Nu	10 L	14
Astor Pl (MI)	Nu	20 M	15
Astor Pl (bh)	Hu	23 O	24
Astor Pl (rv)	Hu	31 Q	20
Astor St	Hu	4 E	19
Astronomy La	Hu	38 W	16
Athem Dr	Ou	16 N	3
Atherton Av	Hu	4 F	18
Atkinson Rd	Hu	22 M	20
Atlanta Av	Nu	19 M	14
Atlantic Av	Hu	4 E	17
Atlantic Av (CH)	Hu	6 D	25
Atlantic Av (LW)	Hu	7 E	25
Atlantic Av (GA)	Nu	11 J	16
Atlantic Av (GA)	Hu	21 L	17
Atlantic Av (cp)	Nu	20 O	15
Atlantic Av (LB)	Hu	13 J	22
Atlantic Av (ER)	Hu	14 K	23
Atlantic Av (bw)	Hu	23 N	23
Atlantic Av (LB)	Hu	24 L	28
Atlantic Av (nb)	Hu	40 U	20
Atlantic Av (FR)	Hu	23 P	23
Atlantic Av (FG)	Ou	46 BB	16
Atlantic Av (MS)	Ou	47 BB	20
Atlantic Blvd (AB)	Hu	7 C	27
Atlantic Blvd	Hu	40 W	21
Atlantic Pl N	Hu	24 L	26
Atlantic Pl S	Hu	24 L	26
Atlantic St	Hu	12 H	17
Atlantic St	Nu	20 N	15
Atlantic View Av	Hu	40 X	22
Atlas Av	Hu	13 J	20
Atlas Ct	Nu	11 J	15
Atlas Ct	Hu	13 J	20
Atlas La	Ou	29 T	14
Atom Ct	Hu	30 P	19
Attorney St	Hu	21 N	18
Atwater Pl	Ou	48 BB	22
Atwood Rd	Ou	37 X	12
Auburn La (oy)	Ou	35 U	6
Auburn La (hk)	Ou	38 V	14
Auburn Rd	Hu	40 W	20
Auburn St	Hu	12 H	18
Auburn St (EW)	Nu	20 L	14
Audley Cir	Ou	37 Y	14
Audley Ct	Ou	37 Y	14
Audrey Av	Hu	13 G	20
Audrey Av (oy)	Ou	35 U	5
Audrey Av (hk)	Ou	37 W	12
Audrey Ct	Hu	13 H	20
Audrey Dr	Hu	24 M	27
Audrey Rd	Ou	28 R	13
Audubon Blvd	Hu	24 L	26
Auerbach Av	Hu	14 H	23
Auerbach La	Hu	7 E	25
August Av	Ou	25 T	2
August La	Nu	28 P	12
August La	Ou	29 T	14
Augusta Ct	Nu	10 H	13
Augusta La	Nu	10 J	12
Augustina St	Hu	6 C	25
Aurelia Ct	Hu	13 H	20
Austin Av	Hu	40 W	21
Austin Blvd	Hu	15 K	26
Austin Pl	Nu	3 E	12
Austin St	Hu	13 F	21
Austral Av	Ou	17 M	5
Autumn La	Ou	38 V	15
Ava Dr	Hu	29 R	16
Ava Dr	Ou	36 W	9
Ava Rd	Hu	31 R	19
Ava Rd	Ou	46 Y	17
Avalon Pl (ML)	Hu	13 H	21
Avalon Pl	Hu	30 T	17
Avalon Rd	Nu	3 E	12
Avalon Rd	Hu	14 G	23
Avalon Rd (WB)	Nu	20 N	15
Avenue A	Nu	8 G	7
Avenue A (in)	Hu	7 B	25
Avenue A (un)	Hu	21 P	19
Avenue A (un)	Hu	30 Q	19
Avenue B	Nu	8 G	7
Avenue B (un)	Hu	21 P	19
Avenue B	Hu	30 Q	19

STREET	MUN.	MAP	GRID
Avenue C	Nu	8	G 7
Avenue C (un)	Hu	30	Q 18
Avenue C (mr)	Hu	31	T 22
Avenue D	Hu	30	Q 18
Avenue M	Hu	20	P 16
Avenue N	Hu	20	P 16
Avenue T	Hu	20	P 16
Avenue U	Hu	20	P 16
Averill Blvd	Hu	12	H 18
Avery La	Ou	37	X 12
Avery Pl	Hu	6	D 25
Avery Rd	Ou	43	AA 8
Avis Dr	Hu	29	T 16
Avoca Av	Hu	38	X 16
Avoca Av (MS)	Ou	47	AA 21
Avon Ct	Hu	14	H 23
Avon Ct	Ou	37	W 11
Avon La (EH)	Nu	18	M 11
Avon La	Hu	24	M 27
Avon La	Nu	28	P 13
Avon Pl	Hu	21	L 18
Avon Rd	Nu	11	H 14
Avon Rd	Hu	14	G 23
Avon Rd	Ou	46	Z 16
Avondale Rd	Ou	45	Z 12
Avondale St	Hu	13	F 22
Axinn Av	Hu	20	O 15
Ayers Pl	Hu	23	N 23
Ayers Rd	Ou	26	Q 4
Aylwood Dr	Hu	29	T 16
Azalea Ct (FG)	Ou	37	X 13
Azalea Ct	Ou	46	BB 16
Azalea Ct	Hu	40	W 21
Azalea Dr	Ou	36	X 8
Azalea Rd	Hu	38	U 16
Azalia Ct	Hu	21	L 18
Azure Pl	Hu	14	H 24

B

STREET	MUN.	MAP	GRID
B Gate	Nu	28	Q 12
B St	Hu	12	G 19
B St (FR)	Hu	32	R 23
Babcock Pl	Hu	13	J 21
Babs La	Hu	31	S 20
Babylon Rd	Hu	31	S 22
Babylon St	Hu	40	V 22
Babylon Tpke (rv)	Hu	31	Q 20
Babylon Tpke (mr)	Hu	31	R 21
Bach Ct	Hu	29	R 15
Backus Farm La	Nu	1	E 6
Bacon Rd	Nu	19	N 12
Baer Pl	Hu	11	H 16
Bagley Av	Nu	19	L 13
Bailey Av	Hu	29	S 16
Bailey Dr	Ou	47	CC 19
Bainbridge St	Hu	31	Q 20
Baird Ct	Ou	36	W 10
Baird Ct (wy)	Ou	44	Z 10
Baird Pl	Hu	40	W 20
Baisley Av	Hu	14	J 23
Baker Av (in)	Hu	6	C 24
Baker Av (ne)	Hu	31	S 20
Baker Ct	Hu	15	K 27
Baker Hill Rd	Nu	2	D 11
Baker La	Hu	39	V 18
Balchen St	Ou	47	BB 18
Balcom Rd	Ou	46	BB 15
Baldwin Av (lv)	Ou	16	P 4
Baldwin Av (bw)	Hu	22	N 22
Baldwin Av (mr)	Hu	33	Q 27
Baldwin Av (mq)	Ou	48	Z 22
Baldwin Blvd	Ou	25	R 2
Baldwin Ct (un)	Hu	21	P 17
Baldwin Ct (mr)	Hu	31	T 22
Baldwin Dr	Hu	12	J 19
Baldwin Dr (WB)	Nu	28	R 13
Baldwin Dr	Ou	46	Z 17
Baldwin Pl	Hu	23	M 23
Baldwin Pl (bp)	Ou	46	Y 15
Baldwin Pl (mq)	Ou	48	CC 21
Baldwin Rd	Hu	22	N 19
Baldwin St	Ou	46	CC 16
Balfour Dr	Ou	46	Y 16
Balfour St	Hu	13	G 20
Ball Park La	Ou	29	T 14
Ballad La	Ou	38	U 15
Ballantine La	Nu	2	B 9
Ballard Av	Hu	5	F 21
Ballsten Dr	Ou	44	Y 10
Balsam Av	Hu	30	T 18
Balsam Ct	Hu	39	W 19
Balsam Dr	Ou	37	V 12
Balsam La	Ou	38	V 14
Balsam La	Hu	38	W 16
Balsam Pl	Ou	37	X 14
Balsam St	Hu	23	M 24
Balsams, The	Nu	9	J 11
Balsar Ct	Ou	36	V 8
Baltimore Av	Ou	47	Y 20
Baltustrol Cir	Nu	10	H 13
Bamboo La	Ou	29	T 14
Bambrick St	Hu	14	K 24
Banbury Rd	Nu	20	L 15
Banbury Rd	Hu	22	M 20
Banbury Rd	Ou	47	Y 19
Bancroft Dr	Nu	2	C 9
Bane Rd	Hu	20	P 16
Bangs Av	Hu	31	R 20
Bank La	Ou	29	T 14
Bank St	Nu	8	G 8
Bank St	Hu	5	E 20
Banks Av	Hu	13	K 22
Bannister La	Hu	7	D 27
Bannon Pl	Ou	47	AA 21
Bar Beach Rd	Nu	9	H 8
Barbara Blvd	Hu	12	J 17
Barbara Cir	Ou	47	CC 18
Barbara Ct (nb)	Hu	30	T 19
Barbara Ct (sd)	Hu	40	Y 21
Barbara Dr	Hu	29	S 16
Barbara Dr	Ou	36	W 9
Barbara Dr (sa)	Ou	47	CC 18
Barbara La (GL)	Ou	16	M 3
Barbara La (wh)	Hu	13	K 20
Barbara La (je)	Ou	37	V 12
Barbara La (in)	Hu	39	V 17
Barbara La (ed)	Hu	30	R 19
Barbara La (pv)	Ou	45	Y 11
Barbara Lynn Ct	Ou	45	Z 13
Barbara Rd	Hu	40	V 22
Barbara St	Hu	4	F 19
Barbara St	Ou	46	Y 15
Barberry Ct	Ou	46	BB 15
Barberry Dr	Ou	48	CC 21
Barberry La	Hu	6	F 25
Barberry La	Ou	17	L 7
Barberry La	Nu	18	M 11
Barberry Rd	Hu	39	W 19
Barby La	Ou	45	Y 13
Bard La	Hu	30	R 17
Bard Rd	Nu	28	R 13
Bark La	Hu	39	W 17
Barkers Point Rd	Nu	1	D 7
Barklay Crest	Nu	10	J 12
Barkley Av	Hu	30	R 18
Barlow Av	Ou	8	L 5
Barnard Av	Hu	6	D 23
Barnard Pl	Nu	9	H 10
Barnes Av	Hu	23	N 23
Barnes La	Hu	21	M 17
Barnes Pl	Hu	5	E 21
Barnes St	Hu	12	H 18
Barnes St (LB)	Hu	24	L 27
Barnside La	Ou	27	Q 8
Barnstable Rd	Hu	14	J 24
Barnum Av	Ou	37	X 13
Barnyard La	Nu	19	M 13
Barnyard La	Hu	39	U 17
Baron Hill Colony	Nu	8	J 7
Barr Av	Hu	6	F 23
Barrel La	Ou	38	U 15
Barret Rd	Hu	7	D 26
Barrett St	Ou	48	BB 21
Barrie Av	Hu	39	U 19
Barrie Ct	Ou	47	Z 19
Barrington St	Nu	29	R 14
Barrister Rd	Hu	38	W 15
Barrister Rd	Ou	38	W 15
Barrow Ct	Ou	44	Z 10
Barry Ct	Ou	37	W 13
Barry Ct	Hu	32	S 23
Barry Dr	Hu	13	G 20
Barry Dr (GL)	Ou	8	K 5
Barry Dr	Ou	28	S 13
Barry Dr S	Hu	13	G 20
Barry Dr W	Hu	13	G 20
Barry La	Ou	36	X 9
Barry La E	Ou	45	AA 14
Barry La S	Ou	45	AA 14
Barry La W	Ou	45	AA 14
Barry Park Ct	Nu	10	K 13
Barry Pl	Hu	30	Q 19
Barrymore Blvd	Hu	12	H 18
Barston St	Ou	36	W 10
Barstow Rd	Nu	3	D 11
Bart Ct	Ou	37	X 12
Barter La	Ou	38	U 15
Barth Dr	Hu	22	O 21
Bartlett Dr	Nu	10	J 11
Bartz St	Hu	14	K 25
Barwick Blvd	Nu	19	M 14
Bascom Av	Hu	31	S 20
Basile Ct	Hu	6	D 24
Basket La	Ou	29	U 14
Bass Pond Dr	Nu	19	N 12
Bates Rd	Nu	3	D 13
Bath St	Hu	24	M 27
Battle Row	Ou	45	AA 14
Bauer Av	Hu	31	Q 20
Bauer Ct	Hu	4	F 19
Bauer Pl	Nu	11	K 15
Bauer St	Hu	4	F 19
Baxter Av	Nu	11	H 15
Bay Av (SC)	Ou	8	K 7
Bay Av (oy)	Ou	26	U 4
Bay Av (hk)	Ou	37	V 13
Bay Beach Av	Ou	25	T 2
Bay Blvd	Hu	6	C 24
Bay Ct	Hu	41	W 23
Bay Dr	Nu	1	F 7
Bay Dr (WG)	Hu	14	F 25
Bay Dr (MS)	Hu	32	T 22
Bay Dr	Hu	42	U 27
Bay Dr (MS)	Ou	48	AA 21
Bay Driveway	Nu	2	F 10
Bay La	Hu	24	O 27
Bay Link	Ou	48	AA 22
Bay Pl (sd)	Hu	41	W 23
Bay Pl (sd)	Hu	41	X 22
Bay St	Hu	7	F 27
Bay St (BY)	Ou	25	R 2
Bay St (bm)	Hu	31	T 22
Bay View Cir	Nu	2	F 11
Bay View Pl	Ou	48	Y 22
Bayard Av	Ou	25	R 2
Bayard St	Hu	23	M 24
Bayberry Av (GA)	Hu	20	M 15
Bayberry Av	Hu	32	T 23
Bayberry Dr (HH)	Hu	14	H 24
Bayberry Dr	Ou	45	Z 13
Bayberry Dr N	Hu	14	H 24
Bayberry Dr S	Hu	14	H 24
Bayberry La (in)	Hu	39	V 17
Bayberry La (sd)	Hu	39	X 19
Bayberry Ridge	Nu	9	J 10
Bayberry Rd	Hu	13	H 19
Bayberry Rd E	Hu	7	E 26
Bayberry Rd N	Hu	7	E 25
Bayberry Rd S	Hu	7	E 26
Bayberry Rd W	Hu	7	E 26
Bayfield Blvd	Hu	23	N 24
Bayfront Dr	Hu	23	P 24
Bayfront Pl	Hu	23	P 24
Baylis Av	Hu	4	D 18
Baylis Pl	Hu	14	H 23
Baylis Pl	Ou	36	W 8
Baylis Rd (RC)	Hu	22	M 20
Baylis Rd	Hu	40	X 21
Bayport Ct	Hu	40	V 22
Bayport La	Nu	2	B 11
Bayport La N	Nu	2	B 11
Bayside Av	Nu	8	G 8
Bayside Av	Hu	14	K 23
Bayside Av	Ou	26	T 5
Bayside Ct	Hu	40	V 22
Bayside Dr	Nu	2	F 10
Bayside Dr (hs)	Nu	3	B 12
Bayside Dr (ae)	Hu	7	E 27
Bayside Dr (pl)	Hu	33	Q 27
Bayside Ter (PD)	Nu	3	B 11
Bayswater Blvd	Hu	6	B 25
Bayview Av (ma)	Nu	2	F 11
Bayview Av (pw)	Nu	9	F 8
Bayview Av (GE)	Nu	2	C 11
Bayview Av (mp)	Hu	6	C 24
Bayview Av (CH)	Hu	6	D 24
Bayview Av (VS)	Hu	14	G 22
Bayview Av (in)	Hu	7	B 25
Bayview Av (os)	Hu	14	K 23
Bayview Av (bh)	Hu	23	O 23
Bayview Av (FR)	Hu	22	P 22
Bayview Av (BY)	Ou	25	R 2
Bayview Av (oy)	Ou	26	U 4
Bayview Av (bm)	Hu	32	T 22
Bayview Av	Hu	40	V 21
Bayview Av	Ou	48	Z 22
Bayview Ct (ma)	Nu	2	F 11
Bayview Ct (os)	Hu	23	L 23
Bayview Ct	Hu	41	V 23
Bayview Pl (BY)	Ou	25	Q 2
Bayview Pl	Hu	40	V 21
Bayview Pl	Ou	48	CC 22
Bayview Rd	Nu	2	F 10
Bayview Rd	Hu	14	K 22
Bayview St	Hu	40	X 22
Bayview St E (ba)	Hu	14	J 24
Bayview St E	Ou	48	BB 22
Bayview St W	Ou	48	BB 22
Bayview Ter	Nu	2	F 11
Bayville Av (BY)	Ou	25	Q 2
Bayville Av	Ou	25	R 2
Bayville Pk Blvd	Ou	25	Q 2
Bayville Rd	Ou	25	Q 2
Bea Ct	Hu	24	M 25
Bea Ct (un)	Hu	30	Q 19
Beach Av (IP)	Hu	15	K 27
Beach Av	Ou	34	U 3
Beach Av	Hu	40	V 22
Beach Ct	Hu	14	K 24
Beach Ct	Ou	25	S 1
Beach Ct (bm)	Hu	31	U 22
Beach Dr	Hu	31	S 22
Beach Pa E	Ou	25	S 2
Beach Rd (SP)	Nu	1	F 5
Beach Rd	Nu	2	C 10
Beach Rd (GL)	Ou	16	L 3
Beach Rd (mq)	Ou	48	Z 22
Beach St	Hu	31	T 22
Beach St (sa)	Ou	46	Z 17
Beach St	Ou	48	CC 21
Beach Wy	Nu	2	F 9
Beach Wy	Hu	15	K 26
Beach Wy, The	Nu	2	F 10
Beachview Av	Hu	24	L 26
Beacon Dr	Nu	8	J 7
Beacon Dr	Ou	48	AA 22
Beacon Hill Dr	Hu	30	U 19
Beacon Hill Rd	Nu	8	H 8
Beacon La	Ou	29	T 14
Beacon Rd	Hu	40	X 22
Beacon St (ML)	Hu	13	H 21
Beacon St	Hu	13	H 21
Bear La	Ou	25	P 2
Beatrice Av	Hu	23	M 25
Beatrice Av	Ou	36	W 9
Beatrice Ct	Hu	21	L 18
Beatrice La (GL)	Ou	16	M 3
Beatrice La	Hu	30	U 19
Beatrice La	Ou	45	AA 13
Beaufort La E	Ou	44	Z 10
Beaumont Av	Ou	48	Z 21
Beaumont Ct	Nu	10	J 14
Beaumont Dr	Ou	44	Z 11
Beaver Brook Rd	Ou	26	R 5
Beaver Ct	Ou	17	O 7
Beaver Dr	Ou	25	R 1
Beaver La	Hu	39	W 17
Beaver Rd	Ou	25	R 4
Beaver Turn	Hu	40	X 22
Beck Pl	Hu	31	T 20
Beck St	Hu	21	P 18
Beckman Dr	Hu	39	T 18
Beckman St	Hu	6	C 25
Bedell Av	Hu	21	L 17
Bedell St (HV)	Hu	21	M 18
Bedell St (HV)	Hu	23	M 22
Bedell St (FR)	Hu	31	Q 22
Bedell St (bm)	Hu	41	U 22
Bedell Ter	Hu	21	L 18
Bedford Av (el)	Hu	12	G 18
Bedford Av (gk)	Nu	11	J 15
Bedford Av (RC)	Hu	22	M 21
Bedford Av (rv)	Hu	21	P 18
Bedford Av (WB)	Nu	29	P 15
Bedford Av (rv)	Hu	31	Q 21
Bedford Av (nb)	Hu	30	S 19
Bedford Av (bm)	Hu	40	U 21
Bedford Av (mr)	Hu	31	S 22
Bedford Av (mq)	Ou	47	Y 19
Bedford Ct (un)	Hu	21	O 18
Bedford Ct	Hu	40	U 21
Bedford Pl	Hu	40	U 21
Bedford Rd	Nu	8	H 8
Bedford Rd	Hu	21	O 19
Bedford Rd	Ou	37	X 12
Bee Gee Ct	Hu	13	K 20
Bee St	Hu	5	E 20
Beebe Av	Hu	21	O 19
Beebe Rd	Nu	11	K 15
Beech Blvd	Hu	7	F 28

Nassau Co.

STREET	MUN.	MAP	GRID
Beech Ct	Hu	13 H	20
Beech Ct	Ou	16 M	5
Beech Dr	Nu	2 C	9
Beech La	Nu	2 B	10
Beech La	Hu	29 T	14
Beech La	Hu	30 R	18
Beech St (FP)	Hu	12 F	17
Beech St (NP)	Hu	11 G	15
Beech St (VS)	Hu	5 D	21
Beech St (AB)	Hu	7 E	27
Beech St (ea)	Hu	15 G	28
Beech St (HV)	Hu	21 M	17
Beech St (sh)	Hu	22 M	20
Beech St (bw)	Hu	22 O	22
Beech St (ed)	Hu	30 T	17
Beech St (pl)	Hu	33 Q	27
Beech St (hk)	Ou	37 W	13
Beech St (FG)	Ou	46 Z	16
Beech St (nq)	Ou	47 AA	18
Beech St (wn)	Hu	40 W	21
Beech Tree La	Nu	9 G	9
Beech Tree La	Ou	27 R	10
Beeches, The	Ou	44 AA	10
Beechhurst Av	Hu	11 G	16
Beechwood Av (ma)	Nu	9 G	11
Beechwood Av (pw)	Nu	9 G	9
Beechwood Av	Hu	31 Q	20
Beechwood Ct (GL)	Ou	16 N	4
Beechwood Ct	Hu	47 Y	18
Beechwood Dr	Hu	7 C	26
Beechwood Dr	Ou	17 M	7
Beechwood La	Hu	11 H	14
Beechwood Pl	Ou	47 CC	19
Beechwood Pl	Hu	40 X	20
Beechwood Pl (es)	Ou	48 CC	21
Beechwood Rd	Ou	18 M	10
Beechwood St	Ou	46 BB	15
Behnke Ct	Hu	22 M	20
Belair Ct	Ou	45 Z	14
Bel-Air Ct	Ou	26 S	7
Belair Dr (pv)	Ou	45 Z	13
Belair Dr	Ou	48 CC	21
Belcher St	Hu	23 N	23
Belfry La	Ou	29 T	15
Bell Ct (nv)	Hu	13 G	20
Bell Ct	Hu	31 U	22
Bell Cove	Nu	1 B	8
Bell La	Ou	25 R	2
Bell La	Hu	39 U	17
Bell Pl	Ou	47 Z	19
Bell St	Hu	5 F	21
Bell St (wh)	Hu	12 K	18
Bell St	Hu	21 M	18
Bella Vista Av	Ou	17 N	6
Bella Vista St	Ou	16 P	4
Bellaire Rd	Ou	48 Z	22
Bellaire St	Hu	40 V	22
Belle Ct	Ou	38 U	15
Belle Rd	Hu	41 V	23
Belle Sonia Ct	Ou	27 U	10
Belleview Av	Nu	9 G	8
Belleview Av	Hu	23 L	23
Bellewood Dr	Hu	31 T	21
Bellingham La	Nu	2 D	10
Bellmore Av (nb)	Hu	30 T	19
Bellmore Av (bm)	Hu	40 U	20
Bellmore Av (bm)	Hu	33 Q	27
Bellmore Rd	Hu	30 T	17
Bellmore Rd	Hu	40 U	20
Bellmore St	Hu	4 F	17
Bellows La	Hu	9 H	11
Bellows La	Hu	39 W	17
Bellport Av	Hu	40 V	21
Bellwood Dr	Nu	11 K	15
Belmart Ct	Ou	38 W	15
Belmart Rd	Ou	38 W	15
Belmill La	Hu	31 U	22
Belmill Rd	Hu	31 U	22
Belmond Av	Hu	30 T	18
Belmont Av (FP)	Hu	11 F	16
Belmont Av (el)	Hu	4 E	18
Belmont Av (wh)	Hu	11 H	16
Belmont Av (wh)	Hu	12 K	18
Belmont Av (LB)	Hu	24 L	28
Belmont Av (WB)	Hu	29 T	14
Belmont Av (ed)	Hu	30 R	17
Belmont Av	Ou	37 X	13
Belmont Blvd	Hu	12 F	18
Belmont Cir	Ou	36 W	10
Belmont Dr N	Nu	19 M	13
Belmont Dr S	Nu	19 M	13
Belmont Dr W	Nu	19 M	13
Belmont Pkwy	Hu	21 O	18
Belmont Pl (eg)	Hu	21 P	17
Belmont Pl	Hu	21 P	17
Belmont Pl	Ou	37 U	12
Belmont Rd	Nu	3 D	12
Belmore Av	Hu	30 R	18
Belpark Av	Hu	4 E	18
Belt St	Hu	31 T	20
Beltagh Av	Hu	40 U	20
Beltagh Pl	Hu	40 U	20
Belvedere Dr (sy)	Ou	36 V	8
Belvedere Dr (mq)	Ou	48 AA	21
Bench La	Hu	29 T	15
Bender St	Hu	14 K	24
Benedict Av	Hu	13 F	21
Benedict Ct	Ou	46 AA	16
Benedict Pl	Hu	22 N	21
Benefit St	Hu	31 S	20
Bengeyfield Dr	Nu	19 L	13
Bengeyfield Dr N	Nu	19 L	13
Benine Rd	Nu	28 Q	13
Benito St	Hu	30 S	18
Benjamin Av	Hu	30 R	19
Benjamin Pl	Ou	16 P	4
Benjamin Rd	Hu	23 M	24
Benjamin St (gh)	Ou	17 N	8
Benjamin St (hk)	Ou	28 T	14
Benkert St	Ou	46 Y	15
Benmor Ct	Ou	45 Z	13
Benmore Av	Hu	12 H	17
Benmur St	Ou	37 X	13
Bennett Av (HV)	Hu	21 N	17
Bennett Av (nb)	Hu	31 Q	21
Bennett Av (rv)	Hu	31 T	20
Bennett St (RC)	Hu	22 M	21
Bennett St	Hu	23 M	24
Bennington Av	Hu	31 Q	22
Benris Av	Hu	12 H	18
Benson Av	Hu	12 G	18
Benson La	Hu	31 S	21
Benson Pl (VS)	Hu	5 E	20
Benson Pl	Hu	31 Q	22
Bent La	Hu	38 V	16
Bentley Rd	Nu	2 E	10
Bentley Rd	Ou	37 W	12
Benton Rd	Hu	39 U	18
Benton St	Hu	6 F	24
Berfond Ct	Hu	31 T	22
Berfond Pl	Hu	39 U	18
Berg Dr	Hu	30 R	17
Bergen St (FP)	Hu	11 G	16
Bergen St	Hu	40 U	20
Berger Av	Hu	38 X	16
Bergman Dr	Hu	14 G	23
Bering Ct	Ou	44 AA	10
Berkeley Av	Hu	22 N	21
Berkeley Pl (GL)	Ou	17 M	6
Berkeley Pl (FR)	Hu	31 P	20
Berkeley Pl (bm)	Hu	31 U	22
Berkeley Pl	Ou	40 Y	21
Berkeley St (sh)	Hu	22 N	20
Berkeley St	Hu	30 Q	18
Berkley La (bm)	Hu	41 U	23
Berkley La (lv)	Ou	37 W	11
Berkley La	Ou	37 V	11
Berkley Pl	Hu	6 E	25
Berkley Rd	Hu	20 M	15
Berkley St	Hu	5 F	22
Berkshire Dr	Hu	29 R	15
Berkshire Pl	Hu	7 E	27
Berkshire Pl	Ou	47 Z	20
Berkshire Rd (GN)	Nu	2 D	10
Berkshire Rd (RC)	Hu	22 L	20
Berkshire Rd (mr)	Hu	31 R	22
Berkshire Rd (hk)	Ou	37 W	13
Bermingham Pl	Nu	10 L	14
Bermuda St	Hu	7 C	27
Bernadette Ct	Ou	29 U	14
Bernard Dr (sl)	Hu	29 R	15
Bernard Dr	Hu	39 W	18
Bernard La	Hu	29 T	14
Bernard St (GN)	Nu	2 D	10
Bernard St (pw)	Nu	9 H	8
Bernard St (nv)	Hu	12 G	19
Bernard St (LW)	Hu	6 D	25
Bernard St (ed)	Hu	30 S	18
Bernard St (mr)	Hu	31 S	22
Bernard St (FG)	Ou	46 AA	16
Bernard St (sa)	Ou	46 Z	17
Bernard St	Ou	47 CC	19
Berne Rd	Hu	40 X	20
Bernhard St	Hu	21 N	19
Bernice Dr	Hu	39 U	17
Bernice Pl	Ou	45 Z	13
Bernice Rd (fs)	Hu	12 H	19
Bernice Rd (sd)	Hu	39 X	19
Berry Ct	Hu	13 J	20
Berry Hill Ct	Ou	36 W	8
Berry Hill La	Ou	46 Y	17
Berry Hill Pl	Ou	45 AA	13
Berry Hill Rd	Ou	35 U	5
Berry La (GL)	Ou	17 L	5
Berry La	Ou	38 U	15
Berry Pl	Nu	19 L	13
Berry St (VS)	Hu	13 G	21
Berry St	Hu	14 H	22
Berryhill Ct	Hu	21 L	18
Berrywood Ct	Hu	12 L	19
Berrywood Dr	Hu	39 X	18
Bert Pl	Hu	30 R	17
Bertha Ct	Hu	23 O	25
Bertha Dr	Hu	23 O	24
Bertha La	Ou	47 BB	20
Bertha St	Hu	12 F	17
Bertram Pl	Hu	38 X	16
Berwick Rd	Hu	14 G	23
Beryl La	Ou	46 Z	17
Besade Ct	Hu	14 K	23
Bessels La	Ou	17 M	6
Best St	Hu	31 Q	22
Beth Ct	Hu	41 V	22
Beth La	Hu	6 E	23
Beth La	Hu	44 Z	11
Beth Pl	Ou	36 X	10
Bethel Rd	Nu	19 L	13
Bethlynn Ct	Hu	30 S	18
Bethpage Commons	Hu	38 X	16
Bethpage Ct	Ou	37 V	13
Bethpage Rd (hk)	Ou	37 U	12
Bethpage Rd (FG)	Ou	46 AA	15
Bethpage State Pkwy	Ou	47 AA	18
Bethpage State Pkwy (Assemb Phillip B Healey Memorial Pkwy)	Ou	46 Z	16
Bethpage-Sweethollow Rd	Ou	45 AA	13
Betsy Ct	Nu	3 E	12
Bette Rd	Hu	29 T	16
Betty La	Nu	20 M	14
Betty Rd	Hu	30 R	17
Betty Rd	Hu	37 X	10
Beulah St	Hu	22 N	20
Beverly Av	Hu	12 G	17
Beverly Av	Ou	48 AA	21
Beverly Ct	Nu	10 K	13
Beverly La	Nu	2 E	11
Beverly La	Hu	28 R	13
Beverly La	Ou	29 U	14
Beverly Pkwy	Hu	22 P	21
Beverly Pl (VS)	Hu	5 E	20
Beverly Pl	Hu	29 T	15
Beverly Pl	Ou	48 Z	22
Beverly Rd (pw)	Nu	8 H	8
Beverly Rd (KG)	Nu	3 D	11
Beverly Rd (GL)	Ou	17 L	6
Beverly Rd (ML)	Hu	13 K	21
Beverly Rd (RC)	Hu	22 M	21
Beverly Rd (HV)	Hu	21 O	18
Beverly Rd (os)	Hu	23 M	23
Beverly Rd (BK)	Ou	27 Q	9
Beverly Rd (mr)	Hu	31 S	22
Beverly Rd (bm)	Hu	40 V	21
Beverly Rd (FG)	Ou	46 AA	16
Beverly Rd (MS)	Hu	48 Z	22
Beverly Wy	Hu	31 T	22
Biarritz St	Hu	24 N	27
Bieling Rd	Hu	4 D	18
Biltmore Av	Hu	4 E	18
Biltmore Blvd	Ou	48 Z	21
Bingham Cir	Nu	9 J	10
Bira St	Hu	30 P	19
Birch Av	Hu	39 U	18
Birch Av	Ou	46 BB	17
Birch Bark La	Ou	16 M	3
Birch Ct	Ou	35 X	6
Birch Dale La	Nu	9 J	10
Birch Dr (HH)	Nu	14 H	24
Birch Dr (EH)	Nu	18 M	10
Birch Dr (sg)	Nu	10 J	13
Birch Dr (hr)	Nu	10 J	14
Birch Dr (wn)	Hu	40 V	20
Birch Dr (mr)	Hu	31 S	22
Birch Dr W	Ou	37 X	12
Birch La	Nu	10 J	12
Birch Hill	Ou	35 X	6
Birch Hill Ct	Nu	19 P	12
Birch Hill Rd	Nu	3 E	13
Birch Hill Rd	Ou	16 P	4
Birch La (FH)	Nu	9 H	10
Birch La (NP)	Nu	11 H	15
Birch La (sv)	Nu	5 E	22
Birch La (WB)	Nu	6 F	25
Birch La (FH)	Nu	9 H	10
Birch La (NP)	Nu	11 H	15
Birch La (GA)	Nu	20 L	16
Birch La (ed)	Hu	29 T	16
Birch La (pv)	Ou	45 Z	13
Birch La (sa)	Ou	46 CC	17
Birch La (MS)	Ou	47 BB	20
Birch La (MS)	Ou	48 AA	21
Birch Pl (GL)	Ou	16 M	5
Birch Pl (lg)	Ou	36 V	10
Birch Pl	Hu	40 V	21
Birch Pl (sa)	Ou	46 Z	17
Birch Rd	Hu	13 J	21
Birch St (gg)	Nu	2 E	11
Birch St (pw)	Nu	9 H	8
Birch St (FP)	Hu	12 G	17
Birch St (fs)	Hu	13 J	20
Birch St (LY)	Hu	14 H	23
Birch St	Ou	26 P	4
Birch St (ML)	Hu	13 J	20
Birch St (wh)	Hu	12 L	19
Birch St (un)	Hu	30 Q	18
Birch St (bm)	Hu	31 T	20
Birch Tree Ct	Ou	17 M	6
Birchell La	Ou	17 O	7
Birches, The	Nu	9 K	11
Birchmore La	Ou	37 W	11
Birchwood Ct	Nu	20 M	15
Birchwood Ct E	Ou	37 W	11
Birchwood Dr (nv)	Hu	5 F	20
Birchwood Dr	Nu	11 J	15
Birchwood Dr (sl)	Hu	29 Q	15
Birchwood Dr N	Hu	5 F	20
Birchwood Dr S	Hu	5 F	20
Birchwood Dr W	Hu	5 F	20
Birchwood La	Nu	2 B	10
Birchwood La	Ou	38 W	14
Birchwood Park Ct	Ou	37 V	11
Birchwood Park Cres	Ou	37 V	11
Birchwood Park Dr	Ou	37 U	11
Birchwood St	Nu	9 G	9
Bird Ct	Nu	18 N	10
Bird La	Ou	38 U	15
Bishop Av	Ou	46 Y	15
Bishop Ct	Ou	46 Y	15
Bishop La	Ou	29 U	14
Bishop Pl	Hu	12 K	18
Bishop Rd	Hu	14 L	25
Bismark Av	Hu	13 G	22
Bit Pa	Hu	40 X	21
Bitter Sweet La	Ou	16 N	4
Bittersweet La (sv)	Hu	5 E	22
Bittersweet La	Hu	38 V	16
Bixby Dr	Hu	22 O	22
Bixley Dr	Hu	11 J	15
Bixley Heath	Hu	13 H	22
Black Burn La	Nu	9 J	10
Black Rock Rd	Ou	27 T	9
Blackbird La	Hu	38 U	15
Blackheath Rd	Hu	24 L	27
Blackheath Rd	Hu	23 N	24
Blacksmith Rd	Hu	38 V	15
Blacksmith Rd E	Hu	38 V	15
Blacksmith Rd S	Hu	38 V	15
Blacksmith Rd W	Hu	38 V	15
Blackstone Av	Hu	30 S	18
Blackstone St	Hu	4 E	18
Blaine Av	Hu	30 R	18
Blair Dr	Nu	28 R	13
Blair Rd	Ou	35 V	5
Blair Rd E	Ou	35 V	5
Blair Rd S	Ou	35 V	5
Blake Av	Hu	13 J	22

STREET	MUN.	MAP	GRID
Blakelock Pl	Nu	9	H 11
Blanche La	Hu	32	T 23
Blanche St	Ou	37	W 13
Blemton Pl	Hu	21	N 17
Blendwood Dr	Hu	30	R 18
Blenheim La	Hu	22	N 21
Blenheim Dr	Nu	10	J 11
Bliss Pl	Hu	32	T 23
Block Blvd	Ou	47	BB 20
Block La	Hu	29	T 15
Block Ter	Ou	46	CC 17
Bloodgood La	Nu	19	L 12
Bloomingdale Rd	Hu	38	W 16
Blossom Heath Av	Hu	13	H 22
Blossom La	Hu	11	G 15
Blossom La	Hu	39	V 17
Blossom Rd	Nu	2	D 9
Blossom Row	Hu	5	E 20
Blossom St	Hu	12	G 18
Blue Rd	Hu	40	U 20
Blue Sea La	Nu	2	E 9
Blue Spruce La	Nu	40	V 20
Blue Spruce Rd	Hu	29	T 16
Blue St	Hu	40	U 20
Bluebell Ct	Hu	20	M 15
Bluebell La	Hu	38	V 16
Blueberry La (MN)	Ou	35	U 6
Blueberry La	Ou	28	T 14
Bluebird Dr (SR)	Nu	2	C 11
Bluebird Dr	Hu	19	M 12
Bluebird Dr	Hu	36	W 10
Bluebird Hill Ct	Nu	10	J 11
Bluebird La	Ou	45	Z 13
Bluegrass La	Hu	39	U 17
Bluejay La	Hu	39	V 17
Bluepoint Ct	Hu	40	V 22
Bluff Rd	Ou	16	K 5
Bluth St	Hu	6	C 25
Bly Ct (GN)	Nu	2	E 10
Bly Ct	Hu	11	G 15
Bly Ct	Hu	12	H 19
Bly Rd	Hu	30	R 17
Boardwalk (AB)	Hu	7	C 28
Boardwalk (AB)	Hu	7	D 28
Boat La (PN)	Nu	1	F 7
Boat La	Hu	38	V 16
Bob Reed La	Hu	29	S 15
Boblee La	Ou	37	V 12
Bobolink La	Hu	38	U 15
Bobsbay Rd	Hu	24	O 27
Bobwhite La	Ou	29	T 14
Boden Av (Pvt)	Hu	5	E 21
Boehme Pl	Ou	38	V 14
Boelsen Dr	Hu	29	R 15
Bogart Av	Nu	9	H 8
Bolton Dr	Nu	10	H 12
Bolton Rd	Nu	11	J 15
Bonaparte Pl	Hu	23	O 23
Bond Av	Hu	13	H 21
Bond Ct	Nu	10	J 12
Bond Ct (ne)	Hu	30	R 19
Bond Dr	Hu	32	S 23
Bond La	Ou	38	U 15
Bond St (GP)	Nu	3	D 11
Bond St (un)	Nu	20	O 16
Bond St (bw)	Hu	22	O 20
Bond St	Hu	28	S 13
Bond St (FR)	Hu	31	Q 21
Bondietti Dr	Ou	46	BB 16
Bonnie Ct	Ou	29	T 14
Bonnie Ct (FR)	Hu	31	T 22
Bonnie Dr	Hu	23	N 24
Bonnie Dr	Ou	28	S 13
Bonnie Heights Rd	Nu	9	H 10
Bonnie La	Ou	48	AA 21
Bonnie Lynn Ct	Nu	10	H 13
Bonta St	Hu	4	E 18
Book La	Hu	39	V 18
Boone St	Hu	38	X 16
Boot La	Hu	40	X 21
Booth La	Hu	29	T 15
Booth St	Hu	21	N 19
Border La	Hu	38	V 16
Border St	Ou	29	T 14
Borglum Rd	Nu	9	J 11
Boston Av	Hu	47	Y 20
Boston Rd	Hu	4	E 17
Bostwick La	Nu	19	O 13
Bothner St	Hu	14	K 25
Botsford St	Hu	21	N 19
Boulder La	Ou	29	T 14
Boulder Rd	Nu	9	H 10
Boulevard Dr	Ou	38	U 14
Boulevard Pl	Hu	12	K 17
Boundary Av	Ou	46	Y 17
Boundary La	Hu	40	U 22
Boundary St	Hu	40	U 22
Bounty La	Ou	37	U 11
Bourne Ct	Hu	40	W 20
Bournedale Rd N	Nu	9	F 10
Bournedale Rd S	Nu	9	F 10
Bowden La	Ou	17	O 6
Bowe Rd	Hu	13	F 20
Bowers Dr	Hu	39	X 19
Bowers La	Hu	3	E 12
Bowers Lane Gate	Hu	3	E 12
Bowler Rd	Hu	14	H 23
Bowling Green Dr	Hu	29	R 14
Bowling La	Hu	39	W 17
Bowmans Point Rd	Nu	1	E 7
Bowne St	Ou	17	M 6
Boxwood Dr	Nu	3	C 12
Boxwood Dr W	Hu	14	H 23
Boxwood La	Hu	7	C 25
Boxwood La	Nu	19	M 11
Boxwood La	Ou	29	T 14
Boxwood Rd	Nu	1	F 7
Boyd Dr	Nu	19	O 14
Boyd St	Hu	24	L 27
Boylston St	Hu	20	N 16
Bradford Ct	Hu	22	M 21
Bradford Dr	Hu	10	H 12
Bradford La	Ou	46	Y 16
Bradford Rd	Hu	5	E 20
Bradford Rd	Ou	45	Z 12
Bradley La	Nu	11	K 15
Bradley Ct (nb)	Hu	30	S 19
Bradley Ct	Hu	31	S 22
Bradley Ct	Ou	36	W 8
Bradley Pl	Nu	20	L 15
Bradley St	Hu	12	K 19
Bradley St	Ou	37	X 13
Brae, The	Ou	44	AA 10
Brafmans Rd	Hu	6	C 25
Bramble La	Hu	28	R 13
Brampton La	Nu	2	D 10
Bramshot La	Hu	22	M 21
Branch Av	Hu	23	P 23
Branch Blvd	Hu	6	D 23
Branch Gate	Hu	6	D 23
Branch La	Hu	29	T 15
Branch Pl	Hu	31	Q 20
Brand St	Ou	28	T 13
Branding Iron La	Ou	16	N 4
Brant Pl	Hu	40	X 22
Branton Pl	Nu	19	L 13
Braun Dr	Ou	37	W 12
Braxton St	Hu	30	P 18
Breezy La	Ou	25	T 2
Breezy Pl	Ou	48	CC 21
Breezy Wy	Hu	7	E 26
Bregman Av	Nu	11	G 14
Brendan Av	Ou	47	AA 21
Brengel Pl	Ou	17	L 7
Brennan Pl	Hu	24	L 27
Brenner Av	Hu	38	X 16
Brent Dr	Hu	39	U 18
Brentwood Ct	Hu	40	V 22
Brentwood La	Nu	2	E 11
Brentwood La	Hu	5	E 22
Bretton Rd	Hu	12	G 19
Bretton Rd	Hu	11	J 15
Breuer Av	Nu	2	C 10
Brevoort Pl (RC)	Hu	22	M 21
Brevoort Pl	Hu	40	U 21
Brewster Gate	Ou	47	Y 18
Brewster Pl	Ou	38	V 14
Brewster Rd	Ou	48	AA 22
Brewster Rd W	Ou	48	Z 22
Brewster St	Ou	17	M 5
Brian Ct	Hu	32	S 23
Brian Dr	Hu	31	S 20
Brian La	Hu	39	X 18
Brian St	Nu	11	J 14
Brian St	Hu	23	L 23
Brian St	Ou	45	Y 11
Briar La (KP)	Nu	2	B 10
Briar La (un)	Nu	19	L 11
Briar La	Hu	37	U 11
Briar La	Hu	39	W 17
Briar Pl	Nu	19	N 14
Briar Pl	Hu	30	S 19
Briar Rd	Hu	30	R 19
Briarcliff Dr	Nu	9	G 9
Briarcliff Dr	Hu	31	R 20
Briarcliff Rd (GL)	Ou	17	N 5
Briarcliff Rd (en)	Ou	26	T 7
Briarcliff Rd	Hu	28	R 13
Briard St	Hu	40	W 20
Briarfield Dr	Nu	3	E 12
Briarwood Av	Hu	47	Y 19
Briarwood Ct	Hu	22	M 20
Briarwood Crossing	Hu	6	E 25
Briarwood Dr	Ou	16	N 4
Briarwood La	Hu	6	E 25
Briarwood La	Ou	45	Z 13
Briarwood Rd	Ou	47	Y 18
Brichwood Ct W	Ou	37	W 11
Brichwood Park Dr	Ou	37	V 11
Brickstone Ct	Hu	21	O 17
Bridge La	Ou	29	T 14
Bridge Rd	Nu	9	G 10
Bridge St (wm)	Hu	6	E 23
Bridge St (GL)	Ou	17	M 5
Bridge St	Hu	28	S 13
Bridge St (ne)	Hu	31	R 20
Bridge, The	Nu	1	E 7
Bridle Ct	Ou	35	W 6
Bridle La (SP)	Nu	1	E 6
Bridle La (GL)	Ou	16	N 4
Bridle La	Hu	29	T 14
Bridle Pa (SP)	Nu	8	H 7
Bridle Pa (SP)	Nu	8	H 8
Bridle Pa (KG)	Nu	2	D 11
Bridle Pa (sq)	Nu	10	J 13
Bridle Pa (WB)	Nu	28	P 13
Bridle Pa (bp)	Nu	38	X 15
Bridle Pa (R.O.W.)	Nu	8	H 7
Bridle Path Ct	Ou	27	T 10
Bridle Pa E	Nu	8	H 8
Bridle Path La	Nu	3	E 13
Bridle Path La	Ou	26	T 5
Bridle Path Rd (R.O.W.)	Nu	8	H 7
Briggs Rd	Ou	45	Y 13
Briggs St	Hu	40	U 20
Briggs St	Ou	37	W 12
Bright Av	Hu	30	T 17
Brighton Blvd	Hu	15	J 26
Brighton Pl	Ou	37	U 12
Brighton Rd	Hu	15	K 26
Brighton Rd N	Nu	10	H 12
Brighton Rd S	Nu	10	H 12
Brighton Wy	Hu	31	T 22
Brightwater Pl	Ou	48	BB 22
Brightwaters Ct	Hu	40	V 22
Brill Pl	Hu	11	G 16
Brinkerhoff La	Nu	10	G 11
Brisbane La	Hu	30	R 17
Bristol Dr	Nu	10	J 12
Bristol Dr	Ou	40	U 20
Bristol Dr	Ou	44	Z 10
Bristol St	Hu	13	J 21
Brittle La	Ou	29	T 15
Britton St	Hu	39	W 19
Brixton Av	Ou	37	X 12
Brixton La	Hu	39	V 17
Brixton Rd (GA)	Hu	12	K 17
Brixton Rd (ne)	Hu	30	R 19
Brixton Rd	Ou	45	AA 13
Brixton Rd S	Hu	12	K 18
Broad St (WP)	Nu	19	L 13
Broad St	Hu	21	L 18
Broad St (nb)	Hu	31	T 20
Broad St (wn)	Hu	40	V 22
Broadfield Pl	Ou	16	N 4
Broadfield Rd	Hu	21	O 18
Broadlawn Av	Nu	2	D 9
Broadmoor La	Nu	20	O 15
Broadway (RG)	Nu	3	D 12
Broadway (VS)	Hu	5	D 21
Broadway (WG)	Hu	6	F 24
Broadway (LW)	Hu	7	C 26
Broadway (NP)	Nu	11	H 16
Broadway (MI)	Nu	11	K 15
Broadway (WB)	Hu	20	O 15
Broadway (ny)	Hu	13	J 21
Broadway (wh)	Hu	21	L 18
Broadway (RC)	Hu	22	L 21
Broadway (LY)	Hu	13	H 22
Broadway (ip)	Hu	15	K 26
Broadway (bi)	Hu	24	L 26
Broadway (nc)	Nu	29	R 14
Broadway (hk)	Ou	37	V 13
Broadway (bm)	Hu	40	U 21
Broadway (FR)	Hu	31	Q 22
Broadway (bp)	Ou	45	Y 14
Broadway (pe)	Ou	46	Y 16
Broadway (MS)	Ou	47	BB 19
Broadway (mq)	Ou	48	Z 21
Broadway (MI)	Hu	13	H 21
Broadway Meadows	Hu	14	F 24
Broadway Pl	Ou	37	W 14
Brockmeyer Dr	Ou	48	Y 22
Brody La	Hu	40	U 22
Brokaw La	Nu	2	C 10
Bromleigh Rd	Hu	12	G 17
Bromleigh Rd N	Hu	12	G 17
Bromley La	Nu	2	D 10
Brompton Rd (GP)	Nu	3	D 12
Brompton Rd (GA)	Hu	12	K 17
Brompton Rd (bw)	Hu	22	N 22
Brompton Rd (ne)	Hu	30	R 19
Brompton Rd S	Hu	12	K 17
Bromton Dr	Hu	29	R 15
Brook Av (os)	Hu	23	L 23
Brook Av	Hu	31	T 20
Brook Br Rd	Nu	2	C 11
Brook Ct	Hu	22	O 22
Brook Ct N	Hu	10	H 14
Brook Ct S	Hu	10	H 14
Brook La (SR)	Nu	2	C 11
Brook La (pw)	Nu	9	G 9
Brook La	Ou	27	S 10
Brook La (ed)	Hu	39	U 17
Brook La (sd)	Hu	40	X 21
Brook Park Dr	Hu	32	T 22
Brook Pa	Ou	37	X 12
Brook Pl (VS)	Hu	13	G 22
Brook Pl	Hu	31	T 21
Brook Rd	Hu	5	E 22
Brook Row	Ou	26	Q 4
Brook St (HV)	Hu	21	M 17
Brook St	Hu	29	R 14
Brook Wold Av	Hu	22	O 22
Brookdale Rd	Ou	16	N 5
Brookfield Rd	Nu	10	H 14
Brookfield Rd	Hu	6	F 23
Brookline Av	Hu	15	F 28
Brookline Dr	Ou	47	Z 18
Brooklyn Av (NP)	Nu	11	G 16
Brooklyn Av (VS)	Hu	13	G 22
Brooklyn Av (fs)	Hu	12	K 18
Brooklyn Av (RC)	Hu	22	M 22
Brooklyn Av (bw)	Hu	22	N 22
Brooklyn Av (rv)	Hu	31	R 21
Brooklyn Av (mr)	Hu	31	S 21
Brooklyn Av (FR)	Hu	31	P 22
Brooklyn Av (mr)	Hu	31	S 21
Brooklyn Av (MS)	Ou	47	AA 20
Brooklyn Av (wn)	Hu	40	W 21
Brooklyn Av	Hu	40	X 20
Brooklyn Rd	Hu	21	M 19
Brooks Av	Hu	31	Q 20
Brooks St	Ou	38	V 14
Brooks St S	Ou	38	V 14
Brooks St W	Ou	38	V 14
Brookside Av (ne)	Hu	31	S 20
Brookside Av	Hu	40	V 21
Brookside Ct	Hu	29	R 15
Brookside Dr (PD)	Nu	9	G 10
Brookside Dr (VS)	Hu	13	G 22
Brookside Dr (FH)	Nu	9	J 10
Brookside Av	Hu	22	O 22
Brookside Gardens	Hu	22	O 21
Brooktree La	Hu	40	W 20
Brookville La (OK)	Ou	17	O 6
Brookville La (BK)	Ou	27	R 10

Nassau Co.

STREET	MUN. MAP GRID
Brookville Rd	Ou 27 R 8
Brookwold Ct	Hu 22 O 22
Brookwood Dr	Nu 9 G 10
Brookwood Dr	Hu 22 O 22
Brookwood Dr	Ou 47 CC19
Brookwood St	Ou 17 M 8
Broome Av	Hu 7 D 27
Broomleigh Rd N	Hu 12 H 17
Brouwer La	Hu 22 M 21
Brower Av (WG)	Hu 6 F 24
Brower Av (ML)	Hu 13 J 20
Brower Av (RC)	Hu 22 M 21
Brower Av (RC)	Hu 23 M 23
Brower La	Hu 21 O 18
Brower Pl	Hu 13 J 22
Brower Rd	Hu 6 F 24
Brower's La	Hu 10 K 12
Brown Av	Hu 21 N 19
Brown Ct	Nu 2 C 10
Brown Ct (ER)	Hu 14 K 25
Brown Ct	Hu 30 P 19
Brown Dr	Ou 45 Z 13
Brown Pl	Nu 11 G 16
Brown Rd	Nu 2 C 10
Brown St	Hu 5 E 21
Brown St	Ou 17 L 7
Brown St	Nu 19 L 14
Browning St	Hu 22 O 21
Bruce Av	Ou 37 W 12
Bruce Ct	Hu 12 J 19
Bruce Ct (rv)	Hu 31 R 20
Bruce Dr (ed)	Nu 30 S 18
Bruce Dr	Hu 39 U 18
Bruce La	Nu 10 J 11
Bruce La	Hu 31 S 20
Bruce La	Ou 46 Z 17
Bruce Pl	Hu 47 Y 19
Bruce Rd	Ou 28 R 12
Bruce St	Hu 12 G 18
Bruce St	Ou 36 W 10
Bruce Ter	Nu 20 N 15
Brunella St	Hu 23 P 24
Brunswick Av	Nu 10 K 14
Brunswick Pl	Hu 12 F 18
Brush Hollow Rd	Ou 28 R 13
Brush Hollow Rd (Union Av)	Nu 28 Q 14
Brussel Dr	Nu 11 J 15
Bryant Av (NP)	Nu 11 F 16
Bryant Av (wm)	Hu 6 E 24
Bryant Av (RH)	Nu 18 L 9
Bryant Av (nw)	Nu 39 X 17
Bryant Dr	Nu 40 X 22
Bryant Pl	Hu 22 N 21
Bryant Rd	Ou 17 O 6
Bryant Rd	Nu 15 L 25
Bryant St (ed)	Nu 30 S 18
Bryant St (bh)	Hu 32 P 24
Bryant St (pe)	Nu 38 X 16
Bryce Av	Ou 16 M 4
Bryn Mawr	Nu 11 J 14
Buchanan Av	Nu 11 K 15
Buchanan Rd	Nu 30 R 18
Buchanan St	Hu 23 P 24
Bucket La	Nu 19 M 13
Bucket La	Hu 38 V 16
Buckeye Rd	Ou 16 M 4
Buckingham Ct	Hu 6 D 25
Buckingham Gate	Ou 37 X 13
Buckingham Pl (mq)	Nu 2 F 11
Buckingham Pl	Nu 3 D 12
Buckingham Pl	Hu 13 J 22
Buckingham Rd (CH)	Hu 6 D 24
Buckingham Rd (wh)	Hu 21 L 18
Buckingham Rd (bw)	Hu 22 N 21
Buckingham Rd	Hu 31 R 22
Buckley Pl	Hu 29 R 15
Buckminster La	Nu 10 J 11
Buckminster Rd	Hu 22 M 20
Bucknell Dr	Ou 44 AA10
Bucknell Rd	Hu 5 F 21
Buckner Av	Ou 38 U 14
Buckram Rd	Ou 16 P 4
Bud Ct	Ou 25 Q 2
Bud La	Hu 29 T 15
Budd Ct	Ou 46 Y 17
Buena Vista Av	Hu 6 C 25
Buffalo Av (ea)	Hu 15 F 28
Buffalo Av	Hu 32 R 22
Buffalo Avenue Ext	Hu 32 R 23
Buffalo St	Nu 5 F 20
Buffalo St	Ou 29 U 14
Buick Pl	Hu 29 T 16
Bulaire Rd (ba)	Hu 14 J 24
Bulson Rd	Hu 22 M 20
Bungalow Pl	Hu 14 K 23
Bungalow Rd	Hu 14 K 24
Bungtown Rd	Ou 43 Z 5
Bunker Av	Hu 40 W 20
Bunker Ct	Hu 6 D 23
Bunker Dr	Hu 23 M 24
Bunker La	Nu 19 M 13
Bunker La	Ou 38 V 15
Bunker Rd (wm)	Hu 6 D 23
Bunker Rd (LB)	Hu 24 L 28
Bunting La	Hu 29 T 16
Burbank Pl	Ou 45 Z 13
Burbury La	Nu 2 D 10
Burger Pl	Hu 23 N 23
Burke Av	Ou 37 U 12
Burke Ct	Hu 47 Y 20
Burke La	Ou 36 W 10
Burke Pl	Hu 31 S 20
Burkhard Av	Nu 10 L 14
Burkhardt Av	Ou 46 Y 15
Burkland La	Hu 29 U 14
Burling La	Ou 45 AA13
Burlington Pl	Nu 5 D 20
Burn La	Nu 9 H 10
Burnett St	Hu 21 M 19
Burnham Av	Nu 10 K 11
Burnham Pl	Nu 9 H 10
Burns Av (GL)	Ou 17 M 6
Burns Av (hk)	Hu 37 U 12
Burns Av (hk)	Hu 37 U 13
Burns Av	Hu 40 V 21
Burns La	Ou 48 Y 22
Burnside Av	Hu 6 C 25
Burr Av	Hu 21 M 17
Burro La	Hu 39 U 18
Burston St	Hu 21 O 18
Burt Av	Hu 23 M 23
Burt Ct	Nu 5 E 22
Burtis Av	Hu 22 L 21
Burtis La	Ou 35 U 5
Burtis La	Ou 36 W 8
Burtis Pl	Hu 4 F 19
Burtis St	Hu 13 H 21
Burton Av (nv)	Hu 12 G 19
Burton Av (wm)	Hu 6 F 24
Burton Av (fs)	Hu 12 H 19
Burton Av	Ou 45 Y 13
Burton La E	Ou 47 BB20
Burton La N	Ou 47 BB20
Burton La S	Ou 47 BB21
Burton St	Hu 13 J 20
Buscher Av	Hu 5 E 21
Bush St	Hu 30 T 17
Bushwick Av	Hu 31 R 21
Butler Blvd	Hu 12 G 18
Butler Ct	Ou 17 N 5
Butler La	Hu 38 W 15
Butler Pl (GA)	Nu 20 M 16
Butler Pl	Hu 21 O 18
Butler St	Hu 17 M 5
Butler St	Nu 19 P 14
Buttercup La	Hu 38 U 16
Butternut La	Hu 38 U 16
Buttonwood Rd	Nu 3 D 13
Buxton Av	Hu 12 J 19
Buxton St	Hu 24 M 27
Byrd Av	Nu 20 O 15
Byrd Dr	Hu 30 S 17
Byrd Pl	Hu 23 O 24
Byrd St (GL)	Ou 17 M 6
Byrd St (HV)	Hu 21 N 17
Byrd St	Hu 23 M 24
Byrd St (MS)	Ou 47 BB18
Byron Av (fs)	Hu 4 E 19
Byron Av (SR)	Hu 12 J 19
Byron La	Nu 3 C 11
Byron La	Ou 46 Y 17
Byron Pl (hk)	Hu 37 U 13
Byron Pl (em)	Hu 30 S 18
Byron Pl (pe)	Hu 39 X 17
Byron Pl	Hu 40 W 22
Byron Rd	Hu 31 S 22
Byron St (LY)	Hu 13 H 21
Byron St	Hu 38 X 16
Byron St	Hu 40 W 22

C

STREET	MUN. MAP GRID
C Gate	Ou 28 R 12
C St	Hu 12 G 19
Cable La	Ou 29 T 15
Cabot Rd	Ou 48 AA22
Cabot Rd W	Ou 48 Z 22
Cadillac Dr	Hu 29 T 16
Caffrey Av	Ou 45 Y 14
Caifornia St	Hu 22 N 21
Cail Dr	Ou 45 AA12
Cain Dr	Ou 45 AA12
Calais Dr	Hu 14 K 23
Caldwell Av	Hu 6 D 23
Caldwell Rd	Nu 5 F 20
Calf Farm Rd	Ou 26 S 5
California Av (HV)	Hu 21 N 17
California Av (FR)	Hu 22 P 21
California Av (un)	Hu 21 P 17
California Pl N	Hu 15 K 26
California Pl S	Hu 15 K 27
California St	Hu 15 G 28
California St	Ou 28 T 13
Calla Av	Hu 4 F 17
Callendar View Dr	Ou 25 R 2
Calliope St	Nu 19 O 13
Calvert Dr	Ou 36 Y 8
Calvin Av	Ou 36 W 8
Calvin Rd	Hu 23 M 23
Calvin St	Hu 13 H 22
Cambria Rd	Ou 37 W 11
Cambria St	Hu 30 P 17
Cambridge Av (MH)	Nu 1 E 7
Cambridge Av (SM)	Hu 12 G 17
Cambridge Av (fs)	Hu 12 H 17
Cambridge Av (GA)	Hu 12 K 17
Cambridge Av	Nu 28 Q 13
Cambridge Av	Ou 46 Y 15
Cambridge Ct	Ou 17 N 6
Cambridge Ct	Hu 14 J 24
Cambridge Ct (bp)	Ou 37 X 13
Cambridge Dr (hk)	Hu 37 W 13
Cambridge Dr	Ou 48 Z 21
Cambridge La	Nu 2 F 11
Cambridge Rd (GN)	Nu 2 D 10
Cambridge Rd (WG)	Hu 6 E 24
Cambridge Rd (ba)	Hu 14 J 24
Cambridge Rd (wn)	Hu 40 V 20
Cambridge St (VS)	Hu 5 F 22
Cambridge St (GL)	Ou 16 N 5
Cambridge St (al)	Nu 10 K 12
Cambridge St (ny)	Hu 13 J 21
Cambridge St (RC)	Hu 22 L 21
Cambridge St (ed)	Nu 30 S 17
Camden La	Hu 32 T 23
Camden Pl	Nu 11 J 15
Camdike St	Hu 5 E 21
Cameo Ct	Hu 39 U 17
Cameo Dr	Ou 48 Z 23
Cameo La	Hu 29 S 15
Cameron Av (HV)	Hu 21 O 18
Cameron Av	Hu 31 S 20
Cameron La	Hu 5 E 22
Cameron St	Hu 12 G 19
Cammerer Av	Hu 14 J 23
Camp Av	Hu 31 R 20
Camp Pl	Hu 31 T 21
Camp Rd	Hu 15 L 25
Camp Rd	Ou 47 CC19
Campbell Av	Nu 10 K 14
Campbell Av	Hu 23 L 24
Campbell Av (nb)	Hu 39 U 19
Campbell Pkwy	Nu 19 L 13
Campbell Rd	Hu 39 W 19
Campbell St	Nu 11 G 15
Campbell St	Ou 17 O 6
Campo Cir	Nu 19 N 14
Campus Dr	Nu 9 H 8
Campus La	Nu 39 U 17
Campus Pl	Hu 22 N 21
Campus Pl	Ou 37 W 13
Campus Rd	Hu 12 J 19
Campus St	Hu 30 P 19
Camsanette Ct	Ou 17 O 6
Canal Pl	Hu 40 W 22
Canal Rd	Ou 48 Z 21
Canandaigua Av	Hu 13 K 20
Canary Cres	Nu 10 J 12
Candee Ct	Hu 23 M 25
Candela La	Ou 36 W 9
Candle La	Hu 39 V 18
Candor Dr	Ou 44 Y 10
Candy La (SR)	Nu 2 B 11
Candy La (OW)	Nu 19 N 12
Candy La	Ou 36 W 10
Candytuft Ct	Ou 48 AA21
Cane La	Hu 29 S 14
Canoe La	Hu 23 N 24
Canoe Pl (sd)	Hu 40 X 22
Canon La	Ou 26 T 5
Canterbury La	Nu 20 O 14
Canterbury Gate	Hu 14 H 22
Canterbury La	Nu 19 M 11
Canterbury Ct	Ou 28 R 11
Canterbury Rd (KG)	Nu 3 E 11
Canterbury Rd (OK)	Ou 17 P 8
Canterbury Rd (WP)	Nu 10 L 14
Canterbury Rd (RC)	Hu 22 M 20
Canterbury Rd	Ou 37 Y 11
Canterbury St	Nu 28 Q 13
Cantiague La	Ou 28 S 13
Cantiague Rock Rd	Ou 28 S 12
Canton Dr	Nu 30 S 19
Canyon La	Ou 29 T 15
Capi La	Nu 9 F 9
Capital Pl	Nu 20 M 15
Capitol Av	Nu 10 L 14
Capitol Ct	Ou 35 U 5
Capitol Heights Rd	Ou 26 T 5
Capitolian Blvd	Hu 22 M 21
Capobianco St	Ou 17 N 6
Capri Dr	Nu 10 K 13
Capri Dr E	Nu 7 F 28
Capri Dr S	Nu 7 F 28
Capri Dr W	Nu 7 F 28
Capri Gate	Ou 45 Z 13
Capri Pl	Nu 30 T 19
Capstain Cir	Nu 30 Q 18
Captains Gate	Nu 29 R 15
Captains Pl	Nu 6 E 23
Cardinal Ct	Ou 16 N 4
Cardinal Dr	Nu 18 N 10
Cardinal La	Hu 29 S 14
Cardinal La	Ou 47 CC18
Cardinal Rd	Nu 9 H 9
Cardinal Rd	Hu 38 W 16
Carel Blvd	Hu 23 M 25
Caren Ct	Ou 36 W 8
Carey La	Hu 23 O 24
Carey Pl	Nu 8 G 7
Carey St	Nu 8 G 7
Carl Av	Hu 12 J 18
Carl Ct	Hu 39 U 18
Carl St (VS)	Nu 5 F 21
Carl St	Nu 18 M 9
Carl St (bi)	Hu 15 K 27
Carla La	Hu 30 R 18
Carle Rd	Nu 19 O 14
Carleton Av	Ou 36 X 10
Carleton Pl	Nu 22 N 21
Carleton St	Nu 29 R 14
Carley Ct (bm)	Hu 31 T 20
Carley Ct (nb)	Nu 30 U 19
Carlin Pl	Nu 2 D 11
Carlin Pl	Nu 30 S 18
Carling Dr	Nu 11 J 15
Carlisle Ct (RC)	Hu 22 M 20
Carlisle Ct	Hu 39 W 18
Carlisle Dr	Ou 27 P 9
Carlisle Pl (ML)	Hu 13 J 21
Carlisle Pl	Hu 31 S 22
Carlisle Rd	Ou 37 V 12
Carlisle Rd	Hu 39 W 18

Nassau Co.

STREET	MUN.	MAP	GRID
Channel Dr (KP)	Nu	2 C	9
Channel Dr	Hu	14 H	24
Channel Rd (HH)	Hu	14 H	24
Channel Rd (WG)	Hu	6 F	25
Channel Rd (ld)	Hu	24 O	27
Channon Rd	Hu	14 H	23
Chanticlare Dr (PD)	Nu	9 G	10
Chanticlare Dr (FH)	Nu	9 H	10
Chapel Gate La	Ou	27 Q	8
Chapel La	Hu	39 V	17
Chapel Pl	Nu	3 E	11
Chapel Rd	Nu	10 H	11
Chapel Rd	Ou	28 R	12
Chapin Av	Hu	31 R	20
Chapin Rd	Ou	46 Z	16
Chapman Av	Hu	40 U	21
Chapman Dr	Ou	48 AA	22
Chapman Rd	Hu	6 F	24
Charing Cross	Hu	13 G	22
Charing-Cross Rd	Hu	22 N	22
Charles Av	Nu	8 G	7
Charles Av (hk)	Ou	37 V	13
Charles Av	Ou	47 BB	20
Charles Ct (VS)	Hu	5 F	21
Charles Ct (nb)	Hu	31 T	19
Charles Ct (wn)	Hu	40 X	20
Charles La	Hu	39 X	18
Charles Lindbergh Blvd	Hu	20 P	16
Charles Pl	Ou	25 T	2
Charles Pl	Hu	30 Q	18
Charles Rd	Nu	11 G	14
Charles Rd	Hu	39 U	18
Charles St (pw)	Nu	9 G	8
Charles St (fs)	Hu	11 G	16
Charles St (VS)	Hu	5 D	20
Charles St (GL)	Ou	17 L	5
Charles St (EW)	Nu	19 L	13
Charles St (MI)	Nu	19 M	14
Charles St (ny)	Hu	13 J	21
Charles St	Hu	12 K	19
Charles St (rv)	Hu	22 P	20
Charles St (LY)	Hu	13 K	21
Charles St (os)	Hu	14 K	25
Charles St (os)	Hu	23 L	23
Charles St (hk)	Ou	37 V	13
Charles St (rv)	Hu	31 R	20
Charles St (bm)	Hu	40 U	20
Charles St (mr)	Hu	32 S	22
Charles St (hk)	Ou	37 V	13
Charles St (sa)	Ou	46 AA	17
Charles Wy	Ou	27 P	8
Charlick Pl	Hu	31 Q	21
Charlotte Avenue Ext	Ou	29 T	14
Charlotte Ct (fs)	Hu	12 G	18
Charlotte Ct (wn)	Hu	40 X	19
Charlotte Dr	Hu	32 T	23
Charlotte Pl	Hu	40 V	21
Charlotte Pl	Ou	45 Y	13
Charlotte St	Ou	28 T	13
Charlson Rd	Hu	31 R	21
Charney Ct	Nu	10 H	12
Charter Ct	Hu	30 P	19
Chase La	Hu	39 U	18
Chase La	Ou	46 Y	17
Chase Rd	Nu	9 G	11
Chase St	Hu	21 M	19
Chase, The	Ou	36 X	9
Chasner St	Hu	21 M	18
Chatham Ct	Ou	38 W	14
Chatham Pl	Hu	21 L	18
Chatham Rd	Hu	14 G	23
Chathm Ct	Hu	14 J	24
Chauncey La	Hu	6 E	25
Chauncey Pl	Ou	44 Y	9
Chautauqua Av	Hu	13 K	21
Chelmsford Dr	Ou	27 S	8
Chelsea Ct	Hu	22 P	21
Chelsea Dr	Nu	9 G	9
Chelsea Dr	Hu	31 S	20
Chelsea Dr	Ou	36 Y	8
Chelsea Dr (wy)	Ou	36 X	8
Chelsea La	Hu	23 L	23
Chelsea La (ln)	Hu	39 V	17
Chelsea Pl	Nu	3 D	12
Chelsea Pl	Hu	21 M	18
Chelsea Rd (gs)	Hu	12 K	17
Chelsea Rd (bw)	Hu	23 N	23
Chelsea Rd	Hu	39 V	19
Chelsea St	Hu	4 F	17
Cheltenham St	Hu	24 M	27
Chemung Pl	Ou	28 T	12
Chenango Dr	Ou	28 S	12
Chernucha Av	Hu	31 S	22
Cherokee St	Ou	48 BB	21
Cherry Av	Ou	45 Y	14
Cherry Ct (ER)	Hu	14 K	23
Cherry Ct	Hu	14 L	25
Cherry Ct	Ou	37 Y	11
Cherry Ct (MS)	Ou	47 CC	19
Cherry Dr E	Ou	45 Y	12
Cherry Dr W	Ou	37 X	12
Cherry Grove Ct	Hu	6 E	22
Cherry La (KP)	Nu	2 C	9
Cherry La (NP)	Hu	11 F	15
Cherry La (wm)	Hu	6 E	23
Cherry La (GL)	Ou	17 N	6
Cherry La (WB)	Nu	19 O	14
Cherry La (HV)	Hu	12 H	17
Cherry La (WB)	Nu	20 O	15
Cherry La (HV)	Hu	21 O	17
Cherry La (HH)	Hu	14 H	23
Cherry La (BY)	Ou	25 S	2
Cherry La (hk)	Ou	29 U	14
Cherry La (OC)	Ou	35 X	7
Cherry La E	Ou	36 X	7
Cherry Pl (FR)	Hu	22 O	21
Cherry Pl (ed)	Hu	30 R	17
Cherry Rd (BY)	Ou	25 R	2
Cherry Rd	Ou	25 Q	2
Cherry St (FP)	Hu	4 F	17
Cherry St (VS)	Hu	13 F	22
Cherry St (HB)	Hu	14 G	24
Cherry St (in)	Hu	6 B	25
Cherry St (MC)	Ou	16 P	4
Cherry St (gh)	Ou	17 N	8
Cherry St	Ou	16 O	4
Cherry St (FG)	Ou	46 BB	16
Cherry St (sa)	Ou	46 CC	17
Cherry St (sd)	Ou	40 Y	21
Cherry Valley Av (MI)	Hu	20 L	15
Cherry Valley Av (GA)	Hu	21 L	17
Cherry Valley Av (wh)	Hu	12 K	18
Cherry Wood La	Nu	9 J	10
Cherrybrook Pl	Nu	3 F	12
Cherrytree La	Nu	19 L	12
Cherrytree La	Hu	38 U	16
Cherrywood Ct	Ou	17 P	6
Cherrywood Dr	Nu	10 H	14
Cherrywood Dr (bh)	Hu	23 O	24
Cherrywood Dr (wn)	Hu	39 V	19
Cherrywood Dr (bh)	Hu	23 O	24
Cherrywood La	Ou	25 Q	3
Cherrywood La	Nu	10 J	12
Cherrywood Pl	Hu	40 X	20
Cherrywood Rd	Ou	17 P	6
Cheryl La E	Ou	46 Z	17
Cheryl La N	Ou	46 Z	17
Cheryl La S	Ou	46 Z	17
Cheryl La W	Ou	46 Z	17
Cheryl Rd (bm)	Hu	32 T	23
Cheryl Rd (pe)	Ou	46 Y	17
Cheryl Rd	Ou	47 Y	18
Cheshire Av	Ou	36 W	10
Cheshire Dr	Hu	23 N	23
Cheshire Rd	Hu	6 B	25
Cheshire Rd	Ou	37 X	13
Cheslan Ct	Hu	23 L	24
Chesman St	Hu	12 K	18
Chesney Rd	Hu	6 E	25
Chess Dr	Hu	23 O	24
Chester Av (SM)	Hu	12 G	17
Chester Av (fs)	Hu	12 J	17
Chester Av (wa)	Ou	48 CC	21
Chester Av (nq)	Ou	47 Y	18
Chester Ct	Hu	23 L	23
Chester Dr (PD)	Nu	9 F	10
Chester Dr (RG)	Nu	3 D	12
Chester Dr	Hu	30 S	17
Chester La	Ou	46 Z	17
Chester Pl	Hu	23 L	23
Chester Rd	Hu	13 K	22
Chester St	Ou	26 Q	4
Chester St (sh)	Hu	22 N	20
Chester St (os)	Hu	23 L	23
Chester St	Ou	26 Q	4
Chester St	Hu	30 Q	18
Chestnut Av (FP)	Hu	4 E	17
Chestnut Av	Ou	17 M	8
Chestnut Av (ed)	Hu	30 R	17
Chestnut Ct	Ou	27 S	9
Chestnut Dr (GN)	Nu	3 C	11
Chestnut Dr	Hu	14 F	23
Chestnut Dr (EH)	Nu	18 L	10
Chestnut Dr	Ou	37 X	11
Chestnut Hill	Nu	10 J	13
Chestnut Hill Ct	Ou	26 R	6
Chestnut Hill Rd	Ou	26 R	6
Chestnut La (VS)	Hu	13 F	20
Chestnut La (un)	Hu	30 R	18
Chestnut La	Ou	44 Y	10
Chestnut La (ln)	Hu	39 W	17
Chestnut Pl	Ou	18 M	8
Chestnut Pl	Nu	11 K	15
Chestnut Rd	Nu	9 H	9
Chestnut Rd	Hu	6 B	25
Chestnut St (ML)	Hu	13 H	20
Chestnut St (CH)	Hu	6 D	25
Chestnut St (GL)	Ou	16 M	5
Chestnut St (EH)	Nu	18 M	10
Chestnut St (WB)	Nu	19 P	14
Chestnut St (MI)	Nu	11 K	15
Chestnut St (HV)	Hu	21 M	17
Chestnut St (ML)	Hu	13 H	20
Chestnut St (ML)	Hu	13 J	20
Chestnut St (wh)	Hu	12 K	19
Chestnut St (LY)	Hu	13 J	22
Chestnut St (RC)	Hu	23 M	22
Chestnut St (bw)	Hu	22 N	22
Chestnut St (WB)	Nu	19 P	14
Chestnut St (hk)	Ou	37 V	13
Chestnut St (mr)	Hu	31 S	22
Chestnut St (mq)	Hu	47 Y	20
Chestnut St (sd)	Ou	47 Y	21
Chestnut St (mq)	Ou	47 Z	19
Chestnut Street Ext	Ou	16 M	4
Chevy La	Ou	46 Y	16
Chicadee La	Hu	38 U	15
Chicago Av	Hu	40 U	20
Chicago Av	Ou	47 Y	20
Chicken Valley Rd	Ou	17 O	8
Childs Av (FP)	Hu	4 F	17
Childs Av	Hu	12 K	17
Chime La	Hu	29 S	15
Chimney La	Hu	39 U	17
Chittendon St	Hu	13 G	20
Choir La	Hu	29 S	14
Choir La E	Hu	28 S	14
Choir La N	Hu	28 S	14
Choir La S	Hu	29 S	15
Choir La W	Hu	29 S	15
Chowan St	Hu	4 F	18
Christabel St	Hu	13 J	21
Christie St	Hu	22 N	20
Christina St	Hu	6 C	25
Christopher Ct	Hu	13 K	20
Christopher St	Hu	23 M	23
Church Av	Hu	6 D	23
Church Rd (hk)	Hu	38 U	16
Church Rd	Hu	40 W	20
Church St (GN)	Nu	2 C	10
Church St (in)	Hu	6 C	25
Church St (MC)	Ou	16 P	4
Church St (RH)	Nu	18 L	10
Church St (rt)	Nu	19 L	11
Church St (ML)	Hu	13 J	20
Church St (HV)	Hu	21 O	19
Church St (bh)	Hu	23 O	23
Church St (oy)	Ou	35 U	5
Church St (WB)	Nu	29 Q	14
Church St (FR)	Hu	31 Q	22
Church St (MT)	Ou	36 W	8
Churchill Dr	Nu	11 J	15
Cinder La	Ou	38 V	15
Cindy Ct	Nu	19 N	14
Cindy Dr	Ou	45 Z	14
Cinnamon Ct	Ou	17 O	7
Cinque Dr	Ou	46 AA	16
Ciper La	Hu	38 V	16
Circle Crest	Nu	10 H	11
Circle Dr (PD)	Nu	9 G	10
Circle Dr (MC)	Ou	17 O	5
Circle Dr (al)	Nu	19 L	12
Circle Dr (HV)	Hu	21 M	19
Circle Dr (nc)	Nu	28 R	13
Circle Dr (bm)	Hu	40 U	20
Circle Dr	Ou	37 W	11
Circle Dr (FG)	Ou	46 BB	16
Circle Dr (MS)	Ou	48 AA	21
Circle Dr E	Hu	4 E	18
Circle Dr E (sh)	Hu	22 O	20
Circle Dr N	Hu	4 E	18
Circle Dr W	Hu	4 E	18
Circle Dr W (sh)	Hu	22 O	20
Circle La	Nu	18 M	11
Circle La	Hu	39 V	17
Circle N	Nu	2 E	11
Circle Pl	Hu	23 P	23
Circle Rd	Ou	36 V	8
Circle S	Nu	2 E	11
Circle Wy	Ou	17 L	7
Circle, The	Nu	3 E	13
Circle, The	Ou	17 N	7
Circle, The (MN)	Ou	35 U	6
Cisney Av (FP)	Hu	12 G	17
Citizen Av	Hu	12 G	19
City Av	Hu	31 S	22
City Pl	Hu	31 S	22
Claflin Blvd	Hu	12 J	18
Claflin Ct	Hu	12 J	19
Clair Pl	Hu	13 F	20
Clair St	Nu	3 D	12
Clapham Av	Nu	10 G	11
Clare Rd	Hu	30 P	19
Claremont St	Ou	45 AA	14
Clarence St	Hu	4 F	17
Clarendon Av	Hu	40 U	21
Clarendon Dr	Hu	5 E	20
Clarendon Rd (HV)	Hu	21 O	18
Clarendon Rd	Hu	23 M	23
Claridge Av	Hu	4 E	18
Claridge Cir	Nu	10 H	12
Clarissa Dr	Ou	29 U	14
Clarissa Dr (MT)	Ou	36 W	9
Clarissa Rd	Nu	11 K	15
Clarissa Rd	Ou	46 Y	17
Clark Av	Hu	13 H	21
Clark Av (ER)	Hu	14 K	23
Clark Av	Ou	47 Y	20
Clark Blvd	Ou	47 AA	20
Clark Dr	Nu	3 F	12
Clark Pl (WG)	Hu	14 F	24
Clark Pl (wh)	Hu	21 L	18
Clark Pl	Hu	21 P	18
Clark St (ER)	Hu	14 J	23
Clark St (ld)	Hu	24 L	27
Clark St (ne)	Hu	31 S	20
Clark St (bp)	Ou	37 X	13
Clark St (wn)	Hu	40 X	20
Clarke St	Hu	12 G	19
Clarkson St	Hu	13 J	20
Clary Pl	Hu	32 S	22
Claudia Ct	Hu	40 V	22
Claudy La	Nu	11 G	14
Claurome Pl	Hu	31 P	21
Clausen Ct	Ou	48 AA	22
Clausen Pl	Nu	11 G	15
Claxton Av	Hu	40 V	22
Clay La	Hu	39 W	17
Clay St (FP)	Hu	12 G	17
Clay St	Hu	23 O	23
Claydon Rd	Hu	20 M	16
Clayton Av (SM)	Hu	12 G	17
Clayton Av	Hu	7 F	28
Clayton Rd	Hu	5 F	20
Clearland Av	Nu	20 O	14
Clearland Rd	Ou	37 W	12
Clearmeadow Ct	Ou	43 AA	8
Clearmeadow Dr	Hu	29 S	16
Clearmeadow La	Ou	43 Z	8
Clearstream Av	Hu	5 E	21
Clearview Ct	Ou	48 Z	22
Clearview La	Ou	48 Z	22
Clearwater Av	Ou	48 BB	22
Clearwater Dr	Ou	45 Z	13
Cleaves Av	Hu	21 O	19
Cleft Rd	Ou	25 S	3
Clemens Rd	Nu	20 M	14
Clement Av	Hu	12 H	19
Clement St	Ou	8 L	5
Clemente Pl	Hu	21 O	18
Clemons St	Hu	40 U	20
Clemson La	Ou	44 Y	10
Clent Rd	Nu	3 D	12

Nassau Co.

Nassau Co.

STREET	MUN.	MAP	GRID
Copperfield La	Ou	17 P	6
Coppersmith Rd	Hu	38 V	15
Coral Ct (ML)	Hu	13 J	20
Coral Ct	Hu	30 T	19
Coral Cove	Ou	26 U	7
Coral Rd	Hu	30 R	17
Corbin Av	Hu	11 J	15
Corchaug Av	Nu	1 F	8
Cord La	Hu	39 V	17
Cord Pl	Ou	35 U	6
Cordwood La	Hu	39 X	18
Corey La	Hu	29 T	16
Coriegarth La	Ou	16 P	4
Cormwell Av	Nu	10 K	14
Corncrib La	Nu	19 M	12
Corncrib La	Hu	38 V	16
Cornegie Ct	Nu	3 E	13
Cornelia Av	Nu	11 K	15
Cornelia Pl	Nu	2 C	10
Cornelia St	Ou	46 BB	16
Cornelius Av	Hu	40 V	20
Cornelius Ct	Hu	21 P	17
Cornelius Pl	Ou	48 Z	21
Cornelius St	Hu	32 Q	23
Cornell Av	Hu	13 K	21
Cornell Av	Ou	29 U	14
Cornell Dr	Ou	45 AA	11
Cornell La	Ou	37 W	13
Cornell Pl (ER)	Hu	14 J	23
Cornell Pl (bm)	Hu	31 T	22
Cornell Pl	Ou	46 Z	17
Cornell Rd	Nu	3 E	13
Cornell Rd	Hu	12 J	19
Cornell St	Nu	10 L	14
Cornell St	Hu	21 N	17
Corner La	Hu	40 V	22
Cornflower Rd	Hu	38 V	16
Cornwall La	Nu	1 E	7
Cornwall La	Hu	21 O	18
Cornwall La	Ou	28 U	14
Cornwell Av (ML)	Hu	13 H	20
Cornwell Av (HV)	Hu	21 P	19
Cornwell Av (bh)	Hu	23 O	23
Cornwell Pl	Hu	23 M	23
Cornwell Pl (bh)	Hu	23 P	23
Cornwell St	Hu	22 L	21
Cornwell St (bw)	Hu	22 N	22
Cornwell's Beach La	Nu	1 D	7
Corona Av (VS)	Hu	13 F	21
Corona Av	Hu	13 G	20
Corona Av N	Hu	13 F	21
Corona Dr	Ou	38 X	16
Coronado St	Hu	7 C	27
Coronet Cres S	Ou	46 Y	15
Coronet Dr	Hu	22 O	20
Coronet La	Ou	37 X	11
Corporate Dr	Hu	29 P	15
Corral La	Hu	38 X	15
Corral Pa	Hu	40 W	21
Cort Pl	Ou	46 AA	17
Cortelyou Rd	Hu	31 R	22
Cortland Av	Ou	28 S	12
Cortland Av (hk)	Ou	29 U	14
Corwin Av	Nu	11 H	15
Cory Ct (BY)	Ou	25 T	2
Cory Ct	Ou	36 V	8
Cosgrove Dr	Ou	17 M	5
Costar St	Nu	29 R	14
Costom Village Dr	Hu	31 R	20
Cotillion Ct	Ou	18 N	10
Cottage Blvd	Ou	38 V	14
Cottage Ct (FR)	Hu	31 Q	22
Cottage Ct	Hu	31 U	22
Cottage Dr	Ou	48 AA	21
Cottage Pl	Nu	20 M	15
Cottage Pl (HV)	Hu	21 O	18
Cottage Pl (bw)	Hu	22 O	22
Cottage Pl (FR)	Hu	31 P	20
Cottage Row	Ou	17 M	5
Cottage Row La	Ou	17 M	5
Cottage St	Hu	30 P	19
Cotton La	Hu	39 W	17
Cottonwood Ct	Hu	39 W	19
Cottonwood La	Hu	29 S	14
Cottonwood Rd	Nu	1 F	7
Council Wk	Nu	8 F	8
Countisbury Av	Hu	5 E	20
Country Club Dr (ma)	Nu	10 G	11
Country Club Dr (pw)	Nu	9 J	10
Country Club Dr	Ou	28 S	12
Country Ct (hk)	Ou	29 U	14
Country Ct	Ou	46 AA	17
Country Dr (pv)	Ou	45 Y	12
Country Dr	Ou	45 Z	12
Country La	Ou	27 R	10
Country Pl	Nu	2 C	11
Country Pl	Hu	32 P	23
Country Squires Ct	Hu	29 T	15
Country Village Ct	Nu	10 H	14
Country Village La	Nu	10 H	14
County Rd	Hu	29 R	15
County Seat Dr	Hu	20 M	15
Court A	Hu	23 P	24
Court Av	Hu	6 D	25
Court B	Hu	23 P	24
Court House Rd	Hu	12 H	18
Court House Rd	Nu	11 K	16
Court La	Ou	35 W	7
Court Pl (CH)	Hu	6 D	25
Court Pl (VS)	Hu	14 G	23
Court Pl (ed)	Hu	30 S	17
Court Rd (HB)	Hu	14 G	23
Court Rd (fs)	Hu	12 J	17
Court St (FP)	Hu	12 G	18
Court St (VS)	Hu	5 F	20
Court St (os)	Hu	23 L	23
Court St (bm)	Hu	40 U	20
Court St (mr)	Hu	31 S	21
Court St E	Hu	14 J	24
Court St W	Hu	14 J	24
Courtenay Rd	Hu	21 O	17
Courthouse Dr	Hu	20 M	16
Courtney La	Hu	38 W	15
Courtney Pl	Hu	23 O	24
Courtyard	Ou	25 P	3
Cove Ct	Hu	41 U	23
Cove Dr	Nu	2 F	10
Cove Dr N	Hu	23 L	25
Cove Dr S	Hu	23 L	25
Cove Edge Rd (Pvt)	Ou	35 Y	5
Cove La (PN)	Nu	1 F	7
Cove La (GN)	Nu	2 B	10
Cove La	Hu	39 W	17
Cove Meadow La	Ou	35 W	6
Cove Neck Rd	Ou	34 W	4
Cove Neck Rd (Pvt)	Ou	34 W	3
Cove Rd	Ou	35 V	5
Cove Run	Ou	35 W	7
Cove St (GL)	Ou	17 M	5
Cove St	Ou	48 CC	21
Coventry Av	Nu	19 L	13
Coventry Dr	Hu	22 N	22
Coventry Garden	Hu	14 G	22
Coventry Pl	Hu	20 M	16
Coventry Rd	Ou	37 X	11
Coventry Rd N	Hu	13 K	20
Coventry Rd S	Hu	13 K	20
Cover St	Hu	12 G	18
Covered Bridge Rd	Hu	32 S	22
Covert Av	Nu	11 G	16
Covert Av (South 7th St)	Hu	11 G	16
Covert La	Nu	29 Q	14
Covert Pl	Hu	12 G	17
Covert St (pw)	Nu	9 F	8
Covert St	Hu	21 M	18
Covert St (WB)	Nu	29 Q	14
Covewoods Rd	Ou	35 W	5
Covey Ct	Ou	27 Q	8
Cow La	Nu	2 D	9
Cow Neck Rd	Nu	1 F	6
Cowl La	Hu	29 S	15
Cowpath	Ou	27 R	10
Cox St	Hu	12 J	19
Crab Av	Hu	13 H	22
Crab Tree La	Nu	9 J	10
Crabapple Dr	Nu	18 M	11
Crabapple La	Ou	26 R	6
Crabapple Rd	Nu	9 H	10
Crabtree La	Hu	29 T	16
Craft Av	Ou	17 M	6
Craft Av	Hu	12 J	19
Craft Ct	Hu	12 J	19
Craft St	Hu	7 B	25
Crafton Ct	Hu	13 H	21
Crag La	Hu	39 W	17
Craig Av	Hu	31 P	21
Craig St	Ou	28 T	12
Cramer Ct	Hu	22 O	20
Crampton Av	Nu	2 C	10
Crampton La	Nu	2 D	10
Cranberry La	Ou	37 Y	14
Crandall Dr	Nu	19 N	14
Crane Pl (ln)	Hu	38 W	16
Crane Pl	Hu	41 X	22
Cranford Av	Hu	6 D	23
Cranford Rd	Ou	45 Z	12
Crans Ct	Hu	4 E	19
Crawford Rd	Hu	6 F	24
Cree Ct	Ou	47 Z	19
Creek Pl	Ou	16 O	3
Creek Ridge Rd	Ou	25 R	2
Creek Rd	Nu	2 C	9
Creek Rd	Ou	25 R	2
Crescent	Nu	10 K	12
Crescent Beach Rd	Ou	16 L	4
Crescent Ct	Ou	45 AA	13
Crescent Dr	Nu	10 K	12
Crescent Dr	Ou	45 AA	13
Crescent La (rt)	Nu	10 K	12
Crescent La	Nu	18 M	11
Crescent La	Hu	39 V	18
Crescent Pkwy	Hu	11 H	16
Crescent Pl	Hu	38 X	15
Crescent Rd (pw)	Nu	8 H	8
Crescent Rd	Nu	3 E	11
Crescent St (WG)	Hu	14 F	24
Crescent St	Hu	6 C	25
Crescent St (BY)	Ou	25 R	2
Crescent St (hk)	Ou	37 W	12
Crescent St (sy)	Ou	36 W	8
Crest Av	Hu	12 G	18
Crest Hollow La	Nu	10 K	13
Crest La	Hu	39 W	17
Crest Rd (mh)	Nu	10 H	14
Crest Rd	Ou	36 V	9
Crest Rd	Hu	39 X	19
Crest Rd E	Hu	30 S	19
Crest Rd S	Hu	30 S	19
Crest Rd W	Hu	30 S	19
Crest, The	Ou	44 AA	10
Crestline Av	Ou	46 Y	16
Crestline Pl	Hu	39 X	19
Crestview Av	Hu	6 D	23
Crestwood Blvd	Ou	47 BB	18
Crestwood La	Hu	5 E	22
Crestwood Pl	Nu	2 B	10
Crestwood Pl	Hu	13 J	20
Crestwood Rd	Nu	9 H	9
Crestwood Rd (WG)	Hu	6 E	24
Crestwood Rd	Ou	45 Z	13
Crestwood Rd (sd)	Hu	40 X	20
Crestwood St	Ou	36 W	8
Cricket Club Dr	Nu	10 J	13
Cricket La	Nu	1 B	8
Cricket St	Nu	1 B	8
Crimson Av	Hu	13 J	20
Crimson Av S	Hu	13 J	20
Cripps La	Hu	14 G	22
Crocker St	Hu	22 L	21
Crocus Av (FP)	Hu	4 E	17
Crocus Av	Hu	30 S	19
Crocus Dr (sy)	Ou	36 X	8
Crocus Dr	Ou	47 Y	19
Crocus La	Hu	38 V	16
Crome Rd	Ou	37 X	11
Cromer Rd	Hu	5 E	19
Cromwell Dr	Hu	6 F	24
Cromwell Pl	Ou	17 L	6
Cromwell Rd	Nu	19 N	14
Crooker Pl	Nu	9 G	8
Crosby Av	Nu	10 K	13
Cross La (gh)	Ou	17 M	7
Cross La	Ou	25 S	2
Cross La	Hu	39 U	17
Cross Rd	Nu	9 F	10
Cross Rd	Ou	25 R	2
Cross Rd	Hu	30 U	19
Cross St (PN)	Nu	8 G	7
Cross St	Hu	12 G	18
Cross St (GL)	Ou	16 N	4
Cross St (gh)	Ou	17 M	8
Cross St (lv)	Ou	16 O	4
Cross St (WP)	Nu	10 L	14
Cross St (WB)	Nu	29 P	14
Crossbow La	Ou	44 Z	8
Crosson Av	Ou	25 R	2
Crossway	Ou	17 O	6
Crossways Pk Dr	Ou	44 Y	10
Crossways Pk N	Ou	36 X	10
Crossways Pk W	Ou	36 X	10
Crosswood La	Ou	27 R	9
Crosswood Rd	Nu	3 C	11
Crow La	Ou	17 M	6
Crowell Pl	Hu	13 F	21
Crowell St (el)	Hu	4 F	18
Crowell St (HV)	Hu	21 N	18
Crowell St (un)	Hu	30 P	18
Crowell St	Hu	21 O	18
Crown Av	Hu	12 G	18
Crown La	Hu	29 S	15
Crown St	Hu	40 U	20
Crown St	Ou	37 W	12
Crowntop Rd	Nu	10 H	11
Crows Nest Ct	Nu	10 J	12
Crows Nest, The	Nu	1 E	7
Croyden Ct	Nu	19 L	13
Croyden Dr	Hu	22 N	22
Croyden Dr	Ou	48 AA	21
Croyden La	Ou	29 U	14
Croyden Pl	Hu	31 T	21
Croyden Rd	Hu	12 K	18
Croyden Rd	Nu	20 M	15
Croyden St	Nu	11 H	15
Croyden St	Hu	13 K	21
Croydon Av	Nu	2 D	10
Croydon Dr	Hu	31 S	20
Croydon Rd	Hu	4 E	19
Cruickshank Av	Hu	21 N	19
Crystal Ct	Hu	14 F	24
Crystal Dr	Nu	3 C	12
Crystal La	Hu	29 S	14
Crystal Pl	Nu	11 K	15
Crystal St	Hu	4 E	19
Cumberland Av	Nu	3 E	12
Cumberland Av	Hu	31 Q	21
Cumberland Pl (VS)	Hu	5 E	20
Cumberland Pl	Hu	7 C	25
Cumberland Rd	Ou	37 V	12
Cumberland St	Hu	22 M	22
Cunningham Av (SM)	Hu	12 G	17
Cunningham Av	Hu	30 P	17
Curlew Pl	Ou	48 BB	22
Curley St	Hu	24 L	27
Curtis Av	Nu	20 O	15
Curtis Av	Hu	21 O	19
Curtis Pl (LY)	Hu	13 H	22
Curtis Pl (bw)	Hu	22 O	20
Curtis Pl (wa)	Hu	40 V	20
Curtis Pl (bp)	Hu	38 X	16
Curtis Rd (HN)	Hu	14 G	25
Curve La	Hu	39 U	18
Cushing Av	Nu	10 K	14
Custer Av	Nu	10 L	14
Custer St	Hu	5 F	20
Custom Village Ct	Hu	30 T	19
Cutler Pl	Hu	12 G	19
Cutter La	Hu	38 W	16
Cutter Mill Rd	Nu	3 D	12
Cutter Rd	Nu	3 D	12
Cynron La	Hu	30 S	18
Cynthia Ct (HH)	Hu	14 H	23
Cynthia Ct (HV)	Hu	21 L	18
Cynthia Dr	Hu	30 S	18
Cynthia Dr	Ou	45 Z	13
Cynthia La	Hu	32 S	23
Cynthia La	Ou	45 Z	12
Cynthia La (MS)	Ou	47 BB	20
Cynthia Rd	Hu	21 P	19
Cypress Av (GN)	Nu	2 D	10
Cypress Av (pw)	Nu	9 G	9
Cypress Av	Ou	18 M	8
Cypress Av (os)	Hu	23 L	24
Cypress Av (ed)	Hu	30 T	18
Cypress Av (bp)	Ou	38 Y	14
Cypress Dr (ML)	Hu	13 H	20
Cypress Dr	Ou	44 Z	9
Cypress La	Nu	18 M	10
Cypress La	Ou	45 Z	12
Cypress Rd	Hu	6 B	25
Cypress St (FP)	Hu	12 G	17
Cypress St (wa)	Hu	40 W	21
Cypress St (sa)	Ou	46 BB	17
Cypress St (MS)	Ou	47 AA	19
Cyrus Point La	Ou	25 S	2

D

STREET	MUN.	MAP	GRID
D St	Hu	12 G	19
Dacosta Av	Hu	14 K	23
Daffodil Av	Hu	12 J	18

STREET	MUN.	MAP	GRID
Daffodil La	Hu	39 V	19
Daffodil La	Hu	35 X	5
Dahill Rd	Ou	45 AA	13
Dahlia Av	Hu	23 O	23
Dahlia La (VS)	Nu	5 F	22
Dahlia La	Hu	39 V	19
Dail St	Nu	11 J	14
Dairy Dr	Ou	16 M	3
Dairy La	Ou	38 U	15
Daisy Av	Hu	4 E	17
Daisy La	Hu	38 V	16
Daisy Rd	Ou	46 Y	17
Dakota Dr	Nu	10 G	14
Dakota Pl	Hu	21 N	17
Dakota St	Ou	28 T	13
Dale Av	Hu	30 R	18
Dale Av	Ou	37 W	11
Dale Ct (bp)	Ou	38 W	15
Dale Ct	Hu	39 X	19
Dale Ct	Ou	48 AA	22
Dale La	Ou	46 AA	16
Dale La	Hu	39 W	17
Dale Pl (VS)	Nu	5 E	21
Dale Pl (un)	Ou	30 Q	19
Dale Pl (wn)	Ou	40 W	21
Daleview Av	Hu	39 X	19
Dalex Ct	Ou	17 N	6
Daley Pl	Hu	13 J	22
Daley St	Nu	11 J	14
Dallas Av	Nu	11 H	15
Dallinger Pl	Hu	13 H	21
Dalor Ct	Ou	44 Y	10
Dalston Cir	Hu	13 J	21
Dalto Ct	Hu	23 M	23
Dalton St	Hu	24 L	27
Daly Blvd	Hu	14 L	25
Daly Pl	Ou	17 L	6
Dambly Av	Hu	23 L	24
Damin Dr	Ou	47 BB	18
Damson La	Hu	5 E	22
Damson St	Hu	21 M	17
Dana Av	Hu	13 G	20
Danas Hwy	Ou	16 M	3
Daniel Cox Rd	Hu	7 E	27
Daniel Cres	Hu	23 P	24
Daniel Dr (GL)	Ou	8 K	6
Daniel Dr	Hu	24 O	27
Daniel Dr (wy)	Ou	37 X	11
Daniel Dr (sa)	Ou	46 CC	17
Daniel Pl	Ou	17 L	6
Daniel Rd N	Ou	47 Y	18
Daniel Rd S	Ou	47 Y	18
Daniel St	Hu	6 D	23
Danis Av	Ou	17 N	6
Dannet Pl	Hu	30 R	17
Dante Av	Ou	38 V	15
Danton La N	Ou	25 P	3
Danton La S	Ou	25 P	3
Danzig Pl	Hu	5 E	21
Darby La	Hu	40 X	22
Darby Pl	Ou	17 M	7
Darby Rd	Hu	40 V	19
Darby Rd	Ou	48 AA	21
Darby Rd E	Hu	40 V	19
Darby Rd W	Hu	40 V	19
Darewood La	Hu	5 E	22
Darina Ct	Hu	21 L	18
Darlene Ter (sa)	Ou	47 BB	18
Darlene Ter	Ou	47 BB	18
Darley Rd	Nu	3 E	12
Darley Rd	Ou	37 X	12
Darling St	Hu	22 O	21
Dart St	Hu	14 J	23
Darters La	Nu	10 J	12
Dartmouth Dr (GL)	Ou	16 M	3
Dartmouth Dr (hk)	Ou	37 W	13
Dartmouth Dr (pv)	Ou	37 Y	11
Dartmouth La	Hu	6 E	23
Dartmouth Pl	Hu	31 S	22
Dartmouth Rd	Nu	9 G	10
Dartmouth Rd	Ou	48 AA	22
Dartmouth St (SM)	Hu	12 H	17
Dartmouth St (VS)	Hu	14 F	23
Dartmouth St (WP)	Nu	10 L	14
Dartmouth St (HV)	Hu	21 N	17
Dartmouth St (RC)	Hu	22 L	21
Dartmouth St (bw)	Hu	22 N	21
Dartmouth St	Nu	28 Q	14
Darwin Dr	Hu	30 S	19
Daub Av	Hu	6 F	23
Dauntless Pkwy	Hu	13 F	20
Davenport Pl	Hu	31 T	20
David Av	Ou	37 V	12
David Ct (GL)	Ou	17 O	6
David Ct (os)	Hu	23 M	24
David Ct (ed)	Hu	29 T	16
David Ct (un)	Hu	30 P	19
David Ct (pv)	Ou	45 Y	13
David Dr (hk)	Ou	37 V	12
David Dr (sa)	Ou	46 CC	17
David Pl (bm)	Hu	40 U	20
David Pl	Hu	39 X	19
David Rd (pv)	Ou	45 Z	13
David Rd	Ou	47 Y	18
David St (fs)	Hu	12 H	19
David St (wh)	Hu	12 K	18
Davie St	Hu	29 R	15
Davis Av (pw)	Nu	9 H	8
Davis Av (in)	Hu	6 B	25
Davis Av (RL)	Nu	9 L	11
Davis Av (HV)	Hu	20 O	16
Davis Av (HV)	Hu	21 O	19
Davis Pl (BY)	Ou	25 Q	2
Davis Pl (bh)	Hu	23 N	24
Davis Pl (ba)	Ou	38 X	16
Davis Pl (lv)	Hu	39 V	18
Davis Rd	Nu	9 G	9
Davis St (fds)	Hu	12 H	18
Davis St (lv)	Ou	16 P	4
Davis St (fs)	Hu	12 H	18
Davis St (ER)	Hu	14 J	23
Davis St (os)	Hu	23 L	23
Davis St (FR)	Hu	31 P	21
Davison Av (HH)	Hu	13 H	21
Davison Av (ER)	Hu	14 J	23
Davison Av (os)	Hu	23 L	23
Davison Ct	Hu	14 K	23
Davison Pl (RC)	Hu	22 L	22
Davison Pl (bw)	Hu	22 O	22
Davison Pl (FR)	Hu	23 P	23
Davison Plz	Hu	14 K	23
Davison St	Hu	14 K	23
Dawes Av (LY)	Hu	13 H	22
Dawes Av	Hu	31 P	21
Dawes Av	Ou	36 W	9
Dawn La	Nu	10 K	13
Dawn La	Ou	38 U	15
Dawson Dr	Hu	6 F	22
Dawson Ct	Ou	37 U	12
Dawson Wy	Ou	18 N	9
Day Ct	Nu	2 D	11
Day St	Hu	47 Y	19
Dayton St	Ou	8 K	7
Dayton St	Hu	29 R	14
Daytona St	Hu	7 C	27
De Forest Rd	Ou	35 Y	5
De Kalb Av	Hu	31 S	21
De Mille Av	Hu	12 F	19
De Mott Av (RC)	Hu	22 L	21
De Mott Av (bw)	Hu	22 N	21
De Mott Av (bw)	Hu	22 O	20
De Mott Pl	Hu	14 K	23
De Mott St	Nu	20 L	15
De Paul St	Hu	12 G	18
De Salle Pl	Hu	31 R	20
De Wolfe Pl	Nu	30 S	17
Deal St	Hu	15 K	26
Dean Dr	Hu	22 N	20
Dean St (VS)	Nu	5 D	21
Dean St (ER)	Hu	14 J	23
Dean St (hk)	Ou	38 V	14
Dean St (FR)	Hu	31 Q	21
Dean St (FG)	Ou	46 BB	16
Dean St (bp)	Ou	38 V	14
Deans La (BY)	Ou	25 S	2
Deasy La	Ou	16 M	5
Deb St	Ou	37 X	13
Debevoise Av	Hu	22 P	20
Debora Ct	Ou	45 Y	13
Deborah Ct (sy)	Ou	37 V	11
Deborah Ct (nq)	Ou	47 Z	18
Deborah Rd	Ou	37 V	11
Debra Ct	Nu	19 O	12
Debra Ct (ne)	Hu	31 S	20
Debra Pl	Hu	39 X	18
Debra Pl	Hu	13 G	20
Debra Pl	Ou	36 X	10
Decatur Av	Hu	30 S	19
Decatur Pl	Hu	15 K	27
Decatur St (bw)	Hu	22 O	21
Decatur St (un)	Hu	30 P	18
Decatur St	Hu	31 Q	20
Dechiaro La	Nu	10 K	14
Decker Av	Hu	31 S	20
Decker St	Hu	13 G	20
Dee Ct	Hu	39 U	18
Dee La	Ou	44 Y	9
Deen St	Hu	23 M	23
Deep La	Hu	39 V	19
Deep Woods Ct	Ou	16 M	3
Deepdale Ct (GL)	Ou	16 N	4
Deepdale Ct	Ou	44 Y	10
Deepdale Dr (GE)	Nu	3 C	11
Deepdale Dr (ma)	Nu	10 G	11
Deepdale Pkwy	Nu	10 K	13
Deepwater Av	Ou	48 BB	22
Deepwood Ct (OW)	Ou	28 P	11
Deepwood Ct	Ou	28 Q	11
Deepwood Rd	Nu	18 M	11
Deer La	Ou	37 V	12
Deer La	Hu	39 V	19
Deer Park Rd	Nu	2 E	9
Deer Path La	Ou	37 W	11
Deer Run	Hu	17 N	8
Deer Run	Nu	10 K	12
Deerfield Rd	Ou	9 H	9
Deering La	Hu	14 H	23
Deerpath	Hu	18 M	11
Deirving St	Hu	14 K	24
Dekoven St	Hu	13 K	21
Delamar Ct	Ou	16 K	5
Delano Ct	Nu	11 H	15
Delaware Av	Nu	8 G	8
Delaware Av (LB)	Hu	15 G	28
Delaware Av (FR)	Hu	22 P	21
Delaware Av (IP)	Hu	15 K	26
Delaware Cir	Ou	22 O	21
Delaware Dr	Nu	10 G	14
Delaware Pl	Hu	21 N	17
Delaware Rd	Hu	4 E	17
Delile Pl	Hu	39 W	19
Delise Av	Hu	31 Q	21
Dell Dr	Hu	14 H	23
Dell La	Hu	39 V	19
Dell, The	Hu	10 K	12
Dell, The	Ou	44 AA	10
Delmar Av	Hu	12 H	17
Delmonico Pl	Hu	13 G	22
Delta Rd	Ou	48 CC	21
Demont Rd	Hu	39 X	19
Demott Av	Hu	40 W	20
Demott Ct (sl)	Hu	29 R	15
Demott Ct	Hu	30 R	19
Demott Pl	Hu	40 W	20
Den Pl	Ou	37 X	11
Denhoff Av	Hu	31 Q	22
Denise St	Ou	47 CC	19
Dennis Ct	Hu	23 M	24
Dennis La	Ou	46 Y	17
Dennis St (ma)	Nu	9 F	11
Dennis St (GA)	Nu	11 J	16
Dennis St	Hu	23 M	24
Denton Av	Nu	11 J	15
Denton Av (LY)	Hu	13 J	22
Denton Ct	Nu	14 J	23
Denton Ct	Nu	2 C	9
Denton Ct	Nu	22 M	22
Denton Dr	Nu	32 T	23
Denton Pl	Nu	31 Q	20
Denton Rd (KP)	Nu	2 C	9
Denton Rd	Nu	10 J	14
Denton St	Nu	31 T	20
Denver Rd	Nu	40 W	20
Depan Av	Hu	11 G	16
Depot Av	Ou	46 BB	16
Depot Pl	Ou	17 M	8
Derby Av (wm)	Hu	6 D	23
Derby Av	Hu	6 E	24
Derby Ct	Hu	13 J	20
Derby Ct	Ou	35 U	5
Derby Dr E	Hu	23 N	23
Derby Dr N	Hu	23 N	23
Derby Dr S	Hu	23 N	23
Derby Dr W	Hu	23 N	23
Derby La	Ou	37 X	13
Derby Rd	Hu	9 H	9
Derby Rd (RC)	Hu	22 M	21
Derby Rd	Hu	22 N	22
Derby St	Ou	38 V	14
Derby St	Nu	5 F	22
Derby St	Nu	19 L	13
Derrick Atkins La	Hu	13 K	20
Desibio Pl	Hu	6 C	25
Desmond Pl	Ou	37 U	13
Desoto Pl	Hu	29 T	16
Detroit Av	Ou	47 Y	20
Deusenberg Dr	Ou	35 U	6
Devereux Pl	Hu	20 N	16
Devine Av	Ou	36 W	9
Devine St	Hu	13 J	22
Devon Av	Hu	14 K	25
Devon Dr	Hu	30 S	19
Devon La	Nu	28 P	13
Devon Rd (GN)	Nu	2 D	10
Devon Rd	Nu	19 L	13
Devon Rd (HV)	Hu	21 O	18
Devon Rd	Hu	22 M	21
Devon Rd	Ou	37 X	13
Devon St (LY)	Hu	13 H	22
Devon St (ML)	Hu	13 J	21
Devon St	Hu	30 S	17
Devonshire Ct	Ou	45 Z	12
Devonshire Dr (gk)	Nu	11 J	15
Devonshire Dr	Ou	26 T	7
Devonshire La	Nu	2 D	10
Devonshire Rd	Hu	22 N	22
Devonshire Rd	Ou	48 BB	21
Dewey Av	Nu	10 K	13
Dewey Av	Hu	31 T	20
Dewey Pl	Hu	30 S	19
Dewey St	Nu	2 F	11
Dewey St	Ou	28 T	12
Dewey St E	Hu	14 J	24
Dewey St W	Hu	14 J	24
Dewitt St	Hu	5 E	20
Dexter St	Ou	46 BB	16
Diamond Av	Hu	30 T	17
Diamond Dr	Ou	44 Y	11
Diamond St	Hu	4 E	19
Diana Dr	Ou	47 BB	18
Dianas Cir	Nu	10 K	11
Dianas St	Nu	10 K	11
Dianas Tr	Nu	10 J	11
Diane Ct	Ou	45 Z	13
Diane Dr	Ou	47 Y	18
Diane Dr	Hu	39 X	19
Diane Pl	Hu	6 D	23
Diane St	Hu	4 F	19
Dianne Ct	Hu	30 T	18
Dianne St (VS)	Hu	13 G	21
Dianne St (lv)	Hu	38 X	16
Dianne St (nw)	Hu	39 X	18
Dibblee Dr	Hu	20 O	15
Dickens Av	Hu	12 J	19
Dickens Av	Hu	6 E	24
Dickens St	Nu	29 Q	14
Dickenson Pl	Nu	2 C	11
Dickerson Av	Ou	25 R	2
Dicks La	Nu	9 K	11
Dicks La	Hu	21 M	18
Dickson Cir	Nu	19 L	13
Dickson St	Hu	6 C	25
Dickson St	Ou	17 L	5
Diellen La	Hu	12 G	19
Dieman La	Hu	30 R	18
Dietz St	Hu	22 N	19
Dikeman Ct	Hu	29 T	14
Dikeman St	Hu	21 O	18
Dillon Av	Hu	30 R	18
Dillon Dr	Hu	7 D	25
Dilthy Pl	Hu	23 L	23
Disc La	Hu	39 V	19
Ditmas Av	Hu	22 P	19
Division Av	Nu	28 S	14
Division Av (hk)	Ou	37 U	13
Division Av (hk)	Ou	37 U	14
Division Av	Hu	39 U	17
Division Av (hk)	Ou	37 V	14
Division Av (mq)	Ou	48 Y	22
Division St	Hu	14 F	23
Division St	Ou	46 BB	16
Divot Rd	Hu	23 M	24
Dixon Ct	Ou	17 L	7
Doblin St	Hu	4 E	19
Dobson Av	Hu	31 S	22
Dock Dr	Hu	23 P	23
Dock La (PN)	Nu	1 F	7
Dock La (KP)	Nu	2 C	8
Dock La	Hu	39 V	19
Dock Pl	Hu	16 M	3
Dock Rd	Hu	32 U	22
Dock St	Hu	14 K	23
Dodford Rd	Nu	3 D	12
Dofena La	Hu	29 S	16
Dogleg La	Hu	19 M	13
Dogwood Av	Nu	18 M	10
Dogwood Av	Hu	13 J	20
Dogwood Av (ed)	Hu	30 T	17

Nassau Co.

STREET	MUN.	MAP	GRID
Dogwood Ct	Ou	27 Q	8
Dogwood Hill	Ou	27 R	9
Dogwood La (SP)	Nu	1 E	6
Dogwood La (PD)	Nu	9 G	10
Dogwood La (LW)	Hu	7 D	25
Dogwood La	Ou	26 R	4
Dogwood La (GL)	Ou	17 O	6
Dogwood La (FH)	Nu	9 H	10
Dogwood La (GL)	Hu	17 M	8
Dogwood La (hr)	Nu	10 J	14
Dogwood La (RC)	Hu	22 M	20
Dogwood La (nc)	Nu	28 S	13
Dogwood La (sl)	Hu	29 R	15
Dogwood La (hk)	Hu	29 T	16
Dogwood La (sd)	Hu	40 X	20
Dogwood La (mq)	Ou	47 Y	19
Dogwood Pl	Ou	47 Y	19
Dogwood Rd (GN)	Nu	2 D	10
Dogwood Rd	Hu	5 F	21
Dogwood Rd (sg)	Nu	10 J	13
Dogwood St	Hu	31 T	20
Dogwoods, The	Nu	9 K	11
Doherty La	Hu	12 G	19
Dolly Cam La	Ou	17 N	8
Dolores Dr	Hu	5 E	22
Dolores La	Hu	38 X	15
Dolores Pl (ML)	Hu	13 H	20
Dolores Pl	Ou	45 Y	13
Dolores Pl (nw)	Hu	39 X	19
Dolphin Ct	Hu	41 U	23
Dolphin Dr	Hu	14 G	25
Dolphin Dr	Ou	46 Z	16
Dolphin Dr (mq)	Ou	48 Y	22
Dolphin Green	Nu	9 F	8
Dome La	Hu	39 V	19
Donahve St	Ou	17 M	6
Donald Ct	Hu	4 E	19
Donald Dr (wy)	Ou	46 AA	16
Donald Dr	Ou	36 X	10
Donald Dr	Ou	45 AA	14
Donald La	Hu	6 E	23
Donald Pl (nv)	Hu	13 G	20
Donald Pl	Hu	14 J	23
Donald St	Ou	25 Q	2
Donald St (rt)	Nu	19 L	11
Donald St (EW)	Nu	19 M	14
Donald St	Ou	25 R	2
Donaldson Pl	Nu	10 L	11
Doncaster Rd	Hu	13 H	20
Donegar Pl	Hu	14 L	25
Donlon Av	Hu	13 K	20
Donlon Pl	Hu	13 K	20
Donmoor Rd	Hu	7 D	25
Donna Ct (LY)	Hu	14 H	23
Donna Ct	Hu	23 O	23
Donna Dr (UB)	Ou	26 S	7
Donna Dr	Hu	41 U	23
Donna Dr	Ou	45 Z	12
Donna La	Nu	20 N	14
Donna La	Ou	24 O	27
Donna La	Ou	36 W	10
Donohue Av (Finger Island Rd)	Hu	6 B	25
Donovan St	Hu	12 G	19
Doone Dr	Ou	37 X	11
Doral Ct	Nu	10 J	13
Doral Ct	Ou	28 R	12
Doral Dr	Nu	10 J	12
Dorcas Av	Ou	36 W	9
Dorchester Dr	Nu	9 J	11
Dorchester Dr	Ou	27 S	8
Dorchester Rd	Hu	22 L	21
Dorchester Rd S.	Hu	12 K	17
Doria La S	Hu	40 U	20
Doris Av (fs)	Hu	12 H	19
Doris Av	Nu	30 U	19
Doris Dr	Nu	19 O	13
Doris Dr	Hu	21 L	19
Doris Pl (ML)	Hu	13 J	21
Doris Pl	Hu	31 S	21
Doris Pl	Ou	47 AA	19
Doris Rd	Ou	38 U	14
Dorlan Pl	Hu	23 O	23

STREET	MUN.	MAP	GRID
Dorlon St	Hu	21 N	19
Dorothea La	Hu	12 G	19
Dorothea St	Ou	45 Y	13
Dorothy Ct (mr)	Hu	32 S	22
Dorothy Ct	Ou	46 AA	17
Dorothy Ct	Hu	40 X	20
Dorothy Dr	Hu	29 S	16
Dorothy Dr	Ou	36 W	9
Dorothy Gate	Ou	47 CC	18
Dorothy La	Ou	26 T	5
Dorothy Pl	Hu	14 G	23
Dorothy St (hk)	Ou	37 V	12
Dorothy St	Hu	41 U	23
Dorothy St (wy)	Ou	36 X	10
Dorothy St (bp)	Ou	46 Y	15
Dorset La	Nu	19 L	13
Dorset La (bw)	Hu	22 N	22
Dorset La	Hu	39 V	17
Dorset La (bp)	Ou	37 X	13
Dorset La	Ou	47 CC	18
Dorset Pl	Hu	30 U	19
Dorset Rd	Nu	3 D	13
Dorset Wy	Ou	8 L	5
Dory La	Ou	48 Y	22
Dosoris La	Ou	17 M	5
Dosoris Wy	Ou	17 M	5
Dot Ct E	Hu	23 M	25
Doud St	Ou	46 BB	16
Dougherty St	Ou	17 O	6
Doughty Av	Hu	13 J	19
Doughty Blvd	Hu	6 C	25
Douglas Av	Hu	39 V	19
Douglas Ct	Hu	30 T	17
Douglas Dr	Ou	17 M	5
Douglas Dr	Hu	30 T	17
Douglas Pl	Hu	47 Y	19
Douglas La	Hu	6 C	25
Douglas St	Nu	20 O	15
Dove Hill Dr	Nu	10 J	12
Dove La	Hu	38 U	15
Dove St	Ou	37 W	13
Dover Av	Hu	11 K	16
Dover Av	Ou	47 Y	18
Dover Ct	Hu	22 M	21
Dover La (ob)	Ou	45 AA	14
Dover La	Ou	37 W	11
Dover La (wa)	Ou	47 CC	18
Dover Pkwy	Hu	12 H	17
Dover Pkwy N	Hu	12 H	17
Dover Pl	Hu	21 L	18
Dover Rd (st)	Nu	9 J	11
Dover Rd (st)	Nu	10 H	11
Dover Rd (os)	Hu	14 K	23
Dover Rd	Ou	48 AA	21
Dover Rd	Hu	40 W	20
Dover St	Nu	29 Q	14
Dover St	Ou	47 CC	20
Dow Av	Nu	20 M	15
Dow Av	Nu	31 S	20
Dowling Ct	Nu	10 Q	12
Downhill La	Hu	39 V	19
Downing Av	Ou	17 L	7
Downing Rd	Hu	13 G	20
Downing St	Nu	19 M	14
Downs Rd	Hu	21 N	19
Doxey Dr	Hu	17 M	6
Doxsee Dr	Hu	32 R	23
Doxsey Pl	Hu	13 J	22
Doyle St	Hu	24 L	27
Dragon La	Hu	39 V	19
Drake Ct	Hu	39 X	17
Drake La	Nu	9 H	9
Drake La	Hu	39 W	17
Drake St (ML)	Hu	13 H	20
Drake St (LY)	Hu	13 H	21
Drake St (tr)	Hu	39 X	17
Drawbridge, The	Ou	36 Y	8
Drew Av	Hu	12 G	17
Drew St	Hu	14 F	22
Drexel Av	Nu	29 P	14
Driftwood Dr	Nu	1 F	7
Driftwood Dr	Ou	16 N	4
Driftwood La	Hu	41 U	23
Driscoll Av	Hu	23 L	23
Driscoll La	Hu	47 Y	19
Drive, The	Ou	17 L	6
Drive, The	Hu	31 S	20
Driving Park Av	Hu	13 J	21
Droesch St	Nu	20 M	15
Drumlin La	Ou	35 X	6
Drury La (GN)	Nu	2 D	10
Drury La (pw)	Nu	9 G	9
Drury La	Ou	37 X	11
Dryden St	Nu	29 Q	14
Duane La	Ou	25 S	2
Duane St	Ou	46 BB	16
Dubois Av	Hu	6 F	23

STREET	MUN.	MAP	GRID
Dubois Av	Ou	17 L	6
Dubois Ct	Ou	17 L	6
Dubonnet Rd	Hu	14 G	23
Duck Pond Rd (GL)	Ou	17 N	5
Duckpond Dr	Nu	10 J	12
Duckpond Dr E	Hu	39 W	19
Duckpond Dr N	Hu	39 V	19
Duckpond Dr S	Hu	39 V	19
Duff Pl	Ou	47 Y	18
Duffe Pl	Hu	5 F	22
Duffys Av	Ou	29 T	14
Duffys La	Ou	29 T	14
Duke Ct	Hu	39 X	17
Duke Dr	Ou	17 M	6
Duke St	Ou	28 Q	13
Duke St	Hu	40 U	20
Dumond Pl	Ou	18 M	8
Dumont Pl	Hu	6 D	23
Duncan Av (LY)	Hu	13 J	21
Duncan Av (eg)	Hu	20 P	16
Duncan Ct	Hu	39 V	19
Duncan Dr	Hu	28 R	13
Duncan Dr W	Ou	28 Q	13
Duncan Pl	Hu	23 L	23
Duncan Rd	Hu	21 O	18
Dune Rd	Hu	14 H	24
Dunes La	Nu	1 E	7
Dunhill Rd (hr)	Nu	10 J	14
Dunhill Rd	Hu	39 X	18
Dunne Pl	Hu	14 H	23
Dunstan Dr	Hu	30 S	19
Dunster Ct	Hu	12 J	19
Dunster Dr	Hu	12 J	19
Dunster Rd	Nu	3 E	12
Dunwood Rd	Nu	1 E	7
Dupont St	Ou	44 Z	11
Durand Pl	Nu	9 H	10
Durbyan St	Nu	8 G	7
Durham Pl	Hu	37 X	13
Durham Rd (LY)	Hu	14 G	23
Durham Rd (un)	Hu	30 R	18
Durland Rd	Hu	14 H	23
Dury St	Ou	48 CC	22
Duryea Av	Hu	21 P	18
Duryea Pl (LY)	Hu	14 H	23
Duryea Pl	Hu	21 N	18
Duryea Ter	Hu	12 K	19
Duston Rd	Hu	6 E	23
Dutch Broadway	Hu	4 E	19
Dutchess Blvd	Hu	7 D	28
Dutchess St	Hu	31 P	21
Duxbury Rd	Nu	2 E	10
Dwarf La	Hu	39 W	19
Dwight La	Nu	2 B	10
Dwight St	Hu	23 M	24
Dwyer Pl	Nu	28 R	13
Dyckman Av	Nu	11 J	15

E

STREET	MUN.	MAP	GRID
E Euclid St	Hu	13 H	21
Eab Plz	Hu	30 Q	17
Eagle Av (el)	Hu	12 G	18
Eagle Av	Hu	13 K	19
Eagle Chase	Ou	44 Y	10
Eagle Ct	Ou	36 W	9
Eagle Dr	Hu	6 D	23
Eagle La	Nu	18 N	10
Eagle La	Hu	38 V	16
Eagle La	Ou	47 BB	18
Eagle Point Dr	Nu	1 C	8
Eagles Cres	Nu	10 J	12
Eakins Rd	Nu	9 G	10
Earl Dr	Hu	31 S	20
Earl Pl	Hu	30 T	17
Earl Pl E	Hu	30 T	17
Earl Pl W	Hu	30 T	17
Earl Rd	Hu	40 W	20
Earl St (FP)	Hu	12 G	17
Earl St (EW)	Nu	20 M	14
Earl St	Nu	20 O	14
Earl St	Nu	30 S	19
Earle Av (RC)	Hu	22 M	21
Earle Av	Hu	13 J	22
Earle Ovington Blvd	Hu	20 P	17
Early Pl	Nu	9 H	11
Early Pl (bw)	Hu	22 O	21
Easa Pl (bm)	Hu	41 V	23
East 1st St	Hu	32 R	23

STREET	MUN.	MAP	GRID
East 2nd St	Hu	32 R	23
East Ames Ct	Ou	44 Z	11
East Argyle La	Hu	13 G	21
East Atlantic Av	Hu	23 L	23
East Av (VS)	Nu	5 F	21
East Av (in)	Hu	6 C	24
East Av (gh)	Ou	17 M	7
East Av (GL)	Ou	17 O	6
East Av (BY)	Ou	25 S	2
East Av (hk)	Ou	29 U	14
East Av (FR)	Hu	32 Q	23
East Barclay St	Ou	37 U	13
East Bay Ct	Hu	41 U	23
East Bay Dr	Hu	15 K	27
East Beach Dr	Ou	16 N	3
East Bedell St	Hu	32 Q	23
East Beech St	Hu	15 K	28
East Berkshire Rd	Hu	31 S	22
East Bethpage Rd	Ou	45 AA	12
East Beverly Pkwy	Hu	13 G	21
East Blvd	Hu	14 J	24
East Blvd	Ou	47 AA	19
East Boxwood Dr	Hu	14 H	23
East Broadway (RH)	Hu	18 L	10
East Broadway	Hu	15 J	28
East Broadway	Nu	28 S	13
East Cabot La	Nu	29 T	15
East Carl Av	Ou	22 O	21
East Carl St	Ou	37 V	13
East Carpenter St	Hu	13 G	21
East Cedar St	Ou	47 CC	20
East Centennial Av	Hu	31 P	20
East Cherry St	Hu	12 G	17
East Cherry St	Ou	37 V	13
East Chester St (VS)	Hu	13 G	21
East Chester St (LB)	Hu	15 J	27
East Chester St	Hu	24 L	27
East Chestnut St	Ou	47 CC	20
East Clinton Av	Hu	22 P	20
East Coronet Cres	Ou	46 Y	15
East Ct	Nu	19 L	12
East Ct	Ou	37 X	11
East Ct (bp)	Ou	46 Y	15
East Crest Rd	Nu	8 G	8
East Cypress La (sl)	Hu	29 S	14
East Dean St	Hu	31 Q	21
East Dover St	Hu	13 G	21
East Dr (PD)	Nu	9 G	10
East Dr (ma)	Nu	10 F	11
East Dr (HV)	Hu	20 N	15
East Dr (mr)	Hu	31 S	20
East Dr (bm)	Hu	31 T	21
East Dr (MT)	Ou	36 X	10
East Dr (nq)	Ou	46 AA	17
East Elder Av	Hu	4 E	17
East End	Hu	40 X	21
East End Av	Ou	37 W	12
East Euclid St	Hu	13 G	21
East Fairview Av	Hu	13 G	21
East Fenimore St	Hu	13 G	21
East Fletcher Av	Hu	31 R	20
East Fulton Av	Hu	31 Q	20
East Fulton St	Hu	15 J	27
East Garfield St	Hu	31 S	20
East Gate (st)	Nu	9 H	11
East Gate (nv)	Hu	13 G	20
East Gate (pv)	Ou	37 X	12
East Gate (RC)	Hu	22 L	21
East Gate (FG)	Ou	46 AA	16
East Gate Blvd N	Ou	20 O	15
East Gate Rd	Nu	9 J	10
East Graham Av	Hu	21 N	19
East Grant Dr	Hu	13 F	20
East Greenwich Av	Hu	22 P	20
East Grove St	Ou	47 CC	21
East Harrison St	Hu	15 J	27
East Hawthorne Av	Hu	13 G	22
East Hemlock St	Ou	47 CC	20
East High Rd	Nu	9 J	10
East Hitchcock Av	Hu	11 G	16

STREET	MUN.	MAP	GRID
East Horseshoe Dr	Nu	19 M	12
East Hudson St	Hu	15 J	27
East Jackson Ct	Hu	21 N	18
East Jamaica Av	Hu	13 G	22
East John St	Ou	37 U	13
East Lake Av	Hu	47 BB	20
East La	Nu	10 H	14
East Lexington Av	Hu	23 L	24
East Lincoln Av (VS)	Hu	13 G	21
East Lincoln Av (rv)	Hu	31 Q	20
East Main St	Ou	35 U	5
East Mall	Ou	45 AA	12
East Maple St (VS)	Hu	13 G	21
East Maple St	Ou	47 CC	20
East Market St	Hu	15 J	27
East Maujer St	Hu	13 G	21
East Meadow Av	Hu	30 S	18
East Meadow Knolls #1	Hu	29 T	16
East Meadow Knolls #4	Hu	29 S	16
East Meadow Rd	Hu	30 R	19
East Melrose St	Hu	13 G	21
East Merrick Rd (VS)	Hu	13 G	21
East Merrick Rd (FR)	Hu	31 Q	22
East Mill Dr	Nu	3 D	12
East Mill Page Dr	Ou	46 Y	16
East Milton St	Hu	31 Q	21
East Mineola Av	Hu	13 G	21
East New York Av	Hu	13 G	22
East Nicholai St	Ou	37 V	13
East Norwich Rd	Ou	28 T	11
East Old Country Rd	Ou	37 V	13
East Olive St	Hu	15 J	28
East Oxford St	Hu	13 G	21
Park E	Nu	11 J	14
East Park Av (LB)	Hu	15 H	27
East Park Av	Hu	15 K	27
East Park Ct	Ou	6 D	23
East Park Ct	Ou	45 AA	13
East Park Dr	Ou	45 AA	13
East Park Pl	Nu	2 D	10
East Penn St	Hu	15 J	28
East Pennywood Av	Hu	31 P	20
East Pine Hill Rd	Hu	3 F	13
East Pine St	Hu	15 J	27
East Pine St	Ou	47 CC	20
East Poplar St	Hu	11 F	17
East Raymond Av	Hu	22 P	20
East Ridge Dr	Nu	3 C	11
East Rd (SP)	Nu	8 H	7
East Rd	Nu	2 D	10
East Rd	Ou	20 P	16
East Rockaway Rd	Hu	14 G	23
East Roosevelt Av	Hu	31 P	20
East Saint Marks PlHu		13 G	21
East Sally Ct	Hu	30 R	19
East Seaman Av	Hu	31 Q	21
East Shelley Rd	Hu	30 U	19
East Shore Rd (KP)	Nu	2 D	9
East Shore Rd	Nu	10 F	11
East Slope Rd	Ou	25 S	2
East Smith St	Hu	31 P	22
East Stewart Av (HV)	Hu	20 M	16
East Stewart Av	Hu	20 O	16
East St	Hu	12 G	19
East St (RL)	Nu	18 L	10
East St	Nu	10 J	14
East St (hk)	Ou	37 V	13
East St	Ou	36 W	8
East Tompkins Pl	Hu	21 N	19
East Valley Stream Blvd	Hu	13 G	22
East View Av	Ou	18 N	8
East View Av	Hu	39 X	19
East View Ct	Ou	28 T	11
East View Ct (Pvt)	Nu	9 H	10
East View Ct (Pvt)	Nu	9 H	10
East Voss Av	Hu	14 H	23
East Walnut St	Hu	15 J	27
East Walnut St	Ou	47 CC	20
East Webster St	Hu	31 S	21
East Williston Av	Nu	19 M	14
East Willow St	Ou	47 CC	20
East Windsor Rd	Hu	22 O	22
East Woodbine Dr	Hu	31 P	21
East Wood Rd	Hu	22 N	21
East Zoranne Dr	Ou	46 Z	17
Eastern Av	Hu	40 V	21
Eastern Blvd	Hu	23 O	23
Eastern Dr	Nu	11 J	15
Eastern Pkwy	Hu	23 O	24
Eastern Pkwy	Ou	46 BB	16
Eastern Pl	Hu	40 V	21
Eastfield Rd	Nu	28 R	13
Eastgate Rd	Ou	47 BB	20
Eastland Dr	Ou	16 M	2
Eastover Gardens	Hu	39 X	19
Eastwood Dr	Ou	47 CC	19
Eastwood La	Nu	5 E	22
Eastwood Rd	Hu	6 E	23
Eastwoods Rd	Ou	36 U	9
Eaton Ct	Nu	10 J	12
Eaton Rd	Ou	37 W	11
Eaton Rd E	Hu	40 V	20
Eaton Rd W	Hu	40 V	20
Eaton St	Hu	23 M	24
Echo Home Rd	Ou	43 Z	7
Echo La	Nu	39 X	17
Echo Pl	Nu	9 G	9
Echo Pl	Ou	32 S	23
Eddy Rd	Hu	31 Q	20
Eden Av	Ou	48 BB	21
Eden Ct	Hu	6 D	23
Eden La	Nu	39 X	17
Eden Rd	Hu	24 M	27
Eden Rock Dr	Ou	25 P	3
Eden Wy	Ou	18 L	8
Edge Ct	Ou	36 U	9
Edge La	Nu	39 X	17
Edge Rd	Ou	36 U	9
Edgehill Rd	Ou	17 N	5
Edgemere Av	Hu	21 P	18
Edgemere Dr	Nu	10 J	12
Edgemere Rd	Hu	12 J	17
Edgerton Av	Hu	40 W	20
Edgewater Av	Ou	48 BB	22
Edgewater La	Nu	3 B	11
Edgewood Av	Ou	17 L	8
Edgewood Av	Hu	13 K	21
Edgewood Ct	Hu	21 O	19
Edgewood Dr (gh)	Ou	17 N	7
Edgewood Dr	Nu	11 J	15
Edgewood Dr	Ou	38 U	14
Edgewood Dr	Hu	29 R	15
Edgewood Dr (sy)	Ou	36 W	9
Edgewood Gate	Ou	45 Z	12
Edgewood La	Nu	18 M	10
Edgewood Pl	Nu	2 C	10
Edgewood Pl	Ou	16 P	4
Edgewood Rd	Nu	1 E	7
Edgewood Rd	Hu	13 F	21
Edgeworth St	Hu	6 F	23
Edi Av	Ou	45 Y	11
Edi Ct	Ou	45 Y	11
Edison Dr	Ou	45 Z	13
Edison Pl	Hu	40 U	20
Edith Dr	Ou	45 Z	13
Edith Pl	Hu	31 S	21
Edith St	Hu	13 H	21
Edlu Ct	Hu	13 F	20
Edmund St	Hu	13 J	21
Edna Ct (VS)	Hu	5 E	21
Edna Ct (bw)	Hu	23 N	22
Edna Ct (ed)	Hu	29 T	16
Edna Ct (pe)	Hu	38 X	16
Edna Dr	Ou	36 W	9
Edna Pl	Hu	5 E	21
Edro Ct	Hu	30 R	17
Edson La	Ou	18 O	8
Edward Av	Hu	6 E	24
Edward Av (lg)	Ou	36 W	10
Edward Av	Ou	37 W	13
Edward Bentley Rd	Hu	7 D	27
Edward Ct (lk)	Hu	12 K	19
Edward Ct	Hu	22 O	21
Edward Ct	Ou	46 AA	16
Edward La	Hu	32 S	23
Edward La	Ou	36 X	8
Edward St (ny)	Hu	13 H	21
Edward St (LY)	Hu	13 J	21
Edward St (bw)	Hu	22 N	20
Edward St (pe)	Hu	38 X	16
Edward Ter	Hu	12 J	19
Edwards Blvd (VS)	Hu	13 F	20
Edwards Blvd	Hu	15 J	28
Edwards La	Ou	17 O	5
Edwards Pl (VS)	Hu	5 E	21
Edwards Pl	Hu	31 S	22
Edwards St	Nu	9 L	11
Edwards St	Hu	23 N	23
Edwards St	Ou	46 AA	17
Edwin Ct	Nu	8 G	7
Edwin Ct	Hu	14 J	24
Effron Pl	Nu	3 E	12
Egil Ct	Nu	18 L	9
Eglon Ct	Hu	30 R	19
Egypt La	Ou	25 Q	3
Eider Hill Ct	Nu	10 J	12
Eiffel Gate	Ou	46 Y	16
Eileen Av	Ou	37 X	13
Eileen Ct (fs)	Hu	12 J	19
Eileen Ct	Hu	30 T	19
Eileen Rd	Hu	23 M	23
Eileen St	Hu	12 J	19
Eileen Ter	Hu	6 E	23
Eisenhower Dr	Hu	13 K	20
Eisenhower Pl	Hu	30 Q	18
Elaine Ct	Hu	13 K	21
Elaine Dr	Hu	14 L	25
Elaine Dr	Ou	46 Y	17
Elaine Pl	Hu	45 Y	12
Elaine Pl	Hu	40 V	22
Elayne Ct	Hu	40 X	22
Elbert Av	Hu	31 T	20
Elbert Pl	Hu	14 J	23
Elbow La	Hu	39 X	17
Elda La	Hu	29 R	15
Elder La	Hu	38 W	15
Elder La	Hu	29 R	15
Elder Pl	Hu	4 E	17
Elderberry Dr	Hu	29 R	15
Elderberry La	Hu	5 E	22
Elderberry La E	Hu	5 E	22
Elderberry Rd	Nu	11 L	14
Elderberry Rd	Hu	30 T	19
Elderberry Rd	Ou	37 W	11
Elderd La	Hu	6 E	25
Elderfields Rd	Nu	9 H	10
Eldert La	Hu	13 J	22
Eldorado Blvd	Ou	37 W	13
Eldorado St	Hu	7 C	27
Eldridge Av	Hu	21 N	18
Eldridge Pl	Hu	17 M	6
Eldridge Pl	Hu	21 N	18
Eleanor Dr	Ou	46 Y	17
Eleanor La	Ou	45 Y	13
Eleanor Rd	Ou	45 Y	13
Elf Rd	Ou	37 X	11
Elfland Ct	Ou	34 W	4
Elgin Av	Hu	30 R	18
Elgin Rd	Hu	14 G	22
Elice Pl	Hu	23 O	23
Elin Pl	Ou	18 M	8
Elinor Rd	Hu	23 P	23
Elinor Rd	Hu	14 G	24
Elinore Av	Hu	31 S	22
Eliot Ct	Ou	36 W	9
Elise Av	Hu	30 T	19
Elizabeth Av (HV)	Hu	21 N	19
Elizabeth Av	Hu	23 M	23
Elizabeth Ct (eg)	Hu	21 O	18
Elizabeth Ct	Hu	32 S	22
Elizabeth Dr (LH)	Ou	43 Z	7
Elizabeth Dr (FP)	Hu	11 F	16
Elizabeth St (VS)	Nu	5 E	20
Elizabeth St (in)	Hu	7 C	25
Elizabeth St (GL)	Ou	17 L	5
Elizabeth St (bh)	Hu	23 O	23
Elizabeth St (hk)	Hu	28 S	13
Elizabeth St (FR)	Hu	31 Q	21
Elizabeth St (FG)	Ou	46 BB	16
Elizabeth St (wa)	Ou	48 CC	21
Elk Ct	Hu	30 T	18
Elk Ct (Pvt)	Hu	21 N	18
Elk Pa	Nu	10 K	11
Elk St	Hu	21 N	18
Ell Ct	Hu	32 S	23
Ella Rd	Hu	40 W	20
Ella St (VS)	Hu	5 E	20
Ella St	Hu	13 J	22
Ellard Av	Nu	2 D	10
Ellen Ct (GL)	Ou	16 M	4
Ellen Ct (gh)	Ou	17 M	8
Ellen Ct (sa)	Ou	46 CC	17
Ellen Dr	Hu	32 T	23
Ellen Pl	Hu	6 D	23
Ellen Pl	Ou	37 U	11
Ellen Rd	Hu	41 V	23
Ellen St (bp)	Ou	46 Y	15
Ellen St	Ou	48 CC	21
Ellen Terry Dr	Hu	23 M	24
Elliman Pl	Ou	36 W	8
Ellington Av E	Hu	20 P	16
Ellington Av W	Hu	20 O	16
Elliot Blvd	Hu	14 K	24
Elliot Dr	Ou	38 W	15
Elliot Pl	Nu	10 K	12
Elliot Rd	Nu	2 E	11
Elliot St	Hu	31 T	22
Elliott Pl	Ou	16 M	5
Elliott Pl	Hu	31 S	21
Elliott Pl (FR)	Hu	23 P	23
Elliott St	Hu	12 G	18
Ellis Dr	Ou	37 V	11
Ellison Av (WB)	Hu	19 O	14
Ellison Av	Hu	31 Q	20
Ellison La	Hu	25 R	2
Ellison St	Ou	25 R	2
Ells St	Hu	4 F	18
Ellsworth Av	Nu	20 L	14
Ellsworth Pl	Hu	40 X	22
Ellwood St	Ou	17 L	5
Elm Av (FP)	Hu	4 E	17
Elm Av (GL)	Ou	17 N	6
Elm Av (HV)	Hu	21 M	19
Elm Av	Ou	26 Q	4
Elm Av (GL)	Ou	17 O	6
Elm Av (sa)	Ou	46 BB	17
Elm Ct	Nu	8 G	6
Elm Ct	Hu	30 T	18
Elm Dr (nn)	Nu	11 H	15
Elm Dr (EH)	Nu	18 M	11
Elm Dr (NL)	Nu	10 J	12
Elm Dr (ed)	Hu	30 T	18
Elm Dr (ob)	Ou	45 BB	13
Elm Dr (FG)	Ou	46 Z	16
Elm Dr E	Hu	39 X	17
Elm Dr N	Hu	39 X	17
Elm Dr S	Hu	39 W	17
Elm Dr W	Hu	39 W	17
Elm La (FH)	Nu	9 J	10
Elm La (LS)	Nu	3 F	13
Elm La (hr)	Nu	10 J	14
Elm Pl (GN)	Nu	2 C	10
Elm Pl (SC)	Ou	17 L	7
Elm Pl (ob)	Ou	18 M	9
Elm Pl (MI)	Nu	20 M	15
Elm Pl (HV)	Hu	21 O	18
Elm Pl (bw)	Hu	22 N	22
Elm Pl (lg)	Ou	36 V	10
Elm Pl (wa)	Ou	40 V	21
Elm Pl (FR)	Hu	31 P	22
Elm Pl (bm)	Hu	31 T	22
Elm Pl (ln)	Hu	39 X	17
Elm Pl (MS)	Ou	47 BB	19
Elm Ridge Rd	Nu	2 B	9
Elm Sea La	Nu	6 B	25
Elm St (pw)	Nu	9 H	8
Elm St (GE)	Nu	3 D	12
Elm St (VS)	Nu	5 D	21
Elm St (LY)	Hu	13 H	21
Elm St (WG)	Nu	6 E	24
Elm St (v)	Ou	16 O	5
Elm St (gv)	Ou	18 M	9
Elm St (ob)	Ou	17 N	8
Elm St (rt)	Nu	9 K	11
Elm St (fs)	Hu	12 J	18
Elm St (GA)	Hu	21 M	17
Elm St (lk)	Hu	13 L	19
Elm St (LY)	Hu	13 J	22
Elm St (os)	Nu	14 K	23
Elm St (WB)	Nu	19 P	14
Elm St (hk)	Ou	37 V	13
Elm St (FR)	Hu	31 Q	21
Elm St (bm)	Hu	31 T	20
Elm St (wy)	Ou	44 Z	9
Elm St (nq)	Ou	47 AA	18
Elm St (mq)	Ou	40 Y	21
Elmer Av	Hu	13 J	21

Nassau Co.

STREET	MUN.	MAP	GRID
Elmer St	Hu	40	X 20
Elmhurst Dr	Nu	18	P 11
Elmira St (hk)	Ou	29	U 14
Elmont Av	Hu	4	F 18
Elmont Rd (FP)	Hu	4	F 18
Elmont St	Hu	5	E 20
Elmore Av	Hu	30	R 18
Elmtree La	Ou	37	U 12
Elmwood Av (HV)	Hu	21	O 18
Elmwood Av	Hu	31	Q 20
Elmwood Ct	Nu	19	N 14
Elmwood Ct	Ou	45	Z 12
Elmwood La	Ou	37	W 11
Elmwood St (VS)	Hu	5	F 22
Elmwood St (bw)	Hu	22	O 21
Elmwood St	Nu	20	P 14
Elmwood St	Ou	37	X 12
Elsie Av	Ou	35	U 5
Elsie Av	Hu	31	R 21
Elsie La (FG)	Ou	46	AA 16
Elsie La	Ou	46	Z 17
Elsinore Av	Ou	17	M 5
Elton Av	Hu	21	L 18
Elton Rd	Hu	12	H 17
Elton Rd N	Hu	12	H 17
Elton St	Nu	29	R 14
Elves La	Hu	39	X 17
Elwood Av	Ou	38	U 15
Ely Ct (el)	Hu	4	E 19
Ely Ct	Hu	21	P 19
Elysian St	Hu	22	P 20
Elzey Av	Hu	4	E 18
Embassy Ct	Nu	2	D 11
Emerald Dr	Ou	17	M 6
Emerald La	Hu	39	X 17
Emeric Av	Hu	40	W 20
Emerson Av	Nu	11	F 16
Emerson Av (bw)	Hu	22	N 21
Emerson Av	Hu	39	X 17
Emerson Ct	Nu	29	Q 14
Emerson Dr	Nu	3	B 11
Emerson Dr	Hu	13	K 20
Emerson La	Ou	46	Y 17
Emerson Pl (VS)	Hu	13	G 21
Emerson Pl (ML)	Hu	13	H 21
Emerson Pl (un)	Hu	30	P 18
Emerson Pl (wa)	Hu	40	V 21
Emerson Rd	Ou	27	S 10
Emerson St (CH)	Hu	6	D 24
Emerson St	Hu	30	Q 18
Emery St	Hu	21	N 19
Emily Av	Hu	4	E 19
Emily St	Ou	47	CC19
Emm La	Nu	9	K 11
Emma Pl	Hu	12	H 19
Emma St (FP)	Hu	4	F 17
Emma St	Ou	46	Y 16
Emma St	Hu	40	X 20
Emmet Av	Hu	14	J 23
Emmet Pl	Nu	20	N 16
Emmet Pl	Ou	37	W 13
Emmett St	Nu	10	J 14
Emory Rd	Nu	11	K 15
Empire Blvd	Hu	15	L 25
Empire St	Hu	4	F 19
Emporia Av	Hu	4	F 18
Enclave, The	Nu	10	H 12
End La	Hu	39	X 17
End View Av	Hu	13	H 22
Endo Rd	Hu	29	P 16
Endo Boulevard Ext	Nu	29	P 16
Engel St	Ou	28	T 13
Engineers Dr	Ou	38	W 15
Engineers Rd	Nu	18	L 9
Enid Ct	Hu	23	O 23
Enman Rd	Hu	24	L 25
Ennebrock Rd	Hu	30	S 18
Enness Av	Ou	46	Y 15
Enness St	Hu	30	Q 19
Enos St	Ou	41	V 23
Ensign Dr	Ou	48	Y 22
Ensign La	Ou	48	Y 22
Enter Library La	Ou	25	Q 2
Enterprise Pl	Ou	38	W 14
Entrance Rd	Nu	18	L 11
Entry La	Hu	39	W 17
Epic La	Nu	9	K 12
Equestrian Ct	Ou	27	Q 9
Ercell Dr	Hu	40	W 20
Eric Ct	Hu	39	W 19
Eric La	Nu	11	G 15
Eric La	Hu	30	R 18
Eric La (un)	Hu	30	Q 18
Erick Av	Hu	14	F 23
Erick Ct	Hu	31	U 22
Erie Av	Hu	7	D 28
Erie Dr	Ou	28	S 12
Erie Rd	Hu	13	K 20
Erlwein Ct	Ou	48	CC21
Erma Dr	Hu	29	S 16
Ernest Ct	Hu	39	U 17
Ernest St	Ou	47	AA 18
Ernst Av (hk)	Ou	37	V 14
Erwin Av	Ou	37	U 12
Erwin Pl	Hu	23	M 24
Eschol Av	Hu	31	R 20
Esposito Ct	Hu	30	S 18
Esquire Ct	Nu	10	H 13
Essen Pl	Ou	46	Y 16
Essex Ct	Nu	9	H 9
Essex Ct	Hu	13	K 20
Essex Ct (bw)	Nu	23	N 23
Essex Ct	Hu	31	P 21
Essex La (RC)	Ou	38	V 14
Essex La	Hu	39	V 17
Essex Pl	Hu	5	D 20
Essex Pl	Ou	28	T 12
Essex Rd	Nu	2	D 10
Essex Rd	Hu	4	E 18
Essex Rd	Hu	40	V 20
Essex Rd (hk)	Ou	37	X 12
Essex Rd (bp)	Ou	37	X 13
Estate Ct	Ou	44	Y 10
Estate Dr	Ou	28	R 12
Estates Dr	Nu	18	N 10
Estates Ter N	Nu	10	J 12
Estates Ter S	Nu	10	J 12
Estella La	Hu	21	P 19
Estella St	Hu	40	X 21
Estelle Av	Hu	12	F 18
Estelle Ct	Hu	39	X 19
Esther Pl	Hu	23	M 23
Esther St	Hu	12	H 18
Ethel St	Hu	5	E 20
Ethel T. Kloberg Dr	Hu	22	O 21
Eton Ct (pv)	Ou	45	AA 12
Eton Ct	Ou	47	Z 18
Eton Crest	Ou	13	U 13
Eton La	Ou	37	W 14
Eton Pl	Hu	21	L 18
Eton Pl	Ou	37	Y 13
Eton Rd	Nu	18	N 11
Eton Rd (WG)	Hu	6	E 24
Eton Rd (GA)	Hu	12	K 17
Eton Rd (fs)	Hu	12	J 19
Eton Rd (RC)	Hu	22	M 20
Eton St	Hu	14	F 22
Etta Pl	Hu	13	J 22
Euclid Av	Hu	12	J 19
Euclid Av (MS)	Ou	47	BB 19
Euclid Av	Ou	47	Y 20
Eureka Av	Hu	12	G 19
Euston La	Hu	39	V 17
Euston Rd (GA)	Hu	12	K 17
Euston Rd N	Hu	30	R 19
Euston Rd S	Hu	30	R 19
Eva Ct	Hu	22	O 20
Eva Dr	Hu	24	M 28
Eva La	Ou	45	Y 11
Evans Av (fs)	Hu	12	G 18
Evans Av	Nu	10	K 13
Evans Av (HV)	Hu	21	M 19
Evans Av (os)	Hu	14	K 24
Evans Av (FR)	Hu	22	P 21
Evans Av	Ou	46	BB17
Evans Ct	Hu	40	X 21
Evans Dr (Pvt)	Ou	27	R 10
Evans Pl	Hu	31	T 20
Evans Rd	Hu	23	N 23
Evans St	Ou	46	Z 16
Evans St	Nu	11	G 15
Evans St	Hu	14	J 24
Evans St E	Hu	14	J 24
Eve Dr	Ou	47	CC18
Eve Dr	Hu	39	X 19
Eve La	Hu	39	X 17
Evelyn Av	Nu	20	P 15
Evelyn Av	Hu	39	U 18
Evelyn Ct	Hu	12	L 19
Evelyn Ct (hk)	Ou	37	X 12
Evelyn Ct (MS)	Ou	47	CC18
Evelyn Dr (hk)	Ou	37	W 12
Evelyn Dr (bp)	Ou	45	Z 14
Evelyn La	Ou	36	X 10
Evelyn Rd (pw)	Nu	8	G 8
Evelyn Rd (MI)	Nu	20	M 14
Evelyn Rd	Ou	37	X 13
Everdell Rd	Hu	14	J 24
Everett Ct	Hu	22	N 20
Everett Pl	Hu	30	S 18
Everett St	Hu	14	H 22
Evergreen Av (pw)	Nu	9	G 8
Evergreen Av (NP)	Nu	11	H 15
Evergreen Av (LY)	Hu	13	H 22
Evergreen Av (ER)	Hu	14	K 23
Evergreen Av (ed)	Hu	30	R 17
Evergreen Av	Ou	37	V 14
Evergreen Cir	Nu	10	J 12
Evergreen Dr	Hu	13	J 20
Evergreen Dr	Nu	19	P 13
Evergreen Dr	Ou	36	X 10
Evergreen La	Nu	11	G 15
Evergreen La	Hu	30	R 18
Everit Av	Hu	14	F 23
Everit Pl	Hu	14	H 24
Everitt St	Hu	5	E 20
Everly Pl	Hu	40	U 21
Evers La	Hu	23	M 23
Evers St	Ou	29	T 14
Evon Dr	Ou	37	X 11
Eweler Av	Hu	12	G 17
Ewell Pl	Hu	40	V 20
Executive Dr	Nu	10	G 14
Executive Dr	Hu	44	Z 11
Exeter Av	Hu	13	K 22
Exeter La	Nu	2	F 11
Exeter Pl	Hu	17	M 7
Exeter Rd	Hu	14	H 23
Exeter Rd	Ou	48	AA 22
Exeter St	Nu	10	L 14
Exeter St	Hu	22	N 20
Exford Pl	Nu	19	L 13
Exit La	Hu	39	X 17
Express St	Ou	45	Z 12
Eyre La	Ou	17	P 5
Eyre Pl	Hu	31	T 20

F

STREET	MUN.	MAP	GRID
F St	Hu	12	G 19
Factory Pond Rd	Ou	25	Q 3
Fair Ct	Hu	20	M 15
Fair La	Ou	37	V 11
Fair Oaks Pl	Hu	6	D 25
Fairbanks Blvd	Ou	44	Z 10
Fairbanks Ct	Ou	44	Z 10
Fairchild Av	Ou	44	Z 11
Fairchild Ct	Ou	44	AA 11
Fairfax Rd	Ou	48	AA 22
Fairfax St (VS)	Hu	5	E 21
Fairfax St	Hu	4	F 18
Fairfield Av (SP)	Nu	8	G 6
Fairfield Av	Ou	20	M 15
Fairfield Av	Hu	29	R 15
Fairfield Av	Hu	11	F 15
Fairfield La	Hu	18	L 11
Fairfield Rd	Nu	2	D 9
Fairfield Rd	Ou	48	Z 21
Fairfield Rd	Hu	6	F 22
Fairhaven Blvd	Ou	36	X 9
Fairhaven Rd	Hu	30	S 17
Fairlawn Av	Hu	12	K 18
Fairmont Pl	Hu	17	N 6
Fairmont Blvd	Hu	12	H 17
Fairmount St	Hu	5	E 20
Fairmount St	Nu	18	L 11
Fairview Av (GN)	Nu	2	D 10
Fairview Av (pw)	Nu	9	H 9
Fairview Av (VS)	Hu	6	E 22
Fairview Av (EW)	Nu	19	M 14
Fairview Av (os)	Hu	23	L 23
Fairview Av (bw)	Hu	23	N 23
Fairview Av (sl)	Hu	29	R 15
Fairview Av (ed)	Hu	30	T 17
Fairview Blvd	Hu	21	O 17
Fairview Ct (hk)	Ou	38	V 15
Fairview Ct	Ou	44	Z 9
Fairview Dr	Nu	10	J 12
Fairview La (GL)	Ou	8	K 5
Fairview La (MN)	Ou	26	T 5
Fairview La (pv)	Ou	45	Y 13
Fairview La	Ou	17	L 6
Fairview Pl	Hu	32	P 24
Fairview Rd (MN)	Ou	26	T 5
Fairview Rd (FG)	Ou	46	AA 15
Fairview Rd (MS)	Ou	48	AA 22
Fairview Rd W	Ou	48	Z 22
Fairwater Av	Ou	48	BB 22
Fairway Cir N	Nu	10	H 12
Fairway Cir S	Nu	10	H 12
Fairway Ct	Nu	18	M 9
Fairway Ct	Ou	26	S 7
Fairway Dr (LS)	Nu	3	F 13
Fairway Dr (NL)	Hu	11	H 12
Fairway Dr (wm)	Hu	6	E 23
Fairway Dr (in)	Hu	6	B 25
Fairway Dr (fs)	Hu	12	J 17
Fairway Dr (wh)	Hu	21	L 18
Fairway Dr	Ou	45	AA 13
Fairway La	Nu	10	H 11
Fairway Rd (ML)	Hu	13	H 20
Fairway Rd	Nu	18	L 9
Fairway Rd	Hu	23	M 24
Fairway Rd (ld)	Hu	24	M 27
Faith La	Hu	29	T 15
Falcon Ct	Nu	10	J 12
Falcon La	Nu	38	U 15
Falcon Rd	Nu	18	N 10
Falcon St	Ou	37	V 11
Falcon St	Nu	30	T 18
Fall Av	Hu	21	P 19
Fall La	Ou	37	V 11
Faller St	Hu	14	K 24
Fallon Av	Hu	4	F 19
Fallon Ct	Hu	4	F 19
Fallwood Ct	Hu	40	U 20
Fallwood Pkwy	Ou	46	AA 17
Falmouth La	Nu	11	H 15
Falmouth La	Ou	17	M 7
Falmouth Pl	Nu	19	L 13
Family La	Hu	38	V 15
Fams Ct (je)	Ou	28	S 12
Fams Ct (ed)	Hu	30	S 18
Fams Ct (MT)	Ou	36	W 9
Fams Ct (ob)	Ou	45	Z 14
Fams Ct (lv)	Hu	39	W 17
Fams Dr	Ou	45	Z 13
Fanwood Av	Hu	6	D 22
Fargo St	Hu	22	O 21
Farm Ct	Ou	36	V 8
Farm Hill La	Ou	36	U 8
Farm La (TM)	Nu	3	E 12
Farm La (EW)	Nu	19	M 13
Farm La	Ou	38	V 14
Farm La	Hu	39	V 17
Farm View Rd	Nu	9	J 10
Farm, The (Pvt)	Ou	16	P 3
Farmedge Rd	Hu	38	W 16
Farmedge R (lv)	Hu	38	W 16
Farmedge Rd	Hu	38	X 15
Farmers Av	Hu	31	T 21
Farmers Av	Ou	37	Y 14
Farmers Rd	Nu	2	C 9
Farmranch Rd E	Hu	38	X 16
Farmranch Rd S	Hu	38	W 16
Farmranch Rd W	Hu	38	W 16
Farmstead La	Ou	27	R 10
Farmwoods La	Ou	27	Q 8
Farnum Blvd (fs)	Hu	12	H 17
Farnum Blvd (fs)	Hu	12	H 18
Farnum St	Hu	14	H 22
Farragut Rd	Hu	31	R 22
Farragut Rd	Ou	45	AA13
Farrel St	Nu	10	J 14
Farrell Ct	Hu	31	T 22
Farrell St	Hu	24	L 27
Farrell Wy (Pvt)	Ou	37	V 13
Farrington Rd	Hu	14	K 23
Farview Av	Ou	25	S 2
Favorite La	Ou	37	V 11
Fawn La	Hu	29	S 15
Faye Ct	Hu	31	T 20
Faye Ct	Ou	45	Y 11
Faye La	Hu	40	W 20
Fayette Pl	Nu	3	D 13
Fayette St	Hu	21	P 18
Feather La	Nu	19	M 14
Feeks La	Ou	25	Q 4
Felice Cres	Ou	38	V 14
Felice La	Ou	45	Z 13
Felicia Ct	Ou	45	Z 13
Felix Ct	Hu	22	O 22
Felms Ct	Ou	45	Y 14
Felter Av	Hu	6	F 23
Felton Av	Hu	5	F 21
Fen Ct	Ou	36	X 9

STREET	MUN.	MAP	GRID
Fen Wy	Hu	23 N	23
Fen Wy	Ou	36 X	9
Fen Way N	Hu	23 N	23
Fence La	Hu	38 V	16
Fendale St	Hu	12 J	19
Fenimore Av (NP)	Hu	11 H	16
Fenimore Av	Hu	21 P	17
Fenimore Pl	Hu	22 O	20
Fenimore Rd	Nu	9 G	9
Fenimore Rd	Hu	14 G	23
Fenimore St (ML)	Hu	13 H	21
Fenimore St	Hu	40 U	20
Fenton Pl	Hu	14 H	23
Fenway	Hu	22 N	22
Fenway St	Hu	9 K	11
Fenwood Dr	Hu	5 E	20
Fenworth Blvd	Hu	12 H	18
Fern Ct	Ou	37 W	13
Fern Dr	Hu	18 M	11
Fern Dr	Ou	47 Z	19
Fern Dr E	Ou	37 U	11
Fern Dr W	Ou	37 U	11
Fern Pl (pv)	Ou	37 X	13
Fern Pl (bp)	Ou	38 X	16
Fern St (FP)	Hu	12 G	17
Fern St	Hu	22 N	20
Fern St	Ou	37 V	11
Fern Wood La	Nu	9 K	10
Ferncote La	Ou	27 S	9
Ferncroft Rd	Nu	11 L	14
Ferndale Dr	Ou	38 W	14
Ferndale Dr	Ou	39 X	18
Ferney St	Ou	38 W	14
Ferngate Dr	Hu	12 H	19
Fernwood Ter	Hu	12 H	17
Fernwood Ter N	Hu	12 H	17
Ferris Rd	Hu	39 X	17
Ferth Ct	Hu	30 S	19
Fiddler La	Hu	38 W	15
Field Av	Ou	37 W	13
Field Ct	Ou	37 W	13
Field La	Nu	19 M	12
Field La	Hu	29 S	15
Field La (wn)	Hu	40 X	19
Field Pl	Hu	23 O	23
Fieldcrest La	Ou	46 Z	16
Fieldmere St	Hu	4 E	18
Fieldston St	Nu	29 R	14
Field-Stone Dr	Ou	36 W	10
Fieldstone La	Nu	3 E	13
Fieldstone La	Hu	5 E	22
Fieldstone La	Ou	35 U	5
Fiesta Ct	Hu	6 F	23
Fiesta Dr	Nu	10 K	13
Filbert St (VS)	Hu	14 F	22
Filbert St	Hu	21 M	17
Fillmore Rd	Hu	30 R	18
Fillmore St	Hu	22 O	21
Fillmore St	Ou	47 AA	19
Filmore Pl	Hu	32 R	23
Finch Ct	Ou	48 AA	22
Finch Dr	Nu	18 N	10
Finch La	Hu	5 E	20
Finn St	Hu	5 E	20
Finnin Pl	Ou	25 R	2
Finucane Pl	Hu	14 F	24
Fir Ct	Hu	30 T	18
Fir Dr (KP)	Nu	2 D	9
Fir Dr (EH)	Nu	18 M	10
Fir Dr (hr)	Nu	10 J	14
Fir La	Hu	6 E	24
Fir Pl	Hu	23 N	24
Fir St (VS)	Hu	5 D	21
Fir St (VS)	Hu	5 E	21
Fir St (WB)	Nu	19 P	14
Fir St (wn)	Hu	40 W	21
Fire Thorne Dr	Hu	7 E	25
Firemen's Memorial Dr	Hu	23 M	24
Fireplace La	Ou	38 V	15
Firestone Cir	Nu	10 H	13
Firethorne Ct	Ou	48 AA	21
Firethorne La	Hu	5 E	22
Firma La	Hu	39 U	18
Firtree La	Hu	38 V	15
Firwood Rd	Nu	1 E	7
Fish Av	Nu	19 L	13
Fish Av (ne)	Hu	31 S	20
Fish Av	Hu	31 T	20
Fisher Av (un)	Hu	21 P	19
Fisher La	Hu	31 S	21
Fisher La (hk)	Hu	38 V	15
Fisher La	Hu	40 U	22
Fishermans Dr	Nu	1 F	7
Fishermens Rd	Hu	23 N	24
Fisk Pl	Ou	48 Y	22
Fiske La	Hu	21 O	19
Fiske St	Hu	6 E	24
Fitzmaurice St	Ou	47 AA	20
Fitzroy Pl	Hu	15 K	27
Flag La	Nu	10 H	14
Flagstaff Pl	Hu	22 M	22
Flagstone La	Hu	29 T	15
Flamingo La	Ou	45 Y	14
Flamingo Rd	Nu	18 N	10
Flamingo Rd	Hu	38 U	15
Flamingo Rd N	Nu	18 N	10
Flamingo St	Hu	7 C	27
Flanders Dr	Hu	6 D	23
Flax La	Hu	39 W	17
Fleet Pl	Nu	20 L	15
Fletcher Av	Hu	13 F	21
Flint Av	Hu	21 O	19
Flint La	Ou	37 V	12
Flint La	Hu	39 W	18
Flint Pl	Hu	4 F	19
Flint Rd	Hu	14 J	23
Flo Dr	Ou	36 W	9
Flock La	Hu	38 V	16
Flora La	Hu	29 T	16
Floral Av	Ou	37 X	13
Floral Blvd	Hu	4 E	17
Floral Dr E	Ou	45 Y	12
Floral Dr W	Ou	37 X	12
Floral La	Nu	28 S	13
Floral Park Rd	Hu	12 J	17
Floral Pkwy	Hu	11 F	17
Floral Pl	Hu	40 U	20
Floral Pl	Ou	38 Y	14
Florence Av (SC)	Ou	17 L	7
Florence Av (HV)	Hu	21 O	18
Florence Av (MN)	Ou	35 U	5
Florence Av (bh)	Hu	23 P	24
Florence Av (lg)	Ou	36 W	10
Florence Av (mq)	Ou	48 Y	22
Florence Ct	Hu	29 S	16
Florence Dr	Ou	36 W	10
Florence La	Ou	45 Z	12
Florence Pl	Hu	31 T	21
Florence Rd (se)	Nu	2 C	11
Florence Rd (MI)	Nu	11 K	15
Florence Rd	Ou	46 Y	17
Florence St (FP)	Hu	4 F	16
Florence St (bw)	Hu	22 O	22
Florence St (mr)	Hu	32 S	23
Florgate Rd	Ou	46 Z	16
Florida Av	Hu	15 L	25
Florida St	Hu	15 G	28
Florin Ct	Hu	41 U	22
Flower Av	Hu	11 F	16
Flower Dr	Ou	37 X	13
Flower La (GN)	Nu	2 B	10
Flower La (st)	Nu	10 H	11
Flower La (NP)	Nu	11 G	15
Flower La (GL)	Ou	16 M	4
Flower La (al)	Nu	19 L	12
Flower La (je)	Ou	37 U	11
Flower La (nw)	Hu	39 W	19
Flower La (nw)	Hu	39 X	19
Flower Rd	Hu	6 E	22
Flower Rd (WB)	Nu	20 N	15
Flower Rd	Ou	47 Y	19
Flower St (HV)	Hu	22 M	19
Flower St	Nu	29 S	14
Flower St (hk)	Ou	29 U	14
Flower St	Ou	37 X	13
Flowerdale Dr	Ou	47 Y	18
Flowerhill Av	Nu	9 G	8
Floyd La	Ou	47 BB	21
Floyd Pl	Nu	2 D	10
Floyd Pl	Ou	26 U	7
Foch Blvd	Nu	10 K	14
Folie Ct	Nu	10 H	12
Fonda Rd	Hu	22 M	21
Foran Pl	Ou	37 U	13
Forbes Pl	Hu	23 P	23
Ford Dr N	Ou	47 CC	19
Ford Dr S	Ou	47 CC	19
Ford Dr W	Ou	47 CC	19
Ford Pl	Nu	1 E	7
Ford St	Ou	17 N	5
Fordham Av	Ou	28 U	14
Fordham Ct	Hu	6 E	23
Fordham Dr	Ou	37 Y	11
Fordham Pl	Hu	6 E	23
Fordham Pl	Hu	21 O	18
Fordham Rd	Ou	38 W	14
Fordham St	Hu	6 F	23
Fordham St	Nu	10 L	14
Foreman Pl	Hu	31 S	21
Forest Av (TM)	Nu	2 E	11
Forest Av (WG)	Hu	6 E	24
Forest Av (VS)	Hu	13 G	22
Forest Av (GL)	Ou	17 M	5
Forest Av (bw)	Hu	22 O	20
Forest Av (LY)	Hu	13 J	22
Forest Av (ed)	Ou	30 T	17
Forest Av (FR)	Hu	31 P	21
Forest Av (mq)	Ou	47 Y	20
Forest Ct	Ou	35 X	7
Forest Dr (SP)	Nu	8 G	7
Forest Dr (RL)	Nu	18 L	10
Forest Dr (je)	Ou	37 U	11
Forest Dr	Ou	37 X	13
Forest Lake Blvd	Hu	40 V	20
Forest La	Nu	2 D	10
Forest La (LW)	Hu	7 C	26
Forest La (sl)	Hu	29 S	15
Forest La (bm)	Hu	31 T	21
Forest Pl	Ou	16 N	5
Forest Pl (lk)	Hu	12 L	19
Forest Pl (RC)	Hu	22 M	22
Forest Rd (VS)	Hu	5 E	22
Forest ROW	Nu	2 D	10
Forest St	Nu	10 L	11
Forest St	Hu	23 M	24
Forest St	Ou	25 R	2
Forest Tr	Ou	17 M	6
Forest Turn	Nu	10 H	11
Forestdale Rd	Hu	22 M	21
Forester La	Hu	38 W	15
Forester St	Ou	24 L	27
Forge La	Hu	39 W	17
Fork La	Ou	38 U	15
Forsythia La	Ou	37 V	11
Fort Hamilton Av	Hu	15 K	26
Forte Av	Ou	45 AA	13
Forte Blvd	Hu	12 J	19
Forte Dr	Nu	19 N	12
Fortesque Av	Ou	38 Y	23
Fortesque Gate	Ou	47 CC	18
Fortune Ct	Nu	39 W	19
Fortune La	Ou	37 V	11
Foster Av (VS)	Hu	5 E	20
Foster Av	Hu	13 H	21
Foster Ct	Nu	30 T	19
Foster La	Hu	29 T	15
Foster Pl	Ou	8 K	6
Foster Pl (HV)	Hu	21 O	18
Foster Pl	Hu	23 N	23
Foster St	Hu	12 H	18
Fountain Av	Nu	22 L	20
Fountain La	Ou	37 V	11
Fountain St	Ou	37 V	13
Fowler Av (fs)	Hu	12 H	19
Fowler Av	Hu	13 H	22
Fowler St	Hu	31 T	20
Fox Av	Nu	22 N	22
Fox Blvd	Hu	31 T	21
Fox Blvd	Ou	48 Z	21
Fox Ct (hk)	Ou	38 U	15
Fox Ct	Hu	31 R	20
Fox Ct (OC)	Ou	36 X	7
Fox Hill Dr	Ou	44 Y	9
Foxboro La	Ou	18 N	8
Foxcroft Rd (st)	Nu	9 H	11
Foxcroft Rd (se)	Nu	19 L	13
Foxcroft Rd (lk)	Hu	22 L	20
Foxdale Rd	Hu	23 M	22
Foxfield La	Ou	35 V	6
Foxglove Rd	Hu	30 S	19
Foxhunt Cres E	Ou	35 X	7
Foxhunt Cres N	Ou	35 W	7
Foxhunt Cres S	Ou	35 X	7
Foxhurst Av	Hu	23 N	23
Foxhurst La	Nu	10 H	14
Foxhurst La	Nu	9 G	11
Foxhurst Rd	Hu	23 M	23
Foxmount Farm	Nu	28 Q	12
Foxwood Dr	Ou	28 T	11
Foxwood Pa	Ou	16 O	4
Foxwood St	Ou	45 AA	13
Foxwood Twin Ponds	Nu	2 D	9
Frame St	Hu	12 J	18
Frances Ct	Hu	29 T	15
Frances Dr	Hu	13 H	20
Frances Dr	Ou	36 U	9
Frances Dr	Ou	28 R	13
Frances La (hk)	Ou	37 W	13
Frances La	Hu	48 BB	21
Frances St	Hu	41 V	23
Francesca Dr	Ou	35 U	6
Francine Av	Hu	22 N	21
Francine Dr N	Ou	47 CC	19
Francis Av	Hu	22 N	21
Francis Ct	Hu	12 G	18
Francis Ct	Ou	17 O	6
Francis Dr	Nu	8 G	7
Francis Dr	Hu	30 R	17
Francis Dr (ln)	Hu	39 U	18
Francis St	Hu	13 J	20
Francis Ter	Ou	17 N	5
Frank Av	Nu	19 M	14
Frank Av	Ou	37 V	12
Frank Av	Hu	31 T	21
Frank Av (sa)	Ou	46 BB	17
Frank Ct	Ou	47 Y	19
Frank Rd	Ou	29 T	14
Frank St (VS)	Hu	5 E	20
Frank St	Hu	14 K	24
Frankel Av	Hu	23 P	23
Frankel Blvd	Hu	31 T	21
Frankel Rd	Ou	48 Z	21
Frankie La	Ou	45 AA	14
Franklin Av (pw)	Nu	9 G	8
Franklin Av (NP)	Nu	11 G	15
Franklin Av (fs)	Hu	13 H	19
Franklin Av (WG)	Hu	6 F	23
Franklin Av (LY)	Hu	14 H	23
Franklin Av (SC)	Ou	17 L	7
Franklin Av (GL)	Ou	17 N	5
Franklin Av (MI)	Nu	20 L	15
Franklin Av (fs)	Hu	12 H	19
Franklin Av (hi)	Nu	15 J	26
Franklin Av (BY)	Ou	25 S	2
Franklin Av (ed)	Ou	30 R	17
Franklin Av (wn)	Hu	40 X	20
Franklin Av S	Ou	47 Z	19
Franklin Blvd	Hu	15 K	28
Franklin Ct	Ou	37 U	12
Franklin Ct E	Hu	21 M	17
Franklin Ct W	Hu	21 M	17
Franklin Gate	Hu	12 H	19
Franklin Pl (GN)	Nu	2 D	10
Franklin Pl (WG)	Hu	6 F	24
Franklin Pl (fs)	Hu	12 J	17
Franklin Pl (os)	Hu	23 M	23
Franklin Pl (FG)	Ou	46 BB	16
Franklin Pl (mq)	Ou	48 Y	22
Franklin Rd	Nu	2 D	10
Franklin Rd	Hu	5 E	20
Franklin Sq	Hu	32 Q	22
Franklin St (fs)	Hu	12 J	18
Franklin St (el)	Hu	4 F	18
Franklin St (WP)	Nu	10 L	14
Franklin St (ER)	Hu	14 J	23
Franklin St (os)	Hu	14 K	24
Franklin St (MS)	Nu	28 Q	13
Franklin St (hk)	Ou	37 U	13
Franklin St (MS)	Ou	47 BB	19
Franklin St (wn)	Hu	40 W	20
Frantone Ct	Hu	12 L	19
Fraser Av	Hu	31 R	20
Fraser Pl	Hu	6 F	22
Frazier St	Hu	21 N	19
Frederick (FP)	Hu	12 F	18
Frederick Av (rv)	Hu	31 Q	20
Frederick Av (mr)	Hu	31 R	21
Frederick Av (mr)	Hu	31 S	21
Frederick Av (bm)	Hu	40 U	21
Frederick Av (FR)	Hu	31 Q	21
Frederick Ct	Hu	31 U	22
Frederick Dr	Ou	45 Y	13
Frederick Pl	Hu	14 G	22
Frederick Pl	Hu	23 N	24
Frederick St	Ou	37 U	13

Nassau Co.

STREET	MUN.	MAP	GRID
Freedom Dr	Ou	37 V	11
Freeman Av (el)	Hu	4 E	19
Freeman Av (os)	Hu	23 N	24
Freeman Av (ed)	Hu	30 S	17
Freeman Av (bm)	Hu	31 T	21
Freeport Av (pl)	Hu	33 Q	27
Freeport Plz E	Hu	31 P	22
Freeport Plz N	Hu	31 Q	22
Freeport Plz W	Hu	31 P	22
Freeport St	Hu	40 V	22
Freer St	Hu	13 H	22
Fremont Rd	Hu	14 G	22
French St	Ou	26 R	4
Fresno Dr	Ou	45 Z	13
Frevert Pl	Ou	37 V	13
Frey Rd	Ou	46 Z	17
Frick St	Hu	5 E	19
Frieda La	Hu	39 W	19
Friendly La	Ou	37 V	11
Friendly Rd (UB)	Ou	26 R	7
Friendly Rd	Ou	38 V	15
Friends La (sl)	Hu	29 S	15
Friends La	Hu	29 T	16
Frisch Pl	Hu	31 T	19
Fritchie Pl	Hu	5 E	20
Frochan Ct	Hu	14 F	24
Froehlich Farm Blvd	Ou	44 Y	10
Froehlich Farm Rd	Ou	37 W	13
Froelich Pl	Hu	4 E	19
Front St (MI)	Nu	20 L	15
Front St (HV)	Hu	21 N	18
Front St (HV)	Hu	21 M	18
Front St (ER)	Hu	14 K	23
Front St (RC)	Hu	13 L	22
Front St (ed)	Hu	30 Q	17
Front St (FR)	Hu	32 P	23
Front St (bm)	Hu	31 U	22
Front St (MS)	Ou	47 AA	20
Frost Creek Dr	Ou	16 O	2
Frost La (WG)	Hu	6 F	24
Frost La	Hu	6 D	25
Frost Mill Rd	Ou	26 R	5
Frost Pond	Nu	10 J	13
Frost Pond Rd	Ou	26 P	6
Frost St	Nu	29 S	14
Fruitledge Rd	Ou	27 S	10
Fuchia La	Ou	37 W	12
Fuller Av	Hu	11 G	16
Fullerton Av	Hu	21 P	19
Fulton Av (AB)	Hu	7 D	28
Fulton Av (GA)	Nu	11 J	16
Fulton Av (HV)	Hu	21 M	18
Fulton Av (os)	Hu	23 L	24
Fulton Av (eg)	Hu	21 O	17
Fulton Av (wn)	Hu	40 X	20
Fulton Pl	Hu	5 D	21
Fulton Pl	Ou	28 T	12
Fulton St (VS)	Hu	13 F	20
Fulton St (WG)	Hu	14 F	24
Fulton St (in)	Hu	7 C	25
Fulton St (WB)	Nu	29 P	14
Fulton St (FG)	Ou	46 AA	16
Fulton St (MS)	Ou	47 AA	20
Fulton St E	Hu	14 J	24
Fulton St W	Hu	14 J	24
Funston Av	Nu	10 K	13
Furman Pl	Ou	26 U	7
Furrow La	Hu	38 V	16
Furth Rd	Hu	5 E	22

G

STREET	MUN.	MAP	GRID
G St	Hu	12 G	19
Gabel Gate	Ou	45 AA	13
Gables Av	Hu	31 T	22
Gables Dr	Ou	37 W	13
Gables Rd	Ou	37 W	13
Gabriel Av (fs)	Hu	12 H	18
Gabriel Av	Hu	12 J	18
Gabriel Pl	Ou	17 N	6
Gabriele Dr	Ou	26 U	7
Gace Ct	Hu	40 U	22
Gaddis Pl	Hu	13 H	21
Gaffney Av	Ou	17 M	7
Gaffney Avenue Ext	Ou	17 M	7
Gail Ct	Hu	12 G	19
Gail Dr E	Ou	46 Y	17
Gail Dr N	Ou	46 Y	17
Gail Dr S	Ou	46 Y	17
Gail St	Hu	39 Y	19
Gail Ter	Ou	8 L	5
Gailview Dr	Ou	35 U	5
Gainsboro La (lg)	Ou	37 W	11
Gainsboro La	Ou	37 X	11
Gainsnlle Dr	Ou	37 Y	11
Gale Av	Hu	22 N	22
Gale Dr	Hu	6 E	23
Gallagher Ct	Nu	3 E	11
Galley St	Hu	30 Q	17
Gannet Ct	Nu	10 J	12
Garden Av	Nu	20 O	15
Garden Av	Ou	47 Y	18
Garden Blvd	Hu	12 K	17
Garden Blvd	Ou	38 V	14
Garden Cir	Ou	36 W	10
Garden City Av	Hu	33 Q	27
Garden City Blvd	Hu	12 K	18
Garden City Rd	Hu	12 J	17
Garden Ct (nn)	Nu	11 G	15
Garden Ct (gw)	Ou	18 M	8
Garden Ct (cp)	Nu	20 O	15
Garden Ct	Hu	39 X	19
Garden Dr	Hu	13 H	22
Garden Dr	Nu	10 K	13
Garden Dr (fs)	Hu	12 J	17
Garden Gate	Ou	37 X	13
Garden La (in)	Hu	6 C	24
Garden La	Hu	30 R	18
Garden Pl (GL)	Ou	17 K	5
Garden Pl	Hu	21 L	18
Garden Pl (HV)	Hu	21 M	17
Garden Pl (bw)	Hu	23 O	23
Garden Pl (je)	Ou	37 U	10
Garden Pl (mr)	Hu	31 R	21
Garden Pl (wn)	Hu	39 X	19
Garden St (TM)	Nu	3 E	11
Garden St (VS)	Hu	6 F	22
Garden St (RL)	Nu	10 K	11
Garden St (GA)	Hu	21 M	17
Garden St (wh)	Hu	12 L	19
Garden St (os)	Hu	23 M	24
Garden St (BY)	Ou	25 R	2
Garden St (nc)	Nu	28 R	13
Garden St (ed)	Hu	30 R	18
Garden St (bm)	Hu	31 U	22
Garden St (hk)	Ou	37 W	12
Garden Turn	Nu	10 H	11
Gardenia Av	Hu	31 R	20
Gardenia La	Hu	38 V	16
Gardenia La	Ou	37 W	12
Gardenia St	Hu	12 K	19
Gardiners Av	Hu	39 V	17
Gardner Av	Ou	28 T	12
Garfield Av (FP)	Hu	4 F	16
Garfield Av	Hu	5 D	20
Garfield Av (RH)	Ou	18 M	9
Garfield Av (MI)	Nu	11 K	15
Garfield Av (wh)	Hu	12 K	18
Garfield Av (FG)	Ou	46 AA	16
Garfield Pl (rt)	Nu	10 K	12
Garfield Pl (HV)	Hu	21 N	19
Garfield Pl (ER)	Hu	14 K	22
Garfield Pl (mq)	Ou	48 Y	22
Garfield Rd (bw)	Hu	22 N	20
Garfield Rd	Hu	30 Q	18
Garfield St (fs)	Hu	12 H	17
Garfield St (fs)	Hu	12 J	18
Garfield St (rv)	Hu	31 S	20
Garfield St (ne)	Hu	31 T	20
Garfield St (FR)	Hu	32 Q	23
Garfield St (MS)	Ou	47 AA	19
Garland La	Hu	5 E	22
Garland La	Nu	28 S	13
Garner Pl	Hu	30 R	18
Garnet La	Ou	45 Y	12
Garnet Pl	Hu	4 E	19
Garry Av	Hu	24 O	27
Garson Rd	Nu	19 N	14
Garvies Point Rd	Ou	17 L	6
Gary La (bm)	Hu	41 U	23
Gary La	Hu	40 X	22
Gary Pl	Nu	28 R	13
Gary Pl	Ou	45 Z	12
Gary Rd	Ou	37 W	11
Gary St	Hu	30 R	18
Garynson Ct	Ou	37 X	13
Gaston St	Hu	39 X	19
Gatch Av	Hu	31 S	20
Gate Ct	Ou	37 W	13
Gate La	Hu	29 T	15
Gate Pl	Hu	38 X	16
Gate So	Hu	11 K	16
Gate Wy	Hu	39 U	18
Gate Wy	Ou	47 CC	18
Gate, The	Nu	9 H	11
Gates Av (VS)	Hu	5 F	20
Gates Av (LY)	Hu	13 H	21
Gates Av (ed)	Hu	30 R	17
Gates Av (pv)	Ou	37 X	13
Gates St	Hu	7 B	25
Gates Wy	Ou	17 L	7
Gateway	Nu	19 L	12
Gateway	Hu	22 N	22
Gateway	Ou	46 Y	15
Gateway Ct	Ou	25 S	2
Gateway Dr	Nu	3 D	11
Gateway Dr	Ou	37 X	11
Gatsby La	Nu	1 B	8
Gavrin Blvd	Hu	12 H	19
Gay Dr	Nu	2 C	9
Gaynor Av	Nu	9 F	11
Gaynor Pl	Hu	12 J	19
Gebhardt Plz	Ou	37 V	13
Gehrig Av	Hu	12 H	19
Gem Ct	Ou	38 V	15
Gem La	Ou	48 CC	21
Gene La	Hu	4 F	19
General Pl	Ou	28 R	12
Genesee Blvd	Hu	7 D	28
Genesee St	Ou	29 U	14
Genesee St	Hu	40 U	20
Genevieve Ct	Hu	30 U	19
Genevieve Pl	Nu	3 D	12
Geoffrey Av	Ou	36 W	9
Geoffrey La	Ou	17 N	6
Geofrey Av	Hu	20 O	16
George Av (LY)	Hu	22 P	19
George Av	Ou	38 V	14
George Av	Hu	21 P	19
George Ct	Hu	32 S	23
George Pl	Nu	2 C	10
George Pl	Hu	14 J	23
George Pl (os)	Hu	23 M	24
George Rd	Hu	30 U	19
George Rd (wn)	Hu	40 W	20
George St (ma)	Nu	9 G	11
George St (in)	Hu	7 C	25
George St (BY)	Ou	25 Q	2
George St (GL)	Ou	8 L	5
George St (OW)	Nu	19 N	11
George St (os)	Hu	23 M	23
Georgia Av (LB)	Hu	15 G	28
Georgia Av	Hu	15 L	25
Georgia Dr	Ou	36 W	10
Georgia La	Ou	45 Y	12
Georgia St (VS)	Hu	5 E	20
Georgia St	Hu	22 N	20
Georgia St	Ou	28 T	13
Georgian Ct (EH)	Nu	18 N	10
Georgian Ct	Nu	10 K	13
Georgian La	Nu	2 B	10
Gerald Av (ed)	Hu	30 R	17
Gerald Av (FR)	Hu	23 P	23
Gerald Av	Ou	38 W	14
Gerald Ct	Hu	40 U	20
Gerald La	Ou	45 BB	13
Gerald St	Hu	21 P	17
Geralind Dr	Ou	36 V	8
Geranium Av	Hu	4 F	17
Geranium Av	Nu	20 M	15
Gerard Av	Nu	11 G	14
Gerard Av E	Hu	13 J	20
Gerard Av W	Hu	13 J	20
Gerard St	Hu	23 L	23
Gerhard Rd	Ou	45 Y	13
Gerhard Rd E	Ou	45 Y	13
Gerken Pl	Hu	23 L	23
Germaine St	Ou	8 K	5
Gerose Ct	Hu	30 S	19
Gertmin Pl	Hu	6 F	24
Gertrude Pl	Nu	19 M	14
Gertrude St	Hu	21 O	17
Gervais St	Ou	17 L	5
Gianelli Av	Hu	31 R	21
Giant La	Hu	29 T	16
Gibson Blvd	Hu	14 F	23
Gifford Av	Hu	23 M	24
Gilbert Ct	Hu	12 G	17
Gilbert Ct	Ou	26 U	7
Gilbert La	Ou	45 Z	12
Gilbert Pl (wm)	Hu	6 D	23
Gilbert Pl	Hu	31 P	20
Gilbert Rd	Nu	2 C	10
Gilbert Rd E	Nu	2 C	10
Gilbert Rd W	Nu	2 C	10
Gilbert St	Hu	23 N	23
Gilchrest Rd	Nu	2 E	11
Gildersleeve St	Hu	31 R	21
Gildo Pl	Ou	45 Y	14
Gilford Av	Nu	11 H	15
Gill Av	Hu	31 R	21
Gilling Rd	Ou	39 X	17
Gilmar La	Nu	10 K	12
Gilmartin La	Hu	40 X	21
Gilmore Blvd	Hu	12 H	17
Gilmore St	Nu	11 K	14
Gilroy Av	Hu	30 P	17
Gina Ct	Hu	30 S	19
Gingham La	Hu	39 W	17
Ginny La	Ou	46 Y	17
Gintell St	Hu	23 M	24
Girard Pl	Hu	31 S	22
Glad More St	Hu	30 S	17
Glade La	Hu	39 V	17
Glade, The	Ou	36 X	10
Gladiolus Av	Hu	4 F	17
Gladys Av	Hu	21 N	18
Gladys La	Hu	32 R	23
Gladys Pl	Ou	37 V	12
Gladys St (sv)	Hu	5 E	22
Gladys St	Hu	14 K	25
Glafil St	Hu	4 E	19
Glamford Av	Nu	8 G	7
Glamford Rd	Nu	2 E	10
Glazer La	Hu	38 V	15
Gleaner La	Hu	38 W	15
Glen Av (SC)	Ou	17 L	7
Glen Av	Nu	9 K	11
Glen Av	Ou	18 M	8
Glen Ct	Hu	14 K	23
Glen Ct	Ou	36 X	9
Glen Cove	Ou	16 M	5
Glen Cove Av (GL)	Ou	17 M	6
Glen Cove Dr	Ou	17 N	7
Glen Cove Rd (gh)	Nu	18 M	10
Glen Cove Rd	Nu	20 N	14
Glen Cove Rd (Guinea Woods Rd)	Nu	19 N	12
Glen Curtiss Blvd	Hu	30 Q	17
Glen Dr (fs)	Hu	12 H	19
Glen Dr	Hu	6 E	24
Glen Dr	Ou	45 Z	13
Glen Head Rd	Ou	17 M	8
Glen Keith Rd	Ou	17 M	6
Glen La (PN)	Nu	8 G	7
Glen La (gh)	Ou	17 M	7
Glen La (gw)	Ou	9 L	8
Glen La	Hu	39 U	17
Glen La	Ou	43 Z	7
Glen Rd	Nu	1 E	5
Glen Rd	Hu	11 J	16
Glen Rd (lk)	Hu	13 K	20
Glen Rd	Ou	28 R	13
Glen Rd (wa)	Ou	48 BB	21
Glen St	Ou	17 M	5
Glen St (gw)	Ou	9 L	8
Glen Wy	Ou	36 X	9
Glen, The (gh)	Ou	17 N	7
Glen, The	Ou	26 Q	5
Glen, The (Pvt)	Ou	17 N	7
Glenada	Nu	9 J	11
Glenada Ct	Hu	32 Q	22
Glenbrook Rd	Ou	29 U	14
Glenby La	Ou	27 S	9
Glencove Av	Nu	19 N	14
Glendale Dr	Ou	17 M	6
Glendale Pl	Hu	5 E	20
Glengariff Dr	Ou	16 L	4
Glengariff Rd	Ou	47 Z	20
Glenlawn Av	Ou	17 L	7
Glenlawn Ct	Ou	17 L	7
Glenmare St	Hu	22 O	21
Glenmore Av	Ou	18 L	8
Glenmore Av	Hu	21 M	19
Glenmore Av	Hu	30 R	17
Glenmore St	Nu	19 L	14
Glenn Curtiss Cres	Hu	30 Q	17
Glenn Dr	Hu	41 U	23
Glenn Dr	Ou	44 Y	10
Glenn La	Hu	32 T	23
Glenn Rd	Hu	39 U	18
Glenndale Dr	Ou	35 W	6
Glenns Pl	Ou	18 M	8
Glenola Av	Ou	17 L	7
Glenridge Av	Hu	6 D	23
Glenwood Av (LY)	Hu	14 H	23
Glenwood Av	Hu	33 Q	27
Glenwood Ct	Hu	23 L	23
Glenwood Dr	Nu	3 C	11
Glenwood La	Nu	19 M	12

Nassau Co.

STREET	MUN.	MAP	GRID
Glenwood La	Hu	30 R	18
Glenwood Rd (gw)	Ou	9 L	8
Glenwood Rd (RH)	Nu	18 L	9
Glenwood Rd (lk)	Hu	13 K	20
Glenwood Rd (RC)	Hu	22 M	20
Glenwood Rd (wn)	Hu	39 V	19
Glenwood Rd	Ou	37 X	11
Globe Av	Hu	12 G	18
Gloria Dr	Hu	44 Y	10
Gloria Pl	Hu	12 J	17
Gloria Pl	Hu	45 Z	13
Gloria Rd (Pvt)	Hu	46 Y	17
Gloucester Ct	Nu	3 D	12
Gloucester Ct	Hu	29 Q	15
Gloucester Rd	Ou	48 AA	22
Glover Cir	Hu	13 J	22
Glover Pl	Hu	23 N	22
Glow La	Ou	29 T	15
Godfrey Av	Ou	25 R	2
Gold Cir (ML)	Hu	13 J	20
Gold Cir	Hu	22 O	21
Gold Coast Rd	Ou	18 P	9
Gold Pl	Hu	13 J	20
Gold St	Hu	5 D	21
Gold St (FR)	Hu	31 Q	22
Gold St (nw)	Hu	39 X	19
Goldcoast Ct	Ou	16 L	4
Golden Gate Rd	Ou	45 Z	13
Goldenrod Av	Hu	12 J	18
Goldie Av	Hu	40 U	20
Goldner Ct	Hu	5 E	20
Golf Club La	Hu	20 L	16
Golf Ct	Hu	6 D	23
Golf Ct (Pvt)	Ou	36 V	9
Golf Dr (wm)	Hu	6 D	23
Golf Dr	Hu	23 M	24
Golf La	Nu	3 F	13
Golf La	Hu	14 H	24
Golf View Dr	Ou	28 R	12
Golfwood Ct	Hu	6 C	25
Goliath Rd	Ou	47 Y	18
Gombert Dr	Hu	31 Q	20
Gombert Pl	Hu	31 Q	20
Goodrich St	Nu	10 L	14
Goodrich St	Hu	21 P	18
Goodwin Rd	Hu	4 D	19
Gordon Av	Nu	20 P	15
Gordon Av	Ou	45 Y	12
Gordon Blvd	Hu	12 H	17
Gordon Dr	Hu	10 K	14
Gordon Dr	Ou	36 V	10
Gordon Pl	Hu	32 Q	23
Gormley Av (ne)	Hu	31 Q	20
Gormley Av	Hu	31 R	21
Goroon Rd	Hu	13 G	22
Goshen St	Hu	5 F	20
Gosling Hill Dr	Nu	10 K	12
Gotham Av	Hu	4 E	18
Gotham St	Hu	6 F	23
Gould St (GN)	Nu	2 C	11
Gould St	Nu	11 J	15
Governors Ct	Nu	2 D	11
Governors La	Nu	1 F	6
Grace Av (KG)	Hu	3 D	11
Grace Av (TM)	Nu	3 E	11
Grace Av (LY)	Hu	13 J	21
Grace Av (bm)	Hu	31 T	21
Grace Ct N	Hu	3 E	11
Grace Ct W	Hu	3 E	11
Grace Dr	Hu	19 O	12
Grace La	Ou	35 V	6
Grace La	Hu	29 T	16
Grace St	Hu	23 N	23
Grace St	Ou	35 U	5
Grace St (pv)	Ou	45 Z	12
Gracefield Dr	Nu	2 E	10
Gracewood Ct	Ou	34 W	4
Gracewood Dr	Nu	10 J	12
Gracewood Dr (Pvt)	Nu	10 H	12
Grady Ct	Nu	2 C	10
Graffing Pl	Hu	31 Q	21
Graham Av	Hu	21 M	19
Graham St	Ou	46 AA	17
Gramercy Dr	Ou	37 U	11
Granada Pl	Ou	48 Z	13
Granada St	Hu	7 C	27
Grand Av (LY)	Hu	13 H	21
Grand Av (wh)	Hu	12 K	18
Grand Av (RC)	Hu	13 L	22
Grand Av (os)	Hu	23 N	24
Grand Av (hk)	Ou	37 V	14
Grand Av (bm)	Hu	31 T	21
Grand Av (FR)	Hu	31 Q	22
Grand Av (mr)	Hu	31 R	21
Grand Av (mq)	Ou	47 Z	20
Grand Av (Baldwin Rd)	Hu	22 N	20
Grand Blvd (LB)	Hu	15 H	28
Grand Blvd	Hu	23 O	23
Grand Blvd	Hu	29 Q	14
Grand Blvd	Ou	47 BB	20
Grand Central Pl	Hu	7 B	25
Grand St	Hu	12 G	18
Grand St	Nu	19 P	14
Grand St (nc)	Hu	28 R	13
Grand St	Ou	47 CC20	
Grand Terrace Av	Hu	22 N	20
Grandview Av	Nu	3 E	12
Grandview Cir	Nu	9 F	10
Grange La	Hu	29 T	16
Grange St	Hu	12 J	19
Granger Av	Hu	11 G	16
Grant Av (WG)	Hu	6 E	24
Grant Av (sg)	Nu	10 K	13
Grant Av (lk)	Hu	13 K	20
Grant Av (bw)	Hu	22 N	21
Grant Av (ER)	Hu	14 J	23
Grant Av (ed)	Hu	30 R	17
Grant Av (FR)	Ou	46 BB	16
Grant Av (bp)	Ou	46 Y	15
Grant Av (wn)	Hu	40 X	20
Grant Blvd	Hu	31 T	20
Grant Ct	Ou	28 U	14
Grant Dr N	Hu	13 F	20
Grant Pl (CH)	Hu	6 D	24
Grant Pl	Ou	16 M	5
Grant Pl (HV)	Hu	21 P	19
Grant Pl (ed)	Hu	30 S	18
Grant St (HV)	Hu	21 M	19
Grant St (WB)	Hu	29 Q	14
Grant St (rv)	Hu	31 Q	20
Grant St (FR)	Hu	32 Q	24
Grant St (sa)	Ou	47 CC18	
Grant St (bp)	Ou	46 Y	15
Grant St (MS)	Ou	47 AA	19
Grant St (FG)	Ou	47 BB	18
Grantland Av	Hu	12 K	19
Granz Ct	Hu	39 U	17
Grape La	Ou	29 T	15
Grass Field Rd	Nu	2 D	10
Grasslands, The	Ou	43 AA	8
Grassy La	Hu	38 V	16
Grattan St	Nu	10 J	14
Grayson Dr	Hu	39 U	18
Grayston St	Nu	29 R	14
Graywood Rd	Nu	1 E	7
Great Meadow Rd	Ou	16 O	3
Great Neck Rd	Nu	3 D	12
Great Oak Rd (st)	Nu	9 H	11
Great Oaks Rd	Nu	18 M	11
Greatwater Av	Ou	48 BB	22
Greely Ct	Ou	37 X	13
Greely Sq	Ou	18 M	9
Green Acre Ct	Nu	2 D	11
Green Acres Rd E	Hu	5 E	22
Green Acres Rd W	Hu	5 D	22
Green Av (LY)	Hu	13 H	21
Green Av (HV)	Hu	21 M	19
Green Av (FR)	Hu	22 P	21
Green Av (LY)	Hu	13 J	21
Green Av (ed)	Hu	30 R	17
Green Ct	Hu	23 M	24
Green Dr	Nu	10 K	13
Green La	Hu	39 V	17
Green Pl (WG)	Hu	6 E	23
Green Pl (bh)	Hu	23 O	24
Green Pl (bp)	Hu	38 X	16
Green St	Hu	12 G	17
Green St (VS)	Nu	5 E	21
Green Ter	Nu	10 H	11
Green Tree Cir E	Nu	28 Q	12
Green Tree Cir N	Nu	28 Q	12
Green Tree Cir S	Nu	28 Q	12
Green Tree Cir W	Nu	28 Q	12
Green Valley Rd	Hu	30 R	17
Green Wy (RL)	Nu	18 L	10
Green Wy	Hu	10 K	13
Green Wy	Ou	36 X	9
Greenacre Ct	Ou	37 X	11
Greenbelt La	Ou	29 T	15
Greenbriar La	Nu	9 J	10
Greenbriar La	Hu	30 U	19
Greenbriar La	Ou	38 W	14
Greenfield Rd	Hu	6 E	24
Greenfield Rd	Ou	36 W	10
Greengrove Av	Hu	21 P	18
Greenhays Av	Hu	8 G	8
Greenhouse La (Pvt)	Ou	27 R	10
Greenlawn Blvd	Hu	13 H	20
Greenlawn Ct	Hu	21 O	17
Greenleaf Hill	Nu	2 B	11
Greenman Ct	Hu	39 X	18
Greenridge Av	Hu	11 H	16
Greenridge Park	Hu	11 J	16
Greentree Dr (os)	Hu	23 M	25
Greentree Dr	Hu	39 X	19
Greentree Rd	Hu	19 N	14
Greenvale La	Hu	29 T	16
Greenvale La	Ou	37 W	11
Greenvale-Glen Cove Hwy	Ou	17 N	6
Greenvale-Glen Cove La	Ou	18 M	9
Greenville Ct	Hu	14 J	23
Greenway (pw)	Nu	9 J	10
Greenway (mh)	Nu	10 H	14
Greenway (BK)	Ou	26 S	7
Greenway (wn)	Hu	40 V	20
Greenway Blvd	Nu	5 E	20
Greenway Cir E	Ou	36 X	9
Greenway Cir N	Ou	36 X	9
Greenway Cir W	Ou	36 X	9
Greenway Ct	Hu	39 X	19
Greenway Dr	Hu	24 M	27
Greenway Dr N	Ou	36 X	9
Greenway Dr	Ou	46 Z	16
Greenway E	Nu	10 H	14
Greenway E	Hu	12 K	18
Greenway S	Hu	12 K	18
Greenway So	Nu	12 K	18
Greenway W	Nu	10 H	14
Greenwich Av (BY)	Ou	25 T	2
Greenwich Av	Ou	47 BB	19
Greenwich St	Hu	21 N	18
Greenwood Ct	Hu	12 L	19
Greenwood Dr	Ou	47 Y	18
Greenwood La (SP)	Nu	8 H	6
Greenwood La (EH)	Nu	18 M	10
Greenwood La	Hu	30 S	18
Greenwood La	Ou	44 Z	10
Greenwood Pl	Hu	5 F	22
Greeway	Hu	22 M	22
Gregg Ct (lk)	Hu	12 L	19
Gregg Ct	Hu	39 W	18
Gregory Av	Hu	31 S	22
Gregory St	Hu	5 E	21
Grenada Av	Hu	22 P	20
Grenfell Dr	Nu	3 F	12
Grenwolde Dr	Nu	2 B	10
Greta Pl	Hu	39 U	18
Grey La	Hu	39 W	17
Greyrock Ct	Ou	46 Y	17
Greystone Rd	Hu	22 M	22
Griddle La	Hu	39 W	17
Griffin Av	Ou	26 U	7
Griffin La	Nu	19 L	14
Griffin La	Ou	36 W	10
Griffin Pl	Hu	13 H	22
Grimn Pl	Hu	22 N	22
Grindsted St	Nu	9 F	11
Grist Mill La (pw)	Nu	9 G	9
Grist Mill La	Nu	2 B	11
Grist Mill Rd	Nu	9 G	9
Grohmans La	Ou	45 Y	13
Grosvenor Rd	Nu	3 E	12
Groton La	Nu	2 F	11
Groton Pl	Nu	9 H	9
Groton Pl	Hu	21 L	18
Grouse La	Hu	38 U	15
Grove Av (WG)	Hu	6 E	24
Grove Av	Hu	39 U	18
Grove Ct	Hu	18 M	10
Grove La	Hu	39 U	17
Grove Pl	Hu	8 G	7
Grove Pl	Hu	23 N	24
Grove St (LW)	Hu	7 C	25
Grove St (gh)	Ou	17 M	7
Grove St (GL)	Ou	17 N	6
Grove St (gw)	Ou	9 L	8
Grove St (eg)	Hu	20 O	16
Grove St (HV)	Hu	21 M	18
Grove St (LY)	Hu	13 J	21
Grove St (bw)	Hu	22 N	22
Grove St (BY)	Ou	25 S	2
Grove St (hk)	Ou	37 V	13
Grove St (ne)	Hu	31 S	20
Grove St (wa)	Ou	47 CC21	
Grove St (wn)	Hu	40 W	21
Grove St (mq)	Ou	40 Y	21
Grover Av E	Ou	48 BB	21
Grover Av W	Ou	48 BB	21
Gruber Dr	Ou	17 O	6
Gruber St	Hu	21 L	19
Grumman Rd E	Ou	38 X	15
Grumman Rd W	Ou	38 W	14
Grundy Pl	Nu	31 S	21
Guenther Av	Nu	5 E	21
Guenther Ct	Hu	22 O	22
Guiffoy St	Ou	17 O	6
Guild Ct	Ou	45 Z	12
Guild La	Hu	29 T	16
Guildford Park Rd	Hu	40 X	21
Guilford Ct (fs)	Hu	12 J	18
Guilford Ct	Hu	31 R	21
Guilford Rd	Nu	9 H	9
Guilles La	Ou	44 Y	9
Gull Pl	Ou	47 Z	19
Gull Rd	Ou	38 U	15
Gull Rd	Ou	38 U	15
Gulls Cove	Nu	2 F	9
Gun La	Hu	39 U	17
Gunther Pl	Hu	40 U	21
Gussack Plz	Nu	3 D	12
Gusto La	Hu	31 Q	20
Gutheil La	Nu	2 D	10
Guttenburg Pa	Ou	47 Y	18
Guy Dr	Hu	39 X	19
Guy Lombardo Av	Hu	31 Q	22
Guys La	Hu	19 O	12
Gwenn Gate	Hu	40 X	21
Gwynne La	Ou	46 AA	16

H

STREET	MUN.	MAP	GRID
H St	Hu	12 G	19
H. Harding Blvd	Nu	3 E	13
Haddington Dr	Nu	19 N	13
Haddon La	Hu	30 R	18
Haddon Rd	Nu	11 G	15
Haddon Rd	Hu	6 E	24
Hadley Ct	Nu	2 D	11
Haff Av	Hu	31 T	20
Hahl La	Ou	26 T	7
Hahn Av	Hu	38 X	16
Haig Rd	Hu	13 G	22
Haig St	Hu	22 N	22
Haight Av (mq)	Ou	48 Y	21
Halcourt Dr	Ou	45 Y	13
Hale Dr	Nu	2 D	9
Hale Pl	Hu	31 Q	20
Hale St	Hu	31 T	21
Halevy Dr	Hu	6 D	24
Half Moon La	Nu	1 D	6
Hall Ct	Nu	2 D	9
Hall St	Hu	12 J	19
Hallman Av	Hu	23 L	23
Hallock St	Hu	30 T	18
Hallock St	Ou	46 CC16	
Halsey Av	Hu	12 K	18
Halsey Av (hk)	Ou	37 U	14
Halsey St	Hu	14 F	23
Halsey St (FR)	Hu	32 Q	23
Halter La	Hu	39 V	17
Halyard Dr	Nu	41 U	23
Halyard Rd	Hu	6 E	23
Hamilton Av (VS)	Hu	5 F	21
Hamilton Av (VS)	Hu	6 F	23
Hamilton Av (AB)	Hu	7 D	28
Hamilton Av (wh)	Hu	12 K	18
Hamilton Av (MN)	Ou	35 U	5
Hamilton Av (ne)	Hu	31 S	19
Hamilton Av (mq)	Ou	47 Y	19
Hamilton Av	Ou	48 CC22	

Nassau Co.

STREET	MUN.	MAP	GRID
Hamilton Ct (ob)	Ou	17	O 7
Hamilton Ct	Ou	17	O 7
Hamilton Dr	Nu	10	J 13
Hamilton Pl (VS)	Hu	5	F 21
Hamilton Pl (HV)	Hu	21	M 17
Hamilton Pl (HV)	Hu	21	N 19
Hamilton Rd (un)	Hu	21	O 18
Hamilton Rd	Hu	22	M 21
Hamilton Sq	Ou	18	M 8
Hamilton St (RC)	Hu	22	L 21
Hamilton St (RC)	Hu	13	K 22
Hamilton St (FR)	Hu	32	Q 24
Hamilton St (FG)	Ou	46	AA 16
Hamlet Dr	Ou	28	R 12
Hamlet Rd	Hu	38	W 16
Hammond Rd	Ou	17	L 6
Hampshire Dr	Ou	46	Z 16
Hampshire Rd	Nu	2	D 10
Hampshire Rd	Hu	22	M 21
Hampstead Tpke	Hu	12	H 18
Hampton Av	Nu	19	L 13
Hampton Av	Hu	40	X 21
Hampton Blvd	Ou	48	Z 22
Hampton Ct (pw)	Nu	8	H 8
Hampton Ct (ug)	Nu	3	D 13
Hampton Ct (RC)	Hu	22	L 21
Hampton Ct (sl)	Hu	29	R 15
Hampton Ct (wn)	Hu	40	V 22
Hampton Ct (wy)	Ou	44	Z 9
Hampton Ct (nq)	Ou	47	Z 18
Hampton Dr	Hu	13	K 20
Hampton Pl (LY)	Hu	13	H 21
Hampton Pl	Hu	23	P 23
Hampton Rd (pw)	Nu	8	H 8
Hampton Rd (TM)	Nu	3	E 12
Hampton Rd (WG)	Hu	6	E 24
Hampton Rd (GA)	Hu	11	K 16
Hampton Rd (gs)	Hu	12	K 17
Hampton Rd (LY)	Hu	13	K 22
Hampton Rd (os)	Hu	14	K 24
Hampton Rd (nq)	Ou	47	Y 18
Hampton St	Nu	20	M 15
Hampton St	Hu	30	T 18
Hampton Wy	Hu	31	T 22
Hampton Wy	Ou	44	Z 9
Hampworth Ct	Nu	2	B 8
Hampworth Dr	Nu	2	B 8
Hancock Pl	Hu	5	F 21
Hancock St (FP)	Hu	12	G 18
Hancock St (fs)	Hu	12	H 19
Hancock St (VS)	Hu	14	G 23
Handy La	Hu	29	S 16
Hanington Av	Hu	40	V 20
Hannelore Wy	Ou	44	Z 8
Hanover Ct	Nu	10	J 12
Hanover Pl (RC)	Hu	23	L 22
Hanover Pl	Ou	37	V 13
Hanover Pl	Hu	31	S 21
Hanover St	Hu	12	G 17
Hanscom Pl	Hu	22	M 22
Hanse Av	Hu	32	R 22
Hansen Pl	Ou	17	L 7
Hansen Pl	Hu	13	J 21
Hansen Pl (bw)	Hu	23	O 23
Hansom Pl	Hu	31	Q 20
Hansome Pl	Hu	22	P 22
Hanson Pl	Hu	40	U 21
Hapsburg Pl	Hu	21	N 19
Harbor Blvd	Hu	40	X 21
Harbor Cir	Hu	23	O 23
Harbor Ct	Hu	23	P 24
Harbor Ct E	Nu	18	L 10
Harbor Ct W	Nu	18	L 10
Harbor Dr	Hu	6	D 24
Harbor Dr	Ou	34	V 3
Harbor Hill Rd	Ou	17	L 6
Harbor Hill Rd	Nu	18	L 11
Harbor Hills Dr	Nu	8	G 7
Harbor La (pw)	Nu	18	L 9
Harbor La (gh)	Ou	18	M 8
Harbor La (MN)	Ou	35	U 5
Harbor La (hk)	Hu	39	V 18
Harbor La (bm)	Hu	41	U 23
Harbor La (MS)	Ou	48	AA 21
Harbor La E	Ou	48	AA 22
Harbor La N	Ou	48	AA 22
Harbor Park Dr	Nu	9	K 10
Harbor Pl	Ou	26	U 4
Harbor Point Rd	Hu	23	O 24
Harbor Rd	Nu	8	H 7
Harbor Rd (HH)	Hu	14	H 24
Harbor Rd	Hu	24	M 27
Harbor Rd	Ou	35	V 5
Harbor Rd	Hu	32	T 23
Harbor St	Hu	23	N 24
Harbor View E	Hu	7	D 26
Harbor View N	Hu	7	D 26
Harbor View S	Hu	7	D 26
Harbor View W	Hu	7	D 26
Harbor Wy	Nu	2	E 9
Harbor Wy	Ou	17	L 7
Harborview Ct	Hu	40	V 22
Harborview Pl	Ou	26	T 4
Harborview Rd	Nu	8	G 8
Harborview Rd	Ou	25	S 3
Harbour La	Ou	48	Z 21
Harbour Rd	Nu	2	D 9
Harbour Rd	Ou	48	CC 21
Harbour View Dr	Ou	48	Z 23
Harcourt Rd	Ou	45	Y 13
Harding Av (LY)	Hu	13	H 21
Harding Av (rt)	Nu	10	L 11
Harding Av (MI)	Nu	11	K 15
Harding Av (lk)	Hu	12	K 19
Harding Av (LB)	Hu	24	L 28
Harding Av (hk)	Ou	37	V 13
Harding Av (bm)	Hu	40	U 21
Harding Ct	Hu	30	T 17
Harding Pl	Ou	17	M 8
Harding Pl	Hu	31	Q 22
Harding St (HV)	Hu	21	O 19
Harding St (os)	Hu	23	M 23
Harding St (ed)	Hu	30	T 17
Harding St (bm)	Hu	31	T 20
Harding St (MS)	Ou	47	AA 19
Hards La	Hu	7	C 26
Hardwick Pl	Ou	46	AA 16
Hardy La	Hu	29	S 15
Hardy St	Hu	12	J 19
Hargale Ct (wm)	Hu	6	E 23
Hargale Ct	Hu	22	M 20
Hargale Rd	Hu	23	M 24
Hark La	Hu	29	T 15
Harkin La	Ou	38	V 14
Harland Rd	Hu	47	Y 19
Harlane Cir	Hu	30	T 18
Harless Pl	Hu	13	J 19
Harmon St	Hu	24	L 27
Harmony Ct	Ou	36	W 8
Harmony Dr	Ou	47	AA 21
Harmony La	Ou	17	L 6
Harmony La	Hu	29	T 15
Harnat Ct	Ou	38	V 14
Harness La (ed)	Hu	39	U 18
Harness La	Hu	39	V 18
Harold Av (HV)	Hu	21	N 19
Harold Av	Hu	40	V 20
Harold Ct	Hu	12	H 19
Harold Ct	Ou	45	Y 13
Harold Rd	Hu	14	F 24
Harold Rd	Ou	45	Z 12
Harold St	Hu	23	N 24
Harriad Dr S	Hu	39	X 18
Harriad Dr W	Hu	39	X 18
Harriet Av	Hu	21	O 17
Harriet Av (rv)	Hu	31	Q 20
Harriet Ct	Hu	13	H 20
Harriet Ct	Ou	17	L 6
Harriet Dr	Ou	36	X 10
Harriet La	Ou	45	Y 12
Harriet Pl	Hu	13	J 22
Harriet Pl	Ou	47	Y 18
Harriet Rd	Ou	46	Y 17
Harriet St	Hu	13	F 19
Harriman Av	Hu	21	N 18
Harriman Dr	Nu	1	F 6
Harris Av	Hu	14	F 23
Harris Av (in)	Hu	7	C 25
Harris Av	Hu	31	Q 21
Harris Ct	Hu	40	V 21
Harris Dr	Hu	14	L 25
Harrison Av (fs)	Hu	12	H 19
Harrison Av (GL)	Ou	16	N 5
Harrison Av (fs)	Hu	12	J 18
Harrison Av (MI)	Nu	20	L 15
Harrison Av (HV)	Hu	21	M 19
Harrison Av (ER)	Hu	14	J 23
Harrison Av (os)	Hu	23	L 23
Harrison Av (bh)	Hu	23	O 23
Harrison Av (hi)	Hu	15	J 26
Harrison Av (hk)	Ou	37	V 13
Harrison Av (un)	Hu	30	Q 18
Harrison Av (FR)	Hu	31	Q 21
Harrison Av (bp)	Ou	38	X 15
Harrison Av (wa)	Ou	48	CC 21
Harrison Av (mq)	Ou	48	Y 21
Harrison Pl (sa)	Ou	46	CC 16
Harrison Pl (mq)	Ou	48	Y 22
Harrison St (fs)	Hu	12	G 18
Harrison St (GA)	Hu	12	H 17
Harrison St (LW)	Hu	7	D 26
Harrison St (fs)	Hu	12	H 17
Harrison St (lk)	Hu	13	K 20
Harrison St (HV)	Hu	22	O 19
Harrison St (nb)	Hu	30	U 19
Harrogate St	Hu	24	M 27
Harrow La	Nu	9	J 11
Harrow La	Hu	39	V 18
Harrow La	Ou	45	Z 14
Harrow Rd	Hu	12	H 19
Harry Ct	Hu	22	N 20
Harry La	Hu	31	S 20
Hart Av	Hu	30	T 19
Hart St	Hu	13	J 21
Hart St	Ou	46	AA 17
Harte St	Hu	22	N 21
Hartley Rd	Nu	2	E 10
Harton Av	Hu	30	S 18
Harts Av	Hu	31	P 20
Hartwell Pl	Hu	6	F 24
Harvard Av (VS)	Hu	14	G 23
Harvard Av (LY)	Hu	13	H 21
Harvard Av (RC)	Hu	22	L 21
Harvard Av (bw)	Hu	22	N 22
Harvard Av (mr)	Hu	31	S 22
Harvard Ct (WG)	Hu	6	E 23
Harvard Ct	Hu	30	R 18
Harvard Dr	Ou	44	AA 10
Harvard La	Hu	40	X 22
Harvard Pl	Hu	23	O 23
Harvard Pl	Ou	46	Z 17
Harvard Rd (WG)	Hu	6	E 24
Harvard Rd	Nu	10	J 12
Harvard Rd	Hu	12	J 17
Harvard St (FP)	Hu	11	F 17
Harvard St (NP)	Nu	11	G 15
Harvard St (VS)	Hu	5	D 21
Harvard St (al)	Nu	19	L 12
Harvard St (WP)	Nu	10	L 14
Harvard St (EW)	Nu	19	M 14
Harvard St (WB)	Nu	19	P 14
Harvard St (GA)	Hu	12	H 17
Harvard St (HV)	Hu	21	N 17
Harvard St (MS)	Ou	48	BB 21
Harvest La	Hu	39	V 17
Harvest Rd	Hu	39	V 19
Harvey Av	Hu	23	M 23
Harvey Ct	Hu	22	N 20
Harvey Dr	Hu	39	U 18
Harvey La	Hu	30	S 18
Harwich Rd	Hu	14	J 24
Harwick Rd	Ou	28	R 12
Harwood Dr	Ou	16	L 5
Harwood Dr E	Ou	16	L 5
Harwood Dr W	Ou	16	L 5
Hasket Dr	Ou	36	V 10
Hastings Dr	Hu	30	S 19
Hastings La	Ou	38	U 14
Hastings Pkwy	Hu	23	O 24
Hastings Pl	Hu	21	M 18
Hastings Rd	Nu	18	N 11
Hastings Rd	Hu	15	K 26
Hastings Rd	Ou	47	Y 18
Hastings St	Hu	6	F 23
Hates St	Hu	32	Q 23
Hathaway Av	Hu	4	D 18
Hathaway Dr	Hu	11	H 16
Hattie Ct	Ou	38	V 15
Hausch Blvd	Hu	31	Q 20
Haussner Pl	Nu	11	L 14
Haven Av	Nu	9	G 8
Haven Av	Hu	5	F 20
Haven Av (ne)	Hu	31	S 20
Haven La (ed)	Hu	39	U 18
Haven La	Hu	39	V 18
Haven La	Ou	45	Z 13
Haven Pl	Hu	6	F 23
Haverford Rd	Ou	37	W 12
Hawk La	Hu	39	W 17
Hawk Rd	Hu	38	W 16
Hawke La	Hu	22	L 21
Hawkins Av	Hu	22	N 21
Hawser Cir	Hu	30	Q 18
Hawt La	Hu	6	E 25
Hawthorne Av (pw)	Nu	9	H 9
Hawthorne Av (FP)	Nu	11	F 16
Hawthorne Av (fs)	Hu	12	J 19
Hawthorne Av (HV)	Hu	21	O 18
Hawthorne Av (RC)	Hu	23	L 22
Hawthorne Av (mr)	Hu	31	S 21
Hawthorne Dr E	Hu	39	W 19
Hawthorne Dr N	Hu	39	W 19
Hawthorne Dr S	Hu	39	W 19
Hawthorne Dr W	Hu	39	W 19
Hawthorne La (MK)	Nu	9	G 10
Hawthorne La (SR)	Nu	3	B 11
Hawthorne La (sv)	Hu	5	E 22
Hawthorne La (WG)	Hu	6	E 25
Hawthorne Pl	Nu	9	G 10
Hawthorne Pl	Hu	13	J 21
Hawthorne Rd	Nu	9	G 9
Hawthorne Rd	Hu	11	H 16
Hawthorne Rd (SC)	Ou	17	L 7
Hawthorne Rd	Ou	26	U 7
Hawthorne St (LY)	Hu	13	H 21
Hawthorne St (WP)	Nu	11	L 14
Hawthorne St (bw)	Hu	22	O 21
Hawthorne St	Ou	28	T 13
Hawthorne St (FG)	Ou	46	BB 15
Hawthorne St (MS)	Ou	47	AA 19
Hawthorne St (mq)	Ou	40	Y 21
Hawthorne St (MS)	Ou	47	Z 19
Hawthorne Ter	Nu	3	C 11
Hay Barn Ct	Nu	19	O 12
Hay Path Rd (ob)	Ou	45	AA 13
Hay Path Rd (pv)	Ou	45	Y 13
Hay Path Rd	Ou	45	Z 14
Hayden Av	Nu	2	D 10
Hayden Dr	Ou	38	X 16
Hayes Ct	Hu	30	R 18
Hayes Pl	Hu	23	P 24
Hayes St (GA)	Hu	12	J 17
Hayes St (bh)	Hu	23	O 24
Hayes St	Ou	47	AA 19
Hayloft La	Nu	19	M 12
Haymaker La	Hu	38	V 15
Hazel Av	Ou	46	BB 17
Hazel Dr	Nu	3	C 12
Hazel Dr	Hu	6	E 23
Hazel Pl (FP)	Hu	4	E 17
Hazel Pl (VS)	Hu	6	E 23
Hazel Pl (LY)	Hu	13	H 22
Hazel Rd	Nu	9	G 9
Hazel St (GL)	Ou	17	N 6
Hazel St	Hu	30	U 19
Hazel St (bp)	Ou	38	W 14
Hazelhurst Av	Hu	20	P 16
Hazelwood Ct	Ou	37	U 11
Hazelwood Dr	Nu	19	P 13
Hazelwood Dr	Ou	37	U 11
Hazzard Rd	Hu	24	M 27
Headley Wy	Ou	44	AA 10
Healy Av	Hu	6	B 25
Healy St	Hu	12	G 18
Hearth La	Hu	29	S 15
Heath Pl (HV)	Hu	20	M 16
Heath Pl (HV)	Hu	21	N 19
Heathcliff Dr	Hu	47	Y 18
Heathcote Dr	Nu	19	L 13
Heathcote Rd	Hu	4	D 18
Heather Dr	Nu	18	L 11
Heather Hill Rd	Ou	27	Q 10
Heather La (mh)	Nu	11	H 14
Heather La (HH)	Hu	14	H 24
Heather La (LW)	Hu	6	D 25
Heather La (MN)	Ou	25	S 3
Heather La (je)	Ou	27	U 10
Heather La (ln)	Hu	38	V 16
Heather La	Ou	37	X 13
Heather La (wn)	Hu	39	W 18
Heatherfield Rd	Hu	5	D 22
Hedding Av	Hu	31	S 20
Hedge La (HH)	Hu	14	H 23
Hedge La (hk)	Hu	29	T 15
Hedge La (mr)	Hu	31	S 22

Nassau Co.

STREET	MUN.	MAP	GRID
Intervale	Nu	9	K 11
Intervale	Hu	22	M 22
Intervale Av	Ou	47	BB 18
Inwood Av	Hu	33	Q 27
Inwood Rd	Nu	1	E 7
Inwood Rd	Ou	16	M 4
Iona St	Hu	5	F 21
Ionia St	Hu	40	X 22
Iowa Av	Hu	46	Y 17
Iowa Pl	Hu	15	K 27
Ipswich Av	Nu	3	D 12
Ira Rd	Hu	41	V 23
Ira Rd	Ou	36	W 9
Iram Pl	Hu	46	Y 15
Irene Ct	Hu	13	H 20
Irene Dr	Nu	10	J 13
Irene La	Hu	40	X 22
Irene La E	Ou	37	X 11
Irene La N	Hu	40	X 22
Irene La S	Ou	37	X 11
Irene St (sh)	Hu	22	N 20
Irene St	Hu	32	S 23
Iris Av (FP)	Hu	4	F 17
Iris La	Hu	30	S 19
Iris La (ug)	Nu	3	D 12
Iris La (mh)	Hu	11	H 14
Iris La (sv)	Hu	5	E 22
Iris La (mh)	Hu	11	H 14
Iris La (WB)	Hu	20	N 15
Iris La (bh)	Hu	23	O 24
Iris La (hk)	Hu	38	U 16
Iris La (nb)	Hu	30	T 19
Iris La (MT)	Ou	36	X 8
Iris Pl	Hu	13	K 20
Iris Pl (sl)	Hu	29	S 14
Iris Pl	Ou	46	Y 17
Iris Pl (wa)	Ou	47	CC18
Iris Rd	Ou	45	AA 12
Iris St (WG)	Hu	6	E 25
Iris St	Hu	12	J 18
Irma Av	Nu	8	G 8
Irma Dr	Hu	23	L 24
Irons Pl	Hu	15	F 15
Ironwood Rd	Ou	27	T 9
Iroquois Pl (FG)	Ou	46	AA 16
Iroquois Pl	Ou	48	CC22
Iroquois Pl E	Ou	48	BB 22
Iroquois Pl W	Ou	48	BB 22
Irving Av	Nu	11	F 16
Irving Av	Hu	23	P 24
Irving Ct (MN)	Ou	35	U 5
Irving Ct (hk)	Hu	37	U 13
Irving Ct	Hu	40	U 20
Irving Dr	Ou	44	Z 9
Irving La	Hu	11	F 15
Irving Pl (WG)	Hu	6	F 24
Irving Pl (VS)	Hu	13	G 21
Irving Pl (GL)	Ou	17	L 6
Irving Pl (ER)	Hu	14	J 23
Irving Pl (RC)	Hu	22	L 21
Irving Pl (BW)	Hu	22	N 21
Irving Pl (MN)	Ou	35	U 5
Irving Pl (ed)	Hu	30	S 18
Irving Pl (un)	Hu	21	P 19
Irving Pl (FR)	Hu	31	Q 20
Irving Pl (nq)	Ou	47	Y 18
Irving St (el)	Hu	5	E 20
Irving St (BW)	Hu	22	O 21
Irving St (nc)	Nu	29	Q 14
Irving St (hk)	Ou	37	U 13
Irving St (lv)	Hu	38	X 16
Irving St (wa)	Ou	47	CC20
Irvington St	Hu	6	F 23
Irwin Ct	Hu	13	J 22
Irwin St	Nu	11	J 14
Isabel Ct	Ou	45	BB 13
Isabelle Ct	Hu	30	T 19
Island Av	Hu	6	D 24
Island Channel Rd	Hu	41	X 23
Island Ct	Nu	1	F 7
Island Pkwy N	Hu	15	J 26
Island Pkwy S	Hu	15	J 27
Island Pkwy W	Hu	15	J 26
Island Pl	Hu	40	X 22
Island Plz	Hu	40	U 22
Island Rd	Hu	40	W 20
Island St	Ou	37	W 13
Islip Ct	Hu	40	V 22
Ithaca Av	Hu	7	D 28
Ivan Ct	Hu	15	F 28
Ivanhoe Dr	Hu	31	S 22
Ivanhoe Pl	Hu	5	D 21
Ives La	Ou	37	X 11
Ives Rd	Hu	14	F 24
Ivy Av	Nu	19	P 14
Ivy Ct	Hu	20	M 15
Ivy Ct	Ou	27	R 10
Ivy Ct (pv)	Ou	37	Y 11
Ivy Ct E	Hu	38	W 15
Ivy Ct W	Hu	38	W 15
Ivy Dr	Ou	37	U 11
Ivy Dr	Hu	38	W 15
Ivy Hill Ct	Ou	36	U 10
Ivy Hill Rd	Hu	6	F 25
Ivy La (WG)	Hu	7	E 25
Ivy La (cp)	Nu	20	N 14
Ivy La (ld)	Hu	24	M 27
Ivy La (ed)	Hu	38	U 16
Ivy La (wa)	Hu	39	W 19
Ivy Pl	Hu	5	F 22
Ivy Pl (un)	Hu	21	P 19
Ivy St (WG)	Hu	6	E 25
Ivy St (hr)	Nu	11	J 14
Ivy St (wh)	Hu	21	L 18
Ivy St (MN)	Ou	35	U 5
Ivy St (FG)	Ou	46	BB 16
Ivy Wy	Nu	9	G 9
Ixworth Rd	Hu	12	G 19

J

STREET	MUN.	MAP	GRID
Jackie Dr	Ou	28	S 13
Jackie La	Hu	23	N 24
Jackson Av (el)	Hu	4	E 19
Jackson Av (MI)	Nu	11	K 15
Jackson Av (wh)	Hu	12	K 19
Jackson Av (RC)	Hu	22	M 22
Jackson Av (BY)	Ou	25	S 2
Jackson Av (rv)	Hu	31	P 20
Jackson Av (ed)	Hu	30	R 18
Jackson Av (lg)	Ou	36	W 9
Jackson Av (bp)	Ou	46	Y 15
Jackson Av (MS)	Ou	47	AA 20
Jackson Av (MS)	Ou	47	BB 20
Jackson Av (wa)	Hu	40	W 21
Jackson Av (wn)	Hu	40	X 20
Jackson Av (mq)	Hu	48	Y 21
Jackson Av (mq)	Hu	48	Y 22
Jackson Ct	Ou	36	W 10
Jackson La	Ou	16	L 4
Jackson Pl (LY)	Hu	14	H 23
Jackson Pl (bw)	Hu	23	P 24
Jackson Pl (IP)	Hu	15	K 26
Jackson Pl (ed)	Hu	30	T 18
Jackson Pl (FP)	Hu	31	Q 22
Jackson Pl	Ou	48	Y 22
Jackson Rd	Hu	13	G 22
Jackson St (pw)	Nu	8	F 8
Jackson Pl (GA)	Hu	12	H 17
Jackson St (fs)	Hu	12	H 18
Jackson St (GL)	Ou	8	K 5
Jackson St (WB)	Nu	19	O 14
Jackson St (HV)	Hu	21	M 18
Jackson St (RC)	Hu	22	M 22
Jackson St (bw)	Hu	23	O 24
Jacob Dr	Hu	39	X 19
Jacob Rd	Ou	45	Z 13
Jacob St	Hu	4	F 18
Jacqueline Av	Hu	30	S 18
Jacqueline Rd	Ou	46	Y 17
Jacqueline St	Hu	38	X 16
Jad Ct	Ou	45	Z 12
Jadwin St	Hu	6	F 23
Jaeger Dr	Ou	17	N 8
Jaffa Av	Hu	21	P 19
Jamaica Av	Hu	15	L 25
Jamaica Av	Ou	37	W 12
Jamaica Blvd	Hu	19	N 14
James Av	Nu	8	G 7
James Av (nv)	Hu	13	G 20
James Av	Ou	26	T 7
James Ct (wh)	Hu	12	K 19
James Ct (rv)	Hu	22	P 20
James Ct (sy)	Ou	36	W 8
James Ct (pv)	Ou	45	AA 12
James Doolittle Blvd	Hu	29	P 16
James L.L. Burrell Av	Hu	21	N 17
James La	Hu	38	U 16
James Pl	Hu	30	P 19
James Rd	Hu	40	W 20
James St (el)	Hu	12	G 18
James St (fs)	Hu	12	H 19
James St (in)	Hu	7	C 25
James St (hr)	Nu	10	J 14
James St (ER)	Hu	14	J 23
James St (os)	Hu	14	K 24
James St (os)	Hu	23	M 23
James St (hk)	Ou	37	U 13
James St (rv)	Hu	31	R 20
James St (mr)	Hu	32	S 23
James St (lg)	Ou	36	W 10
James St (nq)	Ou	46	AA 17
James St (FR)	Ou	46	BB 16
Jami St	Hu	41	U 23
Jan La	Ou	44	Y 10
Jane Ct	Nu	28	R 13
Jane Ct (ed)	Hu	29	S 16
Jane Ct	Hu	40	X 22
Jane Ct	Ou	45	AA 13
Jane La	Hu	23	M 25
Jane Pl	Hu	5	F 21
Jane St	Hu	19	L 12
Jane St	Hu	21	O 18
Jane St (wn)	Hu	40	W 20
Janet Av	Ou	30	U 19
Janet Dr	Ou	37	X 13
Janet La	Ou	8	L 5
Janet Pl	Hu	6	E 23
Jano Pl (pv)	Ou	44	Z 11
Janos La	Hu	13	K 20
Janssen Dr	Nu	9	G 10
Jara Ct	Hu	11	G 15
Jarvis Av	Ou	36	W 10
Jarvis Pl	Hu	13	J 22
Jasen Av	Hu	5	E 20
Jasmine Av	Hu	11	H 15
Jasmine La	Hu	5	E 22
Jason Ct	Ou	41	V 23
Jason Dr	Ou	41	V 23
Jasp Ct	Ou	46	Y 16
Jasper St	Hu	5	E 20
Jay Ct	Hu	6	E 23
Jay Ct	Nu	19	N 14
Jay Dr (ed)	Hu	30	T 18
Jay Dr (wn)	Hu	39	U 18
Jay St (hk)	Ou	37	V 14
Jay St (FR)	Hu	31	Q 21
Jay St (bp)	Ou	38	V 14
Jay St (nw)	Hu	39	X 19
Jay Wy	Hu	23	N 24
Jaymie Dr	Nu	28	R 13
Jayne Pl	Hu	22	O 22
Jayson Av	Nu	3	D 12
Jean Av (HV)	Hu	21	O 18
Jean Ct	Ou	38	X 16
Jean Ct	Hu	13	J 21
Jean Pl	Hu	29	T 16
Jean Pl	Ou	37	X 11
Jeanette Av	Hu	23	P 24
Jeanette Dr	Ou	48	Z 23
Jeanette Pl	Hu	6	B 25
Jeanna Ct	Ou	45	AA 14
Jeanna St	Hu	29	T 16
Jeanne La	Ou	46	Y 17
Jeannette Dr	Nu	8	G 8
Jedwood Pl	Hu	5	F 22
Jeff Ct	Hu	29	S 15
Jefferies Rd	Hu	39	V 17
Jefferson Av (VS)	Hu	5	D 20
Jefferson Av (rt)	Nu	10	L 11
Jefferson Av (MI)	Nu	20	L 15
Jefferson Av (LY)	Hu	13	K 21
Jefferson Av (LY)	Hu	13	J 22
Jefferson Av (RC)	Hu	22	M 22
Jefferson Av (BY)	Ou	25	S 2
Jefferson Av (hk)	Ou	29	U 14
Jefferson Av (FR)	Hu	31	Q 21
Jefferson Av (bm)	Hu	40	U 20
Jefferson Av (MS)	Ou	47	AA 20
Jefferson Av E	Nu	20	M 15
Jefferson Blvd	Hu	7	D 28
Jefferson Ct	Ou	30	T 17
Jefferson Pl	Hu	11	K 15
Jefferson Pl	Hu	21	N 19
Jefferson Pl (bh)	Hu	23	O 24
Jefferson Rd	Ou	46	AA 16
Jefferson St (pw)	Nu	9	G 8
Jefferson St (nn)	Nu	11	G 15
Jefferson St (FP)	Hu	12	G 17
Jefferson St (GA)	Hu	12	H 17
Jefferson St (WG)	Hu	6	E 24
Jefferson St (in)	Hu	6	C 25
Jefferson St	Ou	16	L 5
Jefferson St (fs)	Hu	12	H 19
Jefferson St (fs)	Hu	12	J 18
Jefferson St (ML)	Hu	13	J 20
Jefferson St (os)	Hu	23	N 24
Jefferson St (WB)	Nu	28	Q 14
Jefferson St (ed)	Hu	30	S 17
Jefferson St (mr)	Hu	31	S 21
Jefferson St (FR)	Hu	32	Q 23
Jefferson St (mr)	Hu	31	S 21
Jefferson St (es)	Ou	47	CC21
Jefferson St (sd)	Hu	40	X 20
Jeffery La	Nu	10	F 13
Jeffery La	Hu	24	M 25
Jeffrey Av	Hu	30	R 17
Jeffrey Ct (FR)	Hu	32	R 23
Jeffrey Ct (mr)	Hu	31	T 22
Jeffrey Ct	Ou	37	W 11
Jeffrey Ct	Hu	40	X 20
Jeffrey Dr (os)	Hu	23	N 24
Jeffrey Dr	Hu	30	T 19
Jeffrey Pl	Nu	10	H 14
Jeffrey Pl	Ou	44	Y 10
Jefry La	Ou	38	W 14
Jena Ct	Hu	13	K 20
Jenkins Dr	Hu	31	S 20
Jenkins St	Hu	31	S 20
Jennie Ct (bm)	Hu	31	T 20
Jennie Ct	Nu	39	U 18
Jennie Rd	Hu	40	V 20
Jennings Av	Hu	22	L 20
Jennings Ct	Ou	44	Z 10
Jennings La	Ou	44	Y 10
Jenney Av	Ou	45	Y 12
Jericho Rd	Ou	26	U 7
Jericho-Tpke.	Ou	28	T 11
Jericho-Oyster Bay Rd	Ou	27	U 10
Jerold St	Ou	37	X 12
Jerome Av	Nu	20	M 15
Jerome Av	Ou	37	V 12
Jerome Ct (FS)	Hu	12	H 19
Jerome Ct	Ou	36	V 10
Jerome Ct	Nu	29	R 15
Jerome Dr (GL)	Ou	8	K 6
Jerome Dr	Ou	46	AA 16
Jerome Rd	Hu	13	H 20
Jerome Rd	Ou	36	X 9
Jerome St	Hu	23	O 24
Jerome St (lg)	Ou	36	W 10
Jerome St	Ou	47	Y 19
Jerry La	Ou	17	O 6
Jersey St	Ou	28	T 13
Jerusalem Av (HV)	Hu	21	N 18
Jerusalem Av	Ou	38	V 14
Jervis Av	Ou	46	BB 16
Jesse Pl	Hu	29	T 16
Jesse St	Hu	31	R 21
Jessica Pl	Nu	10	K 12
Jester La	Hu	38	W 16
Jetmore Pl	Ou	48	Y 22
Jewel Dr	Hu	6	E 22
Jill Ct (ed)	Hu	30	R 18
Jill St	Hu	31	S 22
Jo Ann Dr	Ou	45	AA 14
Joan Ct (el)	Hu	4	F 18
Joan Ct (lk)	Hu	12	L 19
Joan Ct (FR)	Hu	23	P 23
Joan Ct	Ou	44	Y 10
Joan La (MS)	Ou	47	BB 18
Joan La	Ou	47	CC19
Joan St	Ou	47	Y 18
Joann Ct	Hu	23	L 24
Jodi Ct	Ou	16	L 4
Jody Ct	Hu	30	T 19
Jody La	Ou	45	Z 12
Joel Dr	Hu	30	T 19
Joel Pl	Nu	9	F 9
Joel Pl	Hu	23	M 23
Joel Pl	Ou	45	Z 13
John Av	Hu	12	G 18
John Bean Ct	Nu	9	K 10
John Dr	Ou	45	Z 13

Nassau Co.

STREET	MUN.	MAP	GRID
John La (lv)	Hu	38 U	16
John La	Hu	40 Y	21
John Pl	Hu	30 P	19
John St (LY)	Hu	13 H	22
John St (in)	Hu	6 C	25
John St (GL)	Ou	8 L	5
John St (RH)	Nu	18 M	9
John St (GA)	Hu	20 M	16
John St (bw)	Hu	22 N	21
John St (rv)	Hu	22 P	20
John St (LY)	Hu	13 H	22
John St (os)	Hu	14 K	23
John St (os)	Hu	14 K	24
John St (os)	Hu	23 L	24
John St (lv)	Hu	39 V	17
John St (ne)	Hu	31 R	20
John St (bm)	Hu	40 U	21
John St (rv)	Hu	40 W	20
John St (mr)	Hu	32 S	23
John St (bm)	Hu	40 U	22
John St (pv)	Ou	37 X	12
John St (sa)	Hu	46 AA	17
John St (pe)	Ou	46 Y	16
John St (wn)	Hu	40 W	20
John St (sd)	Hu	40 Y	21
John St (mq)	Hu	48 Z	21
Johnell Pl	Ou	17 N	6
Johns Ct	Hu	22 L	20
Johns Ct (bw)	Hu	22 O	21
Johnson Av	Hu	4 F	18
Johnson Av (LY)	Hu	13 J	21
Johnson Ct	Hu	26 U	7
Johnson La	Hu	12 K	19
Johnson Pl (WG)	Hu	6 F	24
Johnson Pl (HV)	Hu	21 N	19
Johnson Pl (os)	Hu	23 M	22
Johnson Pl (bh)	Hu	23 O	23
Johnson Pl (bm)	Hu	40 U	21
Johnson Pl (wn)	Hu	40 V	20
Johnson Pl (FR)	Hu	23 P	23
Johnson Rd	Hu	6 C	24
Johnson St (BY)	Ou	25 Q	2
Johnson St (GL)	Ou	17 M	6
Johnson St (gw)	Hu	18 L	8
Johnston Av	Hu	39 U	19
Johnston Pl	Hu	31 S	21
Johnstone Rd	Nu	2 E	11
Jolan Av	Ou	37 V	12
Joludow Dr	Ou	48 BB	21
Jomarr Ct	Ou	48 Y	22
Jomarr Pl	Ou	48 Y	22
Jonathan Av	Hu	37 W	13
Jonathan La	Hu	39 V	19
Jonel La	Hu	47 Y	18
Jones Av	Hu	40 V	21
Jones Av N	Hu	40 W	21
Jones Beach Causeway	Hu	41 W	23
Jones Ct	Ou	47 BB	20
Jones Pl	Hu	23 N	23
Jones Pl	Hu	48 AA	21
Jones St	Nu	11 G	15
Jordan Av	Hu	6 E	24
Jordan Dr	Nu	3 C	12
Jordan St (os)	Hu	23 M	24
Jordan St	Ou	35 U	5
Jorgen St	Hu	6 E	25
Joseph Av	Ou	38 X	16
Joseph Ct (sy)	Ou	37 V	11
Joseph Ct	Hu	40 U	22
Joseph Ct (sa)	Ou	46 Z	16
Joseph La (en)	Ou	26 U	7
Joseph La (hk)	Ou	37 W	13
Joseph La	Ou	47 CC	18
Joseph Rd	Nu	11 J	15
Joseph Rd	Nu	11 J	15
Joseph St	Nu	11 G	14
Joslyn Dr	Ou	37 Y	11
Journal Av	Hu	12 G	18
Joy Blvd	Hu	22 N	20
Joy Ct	Hu	40 X	20
Joy Dr	Nu	10 H	14
Joyce Av	Ou	47 CC	19
Joyce Ct	Ou	36 X	10
Joyce La (mr)	Hu	32 T	23
Joyce La	Ou	36 X	10
Joyce La	Hu	39 X	19
Joyce Pl (Cl)	Ou	34 V	3
Joyce Pl	Ou	46 Y	17
Joyce Rd	Ou	45 Y	12
Juanita Av	Hu	23 O	22
Judge Ct (mq)	Hu	47 Y	20
Judith Ct (ER)	Hu	14 H	23
Judith Ct (wn)	Hu	40 V	22
Judith Dr	Hu	39 X	19
Judith Dr	Hu	32 T	23
Judith Dr (wn)	Hu	40 V	22
Judith La	Hu	5 F	21
Judith La (os)	Hu	23 M	24
Judith La	Nu	28 R	13
Judith Pl	Hu	23 P	24
Judith St	Ou	37 X	12
Judson Pl	Hu	22 L	21
Judy Ter	Ou	48 BB	21
Jules La	Hu	39 X	17
Julia La	Hu	30 U	19
Julian La	Hu	32 S	23
Julian St	Ou	37 W	12
Juliana Rd	Ou	47 BB	18
Juliette Rd	Hu	22 L	20
Julius Ct	Hu	30 R	19
Julliard Dr	Ou	37 Y	11
July Av	Ou	25 T	2
Junard Blvd	Ou	12 J	19
Junard Dr	Nu	9 K	11
Junard Dr	Ou	46 BB	17
June Av	Ou	25 T	2
June Ct (wm)	Hu	6 D	23
June Ct	Hu	12 J	19
June Pl	Hu	6 D	23
June Pl (fs)	Hu	12 J	19
Juneau Blvd	Ou	44 Z	10
Juniper Av	Nu	20 M	15
Juniper Av	Hu	31 S	21
Juniper Cir E	Hu	7 D	26
Juniper Cir N	Hu	7 D	26
Juniper Cir S	Hu	7 D	26
Juniper Dr	Nu	3 C	12
Juniper Dr	Ou	26 T	7
Juniper La	Hu	36 V	9
Juniper La	Nu	28 S	13
Juniper Rd	Nu	1 E	7
Juniper St (hk)	Ou	37 W	12
Juniper St	Ou	46 BB	17
Jupiter La	Hu	38 W	16

K

STREET	MUN.	MAP	GRID
K St	Hu	12 G	19
Kaintuck La	Ou	25 Q	4
Kalb Av	Hu	12 H	17
Kalda Av	Nu	11 G	15
Kalda La	Hu	30 R	18
Kalda La	Ou	45 Y	12
Kallas Ct	Hu	13 G	20
Kalman Ct	Ou	37 X	13
Kalmia La	Hu	5 E	22
Kamda Blvd	Nu	11 G	15
Kampfe Pl	Hu	40 U	20
Kampton Rd	Hu	21 P	19
Kane Av	Hu	21 N	19
Kane Ct	Hu	12 J	19
Kansas St	Ou	28 T	13
Karen Av	Ou	45 Y	13
Karen Ct	Nu	19 N	14
Karen Ct	Ou	25 T	2
Karen Ct	Hu	30 S	18
Karen La	Hu	30 S	18
Karen Rd (MC)	Ou	17 O	5
Karen Rd	Ou	17 O	6
Karen St	Hu	41 U	23
Karin Ct	Ou	35 U	5
Karin La	Hu	38 W	14
Karlston Pl	Hu	13 G	22
Karol Pl	Ou	37 U	11
Kate Dr	Nu	11 J	15
Katherine Dr	Ou	45 Y	13
Kathleen Dr E	Ou	36 X	10
Kathleen Dr N	Ou	36 X	10
Kathleen Dr W	Ou	36 W	10
Kathleen Pl	Hu	29 R	15
Kathryn St	Hu	14 H	23
Kathy Ct	Ou	25 P	4
Kathy Dr	Ou	37 U	11
Kay Av	Ou	38 X	16
Kay St	Ou	37 U	12
Kayron La	Hu	30 T	19
Kaywood Rd	Nu	1 E	7
Kearney Av	Ou	46 Y	15
Kearney La	Ou	26 S	7
Kearny Dr	Hu	6 E	23
Keats Ct	Hu	39 X	17
Keats La	Nu	3 B	11
Keats Pl	Ou	37 U	13
Keegan St	Hu	4 F	19
Keel Ct	Ou	35 V	5
Keel St	Hu	6 E	23
Keeler Av	Hu	31 S	22
Keen Gate	Ou	37 W	11
Keen Pl	Hu	30 P	19
Keenan Pl	Hu	20 M	16
Keene La	Hu	6 F	24
Kees Pl	Hu	31 S	21
Keewaydin Pl	Hu	7 D	26
Keil St	Hu	4 E	19
Keily Dr	Hu	40 X	20
Keith Dr	Hu	39 X	18
Keller Av	Hu	12 G	19
Keller St	Hu	13 G	20
Kellogg St	Ou	35 U	5
Kellum La	Hu	20 M	16
Kellum Pl (MI)	Hu	20 L	15
Kellum Pl	Hu	21 M	17
Kelly Ct	Hu	13 G	20
Kelly St	Hu	7 B	25
Kelly St	Hu	17 N	6
Kelsey Pl	Hu	13 H	21
Kemp Av	Hu	17 M	6
Kemp La	Hu	11 K	14
Kendig Pl	Hu	21 M	17
Kenilworth Ct	Hu	11 H	16
Kenilworth Rd	Nu	20 M	15
Kenilworth St (ML)	Hu	13 J	20
Kenilworth St	Hu	23 N	24
Kenmark Pl	Ou	17 M	7
Kenmore Rd (VS)	Hu	13 G	22
Kenmore Rd	Hu	11 J	16
Kenmore St	Hu	30 T	18
Kennedy Av (HV)	Hu	21 N	19
Kennedy Av	Hu	22 M	22
Kennedy Dr	Ou	45 AA	12
Kennedy La	Nu	11 K	14
Kennedy Rd	Nu	19 N	11
Kenneth Av (bw)	Hu	22 N	21
Kenneth Av	Hu	31 T	20
Kenneth Ct	Nu	2 D	9
Kenneth Ct	Hu	12 G	17
Kenneth Ct	Ou	16 M	5
Kenneth Ct (hk)	Ou	37 V	12
Kenneth Dr	Hu	32 T	23
Kenneth Pl	Hu	11 G	15
Kenneth Pl	Hu	23 L	23
Kenneth St	Ou	45 Z	12
Kennilworth Ter	Nu	2 D	9
Kennworth Rd	Nu	9 G	9
Kenny Av	Hu	32 T	22
Kenora Pl	Hu	40 W	21
Kenridge Rd	Hu	7 D	26
Kens Ct	Hu	12 K	17
Kensett Rd	Nu	9 H	10
Kensington La	Hu	38 X	16
Kensington Av	Nu	31 S	20
Kensington Av	Ou	48 AA	21
Kensington Ct	Nu	2 D	11
Kensington Ct	Hu	21 M	18
Kensington Ct (sl)	Hu	29 Q	15
Kensington Dr	Hu	29 Q	15
Kensington Gate	Nu	3 D	11
Kensington Pl	Nu	3 D	13
Kensington Pl	Hu	6 D	24
Kensington Rd (LY)	Hu	13 H	21
Kensington Rd (GA)	Hu	12 K	17
Kensington Rd (ed)	Hu	30 T	17
Kensington Rd S	Hu	12 K	18
Kensington St	Hu	24 N	27
Kent Blvd	Hu	15 J	26
Kent Ct (RC)	Hu	22 M	22
Kent Ct (os)	Hu	23 N	23
Kent Dr	Hu	14 H	23
Kent Dr	Ou	28 R	12
Kent La	Ou	47 CC	18
Kent Pl	Nu	3 E	12
Kent Pl	Hu	12 L	19
Kent Pl	Ou	37 X	12
Kent Rd	Hu	11 H	15
Kent Rd	Hu	5 F	21
Kent Rd (IP)	Hu	15 K	26
Kent Rd E	Hu	40 V	20
Kent Rd W	Hu	40 V	20
Kent St	Nu	10 J	14
Kent St	Hu	29 Q	15
Kent St	Ou	46 AA	17
Kentucky Av	Ou	46 Y	17
Kentucky St	Hu	15 G	28
Kenwood Av	Ou	47 CC	20
Kenwood Ct	Hu	22 M	20
Kenwood Dr	Ou	48 Z	22
Kenwood La	Hu	39 V	17
Kenwood Pl	Hu	31 T	21
Kenwood Rd	Hu	20 M	16
Kernochan St	Hu	21 O	18
Kerrigan St	Hu	24 L	27
Kerry La	Hu	32 U	22
Keswick Av	Ou	45 Y	13
Keswick Rd	Hu	4 D	19
Ketcham Av	Ou	37 V	12
Ketcham La	Ou	46 AA	16
Ketchams Rd	Ou	37 W	11
Keuka Rd	Hu	13 K	20
Kevin Ct	Hu	13 J	21
Kevin Ct	Ou	37 U	11
Kevin La	Hu	46 Y	17
Kevin Pl	Hu	30 R	18
Kevin Rd	Hu	40 X	22
Kew Av	Hu	14 F	23
Key La	Hu	29 T	15
Key Pl	Ou	28 T	12
Keystone Pl	Hu	14 F	24
Kiefer Av	Hu	12 G	18
Kieth Pl	Ou	17 O	6
Kilburn Rd	Hu	12 K	17
Kilburn Rd S	Hu	12 K	18
Kildare Cres Ct	Ou	47 Y	18
Kildare Rd (GA)	Hu	11 J	16
Kildare Rd	Hu	15 K	26
Killians Rd	Ou	47 Y	20
Kilmer La	Hu	6 D	22
Kilmer St	Ou	46 Z	17
Kimberly Ct (wn)	Hu	40 W	20
Kimberly Ct (mr)	Hu	31 S	22
Kimberly Ct (wn)	Hu	40 V	20
Kimson Ct	Nu	9 G	10
King Ct	Ou	28 U	14
King Ct	Hu	39 X	17
King Rd	Ou	25 R	2
King St (FP)	Hu	11 F	16
King St (el)	Hu	4 F	19
King St (WG)	Hu	6 E	24
King St (gs)	Ou	18 L	8
King St (fs)	Hu	13 J	20
King St (os)	Hu	23 M	23
King St (WB)	Nu	28 R	13
King St (FR)	Hu	31 P	21
King St (bm)	Hu	40 U	20
King St (lg)	Hu	36 W	9
King St (hk)	Ou	37 W	12
Kingfisher Rd	Hu	38 U	15
Kings Av	Hu	7 D	28
Kings Av	Ou	47 Y	19
Kings Ct	Nu	2 B	10
Kings Ct	Hu	12 J	17
Kings Ct	Ou	45 Y	13
Kings Dr	Nu	19 N	11
Kings Hwy	Hu	23 L	24
Kings La	Hu	10 J	14
Kings Pkwy	Hu	22 O	21
Kings Pl	Nu	2 B	10
Kings Point Rd	Nu	2 B	9
Kings Rd	Hu	40 W	22
Kings Terrace Rd	Nu	2 D	9
Kingsberry Rd	Ou	39 X	17
Kingsbury Rd	Hu	20 M	16
Kingsland Av	Ou	17 N	6
Kingsley Av	Hu	31 R	20
Kingston Av (FP)	Hu	4 F	17
Kingston Av (bw)	Hu	22 O	20
Kingston Av	Ou	29 U	14
Kingston Av (un)	Hu	39 U	18
Kingston Blvd	Hu	24 L	26
Kingston Ct	Nu	11 H	15
Kingston Pl	Hu	40 U	21
Kingston St	Nu	11 H	15
Kingston St	Hu	5 E	20
Kingswood Cir	Ou	45 BB	12
Kingswood Dr	Ou	45 BB	12
Kinkel St	Nu	28 R	13
Kinloch Rd	Hu	30 U	19
Kinsella Av	Ou	48 AA	21
Kinsley Ct	Hu	23 M	22
Kirby Av	Hu	6 E	24
Kirby Ct	Ou	36 U	10
Kirby Hill	Ou	36 U	10
Kirby La	Ou	36 U	10
Kirgan Ct	Hu	14 J	24
Kirkby Rd	Hu	4 E	19
Kirkman Av	Hu	12 G	19
Kirkwall Ct	Hu	22 L	20
Kirkwood Av	Nu	31 S	22
Kirkwood Dr	Ou	16 N	4
Kirkwood Rd	Nu	31 S	22
Kirkwood St	Hu	24 L	27
Kissam La	Ou	9 L	8
Knabe Rd	Hu	30 Q	19

STREET	MUN. MAP GRID

Knell Dr .... Ou 48 AA 22
Knickerbocker
  Av .... Hu 15 K 26
Knickerbocker
  Rd .... Nu 10 H 11
Knickerbocker
  Rd E .... Ou 37 X 12
Knickerbocker
  Rd N .... Ou 37 W 12
Knickerbocker
  Rd S .... Ou 37 W 12
Knickerbocker
  Rd W .... Ou 37 W 12
Knight Dr .... Nu 28 Q 13
Knight St .... Hu 23 N 24
Knightsbridge
  Rd .... Nu 3 D 12
Knob Hill Dr ...... Hu 30 T 19
Knoll Ct .... Hu 39 X 17
Knoll La (gw) .... Ou 18 M 8
Knoll La (sg) ..... Hu 19 M 13
Knoll La .... Ou 37 V 12
Knoll La .... Hu 39 V 17
Knoll Pl .... Ou 17 M 5
Knoll Rd .... Nu 8 G 6
Knoll St .... Hu 7 B 25
Knoll, The (UB) ... Ou 26 R 7
Knoll, The .... Ou 36 X 9
Knolls Dr .... Nu 10 H 14
Knolls Dr (OW) .. Nu 19 N 13
Knolls Dr N .... Nu 10 H 13
Knolls La .... Nu 9 H 10
Knolls, The .... Ou 26 P 4
Knollwood Av .... Ou 25 R 2
Knollwood Dr .... Nu 19 O 14
Knollwood Dr .... Hu 13 J 19
Knollwood E ...... Nu 9 J 10
Knollwood La
  (MT) .... Ou 36 U 9
Knollwood La .... Ou 39 X 17
Knollwood Rd .... Hu 22 N 21
Knollwood Rd .... Ou 27 T 9
Knollwood S ...... Nu 9 J 11
Knollwood St ..... Hu 12 J 19
Knollwood W .... Nu 9 J 11
Knota Rd .... Hu 6 E 24
Knott Dr .... Ou 17 M 7
Knowles St .... Ou 45 Z 12
Koch Pl .... Nu 20 O 14
Kodiak Dr .... Ou 44 AA 10
Koehl St .... Ou 47 AA 20
Koelbel Ct .... Hu 23 N 23
Koenig Dr .... Ou 35 W 6
Kolmer Av .... Ou 28 T 12
Konig Ct .... Hu 31 Q 20
Kopf Rd .... Hu 40 V 22
Koppell Pl .... Hu 21 N 19
Kowal Ct .... Hu 31 S 22
Kowall Pl .... Hu 13 H 21
Kraemer St .... Ou 37 V 13
Kramer La .... Ou 45 Y 13
Kraus St .... Hu 13 G 19
Kresse St .... Hu 14 K 24
Kristi Dr .... Ou 37 U 11
Kristi La .... Ou 44 Y 10
Kroll Rd .... Hu 30 R 17
Kroll St .... Ou 45 Y 11
Krug Pl .... Nu 20 L 15
Krull St .... Hu 22 P 20
Kruze St .... Hu 12 J 18
Kuhl Av .... Ou 28 T 12
Kulenkampf Pl ... Hu 13 G 22
Kunen Av .... Ou 38 Y 14
Kyle Ct .... Ou 47 Z 19

L

L St .... Hu 12 G 19
La Colline Dr
  (Pvt) .... Ou 26 S 5
La Farge La ...... Nu 9 J 10
Lace La .... Hu 29 S 15
Laclede Av .... Ou 30 Q 17
Ladenburg Dr ... Hu 29 Q 15
Ladew St .... Ou 17 M 5
Ladonia St .... Hu 40 W 22
Lafayette Av
  (SC) .... Ou 17 L 7
Lafayette Av
  (HV) .... Hu 21 N 17
Lafayette Av
  (WB) .... Nu 20 P 15
Lafayette Av
  (LY) .... Hu 13 K 21

STREET	MUN. MAP GRID

Lafayette Av
  (LY) .... Hu 13 J 21
Lafayette Av
  (un) .... Hu 21 P 18
Lafayette Av
  (bp) .... Ou 46 Y 15
Lafayette Blvd ... Hu 15 H 28
Lafayette Dr ...... Hu 6 F 23
Lafayette Dr ...... Ou 36 W 10
Lafayette Pl
  (WG) .... Hu 6 F 24
Lafayette Pl
  (FR) .... Hu 31 P 20
Lafayette Pl
  (FR) .... Hu 31 Q 21
Lafayette Rd ..... Ou 48 Y 22
Lafayette Rd ..... Ou 46 AA 16
Lafayette St ...... Nu 10 K 14
Lafayette St ...... Hu 31 T 20
Lagoon Blvd ..... Ou 48 Z 22
Lagoon Dr .... Nu 2 D 9
Lagoon Dr E ..... Hu 24 M 27
Lagoon Dr W .... Hu 24 M 27
Lahey St .... Nu 11 G 14
Laidlaw Av .... Hu 12 H 19
Lake Av .... Ou 26 T 5
Lake Av .... Hu 31 S 20
Lake Ct .... Ou 48 Z 21
Lake Dr .... Nu 10 H 14
Lake Dr .... Hu 14 H 24
Lake Dr E .... Hu 22 O 21
Lake Dr N .... Hu 13 F 21
Lake Dr S .... Hu 13 F 21
Lake Dr W .... Hu 22 O 21
Lake End Rd .... Hu 31 T 22
Lake La .... Hu 29 S 15
Lake Rd (PR) .... Nu 2 F 10
Lake Rd N .... Hu 3 E 14
Lake Rd S .... Hu 3 F 14
Lake Rd W .... Hu 3 E 14
Lake Shore Blvd .. Ou 47 Z 21
Lake Shore Dr .... Ou 47 AA 20
Lake Side Dr S .. Hu 6 D 23
Lake St .... Hu 23 M 24
Lake St .... Ou 48 CC 21
Lakeside Dr (lk) .. Hu 22 L 21
Lakeside
  (bw) .... Hu 22 N 22
Lakeside Dr
  (FR) .... Hu 31 Q 20
Lakeside Dr
  (wn) .... Hu 39 V 19
Lakeside Dr E .... Hu 7 D 26
Lakeside Dr S .... Hu 7 C 26
Lakeside Dr W ... Hu 7 C 26
Lakeside Pl .... Hu 22 O 22
Lakeview Av
  (ML) .... Hu 13 J 21
Lakeview Av
  (mr) .... Hu 31 R 21
Lakeview Av
  (mq) .... Hu 47 Y 20
Lakeview Av ...... Ou 48 Z 21
Lakeview Dr ...... Nu 3 F 14
Lakeview Dr ...... Hu 14 H 23
Lakeview Rd ..... Hu 40 V 21
Lakeville Dr
  (NP) .... Nu 11 G 15
Lakeville Dr ...... Nu 18 M 10
Lakeville La ...... Hu 30 R 18
Lakeville La ...... Ou 37 X 12
Lakeville Rd
  (TM) .... Nu 3 E 12
Lakeville Rd ...... Nu 11 G 15
Lakewood Av .... Hu 31 P 20
Lakewood Blvd .. Nu 13 K 22
Lamarcus Av .... Ou 17 M 6
Lamberson St ... Hu 15 K 27
Lambert Av .... Ou 46 AA 17
Lambert St .... Nu 11 L 12
Lambeth Rd ...... Hu 5 F 20
Lamp La .... Hu 29 S 15
Lamplighter La ... Ou 48 CC 21
Lancaster Av .... Hu 22 N 22
Lancaster Pl
  (HV) .... Hu 22 N 19
Lancaster Pl ..... Hu 15 K 27
Lancaster St
  (ML) .... Hu 13 J 21
Lancaster St ..... Hu 30 S 17
Lancia Dr .... Ou 35 U 6
Land La .... Hu 29 S 15
Land Pl .... Hu 23 L 24
Landau Av .... Hu 12 G 18
Landford Dr ...... Hu 4 E 19
Landing Av .... Hu 40 U 22

STREET	MUN. MAP GRID

Landing Rd (GL) . Ou 8 K 5
Landing Rd .... Nu 9 K 10
Landing Rd .... Ou 35 W 5
Landman La ...... Hu 30 U 19
Landomus Rd ... Hu 15 L 25
Lands End Rd ... Ou 16 P 2
Lane .... Ou 16 P 5
Lane Av .... Ou 37 X 13
Lane Pl .... Ou 37 Y 11
Lane, The .... Ou 35 X 6
Langdon Dr ...... Hu 13 K 21
Langdon Pl .... Hu 13 H 22
Langdon Rd ...... Nu 19 N 14
Langdon Rd ...... Ou 46 Z 17
Langdon St .... Hu 12 G 18
Langen Dr .... Hu 40 W 21
Langley Av .... Hu 12 K 19
Langley La .... Nu 28 Q 13
Lanier Pl .... Nu 19 P 14
Lannon Pl .... Nu 8 G 8
Lansdowne Av ... Nu 20 O 15
Lansdowne Av ... Hu 31 S 22
Lansing Pl .... Ou 36 V 9
Lantern Rd .... Ou 38 U 15
Laplaca Ct .... Nu 2 F 11
Lapwing Ct .... Nu 10 J 12
Larboard Ct ...... Hu 30 Q 18
Larch Av .... Hu 4 E 17
Larch Dr (GN) ... Nu 3 D 12
Larch Dr (EH) ... Nu 18 M 11
Larch Dr (hr) ..... Nu 10 J 14
Larch Hill Rd ..... Hu 7 D 26
Larch La .... Hu 30 R 18
Larch La .... Ou 48 AA 21
Larch Pl .... Ou 16 M 5
Larch St .... Ou 37 V 13
Larch St .... Hu 40 W 21
Lariat La .... Hu 38 W 15
Lark Av .... Ou 45 Z 13
Lark Ct .... Hu 6 E 24
Lark Ct .... Ou 45 Z 13
Lark Dr .... Ou 37 Y 11
Lark St .... Hu 38 W 16
Larkspur Av ...... Hu 30 R 19
Larkspur Ct .... Ou 46 Z 16
Larrabee Av ...... Ou 26 T 5
Larsen Av .... Ou 18 L 8
Latham La .... Nu 19 M 14
Latham Rd (hr) .. Nu 11 K 14
Latham Rd .... Nu 11 K 15
Latimer Ct .... Hu 22 M 22
Lattingtown
  Ridge Ct ...... Ou 16 N 4
Lattingtown Rd
  (GL) .... Ou 16 M 3
Lattingtown Rd ... Ou 16 N 4
Lattingtown
  Woods Ct ..... Ou 16 O 4
Lauman La .... Ou 38 W 15
Laura Ct .... Hu 31 T 20
Laura Dr (wn) .... Ou 28 S 13
Laura Dr .... Ou 48 BB 22
Laura La .... Ou 45 Z 12
Laureen Ct .... Hu 40 X 21
Laurel Av (SC) ... Ou 8 K 7
Laurel Av (GL) ... Ou 8 L 5
Laurel Av (HV) ... Hu 21 M 18
Laurel Av (bh) ... Hu 23 O 23
Laurel Ct (lk) ..... Hu 12 K 19
Laurel Ct (bw) ... Hu 22 O 22
Laurel Ct (MT) ... Ou 26 T 7
Laurel Ct (ed) ... Hu 30 S 19
Laurel Ct (LH) ... Ou 43 Y 7
Laurel Ct (bp) ... Ou 37 X 13
Laurel Ct (sd) ... Hu 40 X 21
Laurel Cove
  R.O.W. .... Ou 35 X 5
Laurel Cove Rd .. Ou 35 W 5
Laurel Dr (GE) ... Nu 3 C 12
Laurel Dr (mh) ... Nu 10 H 14
Laurel Dr .... Nu 20 N 15
Laurel Dr .... Hu 13 J 20
Laurel Dr .... Ou 48 AA 21
Laurel Hill Dr ..... Ou 35 U 6
Laurel Hill Rd ..... Hu 5 E 22
Laurel Hollow
  Rd .... Ou 35 Y 6
Laurel La (PN) ... Nu 1 F 7
Laurel La (in) ..... Hu 7 C 25
Laurel La (EH) ... Nu 19 N 11
Laurel La (OW) .. Nu 19 N 14
Laurel La (MC) ... Ou 26 Q 5
Laurel La (lv) ..... Hu 38 V 16
Laurel La (LH) ... Ou 43 Y 7
Laurel La (lg) ..... Ou 36 X 8

STREET	MUN. MAP GRID

Laurel La (wn) .... Hu 39 W 19
Laurel La E .... Nu 19 N 14
Laurel Pl (VS) .... Nu 5 D 21
Laurel Pl (nv) ..... Hu 13 G 20
Laurel Pl (BY) .... Ou 25 R 2
Laurel Pl (bp) .... Ou 38 X 15
Laurel Rd (lk) ..... Hu 12 K 19
Laurel Rd (RC) ... Nu 22 M 20
Laurel Rd (FR) ... Hu 32 Q 23
Laurel St (FP) .... Nu 12 G 17
Laurel St (rt) ...... Nu 19 L 11
Laurel St (HV) ... Nu 20 N 15
Laurel St (je) ..... Ou 37 V 11
Laurel St (hk) .... Ou 37 U 13
Laurel St (mr) .... Hu 31 S 22
Laurel St (FG) .... Ou 46 BB 15
Laurel Wy .... Ou 8 K 7
Laurel Woods
  Dr .... Ou 26 R 6
Laurelton Blvd ... Hu 15 J 28
Laurelton St ...... Ou 46 AA 16
Lauren La .... Ou 25 S 2
Laurette La .... Hu 32 R 23
Laurie Blvd .... Ou 45 Y 14
Laurie Dr .... Ou 46 AA 16
Laurie La .... Hu 12 L 19
Laurie Pl .... Ou 17 O 5
Laux Pl .... Hu 30 U 19
Lavenders Ct .... Nu 10 H 12
Law St .... Hu 5 E 20
Lawn Cir .... Hu 39 V 18
Lawn Dr .... Nu 18 M 10
Lawn Dr .... Hu 30 T 18
Lawn La .... Ou 26 T 6
Lawn Pl .... Hu 6 F 24
Lawn Pl .... Ou 38 V 15
Lawn St .... Hu 13 H 20
Lawnside
  (hk) .... Ou 37 V 13
Lawnside Dr ...... Ou 37 V 14
Lawnview Av
  (hk) .... Ou 37 V 14
Lawrence Av
  (in) .... Hu 6 C 24
Lawrence Av
  (LW) .... Hu 7 D 26
Lawrence Av
  (ML) .... Hu 13 J 20
Lawrence Av
  (LY) .... Hu 13 J 20
Lawrence Av
  (LY) .... Hu 13 K 21
Lawrence Av
  (sv) .... Hu 23 L 24
Lawrence Ct
  (sv) .... Hu 5 E 22
Lawrence Ct
  (ae) .... Hu 7 E 27
Lawrence Ct
  (ML) .... Hu 13 J 20
Lawrence Ct
  (hk) .... Ou 37 U 13
Lawrence Ct
  (sl) .... Hu 29 R 15
Lawrence Ct
  (ed) .... Hu 30 S 19
Lawrence Ct
  (sy) .... Ou 36 W 8
Lawrence Dr ...... Hu 39 U 18
Lawrence La ...... Ou 17 O 6
Lawrence Pk ..... Hu 6 C 24
Lawrence
  Pkwy E .... Hu 7 D 25
Lawrence Pl
  (RC) .... Hu 22 M 21
Lawrence Pl ...... Ou 28 T 12
Lawrence Pl ...... Hu 40 V 21
Lawrence Rd
  (fs) .... Hu 12 J 19
Lawrence Rd
  (HV) .... Hu 21 O 19
Lawrence Rd
  (nb) .... Hu 30 T 19
Lawrence Rd
  (nw) .... Hu 39 X 18
Lawrence St
  (nn) .... Nu 11 G 14
Lawrence St
  (fs) .... Hu 12 H 18
Lawrence St
  (el) .... Hu 12 G 19
Lawrence St
  (mh) .... Nu 10 H 14
Lawrence St
  (eg) .... Hu 21 O 17
Lawrence St
  (ba) .... Hu 14 J 24

Nassau Co.

STREET	MUN.	MAP	GRID

Nassau Co.

STREET	MUN.	MAP GRID
Links Dr W	Hu	23 M 24
Links Rd	Hu	14 G 24
Linkwood Dr	Hu	22 O 20
Linmouth Rd	Hu	13 J 21
Linnet Ct	Nu	10 J 12
Linstead La	Hu	30 T 18
Linwood Av (CH)	Hu	6 D 24
Linwood Av	Hu	30 U 19
Linwood Av	Ou	46 AA 16
Linwood Dr	Hu	18 M 11
Linwood Pl	Ou	47 CC 19
Linwood Rd N	Nu	1 E 7
Linwood Rd S	Nu	1 E 7
Linwood St	Hu	21 P 19
Lion Ct	Hu	14 H 23
Lion La	Hu	29 S 15
Lippold St	Hu	31 S 22
Lipton La	Hu	19 K 14
Lisa Ct (sy)	Ou	36 V 8
Lisa Ct (bm)	Hu	31 U 22
Lisa Ct (wy)	Ou	43 Z 8
Lisa Ct (pv)	Ou	45 Y 13
Lisa Ct (sa)	Ou	46 AA 17
Lisa La	Hu	21 K 19
Lismore Rd	Hu	7 C 26
Liszt St	Ou	37 W 12
Litchfield Av	Hu	12 G 19
Litchfield Rd	Nu	9 G 9
Little Neck Av	Hu	30 T 19
Little Vikings Cove	Ou	16 N 3
Little Whaleneck Rd	Hu	30 S 19
Littleworth La	Ou	17 L 7
Livengood Ct	Ou	44 AA 10
Livingston Av	Ou	28 S 12
Livingston Pl	Hu	6 D 25
Livingston St	Nu	28 Q 13
Livingstone Pl	Hu	7 E 27
Lloyd Av	Hu	14 H 23
Lloyd Ct (un)	Hu	30 Q 17
Lloyd St	Hu	30 T 19
Lloyd St	Hu	12 H 18
Lloyd St	Nu	18 M 9
Lloyd St (hr)	Nu	10 J 14
Loch Pa	Nu	9 K 11
Loch Pa	Nu	22 N 22
Loch, The	Nu	9 K 11
Loch, The	Nu	22 N 22
Lockwood Av	Ou	46 AA 17
Locust Av	Nu	8 G 8
Locust Av (WG)	Hu	6 E 25
Locust Av (GL)	Ou	17 L 6
Locust Av (gw)	Ou	17 M 8
Locust Av (RC)	Hu	22 L 21
Locust Av (os)	Hu	23 M 23
Locust Av (FR)	Hu	23 P 23
Locust Av (BY)	Ou	25 S 2
Locust Av (Cl)	Ou	34 U 3
Locust Av (MN)	Ou	35 U 5
Locust Av (en)	Ou	26 U 7
Locust Av (un)	Hu	30 P 18
Locust Av (un)	Hu	30 Q 18
Locust Av (nb)	Hu	30 T 19
Locust Av (bp)	Ou	37 X 13
Locust Av (sa)	Ou	46 BB 17
Locust Av (wn)	Hu	40 W 21
Locust Av (sa)	Hu	40 X 21
Locust Ct	Hu	13 K 21
Locust Ct (rv)	Hu	31 R 21
Locust Cove La	Nu	2 B 9
Locust Dr	Nu	3 C 11
Locust La (hr)	Nu	10 J 14
Locust La (EH)	Nu	19 M 11
Locust La (BY)	Ou	25 T 2
Locust La (OK)	Ou	26 Q 7
Locust La (oy)	Ou	26 T 5
Locust La (lv)	Ou	36 W 10
Locust Pl	Nu	9 F 11
Locust Pl (LT)	Ou	16 P 4
Locust Pl (SC)	Ou	8 K 7
Locust Pl	Hu	23 P 23
Locust Rd	Nu	9 G 9
Locust St (gg)	Nu	2 E 11
Locust St (ma)	Nu	9 F 11
Locust St (FP)	Hu	4 F 17
Locust St (LY)	Hu	13 H 21
Locust St (VS)	Hu	14 F 22
Locust St (GL)	Ou	8 L 5
Locust St (gh)	Ou	17 N 7
Locust St (EH)	Nu	18 M 10
Locust St (rt)	Nu	9 L 11
Locust St (WB)	Nu	19 P 14
Locust St (GA)	Hu	21 M 17
Locust St (lk)	Hu	12 K 19

STREET	MUN.	MAP GRID
Locust St (RC)	Ou	22 M 20
Locust St (hk)	Ou	29 U 14
Locust St (bm)	Hu	31 T 20
Locust St (mq)	Ou	40 Y 21
Locust Ter	Hu	12 K 19
Locusts, The	Nu	9 J 11
Locustwood Blvd	Hu	4 E 18
Locustwood La	Hu	38 V 16
Lodge Rd	Nu	3 F 12
Loel Ct	Hu	22 L 21
Loft Av	Hu	22 N 22
Loft Rd	Hu	14 F 24
Loftus Av	Hu	23 M 23
Lofty St	Ou	37 V 11
Logan Rd	Hu	39 U 19
Logan St (bm)	Hu	31 T 20
Logue St	Hu	30 T 19
Loines Av	Hu	31 S 21
Lois Ct	Hu	29 S 16
Lois La (ob)	Ou	45 AA 14
Lois La	Ou	47 CC 18
Lois La (VS)	Hu	13 G 22
Lois Pl	Hu	31 S 21
Lois Pl	Ou	47 CC 19
Lombardi Pl	Ou	45 Z 13
Lombardy St	Ou	28 T 13
London Ct	Hu	31 T 22
London Rd	Ou	37 W 11
Long Beach Blvd	Hu	15 K 28
Long Beach Rd	Hu	15 K 26
Long Branch Rd	Ou	17 M 6
Long Dr	Hu	21 L 18
Long Island Expwy (LS)	Nu	3 E 13
Long Island Expwy (NL)	Nu	10 H 13
Long Island Expwy (al)	Nu	19 L 12
Long Island Expwy (OW)	Nu	19 O 12
Long Island Expwy (je)	Ou	28 S 12
Long Island Expwy (pv)	Ou	44 Y 13
Long La	Hu	29 S 15
Long Meadow La	Ou	16 M 3
Long Ridge La	Ou	18 O 8
Long Ridge Rd	Nu	9 G 10
Long Ridge Rd	Ou	44 AA 11
Longacre Av	Hu	6 D 23
Longbeach Av (FR)	Hu	31 P 22
Longfellow Av	Nu	29 Q 14
Longfellow Av (ed)	Hu	30 S 18
Longfellow Av (ln)	Hu	39 X 17
Longfellow Av	Nu	2 B 11
Longfellow St	Hu	22 N 21
Longman Pl	Hu	21 O 17
Longview Av	Hu	6 E 22
Longview Pl	Nu	3 E 11
Longview Rd	Nu	8 H 8
Longwood Av	Nu	20 O 14
Longwood Crossing N	Hu	7 E 26
Longwood Rd	Nu	1 F 6
Longworth Av	Hu	14 F 24
Lonni La	Hu	32 T 23
Loon Pl	Hu	38 X 16
Loop Pkwy	Hu	33 Q 26
Lord Av (in)	Hu	6 C 25
Lord Av	Hu	7 C 26
Lords Wy	Nu	10 J 14
Lorentz St	Hu	4 E 19
Lorenz Av	Hu	22 O 22
Loretta Dr	Ou	37 W 11
Loretta La	Ou	37 U 13
Loretta St	Hu	6 C 25
Lori Ct	Ou	44 Z 8
Loring Rd	Hu	39 U 17
Lorna Pl	Hu	23 M 23
Lorraine Ct	Nu	18 M 9
Lorraine Ct	Hu	13 H 20
Lorraine Dr	Hu	12 H 19
Lorraine Gate	Hu	39 U 17
Lorraine Rd	Hu	15 K 26
Lorraine St	Ou	37 V 11
Lorrie Dr	Hu	31 T 20
Losee Ct	Hu	31 T 20
Lottie Av	Ou	37 V 13
Lotus La	Hu	29 S 15

STREET	MUN.	MAP GRID
Lotus Oval N	Hu	5 E 22
Lotus Oval S	Hu	5 E 22
Lotus St	Hu	6 E 25
Louden Av	Ou	47 CC 20
Louis Av (FP)	Hu	4 F 18
Louis Av	Hu	12 J 19
Louis Dr	Ou	46 AA 16
Louis Pl	Hu	23 N 24
Louis Rd	Hu	40 X 21
Louis St	Ou	46 AA 17
Louis St	Ou	38 W 14
Louise Av	Ou	47 BB 21
Louise Pl	Hu	5 E 21
Louisiana Av	Hu	24 L 25
Louisiana St	Hu	15 G 28
Lourae Dr	Ou	47 BB 18
Lovers La	Hu	6 F 25
Low La	Hu	39 W 17
Lowell Av (FP)	Hu	11 F 16
Lowell Av (NP)	Hu	11 H 16
Lowell Av	Hu	40 V 21
Lowell Dr	Ou	46 AA 17
Lowell La	Hu	32 T 23
Lowell Pl	Hu	22 N 21
Lowell Rd	Ou	28 T 13
Lowell Rd	Nu	9 H 9
Lowell Rd	Hu	21 P 18
Lowell St (LY)	Hu	13 H 21
Lowell St (CH)	Hu	6 D 24
Lowell St (WB)	Nu	29 Q 14
Lowell St (hk)	Ou	28 T 13
Lowell St (pe)	Ou	46 Y 16
Lower Lincoln Av	Hu	23 L 23
Lowland Rd	Hu	38 W 16
Luchon St	Hu	24 N 27
Lucian St	Nu	19 N 14
Lucille Av	Hu	12 H 19
Lucille Ct	Hu	4 F 19
Lucille Ct	Ou	48 Z 21
Lucille Dr	Ou	36 W 9
Lucille La	Ou	45 BB 13
Lucille St	Hu	21 O 18
Luckenbach La	Nu	8 G 6
Luddington Rd	Hu	30 Q 19
Ludlam Av	Hu	4 D 18
Ludlam Av	Ou	25 S 2
Ludlam La	Ou	16 P 4
Ludlum Pl	Hu	12 G 18
Ludwig La	Hu	19 L 13
Ludwig La	Ou	46 Y 17
Ludwig Pl	Ou	46 BB 17
Ludy St	Ou	38 W 14
Luester T. Mertz Plz	Nu	9 H 8
Lufberry Av	Hu	39 W 19
Lufberry Dr	Nu	18 L 11
Lumber Rd	Nu	9 K 10
Luonga La	Ou	17 O 6
Luquer Rd	Nu	9 F 9
Lutz Dr	Hu	5 E 20
Lutz Rd	Ou	37 X 12
Lutz St	Hu	12 H 18
Lydia Av	Hu	12 G 19
Lydia Ct	Ou	10 K 13
Lydia Ct	Hu	41 V 23
Lydia Dr	Hu	12 H 19
Lydia La (GA)	Hu	12 K 17
Lydia La (sl)	Hu	29 R 15
Lydia La	Hu	41 V 23
Lydia Pl	Hu	23 O 24
Lydia Pl	Ou	37 U 11
Lydia St	Hu	13 H 20
Lyme Pl	Hu	22 P 21
Lynbrook Av	Hu	13 J 22
Lynbrook St	Hu	40 V 22
Lyncrest St	Hu	13 G 22
Lynn Ct (ML)	Hu	13 J 21
Lynn Ct (un)	Hu	30 P 18
Lynn Ct	Hu	32 S 23
Lynn Ct	Ou	37 X 13
Lynn Dr	Ou	36 U 9
Lynn La	Hu	39 W 17
Lynn Pl (VS)	Hu	13 F 20
Lynn Pl (WG)	Hu	14 F 24
Lynn Rd (pw)	Nu	9 H 9
Lynn Rd	Nu	9 H 9
Lynne Rd	Hu	39 X 18
Lynne St	Hu	22 O 20
Lynnwood Dr	Nu	19 O 13
Lynton Rd	Nu	19 L 13
Lynwood Dr	Hu	13 G 20
Lyon Ct	Ou	37 W 13
Lyon Pl (LY)	Hu	13 H 22
Lyon Pl	Hu	40 W 19
Lyon St	Hu	5 E 21
Lyon St	Ou	38 W 13
Lyons Av	Ou	46 BB 17

M

STREET	MUN.	MAP GRID
M St	Hu	12 G 19
Mabel Pl	Hu	31 S 21
Mabel St	Ou	37 V 12
MacArthur Av	Ou	37 X 13
MacAtee Pl	Nu	11 K 14
MacDonald Rd	Hu	14 L 25
MacDonald St	Hu	21 N 18
Mack Av	Ou	37 W 12
Mack Pl	Ou	38 X 16
MacKay Wy	Nu	18 L 10
MacKey Av	Nu	9 G 8
MacLean Dr	Ou	27 S 10
Macon Pl	Hu	21 P 19
Macy Dr	Hu	14 G 24
Madeline Pl	Ou	16 M 5
Madison Av (CH)	Hu	6 D 24
Madison Av (in)	Hu	6 C 25
Madison Av	Ou	17 M 5
Madison Av (rt)	Nu	10 K 11
Madison Av (gk)	Nu	11 J 15
Madison Av (fs)	Hu	12 J 18
Madison Av (wh)	Hu	12 K 19
Madison Av	Hu	21 M 18
Madison Av (bw)	Hu	22 N 21
Madison Av (RC)	Hu	13 L 22
Madison Av (os)	Hu	23 M 23
Madison Av (FR)	Hu	22 P 22
Madison Av (hi)	Hu	15 J 26
Madison Av	Ou	25 S 2
Madison Av (WB)	Nu	29 P 14
Madison Av (je)	Ou	28 S 12
Madison Av (rv)	Hu	31 Q 21
Madison Av (bm)	Hu	40 U 20
Madison Av (bp)	Ou	38 W 14
Madison Dr	Hu	30 S 17
Madison Pl	Nu	10 L 11
Madison Pl (bh)	Hu	23 N 24
Madison Pl	Ou	28 S 12
Madison Pl	Hu	30 S 19
Madison St (pw)	Nu	9 G 8
Madison St (SF)	Hu	12 G 18
Madison St (nv)	Hu	12 F 19
Madison St (fs)	Hu	12 H 19
Madison St (HN)	Hu	14 G 24
Madison St (LY)	Hu	13 K 22
Madison St (bh)	Hu	23 N 24
Madison St (WB)	Nu	29 Q 14
Madison St (mr)	Nu	31 S 21
Madison St	Ou	47 CC 20
Madonia Ct	Nu	9 G 10
Mae Ct	Ou	40 V 22
Maeder Av	Hu	31 R 20
Magee Pl	Hu	14 K 23
Magenta St	Ou	37 W 12
Maggio La	Ou	45 Z 13
Maglie Dr	Ou	38 V 14
Magnolia Av (FP)	Hu	12 G 17
Magnolia Av	Ou	17 M 8
Magnolia Av (HV)	Hu	20 M 16
Magnolia Av	Nu	28 R 13
Magnolia Blvd	Hu	15 J 28
Magnolia Dr (GE)	Nu	3 D 11
Magnolia Dr (VS)	Hu	6 F 23
Magnolia Dr	Nu	11 H 15
Magnolia La	Hu	13 J 20
Magnolia La	Ou	47 Z 19
Magnolia La	Hu	18 M 11
Magnolia La (lg)	Ou	18 L 9
Magnolia La (wy)	Ou	44 AA 9
Magnolia La (sy)	Ou	36 X 8
Magnolia Pl	Hu	6 F 23
Magnolia Rd	Hu	30 U 19
Magnolia St	Nu	19 O 14
Magpie La	Hu	38 U 15
Mahan Rd	Ou	45 AA 13
Mahland Pl	Hu	23 L 23
Mahlon Brower Dr	Hu	23 M 25
Mahopac Rd	Hu	13 K 20
Maiden La (LY)	Hu	13 K 22
Maiden La (in)	Hu	6 C 25

Nassau Co.

137

Nassau Co.

STREET	MUN.	MAP	GRID
Michael Rd	Ou	37	W 11
Michael William Rd	Hu	31	R 20
Michaels La	Ou	18	N 8
Michaelson La	Ou	27	U 10
Michalaki Pl	Hu	31	R 21
Michel Av	Ou	46	AA 17
Michel Ct	Hu	13	H 21
Michele La	Hu	39	W 18
Michele Ter	Ou	48	BB 21
Michelle Dr	Ou	37	U 11
Michelle Pl	Hu	6	D 23
Michigan Av (MS)	Ou	47	BB 20
Michigan Av	Ou	47	Y 20
Michigan Dr	Ou	38	W 14
Michigan Rd	Hu	4	E 17
Michigan St	Hu	15	G 28
Middle Bay Dr	Hu	23	P 25
Middle Cross La	Ou	16	L 4
Middle Dr	Nu	9	F 10
Middle La	Ou	37	U 11
Middle La	Hu	29	S 15
Middle Neck Rd (SP)	Nu	1	E 6
Middle Neck Rd (KP)	Nu	2	D 9
Middle Neck Rd (FH)	Nu	9	H 9
Middle Rd	Nu	8	H 7
Middlecamp Rd	Nu	28	Q 13
Middleton Rd	Hu	12	H 17
Midfarrn Rd	Hu	22	M 21
Midfield Rd	Hu	6	E 24
Midge Av	Ou	17	M 5
Midgely Dr	Hu	14	F 24
Midian St	Hu	30	R 19
Midland Av	Ou	37	V 12
Midland Dr	Nu	11	H 14
Midland Pl	Hu	39	U 18
Midland Rd	Nu	19	M 11
Midland Rd	Hu	30	S 18
Midland St	Hu	21	P 18
Midlane	Ou	36	U 9
Midlane S	Ou	36	V 9
Midlawn Dr	Ou	47	Y 18
Midtown Rd	Nu	19	N 14
Midvale Av	Hu	30	T 18
Midvale La	Hu	13	G 20
Midway Av	Ou	25	Q 4
Midway Ct	Hu	12	H 19
Midway East End	Hu	6	E 23
Midway La	Hu	39	U 17
Midwood Av	Hu	40	V 21
Midwood Av	Ou	47	BB 18
Midwood Cross	Nu	18	M 10
Midwood Dr	Hu	30	U 19
Midwood Dr	Ou	45	Y 12
Midwood Pl (wm)	Hu	6	E 24
Midwood Pl	Ou	17	M 7
Midwood Pl (FR)	Hu	22	P 21
Midwood Rd (wm)	Hu	6	E 23
Midwood Rd	Hu	22	L 21
Midwood St (VS)	Hu	5	E 21
Midwood St (HV)	Hu	21	N 17
Midwood St (un)	Hu	21	P 18
Mikel La	Ou	18	M 8
Milanna La	Hu	39	V 19
Milano St	Ou	38	V 15
Milben Ct	Ou	44	Z 11
Milber Heath	Hu	14	G 23
Milbrock Ct	Nu	2	D 11
Milburn Av (HV)	Hu	21	N 19
Milburn Av (bw)	Hu	22	O 22
Milburn Ct (nv)	Hu	13	H 20
Milburn Ct	Hu	22	O 21
Milburn Rd	Hu	13	H 20
Milburn St	Hu	22	M 21
Milburn St	Ou	29	U 14
Mildred Ct	Hu	12	G 17
Mildred Ct	Ou	45	Z 11
Mildred Dr	Hu	23	P 25
Mildred Pl (ER)	Hu	14	H 23
Mildred Pl (HV)	Hu	21	O 19
Mildred Pl (bm)	Hu	40	U 21
Mildred St	Hu	23	M 23
Miles Av	Nu	10	K 13
Milford Ct	Ou	45	Z 12
Milford Dr	Ou	45	Z 12
Milford La	Hu	5	F 20
Milford Pl (RC)	Hu	22	L 21
Milford Pl	Hu	39	U 18
Milford Pl (sa)	Ou	47	BB 18
Milford Pl	Ou	47	Z 21
Milford St	Hu	21	N 18
Mill Hill Rd (GL)	Ou	17	M 5
Mill Hill Rd	Ou	26	S 5
Mill La	Hu	39	V 17
Mill Pond La	Ou	25	Q 3
Mill Pond Rd	Nu	8	F 8
Mill River Av	Hu	13	K 22
Mill River Hollow Rd	Ou	26	T 6
Mill River Rd	Ou	26	T 7
Mill Rd (VS)	Hu	6	F 22
Mill Rd (gh)	Ou	17	M 8
Mill Rd (hk)	Ou	38	U 15
Mill Rd (ne)	Hu	31	R 20
Mill Rd (FR)	Hu	31	Q 22
Mill Rd (sa)	Ou	46	CC 17
Mill Rd (wn)	Hu	39	X 19
Mill Spring Rd	Nu	9	H 11
Mill St (LW)	Hu	7	C 25
Mill St	Hu	23	M 23
Millang Pl	Hu	31	S 22
Millburn Ct (bw)	Hu	22	O 22
Millburn Ct	Hu	40	V 20
Millburn La	Nu	18	M 11
Miller Av (FP)	Hu	4	F 17
Miller Av (eg)	Hu	20	O 16
Miller Av (os)	Hu	23	L 23
Miller Av (bw)	Hu	22	O 22
Miller Av (FR)	Hu	32	Q 23
Miller Blvd	Ou	36	X 8
Miller Cir	Ou	37	V 12
Miller Pl (VS)	Hu	5	E 20
Miller Pl	Nu	10	L 11
Miller Pl (HV)	Hu	21	M 17
Miller Pl (bw)	Hu	22	O 22
Miller Pl	Ou	37	V 11
Miller Pl (mr)	Hu	31	S 21
Miller Pl (ln)	Hu	39	X 17
Miller Rd (hk)	Ou	37	V 12
Miller Rd (lg)	Ou	37	X 11
Miller Rd (FG)	Ou	46	Z 16
Miller St	Ou	16	L 5
Millers La (NP)	Nu	11	H 16
Millford Dr	Ou	25	Q 3
Millford La	Ou	16	M 4
Millington Pl	Nu	20	L 15
Millpond St	Ou	37	U 11
Millwood Gate La	Ou	38	W 14
Millwood La	Hu	31	R 20
Milne Pl	Ou	45	Y 12
Milton Av	Hu	39	X 17
Milton Ct	Hu	22	M 22
Milton La	Ou	36	W 10
Milton Pl	Hu	6	E 24
Milton St	Hu	13	H 21
Milton St	Ou	37	U 13
Mimosa Dr	Nu	9	L 11
Mimosa La	Nu	8	H 6
Mindy Ct	Ou	16	O 3
Mindy La	Ou	28	R 12
Mineola Av (RL)	Nu	9	K 11
Mineola Av (WB)	Nu	20	N 15
Mineola Av	Hu	33	Q 27
Mineola Av	Ou	38	W 14
Mineola Blvd	Nu	20	L 15
Mingo Av	Ou	34	U 3
Minnesota Av	Hu	15	G 28
Mirabelle Av	Hu	29	R 14
Mirada Dr	Ou	34	W 2
Miramare Ter	Ou	34	V 2
Miravista Rd	Ou	34	W 2
Miriam Ct	Hu	12	F 19
Miriam La	Ou	5	AA 13
Miriam Pkwy	Hu	5	F 19
Miriam St (VS)	Hu	13	G 22
Miriam St	Hu	38	X 16
Mirin Av	Hu	31	Q 20
Mirrielees Cir	Nu	3	C 12
Mirrielees Rd	Nu	3	C 12
Mirschel St	Hu	21	M 18
Mishaupan Pl	Ou	25	R 1
Mist La	Hu	29	S 15
Mistletoe La	Hu	38	V 16
Mistletoe Wy	Hu	7	E 26
Mitchel Av (LB)	Hu	24	L 28
Mitchel Av	Hu	30	Q 18
Mitchel Ct	Ou	38	U 14
Mitchel Ct	Hu	31	T 22
Mitchell Av	Nu	20	O 15
Mitchell Av	Ou	45	Y 11
Mitchell Ct	Hu	21	N 17
Mitchell Dr	Nu	2	C 9
Mitchell La	Ou	36	W 10
Mitchell Pl	Nu	10	G 11
Mitchell Pl	Hu	31	T 21
Mitchell Rd	Nu	9	G 8
Mitchell St	Ou	25	Q 4
Mitchell St (un)	Hu	30	Q 19
Mitchell St (bm)	Hu	31	T 21
Mize Ct	Hu	21	P 18
Mockingbird La	Hu	29	T 16
Moeller St	Ou	37	V 12
Moffat Pl	Hu	21	O 19
Moffett Av	Ou	35	U 5
Moffit Av	Hu	14	G 23
Mogene Dr	Ou	46	Y 17
Mohawk Av	Hu	7	F 28
Mohawk Dr	Ou	46	Y 17
Mohawk Pl	Ou	48	Z 22
Mohawk Rd E	Hu	13	K 20
Mohawk Rd W	Hu	13	K 20
Mohegan Av	Nu	1	F 7
Mohegan Dr	Ou	46	Y 17
Mohring Bay Ct	Ou	25	R 2
Moline Ct	Nu	2	D 9
Mollineaux Pl	Hu	31	P 20
Molyneaux Rd	Hu	5	F 20
Mona Ct	Hu	40	U 20
Monaco Av	Hu	4	E 19
Monette Rd	Ou	45	Y 13
Monfort Pl	Ou	36	W 8
Monfort Rd	Nu	8	H 8
Monika Ct	Ou	38	X 15
Monitor St	Nu	29	Q 14
Monroe Av (BY)	Ou	25	S 2
Monroe Av (hk)	Ou	29	U 14
Monroe Av (rv)	Hu	31	Q 21
Monroe Av (ed)	Hu	30	S 19
Monroe Av (wa)	Ou	47	CC 21
Monroe Av (sd)	Hu	47	Y 20
Monroe Blvd	Hu	15	K 28
Monroe La	Hu	14	G 25
Monroe Pl (in)	Hu	7	C 25
Monroe Pl	Hu	21	N 19
Monroe St (CH)	Hu	6	D 24
Monroe St (LW)	Hu	7	D 26
Monroe St (lk)	Hu	13	K 20
Monroe St	Nu	9	G 8
Monroe St (el)	Hu	12	G 17
Monroe St (GA)	Hu	12	H 17
Monroe St (fs)	Hu	12	J 18
Monroe St (LY)	Hu	13	K 22
Monroe St (RC)	Hu	22	M 22
Monroe St	Ou	47	AA 20
Montague Av	Hu	31	R 20
Montana Ct	Ou	36	X 8
Montana St	Ou	28	T 13
Montauk Av (RC)	Hu	22	M 22
Montauk Av	Hu	31	S 22
Montauk Ct	Nu	28	R 13
Montauk St	Hu	13	H 21
Montclair Rd	Ou	45	Z 11
Montecito Dr	Ou	34	W 2
Monterey Dr	Nu	10	H 14
Monterey Dr	Hu	32	S 23
Montgomery Av	Hu	14	K 24
Montgomery Blvd	Hu	7	D 28
Montgomery Pl	Ou	28	T 12
Montgomery St	Hu	40	U 20
Montrose Ct	Nu	18	L 9
Montrose Dr	Nu	18	L 9
Montrose Rd	Ou	28	S 12
Moody Av	Hu	23	O 22
Moore Av (HV)	Hu	21	M 17
Moore Av (os)	Hu	14	K 24
Moore Av (FR)	Hu	31	P 21
Moore Av	Ou	48	AA 21
Moore Cir	Hu	22	O 21
Moore Dr	Ou	38	X 16
Moore Pl	Ou	37	U 13
Moore St (wm)	Hu	6	D 24
Moore St	Nu	10	J 14
Moore St (ln)	Hu	39	X 17
Moore's Hill Rd	Ou	35	X 6
Mora Ct	Nu	9	F 11
Mora Pl	Hu	6	F 23
Moraine Ct	Ou	27	S 9
Morea St	Hu	14	K 24
Moreland Av	Hu	23	N 24
Moreland Ct	Nu	2	B 10
Morewood Oaks	Nu	1	F 7
Morgan Ct	Nu	9	F 9
Morgan Days La	Hu	13	K 22
Morgan Dr	Ou	18	P 11
Morgan Dr	Hu	30	U 19
Morgan La	Ou	17	O 5
Morgan Pl	Nu	8	F 7
Morgan Pl	Ou	34	V 3
Morgan Pl (WB)	Nu	29	P 14
Morgan St	Hu	5	F 20
Morgan St	Ou	28	U 14
Morley Ct	Nu	10	K 12
Morning Glory Rd	Hu	38	U 16
Morningside Av	Hu	24	L 26
Morningside Dr	Nu	20	O 15
Morrell St	Hu	21	M 17
Morris Av (in)	Hu	7	C 25
Morris Av	Ou	17	L 6
Morris Av (ML)	Hu	13	J 20
Morris Av (RC)	Hu	22	M 21
Morris Av (ne)	Hu	31	R 20
Morris Av W	Hu	13	H 20
Morris Ct	Hu	30	S 18
Morris Ct	Ou	36	X 7
Morris Dr (nv)	Hu	12	G 19
Morris Dr	Nu	11	J 15
Morris Dr (ed)	Hu	29	T 16
Morris Dr	Ou	37	V 11
Morris Gate	Hu	40	X 21
Morris La	Nu	2	B 10
Morris La	Ou	35	X 5
Morris La (MS)	Ou	48	BB 21
Morris Pkwy	Hu	13	G 20
Morris Rd	Ou	46	Y 17
Morris St	Hu	23	P 23
Morris St	Ou	38	W 14
Morrison Dr	Ou	45	BB 12
Morrow Rd	Hu	14	K 23
Morse La	Nu	9	J 11
Morton Av (HV)	Hu	21	M 17
Morton Av (fs)	Hu	12	J 19
Morton Av (wh)	Hu	21	L 18
Morton Av (ER)	Hu	14	K 23
Morton Av (os)	Hu	23	M 23
Morton Av (FR)	Hu	23	P 23
Morton Av	Ou	48	Z 21
Morton Blvd	Ou	45	Y 13
Morton La	Hu	40	X 20
Mosefan St	Hu	12	H 18
Mosher Av	Hu	6	E 24
Moss La	Ou	37	U 11
Moss La	Hu	39	V 17
Motley St	Hu	13	G 21
Motor Av	Ou	46	AA 17
Motor La (ob)	Ou	45	AA 14
Motor La	Ou	46	Y 16
Mott Av	Hu	6	C 25
Mott Av	Nu	9	K 10
Mott Pl	Hu	6	C 25
Mott Pl	Ou	18	L 8
Mott St	Hu	23	M 24
Mott St	Ou	47	CC 21
Motts Cove Ct	Ou	18	L 8
Motts Cove Rd N	Nu	18	L 9
Motts Cove Rd S	Nu	18	M 9
Motts La	Nu	18	L 8
Mount Av	Hu	23	M 23
Mount Av	Hu	31	Q 22
Mount Joy Av	Hu	22	P 21
Mountain Av	Ou	25	R 2
Mountain Avenue Ext	Ou	25	S 2
Mountain Cut	Nu	10	H 11
Mozart La	Ou	46	Y 17
Muir St	Hu	30	S 18
Muirfield Rd	Hu	22	M 21
Mulberry Av	Hu	20	M 16
Mulberry Ct	Ou	37	U 11
Mulberry La	Hu	13	K 19
Mulberry Pl	Hu	6	D 23
Mulberry St	Ou	38	W 14
Mulford Pl	Hu	21	M 18
Muller Pl (VS)	Hu	14	F 23
Muller Pl	Hu	12	L 19
Mullon Av	Nu	8	G 8
Mulry La	Hu	6	D 25
Munro Blvd	Hu	14	F 23
Munsey Pl	Nu	9	G 11
Munson Av	Hu	12	K 18
Munson Pl	Hu	14	K 23
Munson St	Nu	9	H 8
Munster Rd	Ou	37	X 12
Murdock Av	Hu	14	K 24
Murdock Rd	Hu	14	H 23
Murdock Rd (nb)	Hu	39	V 19
Murel Ct	Nu	18	L 9
Muriel Av	Hu	6	D 25
Muriel Rd	Nu	9	G 9
Muriel St	Hu	23	P 24
Murray Av	Nu	9	G 8
Murray Ct	Ou	16	L 4
Murray Ct	Hu	23	L 23
Murray Dr (os)	Hu	23	L 24

STREET	MUN.	MAP	GRID
Murray Dr	Hu	29 S	15
Murray Hill St	Hu	4 E	18
Murray Pl	Hu	31 R	21
Murray Rd	Ou	38 V	14
Murray St	Ou	25 S	2
Murry La	Nu	19 L	12
Museum Dr	Nu	18 L	10
Museum La	Hu	20 P	16
Musgnug Av	Nu	20 L	15
Muttontown La	Ou	26 U	7
Muttontown Rd (MT)	Ou	27 S	9
Muttontown Rd	Ou	36 V	8
Myles La	Hu	29 T	15
Myrna Dr	Hu	13 J	20
Myron Rd	Hu	29 R	15
Myron Rd	Ou	45 Z	13
Myron St	Hu	21 P	17
Myrtle Av	Hu	21 O	17
Myrtle Av	Nu	29 P	15
Myrtle Dr	Nu	3 D	12
Myrtle La	Hu	38 V	16
Myrtle Rd	Nu	3 C	11
Myrtle St	Nu	9 F	11

STREET	MUN.	MAP	GRID
N St	Hu	12 G	19
Nan Rd	Ou	45 Y	14
Nana Pl	Ou	36 X	10
Nancy Blvd	Hu	31 S	21
Nancy Ct	Ou	9 H	9
Nancy Ct	Ou	17 O	6
Nancy Dr	Hu	30 P	19
Nancy Dr	Nu	19 P	14
Nancy Dr	Hu	29 T	16
Nancy Dr	Ou	46 CC17	
Nancy La	Ou	38 W	15
Nancy La	Hu	40 X	22
Nancy Pl	Hu	6 D	23
Nancy Pl	Ou	47 CC19	
Nancy Rd	Hu	11 K	15
Nantucket La	Hu	23 M	24
Nantucket Rd	Hu	30 S	19
Nantwick St	Hu	24 N	27
Naomi Pl	Hu	40 W	21
Naomi St	Hu	41 X	23
Naple Av	Hu	12 H	18
Napoleon St	Hu	6 D	24
Narcissus Dr	Ou	36 X	8
Narcisus Av	Ou	37 U	12
Narkin Ct	Ou	38 U	14
Narragansett Av (LW)	Hu	7 E	26
Narrangaset Av	Hu	40 X	21
Narrow Ct	Hu	6 E	24
Narrow La (wm)	Hu	6 E	24
Narrow La	Hu	6 C	25
Narrows	Hu	30 Q	17
Narwood Av	Hu	31 S	22
Narwood Ct	Hu	31 S	22
Narwood Rd	Ou	48 Z	21
Nassau Av	Nu	9 G	11
Nassau Av (in)	Hu	7 B	25
Nassau Av (AB)	Hu	7 D	28
Nassau Av (GL)	Ou	17 N	6
Nassau Av (ML)	Hu	13 J	20
Nassau Av (FR)	Hu	32 Q	23
Nassau Av (wn)	Hu	40 V	22
Nassau Av (pv)	Ou	37 W	12
Nassau Av (mq)	Ou	47 Z	19
Nassau Blvd (ug)	Nu	3 D	13
Nassau Blvd (MI)	Nu	19 L	14
Nassau Blvd (gk)	Nu	11 J	15
Nassau Blvd	Hu	13 J	21
Nassau Boulevard Ext	Nu	10 K	12
Nassau Blvd S	Nu	12 K	18
Nassau Ct	Hu	5 E	21
Nassau Dr (KG)	Nu	3 D	11
Nassau Dr (hr)	Nu	10 J	14
Nassau Dr (sg)	Nu	10 K	13
Nassau Expwy	Hu	6 C	24
Nassau La	Hu	15 K	26
Nassau Pkwy (HV)	Hu	21 N	19
Nassau Pkwy (os)	Hu	23 M	23
Nassau Pl (gs)	Hu	12 K	17
Nassau Pl (HV)	Hu	21 N	18
Nassau Pl (IP)	Hu	15 K	22

STREET	MUN.	MAP	GRID
Nassau Plz	Hu	11 H	16
Nassau Rd	Nu	3 C	12
Nassau Rd (lv)	Ou	16 O	5
Nassau Rd (un)	Hu	21 O	19
Nassau Rd (ns)	Ou	48 BB22	
Nassau St (FP)	Hu	11 F	17
Nassau St (el)	Hu	4 F	19
Nassau St (wm)	Hu	6 F	24
Nassau St (RC)	Hu	13 K	22
Nassau St (WB)	Hu	29 P	14
Nassau St (WB)	Hu	29 Q	14
Nassau St (mr)	Hu	31 S	21
Nassau St (bm)	Hu	40 U	21
Nassau St (sy)	Ou	36 W	8
Nassau St (MS)	Ou	48 AA21	
Nassau Terminal Rd	Nu	11 J	16
Nat. Blvd	Nu	19 O	14
Natalie Blvd	Hu	40 X	21
Nathan Ct	Ou	36 X	9
Nathan Dr	Ou	37 X	13
National Blvd	Hu	15 J	28
National Ct	Nu	10 H	13
Natta Blvd	Hu	31 T	20
Natta Ct	Hu	31 T	20
Nautilus Av	Ou	45 Z	13
Navy Ct	Hu	31 U	22
Navy Pl	Hu	31 U	22
Nearwater Av	Ou	48 BB22	
Nebraska St	Hu	15 G	28
Neck Rd	Nu	2 D	9
Neck, The	Nu	2 F	10
Needle La	Hu	39 W	17
Neil Ct (os)	Hu	23 M	25
Neil Ct	Ou	28 S	13
Neil Ct (sl)	Hu	29 T	15
Neil Ct (ln)	Hu	29 T	15
Neil Dr	Ou	45 AA13	
Nelson Av	Hu	22 N	20
Nelson Av	Ou	37 U	13
Nelson Ct (VS)	Hu	14 G	23
Nelson Ct	Ou	36 U	10
Nelson Ct (mr)	Hu	32 T	23
Nelson Dr	Hu	40 X	22
Nelson La	Hu	36 W	10
Nelson Pl	Nu	28 R	13
Nelson Pl	Hu	29 R	15
Nelson Rd	Hu	14 G	23
Nelson St	Ou	46 BB16	
Nelson St (wn)	Hu	40 W	21
Nelson St (el)	Hu	4 F	19
Nelson Verity Plz	Hu	40 Y	21
Nemeth St	Hu	13 H	20
Neptune Av (wm)	Hu	6 F	24
Neptune Av (os)	Hu	23 M	24
Neptune Av (sd)	Hu	40 X	21
Neptune Blvd	Hu	15 L	28
Neptune La	Hu	38 W	16
Neptune Pl (ns)	Ou	48 CC22	
Neptune Pl	Ou	48 Z	22
Neptune Rd	Hu	24 O	27
Nesaquake Av	Nu	1 F	7
Nestor St	Hu	14 F	24
Netherwood Dr	Nu	10 K	13
Netto Ct	Ou	45 Z	12
Netto La	Ou	45 Z	12
Netz Pl	Nu	19 L	12
Neubrech Ct	Ou	28 S	13
Neulist Av	Nu	9 H	9
Nevada Av (ea)	Hu	15 F	28
Nevada Av	Hu	24 L	25
Nevada Dr	Nu	10 G	14
Nevada St (hk)	Ou	28 T	13
Nevada St	Ou	36 X	8
Nevin Ter	Ou	47 BB21	
New Bridge Rd	Hu	31 U	22
New Ct	Hu	21 L	18
New Hampshire Av	Ou	47 Y	19
New Hampshire St	Hu	15 G	28
New Hyde Park Rd	Nu	10 G	14
New Jersey Av	Hu	30 P	18
New McNeil Av	Hu	7 C	26
New Pl (bm)	Hu	31 U	22
New Pl	Hu	39 X	18
New Rd	Hu	39 X	18
New South Rd	Hu	37 W	13
New Rd S	Ou	38 W	14
New St	Nu	9 F	8
New St (ML)	Hu	13 H	21
New St (wm)	Hu	14 F	24
New St (LY)	Hu	13 H	22

STREET	MUN.	MAP	GRID
New St (os)	Hu	14 K	24
New St (FR)	Hu	23 P	22
New St (un)	Hu	21 P	19
New St	Ou	47 CC21	
New Town Plz	Ou	45 AA	12
New Villa Ct	Hu	23 M	23
New York Av (el)	Hu	12 G	19
New York Av (LB)	Hu	15 G	28
New York Av (wh)	Hu	12 K	18
New York Av (RC)	Hu	22 M	22
New York Av (bw)	Hu	22 N	22
New York Av (FR)	Hu	22 P	21
New York Av (bi)	Hu	24 L	26
New York Av	Nu	28 S	13
New York Av (un)	Hu	30 P	18
New York Av (bm)	Hu	31 T	20
New York Av (mp)	Ou	47 AA	20
New York Av (wn)	Hu	40 X	20
New York Av (mq)	Ou	47 Y	20
New York Dr	Ou	46 AA	17
Newberry Ct	Nu	19 L	13
Newbould Av	Hu	13 G	22
Newbridge Rd	Ou	29 U	14
Newbridge Rd	Hu	30 T	17
Newburg Av	Hu	6 D	23
Newburg St	Hu	5 F	20
Newbury Rd	Nu	9 J	9
Newcastle Av	Ou	37 X	12
Newell Rd	Hu	31 S	19
Newhall Pl	Hu	7 B	25
Newkirk Av	Hu	14 H	23
Newland Pl	Hu	40 U	21
Newman Ct	Hu	30 S	18
Newman Rd	Hu	30 S	19
Newmans Ct	Hu	21 M	18
Newmarket Rd	Hu	11 J	16
Newmarket Rd	Ou	37 W	11
Newport Dr	Hu	6 F	23
Newport Dr	Ou	45 AA	12
Newport Rd	Hu	15 K	26
Newport Rd	Hu	20 P	17
News Av	Hu	12 G	19
Newton Av (LY)	Hu	13 K	22
Newton Av (bw)	Hu	22 O	21
Newton Av (un)	Hu	21 P	19
Newton Blvd	Hu	31 Q	22
Newton Pl	Hu	31 Q	20
Newton St	Hu	29 P	14
Newtown Rd	Ou	45 AA12	
Neylon Ct	Hu	22 M	20
Niagara Av	Hu	32 R	22
Niagara Dr	Ou	28 S	12
Niagara St	Hu	5 F	20
Niami St	Hu	40 X	22
Nibbe La	Ou	46 Y	15
Nichalai St	Ou	28 U	14
Nicholas Av	Hu	14 J	23
Nicholas Ct	Ou	46 Y	16
Nichols Ct	Hu	21 N	18
Nichols Ct	Ou	27 S	8
Nichols La	Hu	23 P	23
Nick Pl	Ou	45 Z	12
Nicole Ct	Hu	23 M	23
Niemann Av	Hu	13 H	22
Nightingale Ct	Hu	10 J	11
Nightingale Rd	Hu	13 K	20
Niles St	Hu	23 M	24
Nimitz St	Ou	28 T	11
Nimrod St	Hu	41 X	23
Nira Av	Hu	39 U	18
Nirvana Av	Nu	2 C	11
Nitas Pl	Hu	40 X	20
Nixon Dr	Ou	37 X	13
Nob Hill Gate	Nu	18 M	10
Noble St (LY)	Hu	13 J	22
Noble St (ed)	Hu	30 S	18
Nocella Ct	Hu	12 K	19
Noel Av	Hu	14 F	23
Noel Ct (ed)	Hu	30 R	19
Noel Ct (wn)	Hu	40 V	22
Noel La	Ou	27 U	10
Noell St	Hu	39 V	17
Nome Dr	Ou	44 AA	9
Noon Pl	Hu	23 P	23
Nora La	Ou	45 Y	12
Norbay St	Hu	12 H	18

STREET	MUN.	MAP	GRID
Norcross Av	Ou	46 Y	15
Norcross St	Hu	22 L	21
Norden Dr	Ou	27 S	10
Norfeld Blvd	Hu	4 E	19
Norfolk Dr	Hu	4 E	19
Norfolk La (GL)	Ou	17 N	5
Norfolk La	Ou	37 X	13
Norfolk Rd	Nu	3 D	12
Norfolk Rd	Hu	15 K	26
Norgate Rd	Nu	9 F	11
Norgate Rd	Ou	18 O	9
Norm Pl	Hu	40 X	20
Norma Ct	Ou	37 W	13
Norma La	Ou	46 Z	17
Norma St	Hu	4 F	19
Norman Ct	Ou	16 M	4
Norman Dr (ed)	Hu	30 R	17
Norman Dr	Hu	39 U	18
Norman La	Hu	29 T	15
Norman Pl	Hu	10 K	12
Norman Pl	Ou	47 Y	18
Norman St	Hu	13 H	22
Norman St	Hu	10 K	14
Norman Wy	Hu	6 E	23
Normandy Dr (FG)	Ou	46 BB	15
Normandy Dr	Ou	46 Y	17
Normandy La	Nu	9 F	11
Normandy Rd	Ou	47 Y	19
Norris Av	Hu	21 P	19
Norshon Rd	Hu	31 T	22
Nortema St	Hu	10 H	14
North 1st St	Hu	11 G	15
North 1st St	Ou	46 Y	15
North 2nd St	Hu	11 G	15
North 2nd St	Ou	46 Y	15
North 3rd St	Hu	11 G	15
North 3rd St	Ou	46 Y	15
North 4th St	Hu	11 G	15
North 4th St	Ou	46 Y	15
North 5th St	Hu	11 G	15
North 5th St	Ou	38 X	15
North 6th St	Ou	38 X	15
North 6th St	Hu	11 G	15
North 7th St	Hu	11 G	15
North 9th St	Hu	11 G	16
North 10th St	Hu	11 G	16
North 11th St	Hu	11 H	16
North 12th St	Hu	11 H	16
North Ascan St	Hu	13 G	20
North Atlanta Av	Ou	47 Y	18
North Av (SM)	Hu	12 G	17
North Av (mp)	Hu	6 C	24
North Av (GA)	Hu	12 K	17
North Av (eg)	Hu	20 O	15
North Bay Av	Ou	47 Z	18
North Bay Dr	Ou	46 Z	17
North Bayles Av	Hu	8 G	8
North Bayview Av	Hu	22 O	22
North Beech St	Ou	47 Z	18
North Bellmore Rd	Hu	29 T	16
North Bergen Pl	Hu	31 P	22
North Bleecker Dr	Ou	46 Z	17
North Boston Av	Ou	46 Y	17
North Blvd	Hu	14 J	24
North Branch	Nu	9 J	11
North Brittany Dr	Ou	46 Y	17
North Broadway	Ou	28 T	11
North Broadway (nq)	Ou	46 AA	17
North Brook Dr	Hu	14 F	23
North Brookside Av	Hu	22 O	21
North Butterhorn St	Ou	38 X	15
North Cambridge St	Hu	13 J	21
North Cedar St	Ou	47 Z	18
North Central Av	Ou	47 Z	18
North Central Dr	Ou	46 Z	17
North Centre Av	Hu	13 K	22
North Cherrybrook Pl	Nu	3 F	12
North Chestnut St	Ou	47 Z	18
North Cir	Nu	3 C	12
North Clover Dr	Nu	3 C	11
North Columbus Av	Hu	31 Q	21
North Copper Beech La	Hu	15 F	26
North Corona Av	Hu	13 G	21

Nassau Co.

STREET	MUN.	MAP	GRID
North Coronet Cres	Ou	46 Y	15
North Cottage St	Hu	13 G	21
North Ct (OC)	Ou	35 V	6
North Ct (pw)	Nu	2 F	8
North Ct (al)	Nu	19 L	12
North Ct (WB)	Nu	19 N	14
North Ct (BY)	Ou	25 R	2
North Delaware Av	Ou	47 Z	18
North Detroit Av	Ou	47 AA	18
North Devon St	Hu	13 J	21
North Dr (PD)	Nu	2 F	10
North Dr (KG)	Nu	2 D	11
North Dr (VS)	Hu	5 E	20
North Dr (hr)	Nu	10 J	14
North Dr (WB)	Nu	19 O	14
North Dr (bh)	Hu	23 P	24
North Dr (hk)	Ou	38 V	14
North Dr (ed)	Hu	30 S	18
North Dr (ne)	Hu	30 R	19
North Dr (nq)	Ou	46 AA	17
North Dr (nw)	Hu	39 X	18
North Dr (sd)	Hu	40 Y	21
North East Shore Dr	Ou	48 CC	21
North Elm St	Ou	47 Z	18
North End Dr	Hu	23 O	24
North Fletcher Av	Hu	13 F	20
North Fordham Rd	Ou	38 W	14
North Forrest Av	Hu	22 L	22
North Franklin St	Hu	13 F	21
North Franklin St	Hu	21 M	17
North Front St	Ou	46 BB	16
North Gate	Hu	32 S	23
North Gate (lg)	Ou	36 W	10
North Gate	Ou	47 CC	19
North Gate Rd	Nu	2 E	10
North Grove St	Hu	13 G	21
North Grove St (FR)	Hu	31 Q	22
Norht Harbor Pl	Ou	48 CC	22
North Hawthorne St	Ou	47 Y	19
North Hempstead Tpke (Northern Blvd) (UB)	Ou	27 R	8
North Hempstead Tpke (Northern Blvd) (en)	Ou	26 T	7
North Herman Av	Ou	46 Y	16
North Hills Rd	Ou	26 U	7
North Hillside Av	Hu	5 E	20
North Idaho Av	Ou	46 Y	17
North Jerusalem Rd	Hu	30 R	19
North King Ct	Hu	4 F	19
North King St (el)	Hu	4 F	19
North King St (ML)	Hu	13 J	20
North King St	Ou	47 Z	19
North La	Ou	17 M	5
North La	Hu	39 X	17
North Lerisa St	Ou	38 X	16
North Lewis Pl	Hu	22 L	22
North Linden St	Ou	47 Z	18
North Long Beach Rd	Hu	22 M	22
North Longbeach Av	Hu	22 P	20
North Longbeach Rd	Hu	22 M	21
North Main St	Hu	31 P	20
North Mall	Ou	45 AA	12
North Maple St	Ou	47 Z	18
North Marginal Rd	Ou	28 S	12
North Marion Pl	Hu	22 L	22
North Maryland Av	Nu	8 H	8
North Meadow Rd	Hu	30 R	19
North Michigan Av	Ou	47 Z	18
North Mill Page Dr	Ou	46 Y	16
North Montague St	Hu	5 E	21
North Montgomery St	Hu	5 F	21
North Nancy Pl	Ou	47 Z	18
North Nassau Av	Ou	47 Z	19
North Nassau La	Hu	15 K	25
North Nassau St	Ou	38 X	15
North Newbridge Rd	Hu	29 T	16
North Oak St	Ou	47 Z	19
North Oakdale Av	Ou	46 Y	16
North Ocean Av	Hu	31 P	21
North Park Av	Hu	22 L	22
North Park Dr (nq)	Ou	47 AA	18
North Peach St	Ou	38 X	16
North Pershing Av	Ou	46 Y	15
North Pine Dr	Ou	47 AA	18
North Pine Hill Rd	Nu	3 E	13
North Pine St	Hu	30 T	17
North Pine St	Ou	47 Y	18
North Pl	Ou	17 M	8
North Plandome Rd	Nu	9 F	8
North Poplar St	Ou	47 Z	18
North Prospect Av	Hu	13 H	22
North Queens Av	Ou	47 Z	19
North Ravine Rd	Nu	2 E	10
North Richmond Av	Ou	47 Z	19
North Rd (SP)	Nu	8 H	7
North Rd (GN)	Nu	2 D	11
North Rd (GL)	Ou	17 M	6
North Rd (eg)	Hu	20 P	16
North Rd (bm)	Nu	40 V	22
North Rd (OC)	Ou	35 X	5
North Rd (ln)	Hu	38 X	15
North Robert Damm St	Ou	47 Z	18
North Rockway Av	Hu	13 J	21
North Service Rd	Nu	3 E	13
North Service Rd	Ou	37 U	12
North Shelley Rd	Hu	30 U	19
North Sheridan Av	Ou	46 Y	15
North Station Plz	Nu	3 D	12
North Strathmore St	Hu	6 E	22
North St (gh)	Hu	11 G	16
North St (mp)	Hu	6 C	24
North St (LW)	Hu	7 D	26
North St (lv)	Ou	16 O	4
North St (GL)	Ou	8 L	5
North St (gh)	Ou	17 N	8
North St (hr)	Nu	10 J	14
North St (sy)	Ou	36 W	8
North St (mq)	Ou	47 Y	19
North Suffolk Av	Ou	47 Y	19
North Summit Dr	Ou	47 AA	18
North Syracuse Av	Ou	47 Y	18
North Terrace Pl	Hu	5 E	21
North Tyson Av	Nu	11 F	16
North View Av	Hu	39 W	19
North Village Av	Hu	22 L	21
North Violet St	Ou	38 X	16
North Virginia Av	Ou	46 Y	17
North Waldinger St	Hu	5 E	21
North Walnut St	Ou	47 Z	19
North Wantage Av	Hu	38 X	16
North Washington St	Nu	8 G	8
North West Dr	Ou	46 AA	17
North William St	Hu	22 N	20
North Windhorst Av	Ou	46 Y	16
North Wisconsin Av	Ou	47 Y	18
North Wood Rd	Hu	22 N	21
North Woods Rd	Nu	9 H	10
North Woodward Dr	Ou	46 Z	17
North Yew	Ou	16 M	5
North Zoranne Dr	Ou	46 Z	17
Northampton Gate	Ou	37 W	13
Northcote Cres	Nu	28 R	13
Northern Blvd	Nu	3 D	13
Northern Blvd	Hu	23 O	24
Northern Pkwy	Hu	21 O	19
Northern Pkwy	Ou	37 X	11
Northern Pkwy E	Ou	37 Y	11
Northern Pkwy W	Ou	37 X	12
Northern State Pkwy	Nu	3 F	14
Northern Woods Dr	Nu	18 N	10
Northfield La	Nu	28 Q	13
Northfield Rd	Hu	6 E	23
Northfield Rd	Ou	17 K	5
Northgate Ct	Hu	30 Q	19
Northgate Ct S	Hu	30 Q	19
Northgate Dr	Hu	30 Q	19
Northgate Dr	Ou	35 W	7
Northgate Rd	Ou	47 BB	20
Northoote Rd	Nu	28 R	13
Northridge Av	Hu	31 R	20
Northridge Gate	Ou	47 Y	19
Northumberland Gate	Hu	13 G	22
Northumberland Rd	Ou	37 V	12
Northwood Ct (je)	Ou	28 S	12
Northwood Ct	Ou	44 AA	8
Norton Av	Nu	11 J	15
Norton Dr	Hu	22 O	20
Norton Pl	Hu	41 V	23
Norton St (in)	Hu	6 C	25
Norton St	Hu	32 Q	24
Norwich Av	Hu	14 H	23
Norwood Av (ML)	Hu	13 J	20
Norwood Av	Hu	30 T	19
Norwood Ct	Ou	47 CC	18
Norwood Rd	Nu	1 E	7
Nostrand Av (os)	Hu	23 L	23
Nostrand Av (ed)	Hu	30 R	17
Nostrand Av (un)	Hu	30 Q	19
Nostrand Pl	Hu	21 N	18
Nostrands La	Ou	46 BB	16
Notre Dame Av	Ou	37 U	13
Notre Dame Ct	Hu	22 O	20
Notre Dame Dr	Hu	14 K	24
Nottingham Av	Hu	5 E	20
Nottingham Ct	Nu	10 H	14
Nottingham Gate	Ou	37 X	13
Nottingham Pl	Nu	3 C	11
Nottingham Rd (ML)	Hu	13 J	20
Nottingham Rd	Nu	10 H	14
Nottingham Rd (RC)	Hu	22 M	20
Nottingham Rd	Nu	29 S	16
Nottinghill Dr	Ou	47 Z	19
Nova Av	Ou	25 T	2
Noye La	Hu	6 F	25
Nugent St	Nu	11 G	15
Nursery St	Ou	16 P	4
Nursey La	Nu	19 P	14
Nutley Ct	Ou	37 X	13
Nutley Pl	Hu	6 D	23

O

STREET	MUN.	MAP	GRID
O St	Hu	12 G	19
Oak Av (CH)	Hu	6 D	25
Oak Av (in)	Hu	6 B	25
Oak Av (HV)	Hu	21 N	19
Oak Brook La	Hu	31 T	21
Oak Ct (ML)	Hu	13 H	20
Oak Ct (CH)	Hu	6 D	25
Oak Ct (os)	Hu	23 M	23
Oak Ct (ne)	Hu	31 S	20
Oak Ct (bm)	Hu	40 U	21
Oak Ct (sd)	Hu	40 X	22
Oak Dr (GE)	Nu	3 C	11
Oak Dr (nn)	Nu	11 H	15
Oak Dr (VS)	Hu	14 F	23
Oak Dr (EH)	Hu	18 M	11
Oak Dr (lg)	Ou	36 V	10
Oak Dr (nb)	Hu	39 U	18
Oak Dr (pv)	Ou	37 X	12
Oak Hill Dr	Ou	35 U	6
Oak La (wm)	Hu	6 E	23
Oak La (GL)	Ou	17 M	5
Oak La (OK)	Ou	17 O	7
Oak La (hr)	Nu	10 J	14
Oak La (rt)	Nu	19 M	12
Oak La (BY)	Ou	25 S	2
Oak La (ed)	Hu	30 R	18
Oak La (ob)	Ou	45 AA	13
Oak La (pe)	Ou	46 Y	17
Oak Lawn Av	Ou	17 M	8
Oak Pl (im)	Hu	6 F	23
Oak Pl (wn)	Hu	6 B	25
Oak Pl (sg)	Nu	10 K	12
Oak Pl (Ml)	Nu	11 K	15
Oak Pl (BY)	Ou	25 R	2
Oak Pl (ed)	Hu	30 R	18
Oak Pl (mq)	Ou	47 Y	20
Oak Ridge La (sg)	Nu	10 J	13
Oak Ridge La	Nu	19 L	13
Oak St (LY)	Hu	13 J	22
Oak St (FP)	Hu	11 F	17
Oak St (el)	Hu	4 E	18
Oak St (mr)	Hu	13 H	20
Oak St (wm)	Hu	6 E	24
Oak St (VS)	Hu	13 G	22
Oak St (eg)	Hu	20 O	16
Oak St (wh)	Hu	21 L	18
Oak St (sh)	Hu	22 M	20
Oak St (bw)	Hu	22 O	21
Oak St (RC)	Hu	22 M	22
Oak St (BY)	Ou	25 R	2
Oak St (hk)	Ou	37 W	13
Oak St (sl)	Hu	29 Q	15
Oak St (rv)	Hu	31 Q	21
Oak St (ne)	Hu	31 T	20
Oak St (bm)	Hu	31 T	21
Oak St (lg)	Ou	36 X	10
Oak St (bp)	Ou	37 W	13
Oak St (sa)	Ou	46 BB	17
Oak St (MS)	Ou	47 AA	19
Oak Tree Ct	Nu	19 L	12
Oak Tree La	Nu	9 J	10
Oak Valley Dr	Ou	17 N	8
Oakdale Av	Ou	47 BB	19
Oakdale Av	Hu	40 X	21
Oakdale Blvd	Ou	46 BB	15
Oakdale Ct	Hu	40 V	22
Oakdale Dr	Nu	28 S	13
Oakdale La	Hu	18 M	11
Oakdale Pl	Ou	47 CC	19
Oakdale Rd	Nu	10 K	12
Oakdale Rd (RC)	Hu	22 M	20
Oakdale Rd (ed)	Hu	30 T	18
Oakfield Av (FR)	Hu	22 O	21
Oakfield Av	Hu	39 U	18
Oakford St	Hu	12 K	19
Oakland Av	Nu	8 G	6
Oakland Av (CH)	Hu	6 D	24
Oakland Av (LY)	Hu	13 H	22
Oakland Av (wh)	Hu	12 K	18
Oakland Av (wn)	Hu	40 W	20
Oakland Ct	Hu	30 S	18
Oakland Dr	Nu	9 G	9
Oakland Pl	Nu	3 D	11
Oakland St	Hu	21 N	19
Oakleigh Rd	Hu	6 E	23
Oakley Av	Hu	12 G	19
Oakley Av	Ou	48 CC	21
Oakley Ct	Ou	26 T	4
Oakley La	Nu	19 L	14
Oakley Pl	Nu	3 D	13
Oakley St	Nu	30 Q	18
Oakley St	Ou	47 CC	20
Oakmere Dr	Hu	22 O	22
Oakmont Av	Hu	21 O	19
Oakpoint Dr N	Ou	25 R	1
Oakpoint Dr S	Ou	25 R	2
Oakpoint Dr W	Ou	25 R	1
Oaks Ct	Hu	12 H	19
Oaks Dr	Hu	12 J	19
Oaks Hunt Rd	Nu	3 D	13
Oaks Pl	Hu	12 G	19
Oaks, The	Nu	9 J	11
Oakshore Dr	Ou	25 S	2
Oaktree Ct	Nu	1 E	6
Oaktree La	Nu	1 E	6
Oaktree La	Hu	29 T	16
Oakview Av	Hu	23 M	23
Oakview Av	Ou	46 BB	16
Oakwood Av (CH)	Hu	6 E	24
Oakwood Av (bw)	Hu	22 N	22
Oakwood Av (mr)	Hu	31 S	21

Index

Nassau Co.

Pa to Pi

STREET	MUN. MAP GRID
Park Av (in)	Hu 6 C 24
Park Av (ma)	Nu 9 G 11
Park Av (pw)	Nu 9 H 8
Park Av (NP)	Nu 11 H 16
Park Av (ML)	Hu 13 H 21
Park Av (CH)	Nu 6 D 25
Park Av (LT)	Ou 25 Q 3
Park Av (SC)	Ou 17 L 7
Park Av (GL)	Ou 16 M 5
Park Av (gv)	Nu 48 W 20
Park Av (WP)	Nu 19 L 13
Park Av (cp)	Nu 20 N 14
Park Av (gk)	Nu 11 J 16
Park Av (GA)	Hu 21 L 17
Park Av (lk)	Hu 12 L 19
Park Av (os)	Nu 23 M 24
Park Av (bh)	Hu 23 O 23
Park Av (FR)	Hu 22 P 22
Park Av (oy)	Ou 35 U 4
Park Av (WB)	Nu 28 P 13
Park Av (nc)	Nu 28 R 13
Park Av (hk)	Ou 37 V 13
Park Av (ed)	Hu 30 S 18
Park Av (un)	Hu 21 P 19
Park Av (mr)	Nu 31 S 21
Park Av (wn)	Hu 40 V 20
Park Av (wy)	Ou 44 Z 9
Park Av (FG)	Ou 46 AA 16
Park Av (bp)	Ou 46 Y 15
Park Av (nq)	Ou 47 Z 18
Park Av (mq)	Ou 48 Z 21
Park Blvd (ML)	Hu 13 J 21
Park Blvd	Nu 29 Q 16
Park Blvd	Ou 47 AA 20
Park Cir (GN)	Nu 2 C 10
Park Cir (pw)	Nu 9 G 9
Park Cir (nn)	Nu 11 G 15
Park Cir (CH)	Hu 6 D 24
Park Cir (MI)	Nu 20 N 14
Park Cir (gk)	Nu 11 J 15
Park Cir (ed)	Hu 30 T 17
Park Cir W	Nu 11 J 15
Park Ct (sv)	Hu 6 E 22
Park Ct (ed)	Hu 30 T 17
Park Ct (bm)	Nu 31 U 22
Park Ct (pv)	Ou 44 Y 11
Park Dr (PD)	Nu 9 F 10
Park Dr (nn)	Nu 11 H 15
Park Dr (nv)	Hu 13 H 20
Park Dr (ld)	Nu 24 M 27
Park Dr (ln)	Hu 39 U 18
Park Dr (ob)	Ou 45 AA 13
Park Dr (sd)	Hu 47 Y 20
Park Dr E	Nu 19 N 11
Park Dr E	Nu 36 X 10
Park Hill Av	Ou 47 Y 20
Park La	Nu 2 D 11
Park La (GA)	Hu 11 H 16
Park La (wm)	Hu 6 D 23
Park La (CH)	Hu 6 D 24
Park La (RC)	Hu 22 M 21
Park La (ln)	Hu 39 U 17
Park La (ed)	Hu 30 Q 18
Park La (pe)	Ou 46 Y 16
Park La (MS)	Ou 47 BB 20
Park Lane Dr	Nu 10 K 13
Park La E	Hu 13 H 20
Park La N	Hu 39 U 17
Park Lane Pl	Ou 48 Z 22
Park La S (fs)	Hu 12 H 19
Park Manor Ct	Ou 17 M 6
Park Pl (GN)	Nu 2 B 10
Park Pl (GP)	Nu 3 B 12
Park Pl (VS)	Nu 5 E 20
Park Pl (CH)	Hu 6 D 24
Park Pl (SC)	Ou 8 K 7
Park Pl (GL)	Ou 17 M 6
Park Pl (al)	Nu 19 L 12
Park Pl (WP)	Nu 19 L 13
Park Pl (HV)	Hu 21 O 18
Park Pl (un)	Hu 21 O 19
Park Pl (LY)	Hu 13 J 22
Park Pl (RC)	Hu 13 L 22
Park Pl (LB)	Hu 15 J 27
Park Pl (MN)	Ou 35 U 6
Park Pl (un)	Hu 21 P 19
Park Pl (rv)	Hu 22 N 20
Park Pl (ne)	Hu 31 T 20
Park Pl (bm)	Hu 40 U 21
Park Pl (bp)	Ou 38 Y 14
Park Pl (MS)	Ou 48 Z 22
Park Plz (gh)	Ou 17 N 7
Park Plz	Nu 17 N 8
Park Rd	Nu 2 E 11
Park Rd	Hu 39 V 19
Park Row	Hu 7 E 25
Park St (wm)	Hu 6 E 24
Park St (AB)	Hu 7 D 27
Park St (ea)	Hu 7 F 27
Park St (sl)	Hu 29 S 15
Park Ter N	Hu 30 T 17
Park View Pl	Hu 4 E 19
Park Wy	Ou 17 L 6
Park W	Nu 11 J 14
Parkdale Dr	Hu 47 BB 18
Parkdale Dr W	Ou 47 BB 18
Parker Av (wh)	Hu 21 L 18
Parker Av	Hu 39 X 17
Parkfield Ct N	Ou 36 W 10
Parkfield Ct S	Ou 35 W 10
Parkhurst Rd	Hu 4 D 19
Parkside Blvd	Ou 47 Z 20
Parkside Dr	Ou 37 V 12
Parkside Dr (ln)	Hu 38 U 16
Parkside Dr (se)	Nu 2 C 11
Parkside Dr (al)	Nu 19 L 12
Parkside Dr (pl)	Hu 33 Q 27
Parkside Dr (sd)	Hu 40 Y 21
Parkside Rd	Hu 13 K 21
Parkview Av	Hu 47 Y 20
Parkview Cir N	Ou 46 Y 15
Parkview Cir S	Ou 46 Y 15
Parkview Ct	Ou 46 Y 15
Parkview Dr	Nu 10 K 12
Parkview Dr (Pvt)	Ou 27 U 10
Parkview Pl (ML)	Hu 13 J 20
Parkview Pl	Hu 22 N 22
Parkview St	Ou 37 W 12
Parkway Dr	Nu 20 M 14
Parkway Dr (al)	Nu 19 M 12
Parkway Dr (WB)	Nu 19 N 14
Parkway Dr	Hu 23 P 24
Parkway Dr (lg)	Ou 37 W 11
Parkway Dr (pv)	Ou 45 Z 13
Parkway Dr E	Ou 37 X 11
Parkwold Dr E	Hu 13 H 20
Parkwold Dr S	Hu 13 H 20
Parkwold Dr W	Hu 13 H 20
Parkwood Ct	Hu 13 K 21
Parkwood Dr	Nu 3 B 12
Parkwood Dr	Hu 30 R 19
Parkwood Rd	Nu 28 R 13
Parkwoods Rd	Nu 9 G 10
Parma Dr	Ou 46 Y 16
Parma Rd	Hu 15 K 26
Parp Dr	Nu 18 M 10
Parsonage Pl	Hu 23 N 24
Parsons Av	Hu 31 Q 22
Parsons Dr	Hu 21 M 18
Parsons La	Hu 38 W 16
Parthage La	Nu 2 C 10
Partridge Av	Hu 22 L 20
Partridge Dr N	Nu 18 N 10
Partridge La	Ou 18 P 10
Pasadena Dr	Ou 37 X 12
Paschal Av	Hu 12 H 17
Pasture Ct	Hu 46 Y 17
Pasture La	Nu 19 M 13
Pasture La	Hu 39 U 17
Pasture La	Ou 45 AA 13
Pasture La (R.O.W.)	Ou 35 X 6
Patience La	Hu 29 R 15
Patricia Ct (pe)	Ou 46 Y 17
Patricia Ct	Ou 47 CC19
Patricia La	Hu 41 Y 23
Patricia La	Ou 37 W 11
Patricia St	Ou 37 X 13
Patsy Pl	Nu 2 D 11
Patt Pl	Hu 13 J 20
Patten Av	Hu 14 K 23
Patterson Av (fs)	Hu 13 J 20
Patterson Av	Hu 21 O 18
Patterson St	Nu 30 S 18
Patti Dr	Nu 30 R 18
Patton Blvd	Nu 11 G 14
Patton Pl	Hu 13 K 20
Patton Pl	Ou 37 X 13
Paul Av	Nu 11 G 15
Paul Ct	Hu 12 J 19
Paul La	Hu 40 X 20
Paul Pl (wh)	Hu 12 J 19
Paul Pl (rv)	Hu 22 P 21
Paul St (bw)	Hu 22 O 21
Paul St	Hu 47 Y 19
Paula Dr	Hu 31 T 20
Paula Dr	Ou 47 CC18
Paula La	Hu 30 R 19
Paula Pl	Ou 17 L 6
Paula St	Ou 28 T 13
Pauley Dr	Hu 12 J 19
Pauline Dr	Ou 46 CC17
Payan Av	Hu 5 F 21
Payne Ct	Hu 14 H 23
Payne Whitney La	Nu 10 H 11
Pea Pond Rd	Hu 39 U 19
Peach Dr	Nu 18 L 11
Peach Grove Dr	Hu 12 K 18
Peach La	Nu 30 R 18
Peach Tree Dr	Ou 35 U 6
Peach Tree La	Nu 9 J 10
Peachtree La (rt)	Nu 19 L 12
Peachtree La (cp)	Nu 19 N 14
Peachtree La	Ou 37 U 12
Peachtree La	Hu 38 U 16
Peack Av	Hu 31 R 20
Peacock Dr	Nu 18 N 10
Peacock La (LT)	Ou 16 N 3
Peacock La (UB)	Ou 27 Q 8
Peacock La	Ou 39 V 17
Peacock Pond Rd	Ou 17 O 5
Peale Rd	Nu 9 H 11
Pearce Pl	Nu 3 D 12
Pearl Dr	Ou 45 Y 12
Pearl Pl	Hu 13 J 21
Pearl St (nn)	Nu 11 H 15
Pearl St (in)	Nu 6 D 25
Pearl St (sv)	Nu 6 E 22
Pearl St (GL)	Ou 17 M 6
Pearl St (MI)	Nu 11 K 16
Pearl St (os)	Nu 14 K 23
Pearl St (oy)	Ou 35 U 5
Pearl St (nc)	Nu 28 S 13
Pearl St (bp)	Ou 45 Y 14
Pearsall Av (LW)	Hu 6 D 25
Pearsall Av (rt)	Nu 19 L 12
Pearsall Av (LY)	Hu 13 K 21
Pearsall Av (LY)	Hu 13 J 21
Pearsall Av (os)	Hu 14 K 24
Pearsall Av (GL)	Ou 17 N 6
Pearsall Av (FR)	Hu 22 P 22
Pearsall Pl (mr)	Hu 31 R 21
Pearsall Pl (wm)	Hu 6 E 24
Pearsall Pl (in)	Hu 7 C 25
Pebble La (hl)	Hu 14 G 23
Pebble La	Nu 19 M 12
Pebble La (ln)	Hu 39 U 17
Peconic Av	Hu 40 X 22
Peconic Ct	Nu 28 R 13
Peconic Dr	Ou 48 BB22
Peekskill St	Nu 5 E 20
Peerless Dr	Ou 35 U 6
Peg Ct	Ou 38 V 14
Peg La	Hu 29 T 16
Peg Pl	Ou 36 X 9
Pelham Av	Nu 1 D 7
Pelham St	Hu 12 F 18
Pelican Ct	Ou 36 X 8
Pelican Rd	Hu 38 U 15
Pell La	Ou 36 X 8
Pell Ter	Nu 20 N 15
Pemaco La	Nu 30 Q 18
Pemaco Rd	Hu 41 U 23
Pembroke Ct	Nu 3 D 13
Pembroke Dr (GL)	Ou 16 K 5
Pembroke St	Ou 47 Y 18
Pembroke Dr	Hu 30 P 17
Pembroke St	Nu 10 L 14
Pembrook Dr	Nu 19 M 14
Pen La	Ou 38 U 15
Pen Mor Dr	Ou 27 R 8
Penatiquit Av	Nu 40 X 21
Pendroy St	Nu 30 T 18
Pengon Cir	Hu 29 S 16
Peninsula Blvd	Hu 6 D 24
Penn Rd	Nu 11 G 15
Penn St	Ou 46 Z 17
Pennsylvania Av (EW)	Nu 19 L 14
Pennsylvania Av (LB)	Hu 15 G 28
Pennsylvania Av (HV)	Hu 21 N 18
Pennsylvania Av (bi)	Hu 15 K 26
Pennsylvania Av (un)	Hu 30 Q 18
Pennsylvania Av (FR)	Hu 22 P 21
Pennsylvania Av (MS)	Ou 47 BB 20
Pennsylvania Av (mq)	Ou 47 Y 20
Pennsylvania Blvd	Hu 4 E 17
Penny Ct	Hu 31 T 21
Penny La	Hu 39 V 17
Peony Dr	Ou 47 Y 19
Peony Rd	Hu 38 V 16
Peppe Dr	Hu 6 B 25
Pepper Cir E	Ou 47 CC18
Pepper Cir N	Ou 47 CC18
Pepper Cir S	Ou 47 CC18
Pepper Cir W	Ou 47 CC18
Pepperday Av	Nu 8 G 7
Pepperidge Rd	Hu 14 H 24
Pepperidge Rd	Nu 28 R 13
Peppermill Rd	Nu 10 J 13
Pequa Pl	Ou 48 Z 22
Pequot Av	Nu 8 F 7
Percheron La	Nu 19 M 13
Peri La	Nu 5 F 22
Perimeter Rd	Hu 20 P 16
Periwinkle Rd	Hu 38 U 16
Perkins Av	Nu 23 L 24
Perkins Ct	Ou 17 M 7
Perry Av	Nu 23 M 24
Perry Av (BY)	Ou 25 R 2
Perry Av	Ou 38 X 15
Perry Ct	Ou 36 X 8
Perry St	Hu 21 O 18
Pershing Av (VS)	Hu 6 F 22
Pershing Av	Ou 26 Q 4
Pershing Av (ed)	Hu 30 S 19
Pershing Blvd (LY)	Hu 13 K 21
Pershing Blvd	Hu 22 N 22
Pershing Pkwy	Nu 20 M 14
Pershing Pl (IP)	Hu 15 K 26
Pershing Pl	Hu 31 Q 21
Pershing St	Hu 5 F 20
Perth Rd	Ou 48 Z 21
Petal La	Ou 29 T 15
Peter Av	Ou 25 R 2
Peter Ct	Ou 37 U 11
Peter La	Nu 11 G 15
Peter La	Hu 30 R 18
Peter La	Ou 45 Y 13
Peter Rd	Ou 29 U 14
Peter St (el)	Hu 4 E 18
Peter St	Hu 39 X 18
Peterhoff Av	Hu 13 H 20
Peters Av (HV)	Hu 21 N 19
Peters Av	Hu 30 R 17
Peter's Gate	Nu 30 Q 17
Peters La	Nu 9 G 10
Peterson Pl	Hu 14 H 22
Petite Pl	Ou 17 M 6
Pettit Av (ne)	Hu 31 S 20
Pettit Av	Hu 40 U 21
Pettit Pl (bi)	Hu 15 K 27
Pettit Pl	Hu 40 U 21
Pewter La	Ou 38 U 15
Pflug Pl	Nu 5 F 21
Pheasant Hill Dr	Ou 17 O 7
Pheasant La	Ou 44 Y 9
Pheasant Run (KP)	Nu 2 E 9
Pheasant Run (NL)	Nu 10 J 13
Pheasant Run	Ou 28 P 11
Philadelphia Av	Ou 47 BB 20
Philip Ct	Hu 5 E 20
Philips La	Hu 14 G 24
Phillip Ct	Ou 40 U 22
Phillip Dr	Ou 46 Z 16
Phillip Rd	Ou 47 BB 21
Phillips Rd (GL)	Ou 16 M 5
Phillips Rd	Ou 47 BB 21
Phipps Av	Hu 14 J 23
Phipps La	Ou 37 X 11
Phoebe St	Hu 12 H 18
Phoebus Ct	Hu 13 H 20
Phoenix St	Hu 21 N 18
Phylis Ct	Hu 4 E 18
Phyllis Dr (bh)	Hu 23 O 23
Phyllis Dr (nb)	Hu 30 U 18
Phyllis Dr	Ou 46 Y 17
Picadilly Rd	Nu 2 D 11
Picardy La	Ou 43 Z 7

STREET	MUN.	MAP	GRID
Piccadilly Downs	Hu	13 G	22
Pickett Ct	Hu	13 H	20
Pickwick Ct	Ou	37 V	12
Pickwick Dr	Ou	45 AA	14
Pickwick Dr E	Ou	37 X	11
Pickwick Dr N (hk)	Ou	37 V	12
Pickwick Dr N	Ou	37 X	11
Pickwick Dr S	Ou	37 V	12
Pickwick Dr W	Ou	37 X	11
Pickwick Rd	Nu	9 H	11
Pickwick Ter	Hu	22 M	21
Pickwood La	Nu	2 B	10
Picture La	Ou	38 W	15
Pierce Av	Hu	30 T	19
Pierce Pl	Hu	30 R	18
Pierce St	Ou	37 V	13
Pierce St	Hu	14 K	24
Piermont Av	Hu	14 F	23
Pierrepont St	Hu	32 Q	22
Pierson Av	Hu	21 N	19
Pilgrim La	Hu	22 O	21
Pilgrim La	Hu	29 R	15
Pilgrim Pl	Hu	5 F	21
Pilgrim St (nn)	Nu	11 H	15
Pilgrim St	Nu	20 M	15
Pilot La	Hu	38 V	15
Pilot St	Hu	21 N	17
Pin Oak Ct	Ou	26 P	7
Pin Oak Dr	Nu	10 K	14
Pin Oak La	Nu	19 P	14
Pine Av (FP)	Hu	4 E	17
Pine Av	Ou	38 X	14
Pine Ct (ed)	Hu	30 Q	19
Pine Ct	Hu	39 U	18
Pine Dr (pw)	Nu	2 F	8
Pine Dr	Nu	3 C	12
Pine Dr (MN)	Ou	35 U	6
Pine Dr (wy)	Ou	44 AA	8
Pine Dr (ob)	Ou	45 AA	13
Pine Dr N	Nu	9 K	11
Pine Dr S	Nu	9 K	11
Pine Hill Rd	Nu	3 E	13
Pine Hollow Rd	Ou	35 U	6
Pine La (VS)	Hu	5 F	22
Pine La	Ou	25 T	2
Pine La	Hu	30 R	18
Pine Low	Ou	16 L	5
Pine Park Av	Ou	25 T	2
Pine Pl	Ou	16 M	5
Pine Pl	Nu	11 K	15
Pine Pl	Hu	21 O	19
Pine Pl (bm)	Hu	40 V	21
Pine Ridge Rd	Ou	18 N	9
Pine Rd	Hu	13 K	20
Pine Rd	Ou	36 W	9
Pine St (ma)	Nu	9 G	11
Pine St (gh)	Ou	17 N	7
Pine St (os)	Nu	23 L	23
Pine St (pw)	Nu	9 G	9
Pine St (el)	Hu	4 E	18
Pine St (ML)	Hu	13 H	21
Pine St (wm)	Hu	6 E	24
Pine St (hr)	Nu	10 J	14
Pine St (fs)	Nu	12 J	18
Pine St (GA)	Hu	21 M	17
Pine St (RC)	Hu	22 L	21
Pine St (sh)	Hu	22 M	20
Pine St (un)	Hu	22 P	20
Pine St (bw)	Hu	22 N	22
Pine St (nc)	Hu	28 R	13
Pine St (hk)	Ou	37 W	13
Pine St (WB)	Hu	29 P	15
Pine St (ne)	Hu	31 T	20
Pine St (FR)	Hu	22 O	22
Pine St (pv)	Ou	45 Y	12
Pine St (FG)	Ou	46 CC16	
Pine St (nq)	Ou	47 AA18	
Pine St (MS)	Ou	47 AA19	
Pine St (wn)	Hu	40 W	21
Pine Tree Dr	Ou	46 Z	17
Pine Tree La	Nu	19 N	12
Pine Valley Rd	Ou	26 R	7
Pinebrook La	Hu	13 K	21
Pinebrook Ct	Hu	13 K	21
Pinecone La	Hu	29 S	15
Pinehurst Rd	Ou	46 BB15	
Pinehurst St	Hu	24 M	27
Pinelake Dr	Hu	13 K	20
Pineneck Rd	Hu	39 X	18
Pines, The (rt)	Nu	10 J	11
Pines, The	Nu	19 N	12
Pinetree Av	Ou	37 V	12
Pinetree Dr	Nu	2 C	9
Pinetree La (FH)	Nu	9 H	10
Pinetree La (al)	Nu	19 L	12
Pinetree La	Hu	29 T	16
Pinetree Rd	Nu	28 S	13
Pinewood La	Nu	11 H	15
Pinewood La	Ou	47 CC21	
Pinewood Rd (PR)	Nu	9 G	10
Pinewood Rd (EH)	Nu	18 M	10
Pinewood Rd (OW)	Nu	19 O	13
Pinewood Rd	Hu	40 X	20
Pink Woods La	Ou	17 P	6
Pintail La	Hu	38 U	16
Pintle Ct	Ou	38 V	14
Pioneer Blvd	Ou	18 P	9
Piper Ct	Nu	9 K	11
Piper Dr	Nu	10 K	13
Piper La	Hu	38 V	15
Piper Pl	Ou	45 Z	14
Piping Rock (In)	Hu	39 X	17
Piping Rock Rd	Ou	16 P	5
Piquet's La	Ou	44 Y	10
Pirates Cove	Ou	48 CC22	
Pironi Ct	Ou	44 Y	9
Pittsburg Av	Ou	47 Y	20
Pittsburgh Av	Ou	47 BB 19	
Pittsburgh Av	Hu	47 Y	20
Piza St	Hu	6 C	25
Place, The	Ou	17 L	5
Placid La	Hu	29 S	15
Placid St	Ou	37 U	11
Plain Ct	Hu	12 J	17
Plain Rd, The	Hu	29 R	15
Plainedge Ct	Ou	39 X	17
Plainedge Dr	Ou	46 Y	17
Plainfield Av (FP)	Hu	4 F	18
Plainfield Av	Hu	14 J	23
Plainfield La	Hu	6 D	23
Plainfield Rd	Nu	11 L	13
Plainfield St	Nu	19 P	14
Plains Rd, The	Hu	38 W	16
Plainview Rd (wy)	Ou	44 AA	9
Plainview Rd (hk)	Ou	37 V	13
Plainview Rd (bp)	Ou	45 Y	14
Plainview Rd (sa)	Ou	46 Z	16
Plaka Ct	Ou	17 O	8
Planders Av	Hu	21 P	19
Plandome Ct	Nu	2 F	10
Plandome Ct N	Nu	2 F	10
Plandome Ct S	Nu	2 F	10
Plandome Dr	Nu	2 F	10
Plandome Rd	Nu	2 F	9
Plane Av	Hu	18 M	9
Plant Ct	Ou	47 AA18	
Plant La	Hu	29 R	15
Planting Field Rd	Nu	19 M	11
Planting Fields Rd	Ou	26 R	5
Plato St	Hu	12 J	19
Plattsdale Rd	Hu	12 H	17
Play La	Hu	39 V	18
Plaza	Nu	20 L	15
Plaza Av	Hu	11 H	16
Plaza Ent	Ou	37 W	11
Plaza Gate	Hu	18 M	9
Plaza Rd	Nu	18 M	9
Plaza Rd (GA)	Hu	12 H	17
Plaza Rd	Hu	6 C	24
Plaza, The	Hu	8 F	7
Pleasant Av	Hu	38 V	15
Pleasant Av (sl)	Hu	29 S	15
Pleasant Av	Hu	31 Q	22
Pleasant Av (pv)	Ou	44 Y	11
Pleasant Av	Ou	46 BB17	
Pleasant Dr	Ou	46 CC17	
Pleasant La	Ou	35 V	6
Pleasant La	Hu	38 V	15
Pleasant Pl	Hu	14 H	23
Pleasant Rd	Hu	39 W	19
Pleasant View Dr	Ou	25 T	2
Plitt Av	Ou	46 AA17	
Plover La	Hu	29 T	16
Plover La	Hu	38 V	14
Plover Pl	Hu	40 X	22
Plow La	Hu	39 V	17
Plum Beach Point Av	Nu	1 D	8
Plum La (ed)	Hu	30 R	18
Plum La	Hu	29 S	15
Plum La	Ou	37 X	12
Plum Pl	Hu	4 E	17
Plum Tree Rd E	Hu	29 R	15
Plum Tree Rd N	Hu	29 R	15
Plum Tree Rd W	Hu	29 R	15
Plumtree La	Hu	21 L	18
Plymouth Av	Nu	20 M	15
Plymouth Ct	Hu	30 P	18
Plymouth Dr N	Ou	17 M	7
Plymouth Dr S	Ou	17 M	7
Plymouth Dr	Hu	29 Q	15
Plymouth Ct	Ou	47 CC19	
Plymouth Pl	Hu	29 S	16
Plymouth Rd (GN)	Nu	2 D	10
Plymouth Rd (PD)	Nu	9 G	10
Plymouth Rd (pw)	Nu	9 H	9
Plymouth Rd (RC)	Hu	22 M	21
Plymouth Rd (ER)	Hu	14 J	23
Plymouth Rd (BY)	Ou	25 R	2
Plymouth Rd (pv)	Ou	37 X	12
Plymouth Rd (wa)	Ou	48 AA 21	
Plymouth Rd (wn)	Hu	40 W	20
Plymouth St	Nu	11 H	15
Plymouth St	Hu	12 K	19
Plymton Av	Nu	10 K	14
Po La	Ou	37 U	13
Pocahontas St E	Ou	48 BB 22	
Pocahontas St W	Ou	48 BB 22	
Pocasset Ct	Hu	14 J	24
Poe Av	Hu	30 S	18
Poe Ct	Hu	40 W	21
Poe Pl (bw)	Hu	22 N	21
Poe Pl	Hu	39 X	17
Poe St	Hu	6 D	24
Poet La	Hu	38 V	15
Point Branch	Hu	14 F	24
Point La	Ou	35 V	5
Point of Woods Rd	Ou	45 AA	13
Polaris Dr	Hu	38 V	16
Polk Av (fs)	Hu	12 H	19
Polk La	Hu	21 M	19
Polk Pl	Hu	30 R	18
Polk St	Hu	32 Q	24
Pollok Pl	Ou	37 W	11
Polly La	Hu	17 M	8
Polo Ct	Ou	43 AA	8
Polo Dr	Ou	18 O	9
Polo Field La	Nu	3 E	13
Polo La (LW)	Hu	7 E	25
Polo Rd	Hu	29 R	15
Polo Rd	Nu	2 C	10
Pond Rd	Ou	48 AA 21	
Pomander Rd	Nu	11 L	14
Pomeroy La	Ou	16 O	3
Pompano La	Ou	47 CC19	
Pond Crossing	Hu	7 D	26
Pond Hill Rd	Nu	3 F	12
Pond La	Nu	11 H	14
Pond La (HH)	Hu	14 G	23
Pond La (SP)	Nu	8 F	6
Pond La (WG)	Hu	6 F	25
Pond La (In)	Hu	39 U	17
Pond Park Rd	Nu	3 C	11
Pond Pa	Ou	44 Z	10
Pond Pl	Ou	35 V	6
Pond Ridge	Ou	44 Y	9
Pond Rd (wn)	Hu	39 V	19
Pond Rd	Nu	1 B	8
Pond Rd (LW)	Hu	7 E	26
Pond Rd	Ou	16 L	3
Pond Rd	Ou	36 X	9
Pond View	Nu	2 C	11
Pond View Dr (BK)	Ou	26 T	5
Pond View Dr	Ou	36 V	10
Ponder La	Hu	38 V	16
Ponds Edge	Ou	26 T	5
Pondview Ct	Ou	28 S	11
Pondview Dr	Ou	16 L	3
Pont St	Nu	3 D	11
Pontiac Pl	Hu	29 S	16
Pontiac Rd	Hu	39 U	18
Pony Cir	Ou	10 K	12
Pool Dr	Nu	9 K	11
Poole St	Hu	23 L	23
Pope St	Hu	39 X	17
Poplar Av	Ou	46 BB17	
Poplar Ct	Nu	2 D	10
Poplar Ct	Hu	39 W	19
Poplar Dr	Nu	18 L	11
Poplar La	Hu	30 R	18
Poplar Pl	Nu	8 G	6
Poplar Pl	Ou	16 M	4
Poplar Pl	Hu	40 V	21
Poplar St (VS)	Hu	13 F	22
Poplar St	Nu	19 P	14
Poplar St (GA)	Hu	21 M	17
Poplar St (wh)	Hu	12 K	18
Poplar St (os)	Nu	23 M	24
Poplar St (nb)	Hu	30 U	19
Poplar St (mr)	Hu	31 S	22
Poplars, The	Nu	10 K	11
Poppy Av	Hu	12 J	18
Poppy Dr	Ou	47 CC18	
Poppy La	Hu	38 U	16
Poppy La	Ou	16 L	5
Poppy La (fs)	Hu	12 J	17
Poppy Pl	Hu	4 E	17
Poppy St	Hu	30 T	18
Port Dr	Nu	8 F	7
Port La	Hu	29 R	15
Port Washington Blvd	Nu	9 J	11
Porter La	Hu	6 E	24
Porter Pl (SC)	Ou	8 K	7
Porter Pl	Ou	17 M	6
Porter Pl (bm)	Hu	31 T	20
Porter Rd	Nu	11 J	15
Porter St (el)	Hu	12 G	19
Porter St	Hu	31 T	20
Porterfield Pl	Hu	22 P	22
Portico Ct	Nu	3 D	11
Portico Pl	Nu	3 D	11
Portland Av	Nu	22 N	22
Portland Av	Nu	29 Q	14
Post Av (el)	Hu	12 G	18
Post Av (EW)	Nu	20 M	14
Post Av (WB)	Nu	28 P	14
Post Av (wn)	Hu	40 V	20
Post Dr	Nu	18 L	9
Post La	Nu	19 L	14
Post La	Ou	18 P	9
Post La	Hu	38 V	16
Post Rd	Nu	28 P	12
Post St	Ou	17 N	8
Post St	Hu	30 T	17
Potter Av	Nu	31 S	20
Potter La	Hu	38 V	15
Potter St	Ou	46 CC17	
Potters Ct	Nu	2 C	10
Potters La (GN)	Nu	2 B	10
Potters La	Nu	19 M	12
Poulson St	Hu	40 W	19
Poultry La	Hu	38 V	16
Pound Hollow Ct	Ou	17 O	7
Pound Hollow Rd (OK)	Ou	17 O	7
Pound Ridge Rd	Ou	44 AA	11
Powell Av (RC)	Hu	22 M	22
Powell La	Hu	31 S	20
Powell Av	Ou	46 Y	15
Powell La	Nu	28 Q	12
Powell Pl (nn)	Nu	11 F	15
Powell Pl (HV)	Hu	21 O	18
Powell Pl (os)	Nu	14 K	23
Powell Pl (ne)	Hu	31 S	21
Powell Pl	Ou	46 BB15	
Powell St	Hu	31 Q	21
Powell St	Ou	46 BB17	
Powells La	Nu	28 Q	13
Power House Rd	Nu	19 L	12
Power St	Ou	38 W	14
Powers Av	Nu	30 S	18
Powers Pl	Nu	30 S	19
Powers Rd	Ou	47 BB20	
Prague St	Hu	13 H	20
Prairie La	Hu	39 V	18
Prairie Pa	Hu	38 W	15
Prato Ct	Hu	23 P	23
Pratt Blvd	Ou	17 M	5
Prayer Pl	Hu	12 F	18
Premier Blvd	Hu	12 G	17
Prentice Rd	Hu	38 W	16
Prescott Ct	Hu	6 D	23
Prescott Pl	Hu	6 D	23
Prescott Pl	Ou	45 AA	13
Prescott St (nv)	Hu	5 D	23
Prescott St (GA)	Hu	20 M	15
Prescott St (ld)	Hu	24 N	27
President Pl	Hu	15 J	26

Nassau Co.

STREET	MUN.	MAP	GRID
President St (LY)	Hu	13 H	21
President St (HV)	Hu	21 M	18
President St (FR)	Hu	32 Q	23
Presidential Dr E	Ou	45 AA	12
Presidential Dr S	Ou	45 AA	12
Press St	Hu	12 F	18
Preston Av	Ou	8 K	7
Preston Ct	Ou	16 M	4
Preston La (hk)	Ou	38 V	14
Preston La	Hu	32 T	23
Preston La	Ou	36 W	10
Preston Pl	Hu	39 U	18
Preston Rd	Nu	2 D	10
Preston Rd	Hu	30 R	18
Preston St	Nu	9 G	8
Prestwick Ter	Ou	16 N	5
Pride La	Hu	29 R	15
Prim La	Hu	29 R	15
Primrose Av		4 E	17
Primrose Av (hk)	Ou	37 U	12
Primrose Av	Ou	48 AA	21
Primrose Ct	Ou	20 M	16
Primrose Dr	Nu	11 H	14
Primrose La (nv)	Hu	13 H	20
Primrose La	Hu	18 M	11
Primrose La (HV)	Hu	21 O	18
Primrose La (rv)	Hu	22 P	20
Primrose La (ln)	Hu	38 U	16
Primrose Rd	Nu	10 L	14
Prince Av	Hu	22 O	21
Prince Ct	Hu	13 H	21
Prince La	Hu	29 R	15
Prince Pa	Hu	19 O	12
Prince St (ML)	Hu	13 H	20
Prince St (in)	Hu	6 C	24
Prince St	Nu	10 K	14
Prince St (bw)	Hu	22 O	20
Prince St (rv)	Hu	22 P	20
Prince St (bm)	Hu	31 U	22
Prince St (hk)	Ou	37 W	13
Prince St (FG)	Ou	46 CC	17
Princess St	Ou	28 T	12
Princess St	Hu	40 U	20
Princetn Rd	Hu	6 E	24
Princeton Av (hl)	Hu	14 G	23
Princeton Av	Hu	12 J	17
Princeton Ct	Ou	48 AA	21
Princeton Dr (hk)	Ou	37 V	12
Princeton Dr	Ou	44 AA	11
Princeton Dr N	Hu	40 W	20
Princeton Dr S	Hu	40 W	20
Princeton Dr W	Hu	40 W	20
Princeton Pl	Hu	31 S	22
Princeton Rd (fs)	Hu	12 J	19
Princeton Rd	Hu	22 M	21
Princeton St (GA)	Hu	12 H	17
Princeton St (VS)	Hu	5 D	21
Princeton St (EH)	Nu	19 L	12
Princeton St (WP)	Nu	19 L	13
Princeton St (HV)	Hu	21 N	17
Princeton St (lk)	Hu	13 K	21
Princeton St (RC)	Hu	22 L	21
Princeton St (WB)	Nu	28 Q	14
Printer La	Hu	38 V	15
Priscilla Pl	Hu	39 X	18
Priscilla Rd	Hu	14 G	25
Privado Rd	Ou	20 P	15
Private Ct	Nu	19 O	13
Private La	Nu	2 C	8
Private Rd (KP)	Nu	2 C	9
Private Rd (PR)	Nu	9 F	10
Private Rd (LT)	Ou	16 O	4
Private Rd (OW)	Nu	19 N	12
Private Rd (BY)	Ou	25 R	1
Private Rd (CI)	Ou	34 U	3
Private Rd (MT)	Ou	27 T	9
Procop Av	Ou	37 U	12
Promenade, The .	Ou	17 N	7
Propp Av (fs)	Hu	12 H	18
Propp Av (fs)	Hu	12 H	18
Prose St	Ou	28 T	13
Prospect Av (CH)	Hu	6 E	24
Prospect Av (WG)	Hu	14 G	23
Prospect Av (wm)	Hu	14 G	24
Prospect Av (SC)	Ou	8 K	7
Prospect Av (GL)	Ou	16 M	5
Prospect Av (GA)	Nu	20 N	16
Prospect Av (LY)	Hu	14 H	23
Prospect Av (ER)	Hu	14 K	23
Prospect Av (nc)	Nu	29 R	14
Prospect Av (ed)	Hu	30 R	18
Prospect Av (rv)	Hu	31 R	20
Prospect Ct (FR)	Hu	31 P	21
Prospect Ct	Hu	31 U	22
Prospect La	Nu	1 D	7
Prospect Pl (gh)	Ou	18 M	8
Prospect Pl (in)	Hu	6 B	25
Prospect Pl (SC)	Ou	17 L	6
Prospect Pl (HV)	Hu	21 N	18
Prospect Pl (bm)	Hu	40 U	21
Prospect Pl (pv)	Ou	45 Y	12
Prospect Pl (FG)	Ou	46 CC	16
Prospect Pl (mq)	Ou	48 Z	15
Prospect Pl N	Nu	3 C	12
Prospect St (pw)	Nu	9 F	8
Prospect St (TM)	Nu	3 E	12
Prospect St (in)	Hu	7 C	25
Prospect St (gh)	Ou	17 M	8
Prospect St (WP)	Nu	10 K	14
Prospect St (bw)	Hu	22 N	22
Prospect St (oy)	Ou	35 U	5
Prospect St (hk)	Ou	37 V	13
Prospect St (FR)	Hu	32 P	24
Prospect St (FG)	Ou	46 AA	16
Prospect St (bp)	Ou	46 Z	15
Prospect Ter	Ou	17 L	7
Provence La	Ou	17 M	7
Provenzano St	Hu	6 C	25
Pubins La	Hu	11 J	15
Public Dock	Nu	2 F	8
Public Wy	Ou	40 V	22
Puca Ct	Ou	17 N	6
Pulaski Pl	Nu	8 G	7
Pulaski St	Ou	17 L	6
Purdue Rd	Ou	16 M	4
Purdy Ct	Hu	22 M	22
Puritan La	Ou	46 AA	16
Putnam Av (VS)	Hu	5 F	20
Putnam Av (LY)	Hu	14 H	22
Putnam Av (GL)	Ou	17 L	6
Putnam Av (je)	Ou	28 T	12
Putnam Av (FR)	Hu	31 P	21
Putnam Av (rv)	Hu	31 Q	21
Putnam Av (ed)	Hu	30 S	19
Putnam Blvd	Hu	7 D	28
Putnam Dr	Hu	30 T	17
Putney Rd	Hu	5 F	20

Q

STREET	MUN.	MAP	GRID
Q St	Hu	13 G	19
Quail Ct	Ou	44 Z	11
Quail La	Hu	38 U	15
Quail Pa	Ou	27 Q	9
Quail Pl	Hu	14 J	23
Quail Ridge Rd	Ou	46 Y	16
Quail Run (OW)	Ou	18 P	10
Quail Run	Ou	48 CC	21
Quaker La	Ou	46 AA	16
Quaker La	Nu	19 O	12
Quaker La	Nu	39 V	17
Quaker Meeting House Rd	Ou	46 AA	16
Quaker Ridge Dr	Ou	27 T	10
Quaker Ridge Rd	Nu	10 H	11
Quaker St	Nu	11 K	14
Quality Pl	Ou	38 W	15
Quannacut Dr	Ou	25 R	1
Quarry La	Hu	39 V	17
Quarry Rd	Ou	25 Q	4
Quarter Deck, The	Nu	1 E	7
Quay Av	Hu	14 G	23
Quay Ct	Hu	14 J	24
Quealy Pl	Hu	13 L	22
Quebec Rd	Hu	15 K	27
Queen Ct	Nu	28 Q	13
Queen Pl	Ou	47 Z	20
Queen St	Nu	28 Q	13
Queen St (FR)	Hu	31 P	21
Queen St	Ou	37 W	12
Queen St (bm)	Hu	40 U	20
Queens Av	Ou	47 Y	19
Queens Av (el)	Hu	4 F	19
Queens Av	Hu	7 E	28
Queens Ct (pv)	Ou	45 Y	13
Queens Ct	Ou	48 AA	22
Queens La	Nu	10 J	14
Queens St	Ou	36 W	8
Quentin Pl	Hu	6 F	23
Quentin Roosevelt Blvd	Hu	20 O	16
Quiet La	Hu	38 V	15
Quincy Av	Ou	25 S	2
Quincy St	Hu	31 S	21
Quintus Dr	Hu	40 U	20

R

STREET	MUN.	MAP	GRID
R St	Hu	13 G	20
Rabbit Run	Ou	17 O	5
Rachel St	Hu	41 V	23
Radam Ct	Hu	31 P	21
Radcliff Av	Hu	8 F	7
Radcliff Dr E	Ou	26 T	7
Radcliff Dr N	Ou	26 T	7
Radcliff Dr S	Ou	26 T	7
Radcliff Dr W	Ou	26 T	7
Radcliff La	Ou	47 CC	18
Radcliffe Av	Ou	46 AA	17
Radcliffe Blvd	Ou	18 M	8
Radcliffe Ct	Ou	37 W	11
Radcliffe Rd	Hu	15 K	27
Radcliffe Rd	Ou	37 Y	11
Radial La	Hu	39 X	18
Radnor Ct	Ou	29 U	14
Radnor Rd	Ou	37 X	11
Radstock Av	Hu	5 E	20
Raemar Av	Hu	38 X	16
Raff Av	Hu	12 G	17
Raff Av	Nu	20 M	15
Railroad Av (LY)	Hu	13 G	21
Railroad Av (SM)	Hu	12 H	17
Railroad Av (wm)	Hu	6 F	24
Railroad Av (WG)	Hu	6 E	25
Railroad Av (gh)	Ou	17 M	8
Railroad Av (rt)	Nu	9 L	11
Railroad Av (GA)	Hu	11 J	16
Railroad Av (eg)	Hu	20 O	16
Railroad Av (oy)	Ou	35 U	5
Railroad Av (nc)	Nu	29 R	14
Railroad Av (hk)	Ou	37 V	13
Railroad Av (sy)	Ou	36 W	9
Railroad Av (bp)	Ou	38 X	15
Railroad Av (wn)	Hu	40 W	21
Railroad Av E	Hu	21 M	17
Railroad Av W	Hu	21 M	17
Railroad Pl	Hu	15 K	27
Rainbow La	Hu	39 W	17
Rainbow Pl	Hu	20 N	16
Rainbow Rd	Ou	48 AA	22
Raisig Av	Hu	5 F	20
Raleigh La	Hu	6 D	23
Raleigh Pl	Hu	31 Q	20
Raleigh St	Hu	6 D	24
Ralph Av (os)	Hu	23 M	24
Ralph Av	Hu	40 U	20
Ralph Ct	Hu	29 R	15
Ralph J Marino Expwy (Seaford-Oyster Bay Expwy)	Ou	37 Y	11
Ralph Pl	Hu	29 R	15
Ralph St E	Hu	47 Y	19
Ralph St S	Hu	39 X	19
Ralph W Young Av	Ou	17 M	6
Ramble La	Hu	39 X	17
Ramona St	Hu	30 T	18
Rams Hill (gh)	Ou	9 L	8
Ramsden Av	Hu	23 M	23
Ramsey Rd	Nu	2 E	10
Ramsey Rd	Ou	45 Z	12
Ranch La	Hu	39 W	17
Ranch Pl	Hu	31 S	21
Rand Ct	Hu	24 M	27
Rand Pl	Hu	7 C	26
Randal La	Ou	46 Y	16
Randall Av (el)	Hu	12 G	19
Randall Av (in)	Hu	6 C	25
Randall Av (LY)	Hu	13 J	22
Randall Av (ed)	Hu	30 S	17
Randall Av (FR)	Hu	22 P	22
Randall Pl	Hu	40 W	20
Randolph La	Hu	12 H	18
Randy La	Hu	41 U	23
Randy La	Ou	45 Y	12
Range Dr	Hu	31 S	21
Range Rd	Hu	40 U	20
Ransom Av	Ou	17 L	7
Ransom Pl	Hu	21 M	17
Raonor Rd	Nu	2 D	10
Rason Rd	Hu	6 C	24
Raspberry La	Hu	39 X	18
Rasweiler Blvd	Hu	13 J	20
Rave St	Ou	38 V	14
Raven St	Hu	38 W	16
Ravine Av	Ou	17 M	5
Ravine Pl	Hu	39 U	18
Ravine Rd	Nu	2 E	11
Ravine Rd	Ou	25 R	2
Ray Av	Hu	31 Q	21
Ray La	Hu	13 J	20
Ray Pl	Hu	30 U	19
Ray Rd	Hu	39 V	18
Ray St	Ou	37 V	13
Ray St (FR)	Hu	23 P	23
Ray St	Hu	40 X	21
Raymond Av	Hu	13 J	22
Raymond Ct	Ou	17 L	7
Raymond Ct	Nu	20 N	16
Raymond Pl	Hu	6 F	24
Raymond Rd	Hu	30 U	19
Raymond St (GL)	Ou	8 L	5
Raymond St (RC)	Hu	22 M	21
Raymond St (hk)	Hu	18 L	11
Raymond St (sd)	Hu	40 Y	21
Raynham Dr	Ou	36 W	9
Raynham Rd	Ou	17 N	5
Raynor St	Ou	32 Q	22
Reading La	Ou	46 Y	17
Reardon Pl	Ou	39 X	17
Rebecca La	Hu	23 N	23
Rebecca St	Hu	41 V	23
Rector St	Hu	30 T	18
Red Brook Ter	Nu	2 C	10
Red Fox La	Ou	26 Q	7
Red Ground Rd	Nu	18 N	11
Red Maple Dr E	Hu	39 W	18
Red Maple Dr N	Hu	39 W	18
Red Maple Dr S	Hu	39 W	18
Red Maple Dr W	Hu	39 W	18
Red Oak Pl	Ou	48 CC	21
Red Pole Pa	Nu	10 K	12
Red Spring La	Ou	8 L	5
Redan Rd	Hu	24 L	28
Redbrook Rd	Nu	2 B	9
Redfield Rd	Hu	15 K	26
Redmond La	Ou	35 W	6
Redmond Rd	Hu	31 S	20
Redmont Rd	Hu	12 K	19
Redpoll La	Hu	38 U	15
Redwing La	Hu	38 U	15
Redwood Av	Hu	7 C	25
Redwood Ct	Nu	1 E	6
Redwood Ct	Ou	17 O	6
Redwood Dr	Hu	6 D	24
Redwood Dr	Nu	18 L	11
Redwood Dr	Ou	37 X	13
Redwood La	Ou	48 CC	21
Redwood Pa	Hu	39 X	18
Redwood Pa	Hu	16 M	4
Redwood Pa	Hu	47 Y	20
Redwood Rd	Hu	11 H	15
Reed Av	Hu	12 G	17
Reed Ct	Nu	2 C	10
Reed Dr	Hu	10 J	13
Reed Dr	Hu	30 R	18
Reed La	Hu	19 P	14
Reed La	Hu	39 V	17
Reed Pl	Ou	47 AA	19
Reese Pl	Ou	46 AA	17
Reeve Rd	Hu	22 M	20
Regal La	Hu	39 X	18
Regent Ct N	Hu	29 R	15
Regent Ct S	Hu	29 R	15
Regent Dr (ld)	Hu	24 M	27
Regent La	Hu	29 R	15
Regent La (RL)	Nu	9 K	11

Nassau Co.

S

STREET	MUN.	MAP	GRID	
Saint Paul St	Ou	46	Z	17
Saint Pauls Cres	Hu	11	K	16
Saint Pauls Pl	Nu	3	E	11
Saint Pauls Pl (GA)	Hu	11	K	16
Saint Pauls Pl	Hu	21	L	18
Saint Pauls Rd N	Hu	21	L	18
Saint Pauls Rd S	Hu	21	M	18
Saint Pauls St	Hu	22	O	20
Saint Regis Pl	Hu	22	M	19
Saint Regis St	Hu	40	V	22
Saint Rocco's Pl	Ou	17	N	6
Saint Rugby St	Hu	30	S	17
Saint Thomas Pl	Hu	13	J	20
Salem Ct (sy)	Ou	36	Y	8
Salem Ct	Ou	45	AA	12
Salem Gate	Hu	5	E	20
Salem Gate	Ou	38	V	14
Salem La	Nu	9	H	9
Salem La	Hu	39	V	17
Salem Rd (el)	Hu	5	E	20
Salem Rd (EH)	Nu	18	M	11
Salem Rd (WB)	Nu	19	P	13
Salem Rd (RC)	Hu	22	M	21
Salem Rd (ER)	Hu	14	J	23
Salem Rd	Ou	38	V	14
Salem Rd (un)	Hu	30	P	18
Salem Rd (ne)	Hu	30	S	19
Salem Wy	Ou	17	M	7
Salisbury Av (SM)	Hu	12	G	17
Salisbury Av	Hu	12	J	17
Salisbury Garden Ct	Hu	29	T	16
Salisbury Park Dr	Hu	29	Q	15
Salisbury Rd	Hu	29	S	15
Sally Ct	Hu	30	R	19
Sally La	Hu	23	M	25
Sally La	Ou	44	Y	11
Sally Rd	Nu	11	K	15
Saltaire La	Ou	25	S	2
Saltaire Pl	Ou	48	Z	22
Salutation Rd	Ou	16	L	3
Sammis Pl	Hu	21	M	17
Sampson Av	Nu	10	K	13
Sampson St	Ou	35	U	5
Sampson St E	Hu	14	J	24
Sampson St W	Hu	14	J	24
Samuel Ct	Ou	36	X	9
Samuel Pl	Hu	14	J	23
San Juan Av	Nu	10	K	13
Sand Hill Rd	Hu	39	W	18
Sand St	Ou	48	CC	21
Sandalwood Av	Hu	13	F	22
Sanders Pl	Hu	30	T	19
Sandpiper Ct	Ou	18	P	10
Sandpiper Rd	Hu	38	U	15
Sandra Ct	Ou	17	O	6
Sandra Ct	Hu	39	X	18
Sandra La	Hu	31	R	20
Sandra La	Ou	46	Y	17
Sands Ct (MH)	Nu	1	E	7
Sands Ct (GN)	Nu	2	D	11
Sands Ct	Hu	24	M	27
Sands La	Nu	1	E	6
Sands La (HB)	Hu	14	G	24
Sands La	Hu	40	X	22
Sands Light Rd	Nu	1	D	5
Sands Pl	Nu	8	G	7
Sands Point Rd	Nu	1	E	6
Sands Rd	Ou	17	O	6
Sandy Ct	Nu	1	F	7
Sandy Ct	Hu	11	K	16
Sandy Ct (sa)	Ou	47	CC	18
Sandy Ct (sa)	Ou	47	BB	18
Sandy Ct (mq)	Ou	48	Y	22
Sandy Hill Rd	Ou	35	V	5
Sandy Hollow La	Nu	8	G	8
Sandy Hollow Rd	Nu	8	G	8
Sandy La	Hu	39	V	17
Sandy La	Ou	48	Y	22
Sanford Pl	Hu	5	F	22
Sans Av	Hu	32	T	23
Santa Barbara Dr	Ou	45	AA	12
Sanzoverino La	Ou	25	S	2
Sapir St	Hu	5	F	21
Sarah Dr	Hu	39	W	18
Sarah Dr	Ou	45	Z	14
Sarah La	Ou	36	X	9
Sarah Pl	Ou	38	W	14
Saranac Rd	Hu	13	K	20
Saratoga Blvd	Hu	24	L	26
Saratoga Cir	Hu	21	N	17
Saratoga Dr	Ou	28	S	12
Saratoga St (os)	Hu	22	M	22
Saratoga St	Hu	24	N	27
Sargent Pl	Nu	9	H	11
Saries Ct	Hu	39	X	18
Satellite La	Hu	38	W	16
Satinwood Rd	Ou	25	Q	2
Satteriee Av	Hu	13	G	22
Saturn Ct	Ou	37	X	11
Saucer La	Hu	39	W	17
Saul Pl	Ou	45	Y	12
Saville Rd	Nu	11	K	15
Savoy Av	Hu	4	E	18
Savoy Pl	Ou	37	U	12
Sawmill Rd	Hu	30	U	19
Saxon Ct	Ou	16	M	4
Saxon Rd	Ou	47	CC	18
Saxony Ct	Nu	10	H	12
Sayre Pl	Hu	5	E	21
Scally Pl	Nu	29	P	14
Scaneateles Av	Hu	13	K	20
Scarcliffe Dr	Hu	13	H	20
Schenck Av (TM)	Nu	3	F	12
Schenck Av	Nu	29	P	14
Schenck Blvd	Hu	12	G	18
Schenck Cir N	Hu	14	G	23
Schenck Cir S	Hu	14	G	23
Schenck Cir W	Hu	14	G	23
Schencks La	Hu	14	G	23
Scherer Blvd	Hu	12	H	18
Scherer St	Ou	38	X	15
Schermerhorn St	Hu	31	R	21
Schernott Pl	Hu	40	U	20
Scherr Pl	Hu	31	Q	20
Schiller Pl	Hu	30	T	19
Schiller St	Ou	28	T	13
Schley Av	Nu	10	K	13
Schmitt Ct	Hu	29	S	15
Schneider Ct	Nu	28	R	13
Schneider La	Ou	46	Y	15
Schoen St	Hu	22	O	21
Schoharie Ct	Ou	28	T	11
Schoharie Dr	Ou	28	T	11
Scholar Ct	Ou	18	P	9
Scholar La	Hu	38	W	15
Scholl Dr	Ou	46	Z	17
School Dr	Nu	10	J	13
School Dr	Hu	22	N	20
School House Ct	Ou	38	V	14
School House Hill Rd	Ou	9	L	8
School House La	Nu	3	E	13
School House La (sy)	Ou	36	W	8
School House La	Ou	45	AA	14
School House Pl	Ou	35	U	6
School La	Hu	24	M	27
School Rd	Hu	4	F	18
School St (SP)	Nu	8	G	7
School St (in)	Hu	7	C	25
School St (GL)	Ou	17	M	5
School St (gh)	Ou	17	N	8
School St (EW)	Nu	19	M	14
School St (ML)	Hu	13	J	21
School St (lk)	Hu	12	K	19
School St (bw)	Hu	22	N	22
School St (BY)	Ou	25	R	2
School St (oy)	Ou	35	U	5
School St (nc)	Nu	28	Q	14
School St (ed)	Hu	30	R	17
School St (bm)	Hu	40	V	22
School St (mq)	Ou	48	Z	21
Schoolhouse La	Nu	19	M	13
Schoolhouse Rd	Hu	38	U	16
Schooner La	Nu	1	F	7
Schraeder Pl	Ou	25	R	2
Schreiber Pl	Hu	23	O	24
Schroeter Av	Hu	12	J	17
Schultz St	Ou	28	S	13
Schumacher Dr	Nu	11	K	14
Schuman Pl	Hu	22	O	21
Schuman St	Hu	13	H	20
Schuster Av	Nu	20	L	14
Schuyler Av	Hu	22	M	21
Schuyler Dr	Ou	28	T	12
Scimitar Av	Hu	12	G	18
Scooter La	Ou	38	V	15
Scott Av	Ou	37	U	12
Scott Dr (nv)	Hu	13	H	20
Scott Dr (ae)	Hu	7	F	28
Scott Dr (wn)	Hu	39	U	19
Scott Pl	Hu	22	O	20
Scott Pl (GL)	Ou	16	M	4
Scott Pl (RC)	Hu	14	L	22
Scott Pl	Ou	45	Z	13
Scott St	Nu	10	J	14
Scott St	Ou	47	BB	21
Scranton Av	Hu	14	H	22
Scriven Av	Hu	40	U	20
Scudders La	Ou	9	L	9
Sculptor La	Hu	38	W	15
Sea Breeze La	Ou	25	R	2
Sea Breeze Rd	Ou	48	Z	21
Sea Cliff Av	Ou	17	L	7
Sea View Dr	Ou	25	S	3
Sea Wall La	Ou	25	S	2
Seabury Av	Hu	13	J	19
Seabury Rd	Hu	20	N	15
Seabury St	Hu	21	M	19
Seacoast La	Nu	1	E	5
Seacrest Pl	Ou	48	Z	22
Seaford Av	Hu	40	W	21
Seaford Av (mq)	Ou	47	Y	20
Seaford Av	Ou	40	Y	21
Seaford Ct	Hu	40	V	22
Seagull La	Nu	1	F	7
Seagull Pl	Ou	48	BB	22
Sealey Av	Hu	21	M	17
Sealy Ct	Hu	6	E	25
Sealy Dr	Hu	6	E	25
Seaman Av	Hu	21	N	17
Seaman Av (RC)	Hu	22	M	22
Seaman Av	Ou	46	Y	15
Seaman Ct	Nu	29	Q	14
Seaman Ct	Hu	31	R	21
Seaman Dr	Hu	31	T	20
Seaman Rd (GL)	Ou	16	M	4
Seaman Rd	Ou	28	T	11
Seamans Ct Rd	Ou	39	X	17
Seamans Neck Ct	Hu	40	X	21
Seamans Neck Rd	Hu	39	X	18
Seamans Neck Rd W	Hu	39	X	19
Sean Micheal Ct	Ou	46	Z	16
Searing Av	Nu	20	L	15
Searing St (bw)	Hu	22	N	21
Searing St	Hu	21	O	19
Searington Dr	Ou	36	Y	8
Searingtown Av	Nu	10	K	13
Searingtown Rd	Nu	9	J	11
Seaton Gate	Hu	5	E	20
Seaton Pl	Hu	5	F	20
Seaton St	Ou	48	AA	21
Seaview Av	Hu	15	K	27
Seaview Av	Ou	47	Z	21
Seaview Blvd	Nu	9	J	9
Seaview La	Nu	8	F	7
Seaview La	Hu	41	U	23
Seaview St	Ou	48	BB	21
Seawane Dr (HH)	Hu	14	G	24
Seawane Dr	Hu	41	U	23
Seawane Pl	Hu	14	G	24
Seawane Rd	Hu	14	H	24
Seawanhaka Pl	Ou	35	U	5
Seawanhaka Rd	Ou	34	V	2
Seaward Av	Ou	16	L	4
Sebree Pl	Ou	45	Z	13
Secatoag Av	Nu	8	F	8
Secatogue Av	Ou	46	BB	16
Secor Dr	Nu	9	F	9
Secor Dr N	Nu	9	F	9
Secor Dr S	Nu	9	F	9
Secor Dr W	Nu	9	F	9
Seebode Ct	Hu	40	U	21
Seele Ct	Hu	13	J	20
Seidman Pl	Hu	12	H	17
Seiffert Ct	Hu	23	M	23
Seitz Av (HV)	Hu	21	M	17
Seitz Av	Hu	23	L	22
Seitz Dr	Ou	46	Y	17
Selfridge Av	Hu	20	P	16
Selma Pl	Hu	4	F	18
Seminole Av	Ou	48	BB	22
Seminole Av	Hu	40	X	22
Seminole Rd	Hu	12	H	19
Semton Blvd	Hu	12	J	18
Senate St	Nu	20	M	15
Seneca Dr	Ou	46	Y	17
Seneca Dr E	Hu	31	T	21
Seneca Dr N	Hu	31	S	21
Seneca Dr S	Hu	31	T	21
Seneca Dr W	Hu	31	S	21
Seneca Gate	Hu	31	S	21
Seneca Pl (je)	Ou	28	T	12
Seneca Pl (mr)	Hu	31	T	21
Seneca Pl	Hu	40	W	20
Seneca Pl	Ou	48	BB	22
Seneca St E	Ou	48	BB	22
Seneca St W	Ou	48	BB	22
Sentinel Pl	Ou	47	CC	20
September La (Pvt)	Ou	16	M	3
Serein Ct	Ou	27	T	8
Serena Rd	Hu	6	F	23
Serenite La	Ou	27	S	8
Serpentine La	Nu	10	K	13
Serpentine La	Ou	45	AA	13
Serpentine La	Hu	39	W	18
Serpentine, The	Nu	9	J	11
Service Rd	Nu	8	J	7
Service Rd (sy)	Ou	36	X	9
Service Rd	Ou	46	Y	17
Seth La	Ou	38	W	15
Seton Ct	Ou	45	AA	13
Seville Pl	Ou	47	BB	18
Seville St	Hu	4	E	18
Sewanee Av	Hu	4	F	18
Seward Av	Nu	20	L	14
Seward Dr	Ou	44	AA	9
Sewell St	Hu	21	M	18
Sexton Rd	Ou	37	W	11
Seymor La	Ou	37	V	12
Shadetree La	Nu	19	L	12
Shadow La (TM)	Nu	3	E	11
Shadow La	Nu	19	M	14
Shadow La	Ou	44	AA	9
Shady Brook Rd	Nu	2	D	10
Shady La (SC)	Ou	17	L	6
Shady La (hk)	Ou	38	V	15
Shady La (LH)	Ou	43	Z	7
Shady Meadows La	Ou	36	W	8
Shady St	Hu	21	O	17
Shadyside Av	Nu	8	G	6
Shafter Av	Nu	10	K	13
Shakespeare Pl	Hu	30	S	18
Shames Dr	Ou	28	S	12
Shamrock Ct	Ou	36	V	8
Shannon Dr	Ou	44	Y	9
Shannon Wy	Ou	44	BB	11
Sharen Dr	Hu	24	O	27
Shari Ct	Ou	37	V	12
Shari La	Hu	30	R	19
Sharon Ct	Ou	45	Z	14
Sharon La	Nu	28	R	13
Shatel Rd	Ou	37	X	12
Shaun Ridge	Ou	18	L	8
Shaw Av	Hu	5	E	21
Shaw Dr	Hu	30	S	19
Shaw Pl	Hu	39	X	19
Shawcrest Pk	Hu	39	X	19
Shawnee Dr	Ou	46	Y	17
Shea Ct	Hu	31	P	22
Sheehey Pl	Hu	13	J	21
Sheep La	Ou	16	P	2
Sheep La	Hu	38	V	16
Sheep Pasture La	Ou	47	Y	19
Sheer Plz	Ou	45	AA	12
Sheffield Hill	Ou	44	Z	10
Sheffield Rd	Nu	3	E	12
Sheila Ct (fs)	Hu	12	H	19
Sheila Ct	Hu	39	U	17
Sheila Dr	Ou	37	W	12
Sheila Pl	Hu	39	W	18
Shelart St	Ou	44	Z	11
Shelbourne Dr	Hu	13	H	20
Shelbourne La	Nu	10	H	14
Sheldon Ct	Hu	13	H	20
Sheldon Dr	Hu	29	R	15
Sheldon Pl (ML)	Hu	13	H	20
Sheldon Pl	Hu	23	M	23
Sheli Dr (ob)	Ou	45	Z	14
Shell Dr	Ou	16	M	3
Shell La	Hu	39	W	18
Shell Pl	Hu	15	L	25
Shell Rd	Nu	8	G	8
Shell St	Hu	22	O	20
Shell St	Ou	48	CC	21
Shellbank Pl	Hu	14	K	22
Shelley Dr	Hu	38	X	16
Shelley La (SR)	Nu	2	B	11
Shelley La	Nu	19	O	14
Shelley Pl	Hu	30	S	18
Shelley Rd	Hu	30	U	19
Shelly Ct	Hu	32	U	22
Shelly Ct	Ou	45	Y	13
Shelly Dr	Ou	48	Z	23
Shelly La	Ou	46	Y	17
Shelly St	Hu	23	P	23

Nassau Co.

STREET	MUN.	MAP	GRID
Shelter Bay Dr	Nu	2 E	10
Shelter Hill Rd	Ou	37 X	12
Shelter La (LT)	Nu	16 P	4
Shelter La	Nu	19 L	12
Shelter La	Ou	27 R	8
Shelter La	Hu	39 U	17
Shelter Rock Rd	Nu	10 H	12
Shelton Ct	Hu	14 K	22
Shepherd La	Nu	19 L	12
Shepherd La	Hu	38 V	16
Shepherd St	Hu	22 M	21
Shepherds La	Nu	8 G	6
Sheppard St	Ou	17 N	8
Sherborn Rd	Hu	15 K	26
Sherbourne Rd	Nu	5 F	20
Sheridan Av	Hu	14 G	23
Sheridan Av	Nu	10 L	14
Sheridan Blvd	Hu	7 B	26
Sheridan Blvd	Hu	19 M	14
Sheridan Ct	Ou	37 X	13
Sheridan La	Ou	8 K	7
Sheridan Pl (hi)	Nu	15 J	27
Sheridan Pl	Hu	31 Q	20
Sheridan St	Nu	28 R	13
Sheridan St	Ou	45 Z	13
Sherman Av (wm)	Hu	6 F	24
Sherman Av	Nu	10 L	14
Sherman Av (RC)	Hu	22 M	22
Sherman Av (bi)	Ou	24 L	26
Sherman Av (ne)	Hu	31 S	20
Sherman Av (bm)	Ou	37 X	13
Sherman Av (pv)	Ou	37 X	13
Sherman Av (bp)	Ou	38 X	15
Sherman Ct	Hu	29 R	15
Sherman Ct	Hu	39 V	15
Sherman Dr	Ou	36 X	9
Sherman Dr	Hu	13 H	20
Sherman Pl	Hu	38 X	16
Sherman Rd (GL)	Ou	17 O	6
Sherman Rd (ob)	Ou	45 Z	13
Sherman Rd (FG)	Ou	46 AA	16
Sherman St (LY)	Hu	13 H	22
Sherman St (nc)	Nu	28 R	14
Sherman St (rv)	Hu	31 Q	20
Sherman St (mr)	Nu	31 S	21
Sherrard St	Nu	19 N	11
Sherrey Ct	Ou	47 Y	18
Sherry Av	Hu	39 W	18
Sherry Hill La	Nu	10 H	11
Sherwood Av	Hu	12 H	18
Sherwood Ct	Nu	6 D	23
Sherwood Ct	Ou	35 U	6
Sherwood Dr	Nu	30 R	18
Sherwood Dr (pv)	Ou	45 Z	12
Sherwood Dr	Ou	38 Y	14
Sherwood E	Ou	35 V	6
Sherwood Gate	Ou	35 V	6
Sherwood La	Hu	6 E	25
Sherwood La	Nu	19 L	12
Sherwood N	Ou	35 V	6
Sherwood Rd	Ou	16 M	4
Sherwood Rd (RC)	Hu	22 M	20
Sherwood Rd	Hu	29 T	16
Sherwood S	Ou	35 V	6
Sherwood St	Hu	6 D	23
Sherwood W	Ou	35 U	6
Shield La	Hu	39 W	18
Shields Av	Nu	11 L	14
Shine Pl	Hu	39 W	17
Shinncock Av	Ou	48 CC22	
Shipherd Av	Hu	13 J	22
Shipley Av	Hu	5 E	20
Ships Point La	Ou	35 U	5
Shirley La	Hu	30 R	19
Shirley Ct	Ou	46 AA	16
Shirley La	Hu	40 U	22
Shonnard Av	Hu	31 Q	22
Shore Av (BY)	Ou	35 U	5
Shore Av	Ou	35 U	5
Shore Dr (KP)	Nu	2 C	8
Shore Dr (PD)	Nu	2 F	10
Shore Dr (GE)	Nu	3 C	12
Shore Dr	Nu	32 T	23
Shore Drive Wy	Ou	25 T	2
Shore Park Rd	Nu	3 B	12
Shore Pl	Hu	41 W	23
Shore Rd (PN)	Nu	1 F	7
Shore Rd (PH)	Nu	2 F	10
Shore Rd (SC)	Ou	8 K	7
Shore Rd (os)	Hu	14 K	24
Shore Rd (LB)	Nu	15 K	28
Shore Rd (BY)	Ou	25 R	2
Shore Rd (BY)	Ou	25 S	2
Shore Rd (bm)	Nu	31 U	22
Shore Rd (sd)	Hu	41 W	23
Shore View La	Nu	2 F	10
Shore, The	Nu	2 F	10
Shorecliff Pl	Nu	3 B	12
Shorecliff Ter	Nu	3 B	11
Shoredale Dr	Nu	2 F	11
Shoreham Wy	Hu	31 T	22
Shorehaven La	Nu	2 F	11
Shoreview Av	Nu	2 F	11
Shoreview Rd	Nu	8 G	8
Shoreward Dr	Nu	3 E	11
Shorewood Dr	Nu	8 G	6
Shorewood Dr	Ou	25 S	2
Short Dr (st)	Nu	9 H	11
Short Dr	Nu	9 K	11
Short La (ln)	Nu	39 W	17
Short La	Nu	40 U	22
Short La	Ou	48 BB 21	
Short Pl (bw)	Hu	22 N	20
Short Pl (HV)	Nu	21 O	18
Short Pl (mr)	Nu	31 R	21
Short St	Ou	38 V	14
Short St	Nu	18 M	11
Short St	Nu	40 V	22
Short Wy	Nu	10 K	12
Shortridge Dr	Nu	19 M	14
Shotgun La	Hu	39 U	17
Shrub Hollow Rd	Nu	10 J	13
Shu Swamp Rd	Ou	25 R	4
Shubert La	Ou	46 Y	17
Shubert St	Hu	22 O	20
Shutter La	Ou	35 W	6
Sicardi Pl	Nu	20 O	14
Sideview Dr	Ou	35 U	5
Sidney Ct	Hu	39 X	19
Sidney Dr	Hu	31 S	19
Sidney Pl (sv)	Hu	5 E	22
Sidney Pl	Hu	32 R	23
Sidney St	Ou	35 U	5
Siegel St	Nu	28 R	14
Siems Ct	Hu	30 T	19
Sierks La (OK)	Ou	18 M	9
Sigmond St	Nu	23 O	23
Sigsbee Av	Nu	10 K	13
Silber Av	Ou	45 Y	14
Silo La	Hu	39 W	18
Silver Birch Rd	Hu	31 T	21
Silver Ct (wm)	Hu	6 E	24
Silver Ct	Nu	39 U	18
Silver La (os)	Hu	14 K	23
Silver La (bm)	Nu	31 T	22
Silver La (lm)	Hu	39 W	17
Silver St (el)	Nu	4 F	19
Silver St	Hu	13 J	20
Silverlake Blvd	Nu	20 O	14
Silverlake Pl	Hu	23 N	22
Silversmith Rd	Hu	38 W	16
Simcoe St	Ou	35 U	5
Simms Av	Hu	31 T	20
Simon Pl	Hu	39 W	18
Simone Ct	Ou	46 Y	16
Simonson Ct	Ou	18 N	8
Simonson Pl	Ou	46 BB16	
Simonson Rd	Ou	18 N	9
Simonson Rd	Nu	20 L	15
Simpson Dr	Ou	45 AA13	
Simpson St	Ou	28 T	11
Sinclair Dr	Nu	2 B	10
Sinclair Martin Dr	Nu	18 L	10
Sinclair St	Ou	46 BB15	
Singer Pl	Ou	17 M	6
Singleton La	Hu	6 F	24
Singley Ct	Nu	3 E	11
Singworth St	Ou	35 U	6
Sintsink Dr E	Nu	1 F	7
Sintsink Dr W	Nu	1 E	7
Sitka Ct	Ou	44 Z	10
Skellington Rd	Ou	45 Y	13
Skelly Pl	Nu	20 L	15
Ski La	Ou	26 T	5
Skidmore La (Pilvins Dr)	Nu	2 B	10
Skidmore Pl	Hu	6 F	22
Skillman Av	Hu	23 M	24
Skillman St	Nu	9 K	10
Skimmer La	Hu	38 U	16
Skipper Ct	Hu	31 T	21
Skunks Misery Rd	Ou	16 O	4
Sky La	Hu	39 W	17
Skylark La	Hu	39 W	18
Skylark Rd	Ou	48 AA 22	
Skyline Dr	Ou	44 Z	11
Skyview Ct	Ou	35 W	7
Slabey Av	Hu	13 H	20
Slate La	Hu	39 V	18
Sleepy La	Ou	38 V	15
Slice Dr	Hu	23 N	25
Sliverton Av	Hu	40 W	19
Sloan Dr E	Hu	13 F	20
Sloan Dr N	Hu	13 F	20
Sloan Dr S	Hu	13 F	20
Sloanes Beach Rd	Nu	1 E	6
Sloanes Ct	Nu	1 E	6
Slocum Av	Nu	8 G	6
Slocum St	Hu	14 G	23
Small St	Nu	29 Q	14
Smith Av	Hu	31 U	19
Smith Ct	Ou	17 O	5
Smith La (HN)	Hu	14 F	25
Smith La	Hu	40 Y	21
Smith Pl (wm)	Hu	6 E	24
Smith Pl	Nu	19 L	13
Smith Pl	Hu	23 N	24
Smith St (in)	Hu	6 C	25
Smith St (VS)	Hu	5 F	21
Smith St (GL)	Ou	17 O	6
Smith St (gh)	Ou	17 M	8
Smith St (HV)	Nu	21 M	17
Smith St (fs)	Hu	12 J	19
Smith St (lk)	Hu	13 K	20
Smith St (LY)	Hu	13 H	21
Smith St (ER)	Hu	14 J	23
Smith St (RC)	Hu	13 L	22
Smith St (bw)	Hu	22 O	22
Smith St (hk)	Ou	37 V	12
Smith St (un)	Hu	22 P	19
Smith St (mr)	Nu	31 S	21
Smith St (FR)	Hu	23 P	22
Smith St (MS)	Ou	47 AA 20	
Smith St (ne)	Hu	40 W	20
Smull La	Nu	9 F	8
Smull Pl	Nu	8 F	8
Snapdragon La	Hu	38 V	16
Snaporagon La	Nu	19 L	12
Snowbird La	Hu	38 U	15
Snugcove La	Ou	25 S	2
Sobo Av	Hu	12 J	18
Sobro Av	Nu	5 D	20
Sohmer Pl	Nu	28 R	14
Solar La	Ou	10 K	13
Solar La	Hu	38 W	16
Soloff Blvd	Hu	6 B	25
Soloff Rd	Ou	47 CC19	
Solomon Av	Hu	6 B	25
Soma La	Hu	31 T	22
Soma Pl	Hu	31 R	21
Soma Pl	Ou	46 AA	16
Soma St	Nu	10 G	14
Somerset Av	Hu	11 J	16
Somerset Av	Ou	38 W	14
Somerset Dr	Hu	14 H	23
Somerset Dr	Hu	41 X	22
Somerset Dr N	Nu	3 D	12
Somerset Pl	Ou	35 V	7
Somerset Rd	Nu	3 D	12
Somerset S Dr	Nu	3 E	13
Soper Av	Hu	22 N	22
Soper St	Hu	23 L	23
Sophia St	Ou	46 Y	16
Sorgi Ct	Ou	44 AA 11	
Sound Beach Av	Ou	25 T	2
Sound Beach Rd	Ou	25 T	2
Sound View	Ou	25 R	1
Sound View La	Nu	1 E	6
Sound View Rd (GL)	Ou	8 K	5
Sound View Rd	Ou	25 S	3
Soundbeach Dr	Ou	16 M	3
Soundside La	Ou	16 K	4
Soundview Av	Ou	35 U	6
Soundview Crest	Nu	10 H	11
Soundview Dr (PN)	Nu	1 F	7
Soundview La	Nu	3 E	13
Soundview La	Nu	2 B	9
Soundview La	Ou	16 P	4
Soundview Rd	Nu	3 E	13
Sousa Dr	Nu	1 E	6
South 1st St	Hu	11 G	16
South 1st St	Ou	46 Y	15
South 2nd St	Hu	11 G	16
South 2nd St	Ou	46 Y	15
South 3rd St	Hu	11 G	16
South 3rd St	Ou	46 Y	15
South 4th St	Hu	11 G	16
South 4th St (lv)	Ou	16 O	4
South 4th St	Ou	46 Y	15
South 5th St	Hu	11 G	16
South 5th St (lv)	Ou	16 O	4
South 5th St	Ou	46 Y	15
South 6th St	Hu	11 G	16
South 6th St (lv)	Ou	16 O	5
South 6th St	Ou	38 X	15
South 8th St	Hu	11 H	16
South 9th St	Hu	11 H	16
South 10th St	Hu	11 H	16
South 11th St	Hu	11 H	16
South 12th St	Hu	11 H	16
South 13th St	Hu	11 H	16
South 14th St	Hu	11 H	16
South 16th St	Hu	11 H	16
South 17th St	Hu	11 H	16
South 18th St	Hu	11 H	16
South Av	Hu	12 J	17
South Baldwin Pl	Ou	48 CC 21	
South Bay Av	Hu	32 P	23
South Bay Av	Ou	48 Y	22
South Bay Dr	Ou	48 BB 22	
South Bay Pl	Ou	48 BB 22	
South Bayles Av	Nu	9 H	8
South Bayview Av	Hu	22 P	22
South Bergen Pl	Hu	31 P	22
South Bismark Av	Hu	30 T	19
South Branch Dr	Nu	9 J	11
South Broadway	Ou	38 V	14
South Brookside Av	Hu	23 O	22
South Butehorn St	Ou	38 X	15
South Carley Ct	Nu	30 U	19
South Central Av	Hu	5 F	22
South Centre Av	Hu	13 K	22
South Centre Island Rd	Ou	25 U	4
South Cherry Valley Av	Hu	12 K	19
South Cherrybrook Pl	Nu	10 F	12
South Cir	Nu	3 C	12
South Columbus Av	Hu	31 Q	22
South Copper Beech La	Hu	15 F	26
South Corona Av	Hu	13 F	22
South Cottage St	Hu	13 G	22
South Ct (pw)	Nu	2 F	9
South Ct	Nu	19 L	12
South Ct	Ou	22 O	20
South Ct	Ou	38 V	15
South Covert Av	Hu	12 G	18
South Cypress La	Hu	29 S	14
South Dean St	Ou	38 V	15
South Dr (PD)	Nu	2 F	10
South Dr (GE)	Nu	3 D	12
South Dr (ma)	Nu	10 F	11
South Dr (mh)	Nu	10 H	14
South Dr (VS)	Hu	13 F	22
South Dr (RL)	Nu	9 K	11
South Dr (sh)	Hu	22 N	20
South Dr (bh)	Nu	29 P	24
South Dr (ne)	Nu	30 R	19
South East Shore Dr	Ou	48 CC22	
South Elm St	Hu	13 K	19
South Elm St	Ou	37 V	13
South Emerson Pl	Hu	13 G	21
South End Ct	Hu	6 F	23
South End La	Hu	6 E	23
South End Pl	Hu	32 Q	23
South Fair Ct	Ou	47 CC19	
South Farms Rd	Nu	1 E	6
South Fordham Rd	Ou	38 W	15

Nassau Co.

STREET	MUN. MAP GRID
Sterling Rd	Hu 4 E 18
Sterling St (un)	Hu 30 Q 18
Sterling St	Hu 30 T 18
Sterlino Pl	Hu 22 P 21
Sterns Ct	Ou 46 BB 15
Steuben Av	Ou 46 Y 15
Steuben Dr	Ou 28 T 12
Stevans Ct	Hu 12 H 17
Stevedore La	Hu 38 W 16
Steven Av	Hu 12 J 19
Steven Ct (ed)	Hu 30 R 18
Steven Ct	Hu 39 U 18
Steven Ct	Ou 46 Y 17
Steven Dr	Hu 6 F 23
Steven La	Nu 2 D 9
Steven La	Ou 37 X 12
Steven Oval	Ou 16 M 5
Steven Pl	Hu 6 E 24
Steven Rd	Ou 23 O 24
Steven St	Ou 45 Y 12
Stevens Av	Ou 10 K 13
Stevens Av (HV)	Hu 21 L 18
Stevens Av (FR)	Hu 31 Q 21
Stevens Av (ne)	Hu 31 S 20
Stevens Ct	Ou 23 L 23
Stevens Pl	Hu 7 C 26
Stevens St	Ou 23 L 23
Stevens St (rv)	Hu 31 Q 20
Stevenson Cir	Hu 14 G 23
Stevenson Dr	Nu 2 B 11
Stevenson Rd	Hu 14 G 23
Stevenson St (LY)	Hu 13 H 21
Stevenson St	Hu 6 D 23
Stewart Av	Hu 11 F 15
Stewart Av (SM)	Hu 11 G 16
Stewart Av (GA)	Hu 12 H 17
Stewart Av (GA)	Hu 20 L 16
Stewart Av (HV)	Hu 21 N 17
Stewart Av (os)	Hu 23 L 23
Stewart Av (sl)	Hu 29 S 15
Stewart Av (hk)	Ou 29 T 15
Stewart Av (bm)	Hu 31 T 20
Stewart Av (bp)	Ou 38 X 14
Stewart Dr	Nu 22 N 20
Stewart Dr	Nu 3 C 12
Stewart La	Ou 35 Y 6
Stewart Pl	Hu 12 H 17
Stewart St (FP)	Hu 12 F 17
Stewart St (el)	Hu 12 F 18
Stewart St (VS)	Hu 13 G 22
Stewart St (hl)	Hu 14 G 23
Stewart St	Hu 31 T 20
Stewart St	Ou 37 X 13
Stillman Rd	Ou 17 O 6
Stillwater Av	Ou 48 CC 22
Stillwell La	Ou 43 Y 7
Stillwell Pl	Hu 32 Q 23
Stirling Av	Hu 23 P 24
Stirrup Dr	Ou 27 P 8
Stirrup Dr	Hu 39 W 18
Stirrup La (GL)	Ou 16 N 4
Stirrup La	Nu 19 L 13
Stirrup La	Hu 36 V 10
Stirrup La	Hu 39 V 18
Stirrup Pa	Hu 40 X 21
Stoddart Ct	Ou 26 P 5
Stokes Av (FR)	Hu 23 P 22
Stokes Av	Hu 38 X 16
Stone Arch Rd	Hu 18 O 11
Stone Av (fs)	Hu 12 H 19
Stone Av	Hu 30 R 17
Stone Blvd	Ou 48 CC 21
Stone Gate Mall	Hu 10 J 14
Stone Hill Dr E	Hu 10 H 12
Stone Hill Dr N	Hu 10 H 12
Stone Hill Dr S	Hu 10 H 12
Stone Hill Gate	Hu 10 H 12
Stone La	Hu 39 U 17
Stone Rd	Ou 37 X 13
Stone St	Hu 12 F 18
Stonecutter Rd	Hu 38 W 15
Stonegate La	Hu 18 O 9
Stonehenge La	Nu 20 O 14
Stonehenge Rd (GN)	Nu 2 C 11
Stonehenge Rd	Nu 9 G 11
Stonehenge Rd	Hu 22 M 21
Stoner Av	Nu 3 D 11
Stoneridge Ct	Ou 36 U 8
Stonewell Rd	Hu 22 M 21
Stony La	Hu 39 W 18
Stony Run Rd	Nu 2 C 11
Stony Town Rd	Nu 10 J 12
Stoothoff Dr	Hu 11 K 14
Store Hill Rd	Ou 19 P 12
Storm St	Hu 14 K 24

STREET	MUN. MAP GRID
Story La	Ou 38 V 15
Stowe Av	Hu 22 N 21
Stowe Pl	Hu 21 M 17
Straight La	Hu 39 X 17
Strand Pl	Nu 20 M 15
Strang Dr	Hu 39 V 18
Stratford Av	Hu 11 H 16
Stratford Av	Nu 19 L 13
Stratford Ct	Hu 29 R 15
Stratford Ct (nb)	Hu 30 U 19
Stratford Dr (sl)	Hu 29 Q 15
Stratford Dr	Hu 30 R 18
Stratford Green	Ou 46 AA 16
Stratford N	Nu 10 K 12
Stratford Pl	Ou 35 W 7
Stratford Rd	Nu 8 H 8
Stratford Rd (LY)	Hu 14 G 22
Stratford Rd (wh)	Hu 21 L 18
Stratford Rd (RC)	Hu 22 M 21
Stratford Rd (sh)	Hu 22 N 20
Stratford Rd	Ou 37 X 12
Stratford Rd (wn)	Hu 40 W 20
Stratford S	Nu 10 K 12
Strathmore La	Hu 22 M 21
Strathmore Rd (GN)	Nu 2 C 11
Strathmore Rd	Nu 9 G 11
Strathmore St	Hu 6 E 23
Strattford Rd	Nu 11 J 15
Straw La	Ou 29 T 15
Strawberry La	Nu 19 L 13
Strawberry La	Hu 38 U 16
Strawberry Pl	Ou 35 U 6
Stream Ct	Nu 2 C 10
Strickland Pl	Nu 9 H 10
Stringham Av	Nu 5 F 21
Strong St	Ou 37 U 13
Strully Dr	Ou 48 AA 22
Stuart Av (el)	Nu 5 E 20
Stuart Av	Hu 13 J 21
Stuart Ct	Hu 6 E 23
Stuart Dr	Ou 36 X 10
Stuart Dr E	Ou 17 M 5
Stuart Dr W	Ou 17 M 5
Stuart Gate	Ou 47 Y 18
Stuart La	Hu 30 T 17
Stuart La	Ou 47 BB 19
Stuart Pl	Nu 9 H 11
Stuart Pl (os)	Hu 22 M 22
Stuart Pl	Hu 47 Y 18
Stuart Rd	Hu 14 G 23
Stuart St	Nu 2 D 10
Stuart St	Hu 13 H 21
Sturl Av	Hu 14 F 23
Sturlane Pl	Hu 6 F 23
Stuyvesant Av (ed)	Hu 30 S 18
Stuyvesant Av	Hu 31 S 21
Stuyvesant Pl	Hu 6 E 25
Stuyvesant St	Hu 12 F 19
Stymus Av	Ou 46 Z 16
Suburban Gate	Nu 10 G 14
Sudbury La	Nu 28 R 13
Suffolk Av	Ou 47 Z 19
Suffolk Blvd	Hu 7 E 28
Suffolk Ct	Hu 23 L 23
Suffolk Dr	Nu 30 S 19
Suffolk La	Nu 20 L 16
Suffolk Rd	Hu 15 K 27
Suffolk Rd	Ou 47 BB 21
Suffolk St	Hu 32 Q 24
Sugar Maple Dr	Nu 10 J 13
Sugar Maple La	Ou 16 N 4
Sugar Maple Rd	Hu 38 U 16
Sugar Tom's La	Ou 26 U 6
Sugar Tom's Ridge	Ou 26 U 7
Suggs La	Ou 28 T 13
Sullivan Av	Ou 46 AA 17
Sullivan Dr	Ou 28 T 12
Sullivan La	Nu 29 Q 14
Sullivan Rd	Ou 46 BB 16
Sully Dr	Nu 10 H 11
Summa Av	Nu 29 S 14
Summer Av	Nu 3 E 12
Summer Av	Hu 21 P 19
Summer Dr	Hu 39 X 19
Summer La	Ou 38 V 15
Summer St	Nu 3 E 12
Summers Pl	Hu 31 R 21
Summers St	Ou 35 U 6
Summerwind Dr	Ou 27 R 8
Summit Av (bw)	Hu 23 N 23

STREET	MUN. MAP GRID
Summit Av (LY)	Hu 13 H 22
Summit Av (LY)	Hu 6 D 25
Summit Av	Ou 8 K 7
Summit Av (RH)	Nu 18 L 10
Summit Av	Nu 19 M 14
Summit Av (MN)	Ou 35 U 6
Summit Ct	Ou 44 Z 11
Summit Dr	Ou 47 AA 18
Summit Driveway	Nu 2 F 10
Summit La (mh)	Nu 10 H 14
Summit La	Nu 19 L 12
Summit La	Hu 38 V 16
Summit Pl	Nu 2 F 10
Summit Pl	Ou 17 M 5
Summit La (KP)	Nu 2 B 9
Summit Rd	Nu 8 H 8
Summit St (oy)	Ou 35 U 5
Summit St (pv)	Ou 44 Z 11
Summit St	Ou 37 W 13
Summit View Dr	Ou 25 Q 2
Summit Wy	Ou 36 X 9
Sumner Av	Hu 31 R 21
Sumter Av	Nu 19 L 14
Sun Av	Hu 12 G 18
Sunapee Rd	Hu 13 K 20
Sunbeam Av	Ou 38 X 15
Sunbeam Rd	Ou 37 X 12
Sundown Dr	Ou 38 X 15
Sunken Orchard La	Ou 35 V 6
Sunny Hill Dr	Ou 35 U 6
Sunny La (fs)	Hu 12 J 17
Sunny La	Hu 39 W 18
Sunny La	Ou 38 X 15
Sunnybrook Dr	Hu 23 N 23
Sunnybrook Dr E	Hu 23 N 23
Sunnybrook Dr W	Hu 23 N 23
Sunnyfield La	Hu 5 E 22
Sunnyfield Rd	Ou 29 U 14
Sunnyhill Dr	Ou 17 O 8
Sunnyside Av	Hu 21 O 18
Sunnyside Blvd	Ou 37 Y 11
Sunnyside La	Ou 28 S 13
Sunnyside Rd	Hu 23 M 24
Sunnyvale Rd	Nu 9 J 10
Sunrise Dr	Nu 31 U 22
Sunrise Dr	Hu 13 H 22
Sunrise Dr	Ou 46 AA 17
Sunrise Hwy (P.O.W.-M.I.A. Memorial Hwy) (VS)	Hu 5 E 21
Sunrise Hwy (P.O.W.-M.I.A. Memorial Hwy) (LY)	Hu 13 H 22
Sunrise Hwy (P.O.W.-M.I.A. Memorial Hwy) (MS)	Ou 47 AA 20
Sunrise La	Hu 39 W 17
Sunrise Plz	Hu 13 F 22
Sunrise St	Ou 37 W 13
Sunrise Wy	Ou 46 Y 15
Sunset Av (LY)	Hu 14 H 22
Sunset Av (GL)	Ou 17 M 6
Sunset Av (gw)	Ou 18 L 8
Sunset Av (bi)	Hu 15 K 27
Sunset Av (hk)	Ou 37 V 12
Sunset Av (sa)	Ou 47 BB 18
Sunset Av (sd)	Hu 47 Y 20
Sunset Blvd	Ou 48 Z 22
Sunset Ct	Ou 38 X 15
Sunset Dr	Nu 9 G 10
Sunset Dr (wm)	Hu 6 E 23
Sunset Rd	Hu 21 M 18
Sunset Rd	Ou 46 AA 17
Sunset La	Nu 8 H 8
Sunset La	Hu 12 K 18
Sunset La	Ou 37 X 12
Sunset La (ln)	Hu 39 W 17
Sunset Rd	Nu 2 B 9
Sunset Rd (VS)	Hu 13 G 21
Sunset Rd	Hu 7 C 25
Sunset Rd (OC)	Ou 35 X 5
Sunset Rd N	Nu 10 K 13
Sunset Rd S	Nu 10 K 13
Sunset Rd W	Nu 10 K 13
Sunset Ter	Nu 11 K 15
Sunshine Av	Hu 13 K 20
Sunshine Rd	Ou 38 X 15
Sunview Dr	Ou 8 K 5

STREET	MUN. MAP GRID
Superior Rd	Hu 4 D 17
Supreme Court Dr	Hu 20 M 16
Surele Rd	Hu 40 W 20
Surf Dr	Hu 41 U 23
Surprise St	Hu 12 G 18
Surrey Commons Reyam Rd	Hu 13 G 22
Surrey Dr (ed)	Hu 30 R 19
Surrey Dr	Hu 31 S 20
Surrey La (GN)	Nu 2 D 10
Surrey La (VS)	Hu 13 H 21
Surrey La (OW)	Nu 18 O 11
Surrey La (gk)	Nu 11 J 15
Surrey La (GA)	Nu 20 N 15
Surrey La (HV)	Hu 21 O 17
Surrey La (sh)	Hu 22 N 20
Surrey La (bw)	Hu 22 N 22
Surrey La (bm)	Hu 31 T 21
Surrey La (bp)	Ou 37 X 13
Surrey La (ln)	Hu 39 W 17
Surrey La (wa)	Ou 47 BB 19
Surrey Pl	Hu 22 N 20
Surrey Pl	Ou 26 U 7
Surrey Rd (ug)	Nu 3 E 12
Surrey Rd	Nu 11 H 14
Surrey Rd	Ou 48 Z 21
Susan Ct (VS)	Hu 13 F 22
Susan Ct (GL)	Ou 17 O 5
Susan Ct (wh)	Hu 12 K 19
Susan Ct (sl)	Hu 29 T 16
Susan Ct (ne)	Hu 30 R 19
Susan Ct (lg)	Ou 36 X 10
Susan Ct (pv)	Ou 37 X 13
Susan Ct (sa)	Hu 39 X 18
Susan Cove	Ou 26 U 7
Susan Dr	Hu 30 T 17
Susan Pl	Hu 30 Q 19
Susan Rd	Hu 41 V 23
Susan Rd	Ou 37 U 12
Susquehanna Av	Nu 3 E 12
Sussex Av	Ou 47 Y 18
Sussex Dr	Nu 9 J 11
Sussex La	Ou 37 X 13
Sussex Rd	Nu 3 E 12
Sussex Rd (el)	Nu 4 E 18
Sussex Rd	Hu 30 T 17
Sussex St	Ou 37 W 13
Sutherland Rd	Ou 37 V 12
Sutton Cir	Nu 10 H 11
Sutton Ct	Nu 2 D 11
Sutton Dr	Ou 37 Y 11
Sutton Hill La	Nu 10 H 14
Sutton La	Hu 14 F 23
Sutton Pl	Nu 2 D 11
Sutton Pl (wm)	Hu 6 E 24
Sutton Pl (LW)	Hu 7 C 26
Sutton Pl	Nu 10 J 12
Sutton Pl (RC)	Hu 22 M 20
Sutton Pl (ne)	Hu 31 R 20
Sutton Pl	Ou 48 Z 21
Sutton Pl S	Hu 7 C 26
Sutton Ter	Hu 21 M 19
Sutton Ter	Ou 28 T 12
Suzane La	Ou 45 Z 14
Suzanne Ct	Ou 48 AA 21
Swale La	Hu 39 W 18
Swale Rd	Hu 13 H 20
Swallow La	Hu 38 U 15
Swalm St	Nu 28 R 13
Swan Ct (GL)	Ou 16 N 3
Swan Ct	Nu 10 J 12
Swan Ct	Ou 45 BB 13
Swan Dr	Ou 48 Y 22
Swan La	Hu 39 W 17
Swan Pl	Hu 38 W 16
Swansdowne Dr (sd)	Hu 39 X 17
Sweetman Av	Hu 12 G 18
Sweezy Av	Hu 23 P 22
Swenson Dr	Ou 44 Y 9
Swenson Pl	Hu 31 T 21
Swing La	Hu 39 W 18
Swirl La	Hu 38 V 15
Switzerland Rd	Ou 37 V 12
Sycamore Av (FP)	Hu 11 G 16
Sycamore Av (gh)	Ou 17 L 8
Sycamore Av (HV)	Hu 21 M 19
Sycamore Av (ne)	Hu 31 T 20
Sycamore Av (wn)	Hu 40 V 21

STREET	MUN.	MAP	GRID
Sycamore Av (bp)	Ou	38 Y	14
Sycamore Dr (SP)	Nu	1 E	6
Sycamore Dr (GE)	Nu	3 C	12
Sycamore Dr (FH)	Nu	9 J	10
Sycamore Dr (EH)	Nu	18 M	10
Sycamore Dr (hr)	Nu	10 J	14
Sycamore Dr (wy)	Ou	44 AA	9
Sycamore La	Nu	19 L	12
Sycamore La (ln)	Hu	38 U	16
Sycamore La	Hu	30 T	19
Sycamore Pl	Hu	31 T	20
Sycamore Rd	Hu	5 E	22
Sycamore Rd	Ou	8 K	5
Sycamore St	Hu	40 Y	21
Sycamore St	Ou	40 Y	21
Sydney Av	Hu	13 J	20
Sydney Pl	Hu	30 S	18
Sydney St	Hu	45 Y	12
Sylvan Ct (el)	Hu	12 F	19
Sylvan Ct	Hu	23 M	23
Sylvan Dr	Hu	13 K	20
Sylvan La	Nu	19 P	14
Sylvan La	Hu	30 R	18
Sylvan Pl	Hu	14 G	22
Sylvan Pl (wy)	Ou	44 Z	8
Sylvan Pl	Ou	47 BB	18
Sylvester Pl	Hu	13 H	22
Sylvester St	Nu	28 R	13
Sylvia Av	Hu	22 N	20
Sylvia Dr	Hu	30 T	18
Sylvia La	Ou	45 Y	12
Sylvia La	Nu	11 G	15
Sylvia La	Hu	30 Q	18
Sylvia Rd	Ou	45 Z	14
Sylvia Rd	Hu	47 Y	19
Sylvia St	Ou	18 L	8
Syosset Cir	Ou	36 W	10
Syosset-Woodbury Rd	Ou	36 X	8
Syracuse St	Nu	19 L	13

T

STREET	MUN.	MAP	GRID
Table La	Ou	38 U	15
Tabor Pl	Hu	30 T	18
Tacoma La	Ou	37 W	11
Tad La	Ou	45 AA	13
Tadmor St	Hu	30 R	19
Taft Av (in)	Hu	6 C	25
Taft Av (LY)	Hu	13 H	21
Taft Av (HV)	Hu	21 M	18
Taft Av (LB)	Hu	15 L	28
Taft Av (ne)	Hu	31 S	20
Taft Av (bp)	Ou	45 Y	14
Taft Av (sd)	Hu	40 X	20
Taft Ct (ed)	Hu	30 R	18
Taft Ct	Hu	47 Y	20
Taft Pl	Ou	16 M	4
Taft Pl	Nu	19 L	13
Taft Pl	Hu	22 P	22
Taft St (lk)	Hu	13 K	20
Taft St (ed)	Hu	30 T	18
Taft St (wn)	Hu	40 W	20
Tailor La	Hu	38 V	15
Tain Dr	Nu	3 D	12
Talbot Av	Hu	6 D	23
Talbot Dr (LS)	Nu	3 E	12
Talbot Dr	Nu	28 R	13
Talbot Pl	Hu	15 K	26
Talbot St	Nu	10 J	14
Talfor Rd	Hu	14 J	23
Tall Oak Ct	Ou	35 X	7
Tall Oak Cres	Ou	35 X	7
Talley Rd	Hu	18 N	10
Talley Rd S	Hu	18 N	10
Tallow La	Hu	39 V	17
Tally La	Hu	39 W	19
Talmadge Dr	Hu	22 O	21
Tameling Rd	Hu	14 J	23
Tammy's La	Ou	36 V	8
Tamwood Ct	Hu	22 M	20
Tanager La (ln)	Hu	38 U	15
Tangle La	Hu	39 X	19
Tanglewood Crossing	Hu	7 E	26
Tanglewood La	Ou	17 L	7
Tanglewood La	Hu	22 O	21
Tanglewood Rd	Hu	13 K	21
Tanners La	Hu	39 W	17
Tanners Pond Rd	Hu	12 J	17
Tanners Rd	Nu	3 F	14
Tanwood Ct	Hu	40 U	20
Tanwood Ct	Ou	46 Y	17
Tanwood Dr (wh)	Hu	12 K	19
Tanwood Dr	Hu	22 O	20
Tappan Rd	Ou	16 N	4
Tappanwood Rd	Ou	16 N	4
Tappentown La	Ou	27 S	9
Tara Dr (EH)	Nu	18 N	10
Tarboro St	Hu	4 F	18
Tardy La N	Hu	39 W	19
Tardy La S	Hu	39 W	19
Tarence St	Hu	22 M	21
Target La	Hu	39 U	17
Tarry La	Hu	39 W	17
Tatterson St	Nu	9 K	10
Taylor Av (WB)	Nu	20 P	15
Taylor Av (ed)	Hu	30 T	17
Taylor Av (rv)	Hu	22 P	21
Taylor Av (ln)	Hu	39 X	17
Taylor Av	Ou	47 AA	20
Taylor Ct	Ou	25 Q	3
Taylor Dr (GL)	Ou	17 M	6
Taylor Dr	Ou	46 AA	16
Taylor La	Ou	25 S	2
Taylor Pl	Hu	21 N	19
Taylor Rd	Hu	13 J	20
Taylor Rd	Ou	46 BB	16
Taylor St	Hu	32 R	22
Teakwood La	Nu	18 M	10
Teal La	Hu	38 V	15
Teamster La	Hu	38 W	15
Teaticket Ct	Hu	14 J	24
Tec St	Ou	29 T	14
Tee Ct	Hu	6 E	23
Teehan La	Hu	22 O	21
Teibrook Av	Ou	36 W	9
Telegram Av	Hu	12 G	18
Temme Ct	Ou	45 Z	14
Temple Ct	Hu	22 O	22
Temple Dr	Nu	9 G	9
Temple Dr	Hu	40 X	20
Temple Dr	Nu	10 L	14
Tenafly Dr	Nu	11 J	14
Teneyck Av	Hu	13 F	21
Tennessee Av (LB)	Hu	15 G	28
Tennessee Av	Hu	21 N	18
Tennessee St	Hu	12 G	17
Tennis Ct	Ou	45 Y	13
Tennis Court Rd	Ou	34 W	4
Tennyson Av	Hu	22 N	21
Tennyson Av	Nu	29 Q	14
Teresa Pl	Hu	21 O	19
Terminal Dr	Ou	44 Z	11
Terra La	Hu	30 T	18
Terra Park La	Hu	39 U	19
Terrace Av (FP)	Hu	11 F	16
Terrace Av (el)	Hu	4 F	18
Terrace Av (gs)	Hu	12 J	17
Terrace Av (HV)	Hu	22 O	22
Terrace Blvd	Nu	11 H	15
Terrace Cir	Nu	3 D	12
Terrace Ct (pw)	Nu	9 G	9
Terrace Ct (sg)	Nu	19 L	13
Terrace Ct (OW)	Nu	19 O	12
Terrace Ct	Hu	21 M	18
Terrace Ct	Ou	44 Z	10
Terrace Dr (pw)	Nu	9 F	9
Terrace Dr	Nu	19 O	14
Terrace La (BK)	Ou	26 T	6
Terrace La	Ou	44 Z	10
Terrace Pk	Hu	11 J	16
Terrace Pl	Nu	9 F	9
Terrace Pl (GL)	Ou	17 L	5
Terrace Pl (bw)	Hu	22 N	21
Terrace Pl	Ou	37 V	13
Terrace Pl	Hu	30 P	19
Terrace Rd	Nu	3 F	11
Terrace Rd	Ou	46 Z	16
Terrace View Rd	Ou	46 BB	17
Terrace, The	Nu	9 F	10
Terrapin Pl	Hu	40 X	22
Terrehans La	Ou	37 U	11
Terrell Av	Hu	23 L	23
Terrell La	Hu	38 U	15
Terrell Pl	Hu	21 P	18
Terry Ct	Ou	17 M	7
Terry Ct	Hu	21 P	19
Terry La	Nu	10 J	13
Terry La (BY)	Ou	25 R	2
Terry La (je)	Ou	37 U	12
Terry La (pv)	Ou	45 Y	13
Terry La	Hu	39 W	19
Terry Pl	Hu	12 H	19
Terry St	Ou	38 V	14
Texas Av	Hu	15 L	25
Texas Ct	Ou	36 X	8
Texas St	Ou	28 T	13
Thatch La	Hu	39 X	19
Thatch Wy	Ou	16 M	3
Thayer La	Nu	8 G	7
Thayer Rd	Nu	9 G	11
Thelma Av	Hu	31 R	21
Thelma Ct	Hu	31 P	22
Thelma St	Nu	19 L	12
Themar Ct	Hu	23 N	23
Theodora St	Hu	12 G	18
Theodore Dr	Ou	45 Z	13
Theresa Av	Hu	12 J	19
Thimble La	Ou	38 U	15
Thistle La	Hu	39 X	19
Thixton Av	Hu	14 J	24
Thixton Dr	Hu	14 H	24
Thoma Pl	Hu	31 Q	21
Thomas Av	Hu	23 N	23
Thomas Av	Ou	38 X	14
Thomas Ct	Hu	7 C	25
Thomas La	Ou	37 X	11
Thomas Pl	Hu	40 U	20
Thomas Pl (bm)	Hu	40 V	21
Thomas Powell Blvd	Ou	46 AA	16
Thomas Rd	Hu	22 N	21
Thomas St (wm)	Hu	14 F	24
Thomas St (HV)	Hu	21 O	17
Thomas St	Hu	31 S	21
Thompson Av	Hu	23 L	24
Thompson Dr	Hu	14 J	23
Thompson Pl	Hu	14 H	23
Thompson Shore Rd	Nu	2 F	11
Thompson St	Hu	13 G	20
Thomson Av	Hu	31 S	20
Thoreau Av	Hu	31 T	21
Thorens Av	Hu	11 K	15
Thorman Av	Ou	37 U	13
Thorn Pl	Hu	47 BB	21
Thorn St	Hu	23 M	24
Thorne Av	Hu	21 N	18
Thorne Av	Ou	47 Y	18
Thorne Ct	Hu	30 R	19
Thorne Ct	Ou	46 Z	16
Thorne Dr	Ou	46 Z	16
Thorne La	Ou	26 Q	6
Thornhill Dr	Nu	19 M	12
Thornwood La	Nu	19 N	11
Thornwood Rd	Ou	48 AA	22
Thorpe La	Ou	45 Y	13
Thrush Av	Hu	13 K	20
Thrush Hollow	Ou	26 T	5
Thrush La	Hu	38 U	15
Tiana St	Hu	40 X	22
Tianderah Rd	Nu	8 G	8
Tibbets Ct	Nu	1 E	6
Tiber Rd	Ou	35 X	7
Tide Wy (SP)	Nu	8 F	5
Tide Wy	Nu	2 B	9
Tide Wy, The	Nu	2 F	10
Tidewater Av	Ou	48 CC	22
Tiffany Cir	Nu	10 J	12
Tiffany Dr	Ou	48 Z	21
Tiffany Rd	Ou	35 W	5
Tildean La	Ou	25 R	2
Tile La	Ou	38 U	15
Tiller La	Hu	38 W	16
Tilley Pl	Ou	8 K	7
Tilrose Av (ML)	Hu	13 J	21
Tilrose Av	Hu	23 L	23
Timber La	Nu	10 H	11
Timber La	Hu	38 V	16
Timber Ridge Dr	Ou	35 Y	6
Timber Rd	Ou	16 N	4
Timberland La	Ou	17 P	7
Times Av	Hu	12 G	18
Timothy Rd	Hu	41 V	23
Tinder La	Hu	38 V	15
Tinker Dr	Hu	23 M	23
Tinker La	Hu	38 W	15
Tinkers Pl	Ou	29 T	14
Tinsel Ct	Hu	39 X	19
Tioga Av	Hu	7 E	28
Tioga Dr	Ou	28 T	12
Tiptop La	Ou	38 V	15
Titus Av	Nu	19 O	14
Titus Pa	Ou	27 U	10
Titus Rd	Ou	16 N	5
Titus Wy	Nu	19 M	14
Tobias St	Ou	38 V	15
Tobie La	Ou	37 U	11
Tobin Av	Nu	3 D	12
Tod Cir	Hu	39 X	19
Todd Ct	Ou	17 M	8
Todd Ct	Nu	19 L	13
Todd Dr	Nu	8 J	7
Todd Dr	Ou	17 M	8
Todd Dr E	Ou	17 M	8
Todd Dr N	Ou	17 M	8
Todd Rd	Hu	13 F	21
Toll La	Hu	39 W	17
Toll Pl	Ou	45 AA	13
Toller La	Hu	38 W	15
Tollgate Ct	Hu	13 H	22
Tollgate La	Hu	39 X	19
Tomes Av	Ou	46 BB	17
Tommy's La	Ou	36 V	8
Tompkins Av	Ou	28 T	12
Tondon La	Ou	25 P	3
Tone Island Rd	Hu	7 B	25
Toni Ann Cir	Ou	45 Z	13
Toni Ct	Ou	45 Y	12
Toni Pl	Ou	45 Y	12
Tonopah St	Hu	40 W	21
Tonquin St	Hu	30 T	18
Tooker Av	Ou	35 U	5
Toomer Pl	Hu	13 H	21
Top La	Hu	39 V	17
Topper La	Hu	38 V	15
Toronto Av	Ou	47 Y	19
Torquay Pl	Hu	14 H	23
Totten St	Hu	21 N	18
Totten St	Ou	46 Y	15
Tottenham Pl	Nu	11 J	14
Tottenham Rd	Hu	13 G	22
Tower Ct (HV)	Hu	21 O	17
Tower Ct	Hu	21 P	19
Tower Ct	Ou	36 X	9
Tower La	Hu	39 V	17
Tower Pl	Nu	9 K	11
Tower Rd	Ou	16 L	4
Towle Pl	Ou	17 L	6
Town Cocks La	Ou	16 P	5
Town House Pl	Nu	3 D	12
Town Pa	Ou	17 L	7
Town Path Rd	Nu	18 M	10
Towne House Dr	Hu	30 T	19
Townhouse Dr	Ou	47 BB	18
Townsend Dr	Ou	36 X	8
Townsend La	Ou	38 V	14
Townsend Pl	Ou	36 W	9
Townsend Rd	Ou	16 N	5
Townsend Rd	Hu	40 Y	21
Townsend St	Ou	18 M	8
Tracy Pl	Hu	14 H	23
Trader La	Hu	38 V	15
Tradewinds Dr	Ou	25 R	2
Trafalgar Blvd	Hu	24 L	26
Trafalgar Sq	Hu	13 G	22
Transverse Rd	Hu	20 M	16
Trap Rd	Hu	23 N	24
Trapper La	Hu	38 W	16
Travers St	Nu	2 F	11
Travis Av	Hu	12 G	19
Traymore Blvd	Hu	15 K	26
Trebor Rd	Ou	47 CC	21
Tredwell Av	Hu	14 J	22
Tredwell Ct	Ou	36 W	9
Tredwell Ct	Ou	36 W	9
Tredwell Dr	Nu	19 N	13
Tredwell Rd	Nu	20 M	14
Tree La	Hu	39 W	19
Trellis La	Hu	39 W	19
Tremont Pl	Hu	31 P	20
Tremont Pl (ed)	Hu	30 T	18
Tremont St	Hu	20 N	16
Tremont St	Nu	29 P	14
Trenton Av	Hu	15 F	28
Trezza Ct	Ou	37 V	12
Trezza Ct	Nu	40 V	21
Tri Harbor Ct	Nu	9 J	10
Triangle La	Nu	23 O	23
Tribune Av	Hu	12 G	18
Trinity Ct	Hu	12 K	19
Trinity Pl (wh)	Hu	21 L	18
Trinity Pl (wm)	Hu	6 F	24
Trinity Pl (ML)	Hu	13 J	20
Trinity St	Hu	23 L	24
Tropical Ct	Ou	45 Z	13
Troscher La	Ou	46 Y	16
Troy Av	Hu	7 F	28
Troy Ct	Ou	44 Y	10

Nassau Co.

STREET	MUN.	MAP	GRID
Troy Pl (FR)	Hu	31 R	22
Troy Pl	Hu	31 S	22
Troy St	Hu	5 F	20
Troyn Ct	Ou	10 H	14
Trubee Pl	Ou	16 N	5
Truman Av	Hu	30 R	18
Trumbull Rd	Nu	9 H	10
Trumpet La	Hu	38 V	16
Truro La	Hu	21 O	18
Trusdale Dr	Nu	19 O	12
Truxton Rd	Hu	15 K	26
Trysting Pl	Hu	6 D	24
Tucker La	Hu	13 J	20
Tuddington Rd	Nu	2 D	10
Tudor Cres	Hu	4 E	19
Tudor Dr	Hu	10 H	14
Tudor Gate	Hu	4 E	19
Tudor La	Nu	1 F	6
Tudor Rd (hk)	Ou	37 W	14
Tudor Rd	Ou	46 AA	16
Tulane Rd	Ou	16 M	4
Tulane St	Ou	46 AA	16
Tulip Av (FP)	Hu	4 F	16
Tulip Av (ML)	Hu	13 J	20
Tulip Av (lk)	Hu	13 K	20
Tulip Av (bh)	Hu	23 O	23
Tulip Av (ed)	Hu	30 R	19
Tulip Cir	Hu	13 F	20
Tulip Ct (hr)	Hu	10 J	14
Tulip Ct	Hu	10 K	13
Tulip Ct	Hu	30 P	18
Tulip Ct	Ou	47 AA	18
Tulip Dr	Nu	3 C	11
Tulip Dr (GL)	Ou	16 M	4
Tulip Dr (sa)	Ou	46 Z	17
Tulip Dr (MS)	Ou	48 AA	21
Tulip La (pw)	Nu	9 H	9
Tulip La (nn)	Hu	11 G	15
Tulip La (hr)	Nu	10 K	14
Tulip La	Hu	36 V	9
Tulip La (ln)	Hu	38 V	16
Tulip La	Hu	39 W	19
Tulip Pl	Hu	11 K	15
Tulip Pl (bm)	Hu	40 U	20
Tulip Pl	Hu	31 S	22
Tulip Rd (Pvt)	Ou	35 Y	6
Tulip St	Hu	5 E	25
Tulips, The	Hu	10 K	11
Tullamore Rd	Hu	11 J	16
Tulsa St	Hu	21 P	17
Tunnel St	Hu	12 G	17
Turf La	Hu	19 M	13
Turf La	Hu	39 V	18
Turf Rd (wm)	Hu	6 D	23
Turf Rd	Hu	23 M	24
Turn La	Hu	39 V	17
Turnberry La	Ou	45 Z	13
Turnbull La	Ou	29 T	14
Turnwood Ct	Hu	21 O	17
Turret La	Hu	44 Z	8
Turtle Cove La	Nu	2 E	9
Tuscala St	Hu	40 W	21
Tusk La	Hu	39 W	19
Tut Basin	Hu	14 K	24
Tuthill Pl	Hu	40 Y	21
Tutor Pl	Hu	12 K	19
Tuttle Pl	Hu	15 K	27
Tuxedo Av	Hu	11 J	14
Tuxedo Dr	Hu	4 F	19
Twain St	Hu	22 O	21
Twig La	Hu	29 T	15
Twin La E	Hu	39 X	19
Twin La N	Hu	39 W	19
Twin La S	Hu	39 W	19
Twin Lawns Av	Ou	37 V	12
Twin Pl	Hu	15 K	26
Twin Ponds La	Ou	35 V	7
Twisting La	Hu	39 X	19
Two Brothers Ct	Hu	23 L	23
Tyler Av (HV)	Hu	21 M	19
Tyler La	Hu	30 R	18
Tyler Pl	Hu	12 K	18
Tyler Rd	Hu	13 K	20
Tyler St (fs)	Hu	5 F	20
Tyler St	Hu	32 Q	24
Tyrconnell Av	Ou	47 AA	20
Tyrus Ct	Hu	30 R	19

U

STREET	MUN.	MAP	GRID
Udall Dr	Nu	3 F	12
Ulster Av	Hu	7 E	28
Ulster Dr	Ou	28 T	12
Under Hill	Ou	26 T	5
Underhill Av (lv)	Ou	16 P	4
Underhill Av (hk)	Ou	37 U	13
Underhill Av	Hu	31 Q	21
Underhill Av (lg)	Ou	36 W	10
Underhill Blvd	Ou	36 V	9
Underhill Rd (gh)	Ou	17 N	7
Underhill Rd	Hu	6 P	5
Union Av (el)	Hu	12 G	18
Union Av	Hu	14 H	23
Union Av (gh)	Ou	17 N	8
Union Av	Nu	29 Q	14
Union Dr	Hu	30 Q	19
Union Pl (os)	Hu	14 K	24
Union Pl (HV)	Hu	21 M	17
Union Pl (LY)	Hu	13 H	22
Union Pl (rv)	Hu	31 P	20
Union St (VS)	Hu	5 E	21
Union St (in)	Hu	6 D	25
Union St (RH)	Hu	18 L	10
Union St (hr)	Hu	10 U	14
Union St (MI)	Hu	20 M	15
Union St (ER)	Hu	14 K	23
Union St (FR)	Hu	31 Q	21
Union Turnpike Ext	Nu	10 G	14
Uniondale Av	Hu	30 P	18
Universal Blvd	Ou	37 W	13
Universe Dr	Hu	38 W	16
University Dr	Ou	18 P	9
University Pl	Nu	3 E	12
University Pl (gh)	Ou	18 M	9
University Pl	Hu	21 N	18
University Pl	Ou	37 W	13
University Rd	Nu	3 E	12
University Rd	Ou	25 Q	2
University St	Hu	6 D	23
Unqua Cir	Ou	48 BB	22
Unqua Rd	Ou	47 BB	21
Uphill La	Ou	43 AA	8
Upland La	Hu	38 W	16
Upland Rd	Ou	35 X	5
Upland Rd	Hu	3 D	13
Upland St	Nu	28 R	13
Upton Pl	Hu	20 M	15
Urban Av	Nu	28 R	13
Ursula Dr	Nu	10 J	12
Ursuline Ct	Ou	35 W	7
Utah Rd	Hu	13 K	20
Utica Av (hk)	Ou	29 U	14
Utica Av	Ou	47 Z	18
Utica St	Hu	5 F	20
Utterby Rd	Hu	13 J	21
Utz St	Hu	31 Q	21

V

STREET	MUN.	MAP	GRID
Val Ct	Hu	13 F	20
Val Park Av	Hu	13 G	20
Valcour Av	Hu	30 P	17
Valdur Ct	Hu	22 P	20
Vale Ct	Nu	11 J	15
Vale, The	Ou	36 X	9
Valentine Av	Ou	17 M	7
Valentine Dr	Nu	19 L	13
Valentine Dr (mh)	Nu	10 H	14
Valentine La	Nu	9 L	11
Valentine Pl (HV)	Hu	21 O	18
Valentine Pl	Hu	40 V	20
Valentine St	Ou	8 L	5
Valentine St	Hu	31 Q	20
Valentines La	Ou	18 N	9
Valentines Rd	Hu	29 Q	15
Valerie Av	Ou	37 U	12
Valerie Ct	Hu	32 T	23
Valerie Dr	Ou	27 Q	9
Valley Av	Ou	25 Q	4
Valley Ct	Ou	38 V	14
Valley Greens Dr	Hu	6 E	23
Valley La	Hu	38 V	15
Valley La E	Hu	6 E	23
Valley La N	Hu	6 E	23
Valley La W	Hu	6 E	23
Valley Rd (PN)	Ou	8 G	7
Valley Rd	Nu	9 F	10
Valley Rd (GL)	Ou	16 L	5
Valley Rd (BY)	Ou	25 S	2
Valley Rd (MN)	Ou	25 S	3
Valley Rd (MC)	Ou	26 R	6
Valley Rd (OW)	Ou	27 Q	10
Valley Rd (ln)	Hu	38 U	16
Valley Rd (wn)	Hu	39 V	18
Valley Rd (lg)	Ou	36 X	9
Valley Rd (pv)	Ou	45 Z	12
Valleyview Rd	Nu	3 F	11
Valmont Pl	Hu	12 F	19
Val-Page St	Hu	14 H	23
Van Arsdale Pl	Nu	2 E	11
Van Buren Av (FP)	Hu	11 F	16
Van Buren Av	Hu	30 R	18
Van Buren Ct	Nu	19 O	14
Van Buren Pl	Hu	23 P	24
Van Buren St (fs)	Hu	12 H	19
Van Buren St (un)	Hu	22 O	20
Van Buren St (bh)	Hu	23 O	24
Van Buren St (FR)	Hu	32 Q	24
Van Buren St	Ou	47 AA	20
Van Cott Av	Hu	21 M	17
Van Cott Av	Ou	46 BB	16
Van Cott Pl	Hu	40 U	20
Van Nostrand Av (GN)	Nu	2 C	10
Van Nostrand Av	Nu	10 K	11
Van Nostrand Pl	Hu	31 S	20
Van Nostrand Pl	Hu	31 S	20
Van Pl	Hu	40 W	20
Van Roo Av	Nu	31 S	21
Van Siclen Av	Hu	4 F	16
Van Sise Ct	Ou	36 W	10
Van Wagner Pl	Nu	20 L	14
Vanad Dr	Nu	18 N	10
Vanata Ct	Hu	21 N	17
Vancott Av	Ou	46 BB	16
Vandam St	Hu	6 D	23
Vanderbilt Av (PD)	Nu	9 F	11
Vanderbilt Av	Nu	11 F	16
Vanderbilt Ct	Hu	15 K	26
Vanderbilt Ct	Nu	20 N	16
Vanderbilt Dr (SP)	Nu	1 D	5
Vanderbilt Dr (LS)	Nu	3 E	13
Vanderbilt Dr (MI)	Nu	20 N	15
Vanderbilt La	Ou	45 AA	13
Vanderbilt Pl	Hu	15 K	26
Vanderbilt Rd	Nu	9 H	11
Vanderbilt Wy	Hu	5 E	22
Vanderlyn Dr	Nu	9 J	10
Vanderveer Dr	Hu	22 M	20
Vanderventer Av	Nu	9 H	8
Vanderwater St	Ou	46 BB	17
Vandewater Av	Hu	12 F	17
Vanguren St	Nu	9 G	8
Varick Ct	Hu	22 L	21
Vassar La	Ou	37 W	12
Vassar Pl (LY)	Hu	13 H	21
Vassar Pl (wh)	Hu	21 L	18
Vassar Pl (RC)	Hu	22 L	21
Vassar Pl (mr)	Hu	31 S	22
Vassar St (GA)	Hu	12 H	17
Vassar St	Hu	13 K	21
Vaughn St	Hu	14 K	25
Veeder Dr	Hu	14 G	24
Vegas Ct	Ou	45 AA	13
Ventana Ct	Hu	7 E	25
Venus Rd	Ou	37 X	11
Vera Av	Ou	45 Y	13
Verbena Av (FP)	Hu	4 F	17
Verbena Av	Hu	30 S	19
Verbena Ct	Ou	37 U	12
Verity La	Nu	9 K	10
Verity La	Hu	23 O	23
Verleye St	Hu	40 X	21
Vermont Av (HV)	Hu	21 N	17
Vermont Av	Hu	23 L	24
Vermont St	Hu	15 G	28
Verna Wy	Ou	44 Y	10
Vernon Av (AB)	Hu	7 E	28
Vernon Av (os)	Hu	14 K	24
Vernon Av (RC)	Hu	23 L	22
Vernon Av	Ou	26 U	7
Vernon Av (ed)	Hu	39 U	18
Vernon Ct	Hu	22 L	22
Vernon Ct	Hu	4 F	17
Vernon St (hk)	Ou	37 W	13
Vernon St	Ou	46 BB	17
Verona Pl (VS)	Hu	5 F	21
Verona Pl	Hu	40 W	21
Verplank Rd	Ou	16 M	4
Versailles Ct	Ou	27 R	9
Very Ct	Ou	46 Y	17
Vestry Rd	Hu	40 W	20
Veterans Blvd	Ou	47 Z	20
Veterans Memorial Plz	Hu	14 F	23
Vian Av (wm)	Hu	14 F	23
Vian Av	Hu	14 G	23
Viceroy Rd	Hu	39 X	18
Victor Ct (UB)	Ou	26 S	7
Victor Ct	Ou	37 V	12
Victor La	Ou	44 Y	8
Victor St	Hu	13 H	20
Victor St	Ou	45 Z	12
Victoria La	Ou	17 N	5
Victoria Pl	Hu	7 E	27
Victoria St	Hu	22 N	21
Victorian La	Ou	27 T	9
Victory Dr	Ou	48 AA	21
Viking Rd	Nu	18 L	9
Villa Ct	Hu	21 N	18
Villa Pl	Hu	6 D	25
Villa Pl	Ou	25 Q	2
Villa Pl (rt)	Nu	10 K	11
Villa Pl	Nu	11 J	15
Village Av (el)	Hu	4 E	19
Village Av (sh)	Hu	22 N	20
Village Av	Hu	13 K	22
Village Av	Hu	22 N	20
Village Dr	Ou	37 U	11
Village Dr	Hu	30 S	17
Village Hall Dr	Ou	36 U	8
Village La	Hu	44 Z	9
Village La N	Hu	40 V	20
Village La S	Hu	40 V	21
Village Rd (st)	Nu	9 H	11
Village Rd	Hu	18 M	11
Village Rd	Ou	37 W	12
Village Wy	Hu	7 E	25
Vin Ct	Ou	46 BB	17
Vincent Av	Hu	13 J	21
Vincent Ct	Hu	40 W	20
Vincent Dr	Hu	30 R	17
Vincent La	Ou	36 U	9
Vincent Pl	Hu	13 J	22
Vincent Rd	Ou	37 V	12
Vincent St	Hu	23 M	22
Vine Ct	Nu	20 N	14
Vine Dr	Hu	41 U	23
Vine St	Hu	13 H	22
Vine St (gh)	Ou	18 L	8
Vine St	Ou	25 R	2
Vinton St	Hu	24 L	27
Vinton St	Ou	46 Y	17
Viola Ct	Hu	23 L	23
Viola Dr	Ou	17 O	5
Viola St	Hu	5 E	21
Viola St	Ou	17 M	8
Violet Av	Nu	20 M	15
Violet Av	Ou	37 U	12
Violet Ct	Ou	25 Q	2
Violet Dr	Ou	47 Y	19
Violet La	Hu	38 U	16
Violet Rd	Ou	25 Q	2
Violet St	Ou	47 BB	18
Virginia Av	Nu	8 G	8
Virginia Av (el)	Hu	4 F	19
Virginia Av (LB)	Hu	15 G	28
Virginia Av (HV)	Hu	21 M	19
Virginia Av (RC)	Hu	22 M	21
Virginia Av (os)	Hu	14 K	24
Virginia Av (vs)	Hu	23 L	24
Virginia Av (FR)	Hu	22 O	21
Virginia Av (nb)	Hu	30 T	18
Virginia Av	Ou	37 W	12
Virginia Dr	Nu	2 F	11
Virginia Dr	Hu	12 G	18
Virginia La	Ou	46 Y	17
Virginia Pl	Hu	5 F	22
Virginia Rd	Hu	4 E	16
Virginia Rd	Ou	36 W	10
Virginia St	Hu	13 G	21
Virginia St	Ou	17 M	8
Vista Ct	Ou	25 R	2
Vista Dr	Ou	28 R	12
Vista Dr	Nu	2 F	11
Vista Dr	Ou	27 R	9
Vista Hill Rd	Nu	2 E	11
Vista La	Hu	39 V	17
Vista La (Pvt)	Ou	27 R	10
Vista Pl	Hu	4 E	19
Vista Rd	Hu	13 F	20
Vista Rd	Nu	10 K	12

STREET	MUN.	MAP	GRID
Vista Rd	Ou	37	X 11
Vista Wy	Nu	9	G 9
Vivian Ct	Hu	23	O 24
Vivian Pl	Ou	44	Z 11
Vivona Ct	Ou	25	T 2
Voice Rd	Nu	20	N 15
Volante Pl	Hu	29	R 15
Vollkommer Pl	Hu	30	T 19
Von Elm Av	Hu	30	S 18
Vonhuenfeld St	Ou	47	AA 20
Voorhees Pl	Hu	13	H 21
Voorhis Av	Hu	22	M 21
Voorhis Dr	Ou	45	AA 13
Voorhis La	Hu	39	X 19
Vosage St	Hu	22	O 21

W

STREET	MUN.	MAP	GRID
Wachusetts St	Hu	22	L 21
Waddell St	Hu	22	O 21
Wadena St	Hu	40	X 22
Wadleigh Av	Hu	13	K 20
Wadsworth Av	Hu	39	X 17
Wadsworth Pl	Hu	22	N 21
Wafer La	Hu	39	V 18
Wagamon Dr	Ou	44	Z 8
Wagg Av	Hu	13	H 21
Wagner Av	Hu	31	Q 20
Wagner St (el)	Hu	4	E 19
Wagner St	Hu	40	X 19
Wagon La	Ou	17	N 7
Wagon La	Hu	38	W 16
Wagon Rd	Nu	18	M 11
Wagstaff Dr	Hu	39	U 18
Wahl Av	Hu	6	C 25
Wake St	Hu	30	P 19
Wakefield Av	Nu	9	H 9
Wakefield Dr	Ou	27	S 8
Walcott Av	Hu	7	C 25
Walden Av	Ou	37	U 12
Walden Pl	Nu	3	D 13
Walden Pl	Hu	13	K 20
Walden St	Nu	28	Q 13
Waldo Av	Nu	18	M 10
Waldo Av	Hu	14	J 23
Waldo Black La	Nu	9	H 10
Waldo La	Nu	9	H 10
Waldorf Av	Hu	4	E 18
Waldorf Pl	Hu	21	P 18
Wales Av	Hu	22	N 21
Wales Pl (wm)	Hu	14	F 24
Wales Pl	Hu	22	N 21
Walker Av	Hu	31	U 19
Walker Av	Ou	36	W 9
Walker Pl	Nu	10	K 13
Walker Pl	Hu	12	K 19
Walker Rd	Nu	20	L 15
Walker St (ML)	Hu	13	H 21
Walker St	Hu	40	U 22
Walker St	Ou	47	BB 19
Wall Ct	Ou	48	BB 22
Wall St	Ou	17	N 8
Wall St	Hu	13	J 20
Wallace Av (bw)	Hu	22	O 21
Wallace Av	Hu	40	U 20
Wallace Ct (VS)	Hu	5	F 21
Wallace Ct	Hu	22	L 22
Wallace Dr	Ou	45	Y 12
Wallace St (RC)	Hu	22	L 21
Wallace St	Hu	22	P 21
Walland Av	Ou	46	AA 17
Walland Ct	Ou	46	AA 17
Wallen La	Hu	31	T 20
Walnut Av (FP)	Hu	4	E 17
Walnut Av (gh)	Ou	17	M 8
Walnut Av (RC)	Hu	22	L 21
Walnut Av (en)	Ou	26	U 7
Walnut Av (ne)	Hu	31	T 20
Walnut Av (sa)	Ou	46	BB 17
Walnut Ct	Ou	37	X 12
Walnut Dr	Nu	18	M 10
Walnut Dr	Ou	36	W 10
Walnut La	Nu	9	H 10
Walnut La	Ou	38	V 15
Walnut Pl	Nu	11	K 15
Walnut Pl (oy)	Ou	26	T 4
Walnut Pl	Ou	47	Y 19
Walnut Rd	Hu	6	B 25
Walnut Rd	Ou	16	N 5
Walnut Rd (ER)	Hu	14	J 23
Walnut St (gw)	Ou	18	L 8
Walnut St (gv)	Nu	18	M 10
Walnut St (wh)	Hu	12	K 18
Walnut St (LY)	Hu	13	J 22
Walnut St (bw)	Hu	22	N 22
Walnut St (WB)	Nu	19	P 14
Walnut St (un)	Hu	30	Q 18
Walnut St (nq)	Ou	47	Z 18
Walsall St	Hu	40	X 21
Walsh Av	Hu	14	F 24
Walsh La	Nu	19	O 14
Walter Av	Hu	7	B 26
Walter Av	Nu	11	K 15
Walter Av (hk)	Ou	37	W 13
Walter Av	Ou	47	Y 18
Walter Ct	Hu	30	R 18
Walter Ct	Ou	45	AA 13
Walter La	Nu	9	H 10
Walter La	Ou	45	AA 13
Walter Pl	Ou	46	BB 16
Walter Rd	Hu	39	U 18
Walter St	Hu	21	P 18
Walters Av	Ou	36	W 9
Walters Av	Hu	40	W 21
Walters Ct	Hu	31	U 22
Walters La	Nu	2	C 11
Waltoffer Av	Hu	30	S 19
Walton Av	Ou	25	Q 2
Walton Av	Hu	21	P 17
Walton Ct	Hu	12	K 19
Walton Pl	Nu	28	Q 14
Walton St	Hu	12	K 19
Wanamaker St	Hu	14	K 24
Wanda La	Ou	36	W 10
Wander La	Hu	39	W 18
Wanser Av	Hu	6	C 25
Wansers La	Hu	40	X 21
Wansor Av	Ou	25	S 2
Wansor St	Ou	25	S 2
Wantagh Av	Hu	39	W 18
Wantagh Oaks Gate	Hu	39	X 19
Wantagh Park Dr	Hu	40	W 21
Wantagh State Pkwy	Nu	28	S 13
Ward La	Hu	39	V 18
Ward Pl	Hu	6	F 24
Ward St	Hu	12	G 17
Ward St (EW)	Nu	19	M 14
Ward St	Nu	20	O 14
Ward St	Ou	37	W 12
Wardwell Rd	Nu	11	K 15
Waring Dr	Nu	9	H 9
Waring St	Hu	31	T 20
Warner Av	Nu	10	K 11
Warner Av	Hu	21	N 17
Warner La	Ou	36	W 8
Warner Rd	Hu	13	G 20
Warren Av	Ou	25	T 2
Warren Av	Hu	31	T 20
Warren Blvd	Hu	12	K 17
Warren Dr	Hu	6	E 24
Warren Dr	Ou	37	X 11
Warren La	Ou	28	T 12
Warren Pl	Hu	31	R 20
Warren Pl	Ou	37	X 12
Warren St (un)	Hu	21	O 17
Warren St (bh)	Hu	23	N 24
Warren St	Nu	28	Q 13
Warren St (ed)	Hu	30	R 17
Warren Wy	Ou	37	X 11
Warting Ct	Hu	14	H 23
Warton Pl	Hu	20	M 16
Warwick Pl	Nu	8	G 7
Warwick Pl	Ou	37	X 13
Warwick Rd	Nu	2	D 10
Warwick Rd (el)	Hu	4	E 18
Warwick Rd (ER)	Hu	14	H 23
Warwick Rd (RC)	Hu	22	M 20
Warwick Rd (hi)	Hu	15	J 26
Warwick Rd (IP)	Hu	15	K 26
Warwick Rd (ed)	Hu	30	T 17
Warwick St	Hu	30	P 17
Washington Av	Nu	11	H 16
Washington Ct	Hu	21	M 17
Wash Hollow Rd	Ou	26	S 5
Washington St	Ou	46	Y 15
Washburn Av	Hu	31	Q 22
Washington Av (NP)	Nu	11	H 16
Washington Av (VS)	Hu	5	D 20
Washington Av (LW)	Hu	6	D 25
Washington Av (gh)	Ou	18	L 9
Washington Av (gk)	Nu	11	K 15
Washington Av (MI)	Nu	20	L 15
Washington Av (lk)	Hu	12	L 19
Washington Av (LY)	Hu	13	J 22
Washington Av (os)	Hu	23	M 23
Washington Av (hi)	Hu	15	J 27
Washington Av (BY)	Ou	25	S 2
Washington Av (sl)	Hu	29	R 14
Washington Av (rv)	Hu	31	Q 20
Washington Av (nb)	Hu	30	S 19
Washington Av (bm)	Hu	40	U 21
Washington Av (pv)	Ou	44	AA 11
Washington Av (hk)	Ou	37	V 12
Washington Av (wa)	Ou	48	CC 21
Washington Av (sd)	Hu	47	Y 19
Washington Av E	Nu	20	L 15
Washington Blvd (LB)	Hu	15	H 28
Washington Blvd	Hu	31	T 20
Washington Dr	Hu	31	S 20
Washington Pkwy	Ou	38	W 14
Washington Pl (pw)	Nu	8	G 8
Washington Pl (in)	Hu	6	D 25
Washington Pl (MI)	Nu	11	K 15
Washington Pl (bh)	Hu	23	O 24
Washington Pl (IP)	Hu	15	K 26
Washington Pl (rv)	Hu	31	P 20
Washington Pl (MS)	Ou	48	Y 21
Washington St (BE)	Nu	8	G 8
Washington St (GL)	Ou	17	N 6
Washington St (fs)	Hu	12	J 18
Washington St (HV)	Hu	21	N 17
Washington St (lk)	Hu	12	J 19
Washington St (RC)	Hu	13	K 22
Washington St (FR)	Hu	22	P 22
Washington St (hk)	Ou	29	T 14
Washington St (mr)	Hu	31	S 21
Washington St (FG)	Ou	46	BB 16
Washington St (sa)	Ou	47	BB 18
Watchtower La	Hu	39	V 18
Water La	Nu	2	F 9
Water La	Hu	39	W 18
Water La N	Hu	39	W 18
Water La S	Hu	39	W 18
Water Mill La	Nu	3	D 12
Water St (LB)	Hu	15	H 27
Water St	Hu	22	M 22
Waterbury Dr	Hu	40	V 20
Waterbury La	Nu	28	R 12
Wateredge Av	Hu	23	N 23
Wateredge Pl	Hu	14	G 24
Waterford Rd	Hu	15	K 26
Waterford Wy	Ou	35	V 7
Waterfront Blvd (in)	Hu	7	B 25
Waterfront Blvd	Hu	15	K 27
Waters Av	Ou	37	V 13
Waters Pl	Hu	6	F 23
Watersedge Ct	Ou	25	P 2
Waterside La (Pvt)	Nu	2	F 10
Waterview Av	Ou	48	CC 22
Waterview Blvd	Hu	15	K 27
Waterview Dr	Nu	1	F 7
Waterview Dr (wm)	Hu	6	D 24
Waterview Dr	Hu	13	K 21
Waterview Pl	Hu	13	J 21
Waterview Rd	Nu	2	E 10
Waterview Rd	Hu	14	K 23
Waterview St	Hu	14	K 24
Waterway, The	Nu	2	F 10
Watkins Dr	Nu	11	K 14
Watkins St	Hu	13	J 22
Watts Pl (VS)	Hu	6	F 23
Watts Pl	Hu	14	J 23
Waugh Av	Hu	31	S 20
Waukena Av	Hu	23	L 24
Wavecrest Pl N	Hu	24	L 26
Wavecrest Pl S	Hu	24	L 26
Wavecrest St	Hu	13	G 22
Waverly Av (ER)	Hu	14	H 23
Waverly Av (os)	Hu	14	K 23
Waverly Av (sd)	Hu	40	W 21
Waverly Pl (VS)	Hu	5	E 20
Waverly Pl (LW)	Hu	6	E 25
Waverly Pl (RC)	Hu	13	L 22
Waverly Pl (bh)	Hu	23	O 23
Waverly Pl (ed)	Hu	30	S 17
Waverly Pl (un)	Hu	21	P 18
Waverly Pl	Ou	46	BB 16
Waverly Rd	Nu	19	P 12
Waverly St (wm)	Hu	6	F 23
Waverly St	Ou	17	L 8
Waverly St	Hu	40	X 21
Wavy La	Hu	39	V 18
Wayaawi Av	Ou	25	R 1
Wayland Rd	Ou	37	X 11
Waylor La	Ou	43	Y 7
Wayne Av (SM)	Hu	11	G 16
Wayne Av	Hu	7	E 28
Wayne Ct	Hu	31	R 21
Wayne Dr	Ou	45	Y 12
Wayne St	Ou	28	T 12
Waypark Av	Hu	21	P 19
Wayside La	Hu	39	W 18
Weather Low La	Ou	27	R 8
Weaver Dr	Ou	48	CC 21
Weaver La	Hu	38	V 15
Weaving La	Hu	39	V 18
Webb Av (HV)	Hu	21	N 17
Webb Av	Hu	31	R 20
Webb Hill Rd	Nu	3	E 13
Webber Av	Hu	22	N 20
Weber Av	Hu	13	J 20
Weberfield Av	Hu	31	R 21
Webster Av (ma)	Nu	9	F 10
Webster Av (pw)	Nu	8	G 8
Webster Av (un)	Hu	21	O 18
Webster Av (ne)	Hu	31	R 20
Webster Av (nq)	Ou	47	Z 18
Webster St (FP)	Hu	12	G 17
Webster St (LY)	Hu	13	H 21
Webster St (wm)	Hu	14	F 23
Webster St (WB)	Nu	19	O 14
Webster St (bh)	Hu	23	O 23
Webster St (ne)	Hu	31	T 20
Wedgewood Cir	Nu	2	F 11
Wedgewood Ct	Nu	2	E 10
Wedgewood Ct E	Ou	17	O 7
Wedgewood Ct W	Ou	17	O 7
Wedgewood Dr	Ou	28	S 13
Wedgewood La (LW)	Hu	7	D 25
Wedgewood La	Hu	39	V 18
Weeks Av (HV)	Hu	21	N 18
Weeks Av	Hu	23	L 23
Weeks Av	Ou	35	U 5
Weeks Rd	Nu	19	L 13
Weeping Willow Ct	Ou	17	P 6
Weeping Willow La	Nu	18	M 10
Weiden St	Ou	46	BB 16
Weidner Av	Hu	14	K 24
Weil Pl	Hu	21	M 18
Weioner Av	Hu	14	K 24
Weir La	Ou	16	O 4
Weir St	Hu	21	N 19
Weirs La	Ou	16	O 4
Welcome La	Hu	39	V 18
Welder La	Hu	38	V 15
Weld-Gilder Rd	Ou	35	X 5
Weldon La	Ou	45	AA 14
Welgt Ct	Nu	3	E 11
Well Ct	Ou	39	X 17
Wellelein Rd	Hu	21	P 19
Wellesley La	Ou	37	W 12

Nassau Co.

We to Wh

154

STREET	MUN.	MAP	GRID
Whitehall Blvd	Hu	12 K	17
Whitehall Blvd S	Hu	12 K	17
Whitehall Dr	Hu	6 E	22
Whitehall La	Nu	11 J	15
Whitehall La	Hu	39 U	19
Whitehall Rd	Hu	22 N	21
Whitehall Rd S	Hu	12 K	17
Whitehall St	Hu	13 H	21
Whitehouse Av	Hu	31 P	20
Whiteside Av	Hu	12 K	17
Whitewood Dr	Nu	10 J	13
Whitewood Dr	Ou	48 AA	21
Whitlock St	Ou	45 Z	12
Whitman Av	Hu	31 T	21
Whitman Av	Hu	36 X	10
Whitman La	Hu	17 L	6
Whitman Rd	Nu	2 B	11
Whitman St	Hu	39 X	17
Whitney Av	Nu	11 F	16
Whitney Av (en)	Ou	26 U	7
Whitney Av	Hu	36 W	9
Whitney Cir	Hu	16 K	4
Whitney La	Hu	18 O	9
Whitney La	Ou	44 Z	8
Whitney Phipps Garvan Rd	Nu	18 N	11
Whitney Pl	Nu	10 F	11
Whitney Rd	Ou	34 U	2
Whitney St	Nu	19 O	14
Whitson St	Hu	21 M	18
Whittier Av	Hu	11 G	16
Whittier Av (ne)	Hu	31 S	20
Whittier Av	Hu	39 X	18
Whittier Dr	Hu	10 J	12
Whittier St	Hu	13 H	21
Whittier St	Hu	29 Q	14
Wickey Av	Nu	19 P	14
Wickham Rd	Nu	18 N	11
Wickham Rd	Hu	11 J	16
Wicks Av (sd)	Hu	39 X	19
Wicks Ct	Ou	38 U	15
Wicks La	Hu	13 J	21
Wicks Rd	Nu	11 K	15
Wickshire Dr	Hu	30 R	17
Widgeon La	Hu	38 U	15
Widgeon Pl	Hu	41 X	22
Wilben Ct	Nu	11 G	15
Wilbur Dr	Nu	3 C	11
Wilbur La	Hu	22 O	20
Wilbur Pl	Hu	40 V	21
Wilbur St	Hu	13 H	22
Wilburne Av (sd)	Hu	40 X	21
Wildacre Av	Hu	7 C	26
Wilddale Rd	Ou	23 O	23
Wildflower La	Hu	39 V	18
Wildwood Ct	Ou	25 P	2
Wildwood Dr	Nu	2 D	9
Wildwood Dr	Ou	43 Y	7
Wildwood La	Ou	18 N	9
Wildwood La	Hu	19 M	11
Wildwood La	Hu	39 V	18
Wildwood Rd	Nu	2 C	9
Wildwood Rd	Ou	29 U	14
Wildwood Rd	Hu	12 J	19
Wilford St	Hu	38 X	15
Wilfred Blvd	Ou	37 V	12
Willa Wy	Ou	48 Z	23
Willada La	Ou	8 L	5
Willard Av (bh)	Hu	23 O	23
Willard Av (os)	Ou	23 L	23
Willard Av	Ou	46 AA	17
Willard Dr	Hu	14 H	23
Willard Pl	Ou	17 M	8
Willard St	Hu	30 T	18
Willben La	Ou	45 Y	11
Willets Av	Hu	21 L	18
Willets Av	Ou	36 W	10
Willets Ct	Hu	22 M	20
Willets Ct S	Nu	2 F	10
Willets Dr	Hu	36 W	9
Willets La	Nu	2 F	10
Willets La (je)	Ou	28 T	11
Willets La	Ou	36 W	10
Willets Pond Pa	Nu	10 J	13
Willets Rd	Nu	19 N	13
Willett Av	Ou	37 U	12
Willett Pl	Hu	31 Q	20
William Av	Hu	12 H	18
William Av	Hu	18 M	8
William Pl (FR)	Hu	23 P	24
William Pl	Hu	31 T	22
William Rd	Ou	47 Y	18
William St (sd)	Hu	40 X	20
William St (nn)	Nu	11 H	15
William St (el)	Hu	5 E	20
William St (VS)	Hu	5 E	21
William St (wm)	Hu	6 F	23
William St (LY)	Hu	13 G	22
William St (LW)	Hu	6 D	25
William St (GL)	Ou	17 M	7
William St (gh)	Ou	17 M	8
William St (WP)	Nu	10 K	13
William St (EW)	Nu	19 M	14
William St (ML)	Hu	13 J	21
William St (wh)	Hu	12 K	18
William St (RC)	Hu	22 M	21
William St (HV)	Hu	21 N	18
William St (bw)	Hu	22 N	21
William St (hk)	Ou	37 U	13
William St (ln)	Hu	38 U	16
William St (rv)	Hu	31 P	20
William St (ed)	Hu	30 R	19
William St (ne)	Hu	31 R	20
William St (wn)	Hu	40 V	21
William St (FG)	Ou	46 BB	16
William St (bp)	Ou	46 Y	15
William St (mq)	Ou	48 Z	21
Williams Av	Ou	36 W	10
Williams Ct	Hu	31 U	22
Williams Dr	Ou	48 AA	22
Williamson St	Hu	14 J	24
Willis Av (FP)	Hu	11 G	16
Willis Av (al)	Nu	10 K	12
Willis Av (MI)	Nu	20 L	15
Willis Av (mr)	Hu	31 R	21
Willis Av	Ou	36 W	9
Willis Barwick St	Nu	11 F	16
Willis Ct	Ou	38 W	15
Willis Ct	Hu	39 W	19
Willis Gate	Ou	36 W	9
Willis La	Ou	36 V	9
Willis Pl	Nu	18 M	10
Willis St	Hu	22 N	20
Willits Rd	Ou	17 O	6
Willoughby Av	Ou	37 U	13
Willoughby Av	Hu	40 W	21
Willow Av	Ou	38 U	14
Willow Av (CH)	Hu	6 D	25
Willow Av (HV)	Hu	21 N	19
Willow Av (mr)	Hu	31 S	21
Willow Av (FR)	Hu	31 R	22
Willow Ct	Nu	2 F	10
Willow Dr	Nu	9 G	9
Willow Dr	Ou	47 CC	19
Willow Gate	Nu	19 L	11
Willow La (GN)	Nu	2 C	10
Willow La (HH)	Hu	14 H	24
Willow La	Nu	19 N	14
Willow Park Ct	Hu	22 O	21
Willow Pl (ma)	Nu	10 G	11
Willow Pl (GE)	Nu	3 D	12
Willow Pl	Hu	13 H	20
Willow Pl (gh)	Ou	18 M	9
Willow Pl (oy)	Nu	19 L	13
Willow Pl (hk)	Ou	37 V	12
Willow Pond La	Hu	14 G	23
Willow Pond Rd	Ou	44 AA	9
Willow Ridge Rd	Ou	25 R	2
Willow Rd	Nu	11 H	15
Willow Rd (WG)	Hu	6 F	24
Willow Rd	Hu	13 H	20
Willow Rd	Ou	45 BB	13
Willow Shore Av	Ou	8 K	7
Willow St (FP)	Hu	12 G	17
Willow St (BY)	Ou	25 Q	2
Willow St (GL)	Ou	17 N	6
Willow St (rt)	Nu	10 K	11
Willow St (GA)	Hu	21 M	17
Willow St (lk)	Hu	12 L	19
Willow St (sh)	Hu	22 M	20
Willow St (WB)	Nu	29 Q	14
Willow St (un)	Nu	30 Q	18
Willow St (bp)	Ou	46 Y	15
Willow St (MS)	Ou	47 AA	19
Willow St (wh)	Hu	40 W	21
Willow Wy	Hu	7 E	26
Willowbend La	Hu	22 O	21
Willowbrook La	Hu	22 O	21
Willowdale Av	Nu	9 G	9
Willowood Dr	Hu	39 V	18
Willowwood La	Hu	39 W	19
Willy La	Ou	38 W	15
Wilmar Pl	Hu	21 M	17
Wilmarth Pl	Hu	40 V	21
Wilmot Dr	Hu	14 H	23
Wilshire Ct	Nu	32 Q	23
Wilshire Dr	Nu	3 E	12
Wilshire Dr	Ou	36 X	8
Wilshire La	Ou	45 Z	13
Wilshire Rd	Ou	45 AA	14
Wilson Av (LY)	Hu	13 H	21
Wilson Av	Ou	25 Q	2
Wilson Av (MI)	Nu	11 K	15
Wilson Av (LB)	Hu	15 L	28
Wilson Av (WB)	Nu	19 P	14
Wilson Av (ed)	Hu	30 S	19
Wilson Av (bm)	Hu	40 U	21
Wilson Blvd	Nu	11 K	15
Wilson Ct	Hu	6 D	23
Wilson Ct	Nu	20 O	15
Wilson Ct	Ou	47 CC	20
Wilson La (RC)	Hu	13 K	21
Wilson La	Ou	25 Q	2
Wilson La	Hu	30 S	17
Wilson La	Ou	46 Y	16
Wilson Pl (gh)	Ou	18 M	9
Wilson Pl (RC)	Hu	22 L	22
Wilson Pl (rv)	Hu	31 Q	20
Wilson Pl (bm)	Hu	40 U	21
Wilson Pl (FR)	Hu	22 P	22
Wilson Pl	Ou	45 Z	11
Wilson Rd (VS)	Hu	14 F	23
Wilson Rd	Hu	30 Q	18
Wilson Rd (wm)	Hu	6 D	23
Wilson St (fs)	Hu	12 J	17
Wilson St (wh)	Hu	12 K	19
Wilson St (bw)	Hu	22 N	21
Wilson St (ER)	Hu	14 J	22
Wilson St (bi)	Hu	15 K	27
Wilson St	Ou	47 AA	20
Wilton Rd	Hu	5 F	20
Wilton St	Nu	12 G	15
Wilwade Rd	Nu	3 E	13
Wimbledon Ct (je)	Ou	28 R	12
Wimbledon Ct	Ou	44 Z	9
Wimbledon Dr	Nu	10 J	13
Wimbleton La	Nu	2 E	10
Winas Pl	Ou	16 P	4
Winchester Dr	Nu	9 J	11
Winchester Dr	Ou	27 S	8
Winchester Pl	Nu	7 C	25
Windemere Ct	Ou	44 AA	9
Windemere Cres	Ou	44 Z	9
Windemere Dr	Ou	44 Z	9
Windemere Wy	Ou	44 Z	9
Windermere Pl	Hu	13 L	22
Windermere Rd	Hu	12 H	19
Windham Ct	Ou	27 R	8
Windham Rd	Hu	22 M	20
Winding La	Nu	19 O	13
Winding La	Hu	39 U	17
Winding Rd	Nu	22 N	22
Winding Rd (hk)	Ou	38 V	15
Winding Rd (ob)	Ou	45 BB	14
Winding Rd (mq)	Ou	47 Y	19
Winding Wy (LT)	Ou	16 O	3
Winding Wy	Ou	17 L	6
Windmill La	Hu	38 W	16
Windsor Av	Nu	20 L	14
Windsor Av	Hu	13 K	22
Windsor Ct	Nu	20 L	14
Windsor Dr	Nu	19 O	13
Windsor Dr	Ou	27 U	10
Windsor Dr	Hu	38 X	16
Windsor Gate	Nu	3 E	13
Windsor La	Hu	12 K	19
Windsor Pkwy (HV)	Hu	21 N	19
Windsor Pkwy	Hu	23 L	24
Windsor Pl (RC)	Hu	13 K	22
Windsor Pl	Hu	31 S	20
Windsor Pl	Ou	48 AA	22
Windsor Rd	Nu	3 E	11
Windsor Rd (bw)	Hu	23 N	22
Windsor Rd	Hu	21 P	18
Windsor Rd	Ou	37 U	13
Windsor St	Hu	29 R	15
Windsorgate Dr	Nu	10 G	13
Windward Waters Edge	Ou	8 K	5
Winfield Pl	Hu	13 H	20
Winfield Ter	Nu	3 C	11
Wing La	Hu	39 V	18
Wingate Dr	Hu	39 U	18
Wingate Rd	Hu	6 F	22
Winifred Dr	Hu	31 S	20
Winnie Ct	Nu	20 O	15
Winona St	Nu	23 N	23
Winter Av	Hu	21 P	19
Winter La	Ou	38 U	15
Winter St	Hu	13 H	22
Winters Ct	Ou	44 Y	11
Winthrop Av (EH)	Nu	18 M	11
Winthrop Av	Nu	29 P	14
Winthrop Av	Hu	40 U	21
Winthrop Av	Ou	36 X	10
Winthrop Dr (un)	Nu	30 Q	19
Winthrop Dr	Nu	30 Q	19
Winthrop Dr	Ou	44 Z	9
Winthrop Pl	Hu	40 U	21
Winthrop Rd	Nu	9 H	9
Winthrop Rd	Ou	37 X	11
Winthrop St (nn)	Nu	11 G	15
Winthrop St (LY)	Hu	13 H	21
Winthrop St (WP)	Nu	10 L	14
Winthrop St	Nu	21 N	19
Winthrop St (WB)	Nu	29 P	14
Winthrope Rd	Nu	9 G	10
Wisconsin Av	Ou	46 Z	17
Wisconsin St	Hu	15 G	28
Wisdom La	Hu	39 U	17
Wishbone La	Hu	39 V	18
Wishing La	Ou	18 N	9
Wishing Well La	Ou	18 N	9
Wisp La	Hu	39 V	18
Wisteria Av	Nu	20 M	15
Wisteria La	Hu	39 W	18
Wisteria Pa	Nu	8 H	6
Wisteria Pl	Ou	36 X	8
Wisteria Rd	Hu	39 W	19
Witley Ct	Hu	21 O	17
Witte La	Nu	18 L	10
Wm. Penn Rd	Nu	2 C	11
Wm. St	Nu	2 C	11
Wolcott Rd	Hu	39 U	17
Wolf Av	Hu	13 H	20
Wolfie St	Ou	17 N	6
Wolfson Dr	Hu	23 O	24
Wolkow Av	Hu	39 X	18
Wolver Hollow Rd	Ou	26 R	7
Wood Acres Rd E	Ou	27 R	9
Wood Acres Rd N	Ou	27 R	9
Wood Acres Rd S	Ou	27 R	9
Wood Acres Rd W	Ou	27 R	9
Wood Av	Nu	10 K	13
Wood Av	Hu	31 U	22
Wood Av	Ou	47 Z	18
Wood Ct (BY)	Ou	25 R	2
Wood Ct (MN)	Ou	35 U	6
Wood Ct (MT)	Ou	27 T	9
Wood Ct (lg)	Ou	37 W	11
Wood Dr	Ou	35 U	6
Wood Edge Rd	Nu	9 G	10
Wood Hill La	Ou	27 Q	8
Wood La (LT)	Ou	16 O	4
Wood La (ln)	Hu	39 W	17
Wood La (wm)	Hu	6 E	24
Wood La (VS)	Hu	5 F	22
Wood La	Ou	37 X	12
Wood Park Dr	Hu	22 O	20
Wood Pl	Nu	10 G	11
Wood Ridge La	Ou	8 K	7
Wood Rd (SP)	Nu	8 H	7
Wood Rd	Nu	2 C	10
Wood St (wm)	Hu	14 F	24
Wood St (LY)	Hu	13 H	22
Wood St (os)	Hu	14 K	24
Wood Valley La	Nu	9 J	10
Woodale Ct	Ou	16 N	4
Woodbine Av (HN)	Hu	14 G	25
Woodbine Av (mr)	Hu	31 S	21
Woodbine Av (wn)	Hu	39 X	19
Woodbine Ct	Hu	11 F	17
Woodbine Dr	Ou	38 W	14

Nassau Co.

STREET	MUN. MAP GRID
Woodbine	
Dr N	Ou 38 W 14
Woodbine	
Dr S	Ou 38 W 14
Woodbine Rd	Nu 18 N 11
Woodbine St	Nu 30 Q 18
Woodbourne	
Rd	Nu 2 E 10
Woodbridge	
La	Ou 37 V 12
Woodbridge	
La E	Nu 39 X 18
Woodbridge	
La N	Nu 39 W 18
Woodbridge	
La W	Nu 39 W 18
Woodbridge	
Rd	Hu 22 M 20
Woodbury Ct	Ou 37 V 12
Woodbury	
Farms Dr	Ou 44 Y 9
Woodbury Rd	
(hk)	Ou 37 V 13
Woodbury Rd	
(wy)	Ou 44 Z 9
Woodbury Rd	
(pv)	Ou 37 W 12
Woodbury Wy	Ou 36 X 8
Woodcleft Av	Nu 8 G 8
Woodcleft Av	Hu 32 Q 23
Woodcliff Ct	Nu 10 H 12
Woodcliff Dr	Hu 13 H 20
Woodcock La	Hu 38 U 15
Woodcock Rd	Nu 19 O 14
Woodcrest Dr	Ou 36 Y 9
Woodcrest Dr	Nu 10 J 13
Woodcrest Rd	Nu 2 D 10
Woodcrest St	Ou 38 W 15
Woodcrest St	Hu 13 G 22
Woodcut La	
(SP)	Nu 8 G 7
Woodcut La	
(ma)	Nu 9 G 11
Woodcut La (al)	Nu 10 K 12
Wooded La	Nu 39 X 19
Woodedge La	Ou 27 R 10
Woodfield Ct	Ou 43 Z 6
Woodfield La	Ou 18 N 9
Woodfield Rd	Hu 13 K 21
Woodgreen La	Nu 19 M 11
Woodgreen La	Hu 39 W 18
Woodgreen Pl	Hu 22 M 20
Woodgreen Wy	Ou 43 Z 6
Woodhall St	Hu 24 N 27
Woodhill La	Nu 9 H 10
Woodhollow La	Ou 18 N 8
Woodhollow Rd	
(sg)	Nu 19 L 13
Woodhollow Rd	
(EH)	Nu 19 M 12
Woodlake Dr	Ou 44 Y 9
Woodland Av	
(gw)	Ou 18 L 8
Woodland Av	
(RC)	Hu 23 L 23
Woodland Av	Hu 40 V 22
Woodland Av	Ou 36 W 8
Woodland Ct	Nu 9 J 10
Woodland Dr	
(SP)	Nu 1 E 6
Woodland Dr	
(PD)	Nu 2 F 10
Woodland Dr	
(gk)	Nu 11 H 15
Woodland Dr	
(NL)	Nu 10 J 13
Woodland Dr	Hu 22 N 20
Woodland Dr	
(OC)	Ou 35 W 6
Woodland Dr	
(wy)	Ou 36 Y 8
Woodland Dr	
(ob)	Ou 45 AA 13
Woodland Estates	
Dr	Hu 22 O 20
Woodland La	
(OK)	Ou 17 P 6
Woodland La	Ou 47 Y 19
Woodland Pl	Nu 2 C 11
Woodland Rd	Nu 5 E 22
Woodland Rd	
(GL)	Ou 8 K 5
Woodland Rd	
(FH)	Nu 9 J 10
Woodland Rd	Nu 19 N 12

STREET	MUN. MAP GRID
Woodland Rd	
(OK)	Ou 17 P 7
Woodland Rd	
(MN)	Ou 35 U 6
Woodland Ter	Hu 31 S 21
Woodland Wy	Nu 10 H 11
Woodlawn Av	Nu 2 E 11
Woodlawn Av	Hu 13 G 22
Woodlawn Pl	Hu 13 H 21
Woodlawn Rd	Hu 21 L 18
Woodlawn Rd	Nu 9 H 8
Woodlea Rd	Ou 36 V 8
Woodmere Av	Ou 17 L 8
Woodmere Blvd	Hu 6 E 23
Woodmere Dr	Hu 6 E 22
Woodmere	
Mews	Hu 6 F 24
Woodmere Pl	Hu 6 E 24
Woodnut Pl	Nu 20 L 15
Woodoak Dr	Nu 19 N 14
Woodoak Dr	Hu 23 O 24
Woodoak Pl	Hu 12 K 17
Woodpecker La	
(In)	Hu 38 U 15
Woodpecker La	Hu 31 T 21
Woods Av (ML)	Hu 13 H 20
Woods Av (ER)	Hu 14 J 23
Woods Av (RC)	Hu 14 L 22
Woods Av (ed)	Hu 30 T 17
Woods Av (rv)	Hu 22 P 20
Woods Ct	Ou 17 N 7
Woods Crossing	
(Pvt)	Ou 27 R 10
Woods Dr	Nu 18 N 10
Woods La (sg)	Nu 10 J 13
Woods La	Nu 19 N 12
Woods Pl	Hu 23 L 23
Woods Rd (st)	Nu 10 H 11
Woods Rd (MC)	Ou 26 P 5
Woods Rd	Ou 26 R 4
Woods Rd	Nu 19 P 13
Woodside Av	
(ML)	Hu 13 J 20
Woodside Av	
(bw)	Hu 22 O 21
Woodside Av	
(FR)	Hu 31 Q 21
Woodside Dr	
(HB)	Hu 14 G 24
Woodside Dr	Hu 39 V 18
Woodside Rd	Hu 14 F 24
Woodstock Ct	Ou 26 T 7
Woodstock St	Nu 5 F 19
Woodtree Dr	Ou 44 Y 9
Woodvale Dr	Ou 43 Y 7
Woodview Rd	Hu 21 L 18
Woodville La	Nu 10 K 12
Woodward Av	Nu 40 W 21
Woodward Dr	Ou 35 V 6
Woodward	
Pkwy	Ou 46 BB 17
Woodward St	Nu 10 K 12
Woodward St	Hu 23 N 24
Woodwaye Rd	Ou 37 W 12
Woody La	Ou 44 Z 10
Wool Av (fs)	Hu 12 H 18
Wooley La	Nu 2 D 11
Wooley La E	Nu 2 E 11
Woolsey Av	
(GL)	Ou 16 L 5
Woolsey Av	Ou 46 Y 15
Woolworth St	Hu 12 G 18
World Av	Nu 12 G 18
Worthmor Dr	Hu 40 X 20
Wren Ct	Ou 18 N 8
Wren Ct	Hu 22 L 20
Wren Dr	Nu 18 N 10
Wren Dr	Ou 44 Y 11
Wren Pl	Hu 38 X 16
Wright Av (LY)	Hu 13 H 22
Wright Av	Nu 20 O 15
Wright Av	Hu 13 J 21
Wright Dr	Ou 47 Y 19
Wright Rd	Hu 22 M 20
Wright St	Hu 13 H 20
Wright St (cp)	Nu 20 O 15
Wright St	Nu 29 R 14
Wright's La	Hu 23 M 25
Wunaquit Dr	Ou 25 R 1
Wyanet St	Hu 40 W 21
Wyatt Rd	Nu 20 M 16
Wycham Pl	Nu 3 E 12
Wyckoff Av	Hu 31 T 21
Wyckoff Pl	Hu 6 E 24
Wyckoff St	Ou 37 U 13

STREET	MUN. MAP GRID
Wydler Pl	Hu 21 M 17
Wyndham Wy	Nu 9 J 9
Wyngate Dr	Hu 13 G 20
Wyngate Dr	Ou 47 Y 19
Wyngate Dr E	Hu 13 G 20
Wyngate Dr W	Hu 13 G 20
Wyngate Pl	Nu 3 E 11
Wynn Ct	Ou 36 V 8
Wynne La	Hu 41 U 22
Wynsum Av	
(mr)	Hu 31 T 21
Wynsum Av	Hu 41 U 23
Wyoler Ct	Hu 12 K 17
Wyoming Av	
(LB)	Hu 15 G 28
Wyoming Av	Hu 14 K 22
Wyoming Av	Ou 46 Z 17
Wyoming Ct	Ou 36 X 8

X

Xavier Ct	Hu 23 M 24
Xavier Pl	Hu 23 M 23

Y

Yacht Basin Rd	Hu 7 D 26
Yacht Club Dr	Nu 9 F 9
Yale Av (wm)	Hu 6 E 24
Yale Av (wm)	Hu 14 G 23
Yale Av (lk)	Hu 13 K 21
Yale Blvd	Nu 11 H 15
Yale Cir	Nu 10 J 12
Yale Ct	Hu 40 W 20
Yale Dr	Nu 10 J 12
Yale Pl (RC)	Hu 22 L 21
Yale Pl (LY)	Hu 13 H 21
Yale Pl (GL)	Ou 16 M 5
Yale Pl (fs)	Hu 12 J 17
Yale Pl (bh)	Hu 23 N 24
Yale Pl (mr)	Hu 31 S 22
Yale Rd (fs)	Hu 12 J 17
Yale Rd	Hu 31 S 22
Yale St (in)	Hu 6 C 25
Yale St (al)	Nu 10 K 12
Yale St (WP)	Nu 19 L 13
Yale St (GA)	Hu 12 H 17
Yale St (HV)	Hu 21 N 17
Yale St (os)	Hu 14 K 24
Yard, The	Hu 6 E 25
Yarmouth Rd	Hu 14 J 24
Yates Av	Hu 7 E 28
Yates La	Ou 28 T 12
Yellow Gate	
Cote	Ou 35 X 6
Yennicock Av	Nu 1 F 8
Yoakum Av	Ou 46 AA 17
Yoakum St	Ou 46 AA 16
York Av	Ou 37 Y 14
York Ct (sh)	Hu 22 N 20
York Ct	Hu 40 X 22
York Dr	Nu 3 F 11
York Pl	Nu 10 K 14
York Pl	Hu 31 S 21
York Pl	Ou 47 Y 18
York St (ML)	Hu 13 J 21
York St	Ou 37 U 13
York St	Hu 30 S 17
Yorkshire Dr	Ou 26 U 7
Yorkshire Rd	Nu 11 J 15
Yorkshire Rd	Hu 22 M 21
Yorktown St	Hu 22 M 22
Yost Blvd	Hu 14 K 24
Yukon Dr	Ou 44 Z 10
Yung Pl	Hu 6 F 24

Z

Z St	Ou 16 O 4
Zadig St	Hu 14 K 24
Zane Ct	Hu 30 S 19
Zavatt St	Hu 6 C 25
Zeckendorf Blvd	Hu 20 O 15
Zemek St	Hu 13 H 21
Zenith La	Hu 38 W 16

STREET	MUN. MAP GRID
Zinnia St	Hu 12 F 17
Ziska Av	Ou 37 U 12
Zola St	Hu 6 D 24
Zoranne Dr	Ou 46 Z 16

NUMBERED STREETS

1st Av (NP)	Hu 11 G 16
1st Av (gk)	Nu 11 J 16
1st Av (fs)	Hu 12 H 19
1st Av (ER)	Hu 14 J 24
1st Av (BY)	Ou 25 T 2
1st Av (nc)	Nu 28 R 13
1st Av (ed)	Hu 30 T 17
1st Av (ne)	Hu 31 S 20
1st Av (sa)	Ou 46 BB 17
1st Av (MS)	Ou 47 BB 20
1st Pl (gk)	Nu 11 J 15
1st Pl (gs)	Hu 12 J 17
1st Pl (GA)	Hu 21 M 17
1st Pl (bw)	Hu 23 N 23
1st Pl (nc)	Nu 28 R 13
1st Pl (un)	Nu 30 P 18
1st Pl (bm)	Nu 40 U 21
1st Pl (sd)	Hu 40 W 22
1st St (el)	Hu 4 E 19
1st St (ma)	Nu 10 G 11
1st St (fs)	Hu 12 H 19
1st St (CH)	Hu 6 D 24
1st St (VS)	Hu 13 F 22
1st St (lv)	Ou 16 O 4
1st St (GL)	Ou 17 N 6
1st St (gw)	Nu 9 L 8
1st St (gv)	Nu 18 M 10
1st St (MI)	Nu 11 J 15
1st St (MI)	Nu 11 K 15
1st St (GA)	Hu 12 K 17
1st St (eg)	Nu 20 O 16
1st St (LY)	Hu 14 H 23
1st St (ER)	Hu 14 J 23
1st St (os)	Hu 23 M 24
1st St (BY)	Ou 25 T 2
1st St (nc)	Nu 28 R 13
1st St (hk)	Ou 37 U 14
1st St (ed)	Hu 30 S 17
1st St (un)	Nu 30 Q 19
1st St (sy)	Ou 36 W 8
1st St (wy)	Ou 44 Z 8
2nd Av (KP)	Nu 2 B 9
2nd Av (pw)	Nu 9 F 8
2nd Av (NP)	Hu 11 G 16
2nd Av (fs)	Hu 12 H 19
2nd Av (gk)	Nu 11 J 16
2nd Av (ER)	Hu 14 J 24
2nd Av (BY)	Ou 25 T 2
2nd Av (nc)	Nu 28 R 13
2nd Av (ed)	Hu 30 T 17
2nd Av (ne)	Hu 31 S 20
2nd Av (sa)	Ou 46 BB 17
2nd Av	
(Oakdale a)	Ou 47 AA 20
2nd Pl (gs)	Hu 12 J 17
2nd Pl (GA)	Hu 21 M 17
2nd Pl (bw)	Hu 23 N 23
2nd Pl (un)	Nu 30 P 18
2nd Pl (rv)	Hu 31 Q 20
2nd Rd	Nu 3 E 11
2nd St (gw)	Nu 9 L 8
2nd St (un)	Nu 30 Q 18
2nd St (ma)	Nu 10 G 11
2nd St (el)	Hu 4 E 19
2nd St (fs)	Hu 12 H 19
2nd St (lv)	Ou 16 O 4
2nd St (GL)	Ou 17 N 6
2nd St (gv)	Nu 18 M 10
2nd St (hk)	Nu 11 J 15
2nd St (MI)	Nu 20 L 15
2nd St (GA)	Hu 21 L 17
2nd St (eg)	Nu 20 O 16
2nd St (ER)	Hu 14 J 23
2nd St (os)	Hu 23 L 24
2nd St (nc)	Nu 28 R 13
2nd St (hk)	Ou 29 T 14
2nd St (hk)	Ou 37 U 14
2nd St (ed)	Hu 30 S 17
2nd St (bm)	Nu 40 U 21
2nd St (wy)	Ou 44 Z 8
2nd St E	Nu 20 M 15
3rd Av (pw)	Nu 9 F 8
3rd Av (NP)	Hu 11 G 16
3rd Av (fs)	Hu 12 H 19
3rd Av (gk)	Nu 11 J 16
3rd Av (MI)	Nu 20 L 15

PLACES

Nassau Co.

■ POINTS OF INTEREST

■ RAILROAD STATIONS

■ SHOPPING CENTER & MALLS

Parks & Recreation to Shopping Center & Malls

Nassau Co.

STREET	MUN.	MAP	GRID

COUNTY & MUNICIPAL BUILDINGS

STREET	MUN.	MAP	GRID
Atlantic Beach VH	Hu	7 D	28
Baxter Estates VH	Nu	8 G	8
Bayville VH	Ou	25 R	2
Cedarhurst VH	Hu	6 E	25
Center Island VH	Ou	34 V	2
East Rockaway VH	Hu	14 J	23
Farmingdale VH	Ou	46 BB	16
Floral Park VH	Hu	4 F	17
Flower Hill VH	Nu	9 H	10
Freeport Administrative Bldg	Hu	31 P	21
Freeport VH	Hu	31 Q	22
Garden City VH	Hu	20 L	16
Glen Cove City Hall	Ou	17 M	5
Great Neck Plaza VH	Nu	3 D	12
Great Neck VH	Nu	2 D	10
Hempstead Court House	Hu	21 M	18
Hempstead TH	Hu	21 N	18
Hempstead Town Hall Annex	Hu	21 N	18
Hempstead VH	Hu	21 N	18
Island Park VH	Hu	15 K	26
Kensington VH	Nu	3 D	11
Lattingtown VH	Ou	16 O	3
Lawrence VH	Hu	7 D	25
Long Beach City Hall	Hu	15 J	27
Lynbrook VH	Hu	13 J	22
Malverne VH	Hu	13 J	20
Manhasset TH	Nu	9 G	11
Manor Haven VH	Nu	1 F	7
Massapequa Park VH	Ou	47 AA	20
Mill Neck TH	Ou	35 U	5
Munsey Park VH	Nu	9 H	10
Muttontown VH	Ou	36 U	8
Nassau Boces	Ou	36 V	10
Nassau Ctr for the Developmentally Disabled	Ou	36 Y	8
Nassau CO Dept of Health	Ou	45 AA	12
Nassau CO Fire Marshal	Hu	30 Q	18
Nassau CO Jail	Hu	29 S	16
Nassau CO of Art Museum	Nu	18 L	10
Nassau CO Office of Cultural Development-Chelsea Center	Ou	27 T	7
Nassau CO Offices Plainview Ctr	Ou	45 AA	12
Nassau CO Veterans Memorial Coliseum	Hu	29 P	17
National Ctr for Devel Disabilities	Nu	10 K	13
New County Court House	Hu	20 M	15
New Hyde Park VH	Nu	11 H	16
Mineola Boro Hall	Nu	20 L	15
Old Brookville Administrative Bldg	Ou	18 P	9
Old Nassau CO Court House	Hu	20 L	15
Oyster Bay TH S	Ou	47 Y	19
Oysterbay TH	Ou	35 U	5
Port Washington VH	Nu	1 F	7
Rockville Centre North VH	Hu	13 L	22
Roslyn Harbor VH	Nu	18 L	9
Roslyn VH	Nu	9 K	10
Russell Gardens VH	Nu	3 D	12
Saddle Rock VH	Nu	2 B	11
Sea Cliff VH	Ou	17 L	7
South Floral Park VH	Hu	4 F	17
Stewart Manor VH	Hu	12 G	17
Thomaston VH	Nu	3 F	11
Valley Stream VH	Hu	5 F	21
Westbury VH	Nu	29 Q	14
Williston Park VH	Nu	10 L	14